T

*Race and War in France*

WAR/SOCIETY/CULTURE
Michael Fellman, *Series Editor*

# *Race and War in France*

## Colonial Subjects in the French Army, 1914–1918

RICHARD S. FOGARTY

The Johns Hopkins University Press

*Baltimore*

© 2008 The Johns Hopkins University Press
All rights reserved. Published 2008
Printed in the United States of America on acid-free paper

2   4   6   8   9   7   5   3   1

The Johns Hopkins University Press
2715 North Charles Street
Baltimore, Maryland 21218-4363
www.press.jhu.edu

Library of Congress Cataloging-in-Publication Data

Fogarty, Richard Standish.
Race and war in France : colonial subjects in the French Army, 1914–1918 /
Richard S. Fogarty.
p.   cm. — (War/society/culture)
Includes bibliographical references and index.
ISBN-13: 978-0-8018-8824-3 (hbk. : alk. paper)
ISBN-10: 0-8018-8824-7 (hbk. : alk. paper)
1. France. Armée. Troupes coloniales—History. 2. France. Armée—Recruiting,
enlistment, etc.—World War, 1914–1918. 3. France. Armée—Minorities—Social
conditions—20th century. 4. World War, 1914–1918—France. 5. France—Race
relations—History—20th century. I. Title.
D548.9.T76F64 2008
940.4′1244—dc22
2007049546

A catalog record for this book is available from the British Library.

*Special discounts are available for bulk purchases of this book. For more information,
please contact Special Sales at 410-516-6936 or specialsales@press.jhu.edu.*

The Johns Hopkins University Press uses environmentally friendly book materials,
including recycled text paper that is composed of at least 30 percent post-consumer
waste, whenever possible. All of our book papers are acid-free, and our jackets and
covers are printed on paper with recycled content.

# CONTENTS

Robert Schumann, whose music often accompanied the writing of this book, once said, "The roots of a piece should be covered like those of a flower, so that we perceive only the blossom." In the case of this work, however, it is a pleasure to reveal its roots, to acknowledge the sources of inspiration, support, guidance and friendship that sustained me along the way. The following institutions provided generous financial support for research and writing: the National Endowment for the Humanities, the Center for German and European Studies at the University of California, Berkeley; the Graduate Division and the Department of History at the University of California, Santa Barbara; the University of California Office of the President; Bridgewater College; and the Department of History and the College of Arts and Sciences at the University at Albany, State University of New York. In France, I benefited from the assistance of the staffs at the Service historique de l'armée de terre, Château de Vincennes; the Archives nationales, Paris; the Archives du Ministère des affaires étrangères, Paris; the Bibliothèque de documentation internationale contemporaine, Université de Paris X–Nanterre; the Bibliothèque nationale, Paris; the Établissement de communication et de production audiovisuelle de la défense (ECPAD), Médiathèque de la défense, Fort d'Ivry, Ivry-sur-Seine; and the Centre des archives d'Outremer, Aix-en-Provence. In the United States, I would like to thank the staffs of the Hoover Institution Library and Archives at Stanford University, the Davidson Library at the University of California, Santa Barbara, and Alexander Mack Memorial Library at Bridgewater College. The Interlibrary Loan Service at both Davidson and Alexander Mack Memorial libraries deserve special mention for tracking down innumerable books and articles, many of them difficult to find. Some material from chapters 6 and 7 appeared previously as, respectively: "Race and Sex, Fear and Loathing in France During the Great War," *Historical Reflections / Réflexions historiques* 34, 1 (Spring

2008), and "Between Subjects and Citizens: Algerians, Islam, and French National Identity During the Great War," in Paul Spickard, ed., *Race and Nation: Ethnic Systems in the Modern World* (New York: Routledge, 2005), 171–94. I thank the publishers for permission to reprint this material.

I have had the good fortune to have known many outstanding teachers, mentors, and colleagues over the course of my academic career, and their examples have helped inspire this book. Professor William Cook and the late Professor Charles Bailey, at the State University of New York at Geneseo, first inspired me to think of translating my interest in history into a career. Their passion for scholarship and teaching was infectious, and their examples still guide me. At the University of Georgia, John Morrow, David Roberts, and Josh Cole began the long and arduous process of turning me into a professional historian, and helped shape how I think about my work. At the University of California, Santa Barbara, John Talbott, Kenneth Mouré, Michael Osborne, and Tsuyoshi Hasegawa provided teaching, mentoring, and friendship in equal measure. Many colleagues have provided advice on various aspects of research and writing over the many years I have been working on this project. In particular, I would like to thank Tyler Stovall, Alice Conklin, Jennifer Keene, Sue Peabody, Matt Matsuda, Alice Bullard, Paul Spickard, Gregory Mann, Dick Van Galen Last, Jean Pedersen, Kim Munholland, Dagmar Herzog, Emma Vickers, Ralf Futselaar, Ken Osgood, and Steve Longenecker. My colleagues Jamie Frueh, Heather Heckel, David McQuilkin, Jim Josefson, Kara Vuic, and Carl Bowman also helped sustain me during the difficult process of balancing teaching and scholarship. Thanks also to President Phil Stone and Dean Art Hessler for their unswerving support during my time at Bridgewater College. Finally, thank you to the late John Colemen, veteran of wars in southeast Asia and Africa, who reminded me very early on to pay careful attention to the particular culture of armies and their officer corps.

At the Johns Hopkins University Press, I must thank Bob Brugger for first showing interest in this project many years ago, then for sustaining that interest and showing great patience while I labored to produce a book worthy of that attention. Thanks also to Michael Fellman, editor of the "War/Society/Culture" series; to Julie McCarthy and Josh Tong for their help in readying the manuscript for publication; and to Bill Nelson for preparing the maps. Special thanks are due to Peter Dreyer, whose copyediting has improved this book immeasurably.

Friends and family have also provided instrumental moral and material support. My *famille française*—Jean Baker, Valerie Austin, and Jacques, Claire, Steven, Stanley, and Laura Ménard—helped with everything from apartment hunting to obtaining various of life's necessities, to understanding and negotiating the often bewildering complexities of French life, language, and culture (and if I still do not always understand them, it is not their fault!). This remarkable group of people provided conversation and fellowship over numerous meals (no small thing to a hungry and lonely scholar far from home), laughter, and even the occasional getaway to Burgundy. They helped as much as anyone else in enabling me to complete my work, and I shall never be able to repay them fully for their kindness. If I have one sadness upon completing this book, it is that Jacques could not live to see it completed. I hope, nonetheless, that he would have been proud of it. Jean and Françoise Welfling, who were the first people I ever met in Paris, became friends and welcomed me into their home numerous times. Their friendship and kindness confirmed my belief that what is greatest and most interesting about France is its people, and taught me more on this subject than I ever could have learned from books or in archives. Anita Guerrini, Isadora, and Mike, Paul, and Henry Osborne provided yet another home away from home in Paris, as well as practical advice about living and working in that city. I cannot thank them enough. I must also thank my friends and colleagues Ellen Amster and Greg Mann, who often shared coffee, food, and ideas in both France and United States. And I could not ask for greater friendship or support than I have received from Denise Polk, Tom Wang, Rachel and Ken Osgood, and Kara Dixon Vuic and Jason Vuic.

I could never have begun, much less completed this project, or anything else for that matter, without the assistance, love, and support of my parents, Susan and David Adsit. I also owe a special debt of gratitude, and much else, to my Aunt Pauline, who first introduced me to foreign travel, supported my education, hosted several visits to Ireland from France, and provided innumerable smaller, but no less important forms of assistance. Thanks also to Art, Jean, and Paula Cogan, Kevin Myers, and Adam Gay, all of whom helped me see this project through to the end.

I began these acknowledgments with Robert Schumann, and I shall end with him. It was his wife Clara, equal and in many ways superior to him in talent, who pushed him to complete his most ambitious works, his symphonies. My situation is analogous. My wife Cathy has lived, not simply lived through, this project as much as I have, and I could not have completed it without her love, help, and support. I dedicate this work to her.

Nomenclature presents difficult problems when discussing colonial subjects who served as soldiers in the French Army. Some obvious terms are confusing or inexact. "Colonial troops" referred to members of the French Colonial Army, which included white Frenchmen as well as colonial subjects. "Nonwhite troops" is cumbersome, and defines the men in terms of what they were not, rather than what they were. I have chosen to employ the French term *troupes indigènes,* and its English translation "indigenous troops," despite the fact that these are somewhat misleading: once colonial soldiers were on French soil, they were no longer technically "indigenous," native Frenchmen were. However, the French Army used the term to designate colonial subjects in uniform, wherever they happened to be, and I have followed the practice.

The term *tirailleur* translates literally into English as "rifleman," or "skirmisher," but in most cases refers specifically to *troupes indigènes* in the infantry. I have retained this usage, as well as the practice of adding a qualifying adjective to denote the area of origin of the soldier. Thus, *tirailleurs indochinois* describes soldiers from Indochina, *tirailleurs malgaches,* soldiers from Madagascar, and so on. All troops from the federation of French West Africa (l'Afrique occidentale française, or the AOF) were known as *tirailleurs sénégalais,* even though the colony of Senegal comprised only a small part of this 1.8 million square-mile territory.

All translations from the original French in the following text are my own, and in all cases where italics indicate added emphasis, that emphasis appeared in the original and indicates the original author's intent.

*Race and War in France*

# Introduction

❖

France in arms counts among its best shock troops indigenous formations and colonial contingents. The new blood of these young races has flowed in streams when, all of the sudden, it had to be offered up with the old Gallic blood for the defense and support of the threatened fatherland. . . . Therefore the same sepulcher today shelters, from the capital to the frontier, our sons of the metropole and our children of the colonies, whites from Gaul, blacks from Africa, browns from Barbary, yellows from Asia, and citizens of color from the Antilles. The proof has thus been made, on the most sacred battlefields, that colonial France and European France are no longer separated. A pact has been signed in blood for the same honor and the same flags. The colonies have entered into the city by the wide door of common sacrifice, for a traditional association of interests and duties.

—*Senator Henry Bérenger, 1915*

The war against Germany and her allies has kindled in the colonies the most beautiful harvest of devotion to France that history has ever known. Muslim Algeria, Morocco, black Africa, Madagascar, and Indochina have, along with Tunisia, provided the assistance of their indigenous populations, either in the army or in munitions factories. The country—metropole and colonies—has thus affirmed its complete unity above any question of origin or race.

—*Deputies Blaise Diagne and Gratien Candace, 1916*

During the First World War, the French Army deployed some 500,000 colonial subjects on European battlefields. These soldiers, known as *troupes indigènes*, made important contributions to the French war effort, though they constituted only a small percentage of the over 8 million men mobilized in France and its empire between 1914 and 1918. Yet the significance of their contribution extended beyond mere numbers. The presence of men from North Africa, West Africa, Indochina, and Madagascar in uniform and on French soil, defending the metropole from the invading Germans, highlighted issues of race and national identity in a particularly striking way.[1]

Fighting and dying in the struggle against a common enemy associated *troupes indigènes* intimately with the French nation—for many in France there could be no greater sign of devotion to the nation than participating in its defense in those years of critical need. Yet the racial and cultural identity of these men set them apart and made their full integration into the French nation, which official rhetoric insisted was their "adopted fatherland," difficult, if not impossible. Racial prejudices competed with strong traditions of republican universalism and egalitarianism in forming attitudes and policies toward these soldiers. These attitudes and policies, often contradictory and paradoxical, revealed the singular nature of French ideas about race and culture. In France, the republican conception of the nation limited membership, not by race or ethnicity, but by willingness to embrace the nation's culture and its revolutionary and democratic heritage. Such openness caused many in France to view nationality as more open and inclusive than did people in many other countries, yet in practice this ideal was complicated by the racial, cultural, and religious differences of colonial subjects, differences that made it difficult to integrate them easily into existing conceptions of the French nation. *Troupes indigènes* occupied an uncertain rhetorical and legal space in French national life: they were not citizens but imperial subjects, yet were theoretically the objects of a process of assimilation that would provide them with the benefits of French history, culture, language, law, and scientific knowledge, eventually raising them to equal status with their French tutors. Participation in the defense of the metropole only reinforced this vision of unity, but essentialist notions of racial and ethnic hierarchies made full assimilation at the very least problematic, and in the minds of many impossible. A real tension existed, and exists, between universal republican ideals and racial prejudice, which leads to the paradoxical blend of universalism and intolerance that troubles French race relations to this day.

France's use of colonial subjects as soldiers between 1914 and 1918 provides a unique opportunity to explore important questions, not only in French cultural, political, and colonial history, but in the history of the Great War. How did France acquire a reputation as a color-blind society—in which, for example, African Americans have historically received a warm welcome—while at the same time showing manifest signs of racial prejudice and intolerance—from colonial domination of nonwhites to a history of discriminatory treatment of immigrants from Africa and Asia? Why were French political and military officials more willing than those of other Great War combatants to arm nonwhites and deploy them in Europe, yet at the same time seeking to limit the opportunities for integration that military service traditionally provided?

Rhetoric of unity and brotherhood, combined with concrete signs of acceptance, seemed to confirm France's openness, yet the racial and cultural identity of these *troupes indigènes* clearly set them apart. Practices often fell short of rhetoric, and examples of discrimination revealed that race did indeed matter in this supposedly color-blind society. By tracing the attitudes and policies that, first, induced French authorities to make use of *troupes indigènes* in Europe and then defined the role they would play in the war effort and in the French nation, I seek in this book to answer these questions and explain the tension between inclusion and exclusion that marked thinking in France about race, empire, and national identity in a time of war.

Not coincidentally, the Great War cemented France's reputation as a color-blind society, especially in contrast with the prevailing racial climate in the United States. In particular, the experience of African American soldiers in France during this time spread this reputation across the Atlantic. Many of the 200,000 African Americans who served in France after the United States entered the war in 1917 were amazed that French people did not seem to harbor racist feelings against them, an entirely novel experience for virtually all African Americans. One soldier wrote home to his mother, "These French people don't bother with no color line business. They treat us so good that the only time I ever know I'm colored is when I look in the glass."[2] White American officers also took note, and they often worried about the effects such egalitarian treatment would have upon the soldiers when they returned home. Having been exposed to such a different racial environment, would these African Americans submit passively to the daily degradations and humiliations of American racism and Jim Crow?

The integration of black American combat units into the French Army epitomized French acceptance of racial difference. French political and military officials repeatedly asked the commander of the American Expeditionary Force, General John J. Pershing, to provide their exhausted and undermanned units with reinforcements, but Pershing neither wanted to break up the AEF nor wanted his troops to serve under French command. The AEF included several black combat regiments, however, and both the men in these regiments and leaders in the African American community demanded that they play a fighting role, despite the preference of most white American officials that black soldiers serve only in support capacities, performing manual labor.

In the end, Pershing sought to satisfy both French military leaders and African Americans by allowing a few black regiments to serve within the French force structure.[3] Four regiments of the U.S. 93rd Division were integrated into the French Army, retaining their American uniforms but wearing French helmets and carrying French rifles, ammunition, and gear. By most accounts, these men served alongside white French troops in conditions of equality and camaraderie.[4]

If many African Americans were astonished by the egalitarian attitudes they encountered in France and in the French Army, many in France were equally struck by the racism and segregation that reigned in the U.S. Army. In one infamous incident near the end of the war, Colonel J. A. Linard, a French liaison officer serving at Pershing's headquarters, drafted a memorandum explaining American racial prejudices to his French colleagues. Although these attitudes might appear "questionable to a good many French minds," his confidential circular urged French military personnel to respect American prejudices lest overly tolerant attitudes upset white American officers. Linard advised French officers to "avoid any too great intimacy" with their black American colleagues. In particular, treating them on an equal footing with white American officers would "deeply offend the latter," as would praising black American troops excessively, especially in front of white Americans. The military, he urged, should warn French civilians not to "spoil" the black soldiers through too great a familiarity, or through "*public* intimacy" with Frenchwomen.[5]

Linard's advice soon became public, and Blaise Diagne, the black African deputy from Senegal and recently appointed Commissaire général des effectifs coloniaux, protested to Prime Minister Georges Clemenceau that Linard's advice would initiate "outrageous prejudices that, manifestly, violate the inviolable principles of our colonial policy and clash with the noblest French ideas about civilization." To see such "anti-democratic" sentiments penned by a Frenchman, sentiments that were insulting to all men of color, and particularly to the thousands of *troupes indigènes* then fighting for France, was especially offensive.[6] Later, in July 1919, when René Boisneuf, the black deputy for Guadeloupe, read Linard's memorandum before the Chamber of Deputies, his fellow legislators responded by passing a resolution affirming France's dedication to equality and the rights of man, and repudiating prejudice and racism.[7]

Many contemporary observers, noting the apparently dramatic contrast between French racial tolerance and American racism, saw in France a color-blind society, one that truly lived up to the republican ideals of egalitarianism and universalism. W. E. B. Du Bois played a prominent role in propagating this view in the United States. In March 1919, remarking upon the award of the Cross of the Legion of Honor to Blaise Diagne, Du Bois wrote in *The Crisis*, "Vive la France! 'Mine eyes have seen' and they were filled with tears. . . . Men of Africa! How fine a thing to be a black Frenchman in 1919! Imagine such a celebration in America!"[8] Many historians have echoed Du Bois's judgment. The standard history of African American soldiers in the Great War claims the willingness of French commanders to deploy black Americans alongside white French soldiers was unsurprising, because France's use of its own black colonial troops demonstrated that the French "labored under no tradition of race prejudice."[9] Many accounts of the period highlight the contrast between the views of white American officers, who feared that tolerance would undermine the racial order when black soldiers returned home, and more liberal French attitudes.[10] Some historians characterize France's treatment of its *troupes indigènes* as manifestly more egalitarian than American treatment of its black soldiers.[11]

Tyler Stovall asserts, however, that the French viewed African American soldiers "through a haze of stereotypes."[12] Moreover, France's "color-blind" reception of black Americans concealed evidence of racism toward soldiers and workers from the colonies. To many French people, "civilized" black Americans had nothing in common with the "primitive" and "savage" peoples of the French colonial empire. Black Africans were "primitive men, without civilization and who cannot be compared from this point of view with colored Americans," Lieutenant Colonel Édouard Réquin, a member of the French military delegation to the United States, argued in 1918.[13] American soldiers also constituted a temporary presence in France, not a more or less permanent colonial problem. And after three years of fighting that had devastated large parts of the country and killed over a million French soldiers, "many would have welcomed the devil himself had he come prepared to fight the Germans." French people therefore often greeted American soldiers, of whatever color, as saviors deserving of gratitude.[14]

Recent scholarship has challenged the notion that France was really color-blind in any era of its recent history, including at the time of the Great War. During this period, official French discourse hid many unofficial comments that revealed racist attitudes toward both colonial subjects and African American soldiers, and the French reacted so positively to black soldiers in part because severe discipline by racist American officers rendered the behavior of black Americans superior to that of their white compatriots. Praise from men like Du Bois and the soldiers themselves also pleased many in France and convinced them that they did indeed live up to republican egalitarian ideals, despite their manifest prejudices.[15]

France's reputation as a color-blind society in fact concealed a great deal of racist thinking and behavior, but the genuine surprise and delight that many African Americans felt upon encountering the relative tolerance prevalent in French society, even after the war, still requires explanation. Though the "myth" of color-blind France is seriously flawed, and though this myth sometimes served as a tool to give some in France a clear conscience while they criticized American race relations, significant evidence points to the undeniable attractions that the French racial context held for African Americans. If French society was racist like any other, or at least like American society, why then did thousands of African Americans immigrate to France after 1918 in order to make a living and find the acceptance that eluded them on the other side of the Atlantic?

Indeed, the end of the war did not bring an end to conflicts between French and American ideas about race and practices of segregation. In August 1923, the American ambassador to France, Myron T. Herrick, informed the secretary of state that "[b]y order of the Prefect of Police, the licence to remain open all night has been withdrawn from the café 'El Garron' from which the French negro colonials Prince Kojo Tovalou Hovenou and his brother were ejected August 3rd after an altercation with some Americans who objected to their presence." In what was probably unintended irony, Herrick went on: "It is furthermore noted that the cross of the Legion of Honor has been conferred upon an American negro, the painter [Henry Ossawa] Tanner."[16] American tourists, used to strict racial segregation, often objected to the more relaxed social intermingling of races they found in Paris, and many in France were pleased to confer upon a black American artist the recognition and honor denied to him in his own country. Such events only served to confirm, to the French and many others, the idea that the rights of man were more fully realized on that side of the Atlantic.

The reality was more complicated. In certain respects, pure self-interest and expediency, rather than color-blindness, lay behind the French Army's willingness to deploy nonwhites in combat in Europe. France sustained horrendous casualties from the opening weeks of the war, and the French Army soon suffered from a manpower crisis, which only became more acute as the war continued. By 1915, many military and political officials were calling for increased recruitment in the colonies to address this crisis, and soon the government turned to the empire to provide badly needed soldiers for the front. In internal army correspondence, officers could often be particularly blunt about French motives. One noted that increased use of West African troops could "economize, in future offensive actions, the blood, more and more precious, of our [white] soldiers."[17] Another officer was even more direct: "The Senegalese have been recruited to replace Frenchmen, they are cannon fodder [*chair à canon*] to use to spare the whites." These men had come to France "in order to be killed instead of and in place of good Frenchmen."[18] Even if these chilling sentiments represented an extreme opinion among the French officer corps, such comments indicate the important role of manpower needs in stimulating the recruitment and deployment of *troupes indigènes*.

From this perspective, the presence of colonial subjects in the French Army is yet another example of the exploitative relationship between metropole and colonies inherent in all imperial systems. This is certainly part of the story, and it is important not to underemphasize exploitation based upon a grossly unequal power relationship and racist assumptions of white supremacy. Yet these factors alone do not explain why France recruited such a large number of *troupes indigènes* to fight in Europe. Training hundreds of thousands of colonial subjects as soldiers, arming them, and conferring upon them the honor and prestige of membership in the French Army—in short, partially sacrificing the European monopoly on modern military force— posed potentially grave risks for French control of the colonies. Deploying these men in Europe against a white enemy was also dangerous, calling into question white supremacy and violating taboos against committing violence against whites, taboos that to a great extent underpinned the entire European colonial enterprise. In the army, though it was no paradise of racial equality, these men found a relatively egalitarian social order, at least when compared to what they had experienced in the colonies. Similarly, colonial subjects also encountered in metropolitan civil society a racial context that was in many ways much less repressive and color-conscious than the regime that prevailed in the colonies.

Many *troupes indigènes* remarked upon these issues, and protests from colonial officials and others who deemed these risks greater than France's dire need for more soldiers confirmed that the potential for trouble was indeed real. Despite the risks, the French Army did deploy *troupes indigènes* in Europe, and the attitudes of other powers highlighted the uniqueness of its doing so. Germany protested vehemently against France's introduction of "uncivilized" warriors from Africa into Europe as an unconscionable attack upon white prestige, and even France's British and American allies viewed the use of *troupes indigènes* in Europe with skepticism and apprehension.

Great Britain, also possessed of an extensive colonial empire, did use 138,000 Indian troops on the Western Front in 1914 and 1915, but the authors of *The Times History of the War* revealed how uncomfortable the British were with arming their colonial subjects for action in France, asserting in 1914, "We British are constitutionally the last people in the world to take unfair advantage in sport, war, or commerce of our opponents. The instinct which made us such sticklers for propriety in all our dealings made us more reluctant than other nations would feel to employ coloured troops against a white enemy." Yet the fighting quality of "our dusky native troops" had compelled Britain to allow the Indian Army "the privilege of taking its place beside British troops" in the opening stages of the war.[19]

This privilege did not last long. Enormous casualties, declining morale, and doubts about the wisdom of deploying nonwhite troops in Europe led to the permanent withdrawal of the Indian Corps from the Western Front by the end of 1915.[20] Manpower needs did impel some British officials to contemplate the use of soldiers from Britain's West African colonies in Europe in 1918, but the war ended before any plans came to fruition. Still, British authorities regarded such a measure as a risk that only extreme circumstances would justify, and the idea sat uncomfortably next to a British imperial ideology that insisted above all on the maintenance of white supremacy.[21] Instead, the British army deployed its Indian troops in a much more traditional manner after 1915, eventually sending over 800,000 to fight in the Middle East. There, far away from Europe, the Indians fought against the Turks, and thus the British avoided the grave implications of using nonwhite colonial subjects in battle against white Europeans.[22]

For many French officials, the use of *troupes indigènes* outside their colonies of origin and against a white enemy posed less of an ideological problem. Other colonial powers—Great Britain, the Netherlands, Belgium, and Germany, as well as France—had employed indigenous troops locally in the conquest and policing of their colonies. Even during the Great War, German forces serving in East Africa included a large contingent of indigenous troops.[23]

France, however, often used indigenous troops as elements of expeditionary forces deployed in other areas of the empire and beyond. West African troops served in Madagascar and North Africa before 1914, and Algerian troops fought in France itself during the war of 1870. From the earliest weeks of the Great War, North and West African soldiers took part in the desperate attempts to stop the invading Germans. This was only the beginning, and many thousands more *troupes indigènes* from all corners of the French empire soon arrived to bolster the war effort. In short, France had a long tradition of risking what other powers would not, making soldiers of conquered peoples and deploying them against white enemies.[24]

It was not merely the need for military manpower after 1914 that allowed the French government to override the doubts and risks that held back other European powers and to deploy *troupes indigènes* on such a large scale in Europe. After all, the other belligerents also suffered manpower crises as their losses mounted on the battlefield. The key to understanding French decisions lay in republican ideology and its influence upon French thinking about empire and race. The Revolution of 1789 and the Declaration of the Rights of Man and Citizen, which crystallized the Enlightenment principles of "Liberty, Equality, and Fraternity," produced a republican culture that demanded respect for basic human freedoms and rights. That these principles remained imperfectly realized, especially during the many years of undemocratic rule between the Revolution and 1870, did not lessen their power.[25] With the advent of the Third Republic, French liberals strove to identify the new regime closely with the ideals of 1789 and saw themselves as completing the work begun almost a century before, fulfilling the promise of the Revolution. Yet it was under the Third Republic that France dramatically expanded its colonial empire, covering vast stretches of the globe. On the face of it, the possession of such an empire violated the most basic republican principles: colonial subjects enjoyed neither true freedom, nor equality with their colonial masters, nor fraternity, since their inferiority and inability to rule themselves justified their subjugation. Yet it was not mere hypocrisy that allowed French republicans to reconcile their values with the acquisition of empire, but an appeal to a "civilizing mission" in the colonies. Government and colonial officials could claim to be living up to republican principles by arguing that they were introducing these very principles into the colonies. That they had to do this largely by force was regrettable, but the process would benefit the colonized in the long run, they believed. In French West Africa, for example, colonial administrators sought to act upon this civilizing mission, building enough schools, hospitals, and railroads to legitimize empire-building (at least in their own eyes), while still professing republican values.[26]

One of the foundations of French colonial ideology was "assimilation," which sought to integrate indigenous societies into the administrative and cultural structures of the metropole. Assimilation and the civilizing mission were closely related, inasmuch as both proposed in theory to raise indigenous peoples in the colonies up to the level of French people in the metropole, until colonial subjects and French citizens truly shared one national culture.[27] This conception of national identity, which was at once relatively open to the integration of outsiders and restrictive in its demand for cultural conformity, had roots in prerevolutionary France. Gallican Catholicism, the Reformation, absolutism, and the Enlightenment all contributed to the curious blend of tolerance and intolerance—racial others are inferior, yet assimilable—that marked French thinking about the nation. More proximately, the Revolution, and especially the Third Republic, decisively shaped French national identity in the twentieth century, particularly in relation to the colonies.[28]

By the outbreak of the First World War, however, assimilationist ideology faced serious competition from the competing vision of "association," which advocated allowing colonial subjects to develop within their own cultures and social institutions while the French co-opted local indigenous elites and associated them with the colonizing project. Association seemed to abandon, at least in part, the republican ideal of civilizing and assimilating indigenous peoples, and to recognize an irreducible difference between the French and their colonial subjects. Subjects would remain associated with the colonial project, not assimilated into an expansive French national community. Yet assimilation had never been unproblematic, and even the most ardent of assimilationists pointed to racial and cultural gaps that would require many years, even centuries, to bridge before true integration could take place. Association also sometimes pointed to some far-off merging of interests, but ultimately emphasized the distance—cultural, spatial, and racial—that separated France from its colonies. In any case, assimilation and association coexisted and often overlapped right up to and through the Great War.[29]

Republican ideology and racialist thinking, then, were interwoven in complex and contradictory ways in the colonial context, helping to justify the republican empire and to define the purposes of imperial policies.[30] Military service, along with education, railroad construction, and medical care, served as an important component of France's civilizing mission and the spread of republican ideals in the colonies. Even within France itself, republican officials argued that the military should be "the school of the nation," bringing together its sons and smoothing over geographic, linguistic, and ideological diversity.[31] Through the gradual institution of universal obligatory military service, the Third Republic did just that, and service in the army helped unify the country as much as the government's aggressive railroad construction and educational reforms.[32] In the colonies, the service of colonial subjects in the French Army stemmed in large part from practical interests of colonial administration. French officials sought to save both money and French lives by using cheaper soldiers more resistant to local diseases, lowering both the financial and human costs of empire. Yet advocates of using *troupes indigènes* also argued that service in the French Army would bring colonial subjects closer to the French nation and aid in their assimilation. It was only right, too, that they share the burden of military service, because this same republican ideal of assimilation meant that they shared French interests and the obligation of defending them.

The German invasion of France in 1914 provided a critical test of this rhetoric. France itself was in grave danger, and if the interests of citizens and colonial subjects were really one, then the direct participation of *troupes indigènes* in its defense would be unproblematic. Ideally, it would matter neither that *troupes indigènes* were not white nor that they would be bearing arms against a white opponent in the heart of Europe. They were, in theory, French soldiers, and what could be more proper than French soldiers taking up arms in defense of *la patrie en danger*, as when the Revolution itself was threatened from across the eastern frontier in 1792?

This was the theory. Practice turned out to be more complicated. The tension between the theory of republican universalism and egalitarianism, on the one hand, and the practices of the French Army and state with regard to the participation of colonial subjects in the war effort in Europe, on the other, is the subject of this study. Racial prejudice, assumptions of white supremacy and nonwhite inferiority that ran directly contrary to the rhetoric of a universal humanity and equality among people, lay at the root of this tension. In short, commitment to the ideals of universalism and egalitarianism pushed French officials to include *troupes indigènes* in both national defense and the national community, while racism pulled these same officials back from measures that would make the full integration of colonial subjects into national life a reality.

The importance of republican values in the official self-image and political discourse of the Third Republic allowed Gratien Candace and Blaise Diagne, both blacks and members of the French Chamber of Deputies (thus living symbols, to many, of the potentialities of the civilizing mission and assimilation), to assert that through the service of *troupes indigènes* in the war in Europe, France had "affirmed its complete unity above any question of origin or race."[33] Adherence to these values allowed Senator Henry Bérenger to evoke the image of one sepulcher sheltering the bodies of "our sons of the metropole and our children of the colonies," soldiers of all colors fallen on European battlefields, proving "that colonial France and European France are no longer separated. . . . A pact has been signed in blood."[34]

Bérenger's striking image of the mixing of French and colonial blood testified to the fundamental importance of an assimilation of identities that went, in theory, much deeper than a mere merging of interests. Yet this republican rhetoric could not overcome the concrete effects of racism. As much as ideology and common sacrifice for and defense of *la patrie* (the fatherland) joined *troupes indigènes* to the French nation, their racial and cultural identity kept them separate. Native French and colonial blood might literally have been spilled and mixed on the battlefield, but the figurative mixing required to integrate *indigènes* into the national community was more problematic. Bérenger's choice of words hint at an irreducible difference between the two types of soldiers. He called native Frenchmen "sons," an appellation they could retain even with ascension to adulthood, but he characterized colonial subjects as "children," implying a perpetual minority and the corresponding need for tutelage. The impulse simultaneously to infantilize and to glorify *troupes indigènes* remained characteristic of such rhetoric throughout the war.

Though it is focused on the French military, this study goes beyond an examination of military attitudes, aiming to illuminate French ideas about race and national identity in general. Armies are unique institutions, with their own cultures, perspectives, biases, interests, and imperatives. The sources for this study are primarily the written words of French officers, as well as of French colonial officials and politicians, who in turn had their own particular agendas and biases. However revealing these words are of the racial attitudes that shaped French policy toward *troupes indigènes* during the war, one must always keep in mind that such words reflect the distinctive perspectives of the men who wrote them.

Yet it would be wrong to assume that these perspectives had no relevance to realities outside military, political, and colonial circles. For one thing, these men were the ones who had the closest contact with *troupes indigènes* and had the most influence on their use. In a very immediate sense, the attitudes of army officers had the most direct and profound impact upon the soldiers themselves, and these attitudes often determined decisions about recruitment, training, deployment, and tactics, and could thus determine life and death. Yet the attitudes that officers and officials expressed in written reports had a relevance that extended beyond the army, the battlefield, and the rooms in which military and political authorities made decisions. Making the army a republican and national institution was a top priority of the leaders of the Third Republic. This was no easy task, and episodes such as the Dreyfus Affair demonstrated the essential conservatism of many members of the officer corps right into the twentieth century.[35]

By 1914, however, politicans had made a great deal of progress in "republicanizing" the army. The position of General Joseph Joffre, whose political orthodoxy was unquestionable (he also, incidentally, made his career in the colonies), as the head of French forces during the early years of the war was emblematic of the new, closer relationship between the Republic and its guardians.[36] Universal military service, fully established by 1905, followed by long periods in the reserves, and the mobilization of over eight million Frenchmen between 1914 and 1918 meant that, in important ways, the army had become a representative national institution by the time of the Great War. And while many of the officers whose words provide evidence for this study made their careers in the army, and many of them did so in the colonies, both of which gave them a particular outlook, what is remarkable about the attitudes they express is the extent to which they reflect common republican assumptions and partake of the predominant political discourse of the day. Their racial attitudes are not those of reactionary figures standing against the tide of liberal democracy, but those of men who had largely accepted prevailing ideas about French national identity, ideas largely consistent with the egalitarian ideals of 1789, albeit limited by racial and cultural prejudices.

In 1914, France called upon its colonial subjects during a period of extreme crisis, four years of war that threatened the existence of the French nation and the republican values for which it stood. These values, especially universalism and equality, opened up a space in the French nation for the participation of colonial subjects in the sacred duty of defending the *patrie*. But the ultimately uncrossable boundaries of racial difference sharply delineated and limited this space, even if it allowed *indigènes* some opportunities. French military and political authorities defined just what those opportunities were, and just where the boundaries lay, by articulating specific policies toward *troupes indigènes* that clearly reflected the acute tension between republican ideals and racial prejudice.

# CHAPTER ONE

# *Reservoirs of Men*

❖

Africa has cost us heaps of gold, thousands of soldiers, and streams of blood. We do not dream of demanding the gold from her. But the men and the blood, she must repay them with interest.

—*Minister of War Adolphe Messimy, 1909*

Recruitment must no longer appear to them like a roundup analogous to the cruel incursions of the old *sofas* [West African mercenaries], but, on the contrary, as a payment of a blood tax, considered among us . . . as an honor and a duty. . . . it will make them understand that this [French] victory, which will save our race, will also save theirs.

—*Minister of the Colonies Henry Simon, 1918*

You have already taken all that I have, and now you are taking my only son!

—*A Senegalese mother's lament to a French officer*

Recruitment was in many ways the most basic issue confronting the military and political officials who turned to France's colonial subjects for help in defending the metropole against the German invaders. In this time of critical danger to the very survival of the French Republic, French authorities based their appeal to the manpower resources of the empire on a powerful sense of entitlement and republican orthodoxy. Colonial subjects, the thinking went, owed France a "blood tax" (*impôt du sang*) in return for the privilege of living under enlightened French rule. Colonial conquest and rule had cost France dearly in treasure and lives, and now it was time to collect on the debt thus accrued. In other words, the civilizing mission came at a price that Africans and Asians would now have to pay. But the rhetoric was not limited only to the language of debt and repayment. The very ideals of the civilizing mission promoted a discourse emphasizing the duties and interests that white French citizens and colonial subjects shared. These duties and interests grew out of service in defense of the state, of equality of sacrifice, of honor in upholding French civilization in the face of the gravest threat that it had yet faced. Republican ideals, which France was busy spreading around the globe in its colonial empire, stressed the fundamental equality of all human beings and the universality of human rights, and this was precisely why colonial subjects should contribute their fair share to the struggle. The fight was "ours," to be sure, but it was "theirs" as well.

This rhetorical and ideological justification, however, contained numerous contradictions and exceptions. Equality of duty and sacrifice in no way implied equality of rights and privileges. Colonial subjects were just that, not citizens. Pressing them into service, or even asking them to volunteer, thus only highlighted the gulf that separated these subject peoples from their French rulers. Moreover, race was never far from the surface in these discussions. The victory that would save the French "race" might also save African and Asian "races" as well, but such a characterization clearly divided European and colonial populations along racial lines. This belied claims about universal humanity, or at least implied the existence of inequalities and hierarchies within that human family. Finally, it was not clear to most people in the colonies why they should have to make such sacrifices. Colonial rule, despite the ideal of the civilizing mission and its alleged benefits, appeared to be burdensome enough without watching sons, brothers, husbands, and fathers march off to hardship and, possibly, death in a faraway land and for a cause that seemed equally remote.

The need for soldiers to defend France overrode such considerations, however, and the effort to recruit among colonial populations during the war was extensive and yielded results that, for some, vindicated the ideological justifications rooted in the civilizing mission and republican ideals. Practices set in place in the colonies before 1914 provided a sturdy foundation upon which to build more intensive recruitment operations, which produced a large force of *troupes indigènes* for service in Europe. Concepts of "race" helped determine where colonial and military authorities recruited and how intensively. These racial preferences could not always be realized, but they still had a powerful effect upon the shape of recruitment efforts, as did the reaction of colonized peoples themselves. In fact, difficulties stemming from indigenous resistance, as well as logistical, political, and economic problems, produced a virtual halt to recruitment in the colonies by the end of 1917. Yet the following year would see one of the most intensive recruiting efforts of the war in several colonies, as the determination of the new Prime Minister Georges Clemenceau to obtain victory at all costs made itself felt everywhere, from the front to the farthest reaches of the French colonial empire.

## *Troupes indigènes* Before the Great War

The era of the Great War was certainly not the first time that France had looked to its colonial populations for soldiers. In some places, during the first phase of French imperialism under the ancien régime, small numbers of indigenous troops garrisoned remote trading posts. It was during the so-called new imperialism of the nineteenth century, however, that the use of *troupes indigènes* expanded dramatically, and these soldiers played an important role in conquering and policing the territories of France's rapidly expanding empire. This prewar experience helped shape wartime efforts to recruit, train, and deploy *troupes indigènes* in Europe, and by 1914, a system was in place throughout the empire that facilitated the recruitment of hundreds of thousands of colonial subjects to defend the metropole

The French Army began to recruit indigenous troops as early as the seventeenth century, forming its first regular indigenous unit in India.[1] By the late nineteenth century, when France began to expand its colonial empire rapidly, the Colonial Army included permanent units of *tirailleurs* in West Africa, Indochina, and Madagascar.[2] During the same period, the army expanded its use of North Africans in the ranks. Unlike West Africans, Indochinese, and Madagascans, *troupes indigènes* from North Africa served not in the Colonial Army, but in the Armée d'Afrique (a branch of the metropolitan army that garrisoned Algeria, Tunisia, and Morocco).[3] Algerians began serving the French as soldiers from the earliest days of the French conquest, which began in 1830, fighting in Algeria, in other colonial possessions, and even in the Crimea, in Italy, and in France itself during the Franco-Prussian War of 1870.[4] After France established a protectorate over Tunisia in 1881, Tunisians also began to serve in the Armée d'Afrique, and Morocco, the last major French colonial acquisition before 1914, provided the final significant source of *troupes indigènes*.[5]

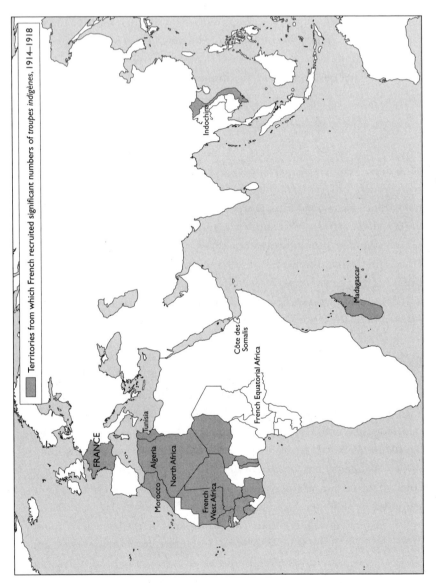

The French empire and its "reservoirs of men"

Territories from which French recruited significant numbers of *troupes indigènes*, 1914–1918

FRANCE

Morocco

Algeria

North Africa

Tunisia

French West Africa

French Equatorial Africa

Côte des Somalis

Madagascar

Indochina

The reasons for recruiting indigenous forces were similar across the different areas of the empire. Administrators in Indochina calculated that the army could employ two indigenous *tirailleurs* for the cost of one European soldier, and this ratio was generally the same in the other colonies as well.[6] Economizing on French lives was even more important. Tropical climates and diseases took a frightening toll on European troops, killing many more men than did armed resistance. Locally recruited troops possessed greater resistance to tropical diseases, and what casualties there were among them were much easier for the French to accept than the loss of their own sons. High European mortality rates in West Africa and Indochina led directly to the expansion of indigenous units. The disastrous experience of French troops during the 1895 conquest of Madagascar—in which the army lost 25 soldiers in combat and over 6,000 to disease, mostly from malaria—was only the most spectacular example of a widespread problem.[7]

Political and national security issues also compelled the army to employ indigenous forces when possible. Given the French public's reluctance to sacrifice its sons in imperial adventures, politicians and military leaders often had to rely on indigenous troops to pursue colonial expansion. Moreover, given the increasingly tense nature of national rivalries within Europe in the decades after the Franco-Prussian war, officials wanted to leave the greater burden of defense and the maintenance of order in the colonies to *troupes indigènes*, the Foreign Legion, and locally recruited Europeans. That way, metropolitan troops could remain in France and face the primary threat to national security, Germany. All of this kept the government and the French people happy, inasmuch as colonial acquisition, never wildly popular with the French public during this period, did not require inordinate sacrifices. Meanwhile, French officers were glad to have troops to command and a theater for action.

Methods of recruiting these troops varied across the different colonies, though officials relied upon a combination of voluntarism and coercion in all areas, setting a pattern they would follow after 1914. In West Africa, for example, early recruitment technically relied on voluntary enlistment, but in reality filling the ranks depended heavily upon the slave trade. Throughout much of the nineteenth century, the military made use of a system known as *rachat* ("repurchase"), in which French military authorities paid an enlistment bonus directly to a slave's master, ostensibly to purchase the former's freedom. Yet, the "freed" slave then owed twelve to fourteen years of service to the army. This system, combined with the opportunity for real soldiering, a colorful uniform, and increased pay, which attracted genuine volunteers, helped transform the *tirailleurs sénégalais* into a sizable force that the French used for conquest and security in West Africa and in other colonies. By the late nineteenth century, the army formally abandoned the system of *rachat*, but similar practices still provided new recruits.[8]

Though voluntarism and less formal methods of coercion such as the *rachat* were important in filling the ranks in West Africa and other areas, political and military officials also employed more systematic systems of compulsion as the French empire and the corresponding need for troops expanded. In many cases, these officials resorted to conscription, and such precedents would in several instances provide a convenient mechanism by which to meet the extraordinary demands of the First World War. In Madagascar, General Joseph Galliéni undertook intensive recruitment as part of the famous "Galliéni method," perfected during his service in West Africa and Indochina, to make extensive use of indigenous troops to secure French control over the territory.[9] Part of this process involved reviving an earlier indigenous system of conscription, and though voluntary enlistment continued to be an important basis of recruitment in Madagascar through and beyond 1914, the French administration retained the ability to draft young Malagasy men into service.[10]

France also made use of an existing indigenous system conscription in Tunisia, instituted by the Tunisian government in 1860.[11] The same was true, briefly, in Morocco. There, the French Army had at first tried to make use of the sultan's army, recruited in part through conscription, but this soon proved impractical and recruitment soon became entirely voluntary.[12] In Indochina, French officials resorted to the draft from the early stages of conquest, employing a form of "indirect administration" and relying on indigenous auxiliaries at the level of the commune to provide a certain quota of recruits as a supplement to voluntary enlistments.[13]

French efforts to institute conscription were the most extensive and controversial in French West Africa (l'Afrique occidentale française, or the AOF) and Algeria. The practice came late in these areas, both seeing their first draft in 1912. The movement to expand the use of *troupes indigènes* had gained significant momentum in the early years of the twentieth century, with the 1905 reduction of obligatory military service for Frenchmen to two years; dramatic diplomatic disputes with Germany over imperial interests in Morocco; heightened fears of Germany's rapidly growing population, larger army, and increased military power; and French fears about their own country's declining birthrate.[14] In this context, new ideas about intensified recruitment in the colonies emerged, and officials turned naturally to the two most important sources of *troupes indigènes,* West and North Africa.

The main impetus to expand the force of West Africans came from Lieutenant-Colonel Charles Mangin, an officer with long experience in West Africa, who in 1909 began to agitate in earnest for what he called a *force noire* (black force).[15] Frustrated by a lack of enthusiasm within the military and colonial administration, Mangin began a public debate in the press that would generate over 4,300 articles before war broke out in 1914.[16] In his book-length manifesto, *La force noire* (1910), Mangin argued passionately that black Africans were "born soldiers," whose warlike past had prepared them well for service in the French Army.[17] Moreover, he argued, black Africans would provide the ideal solution to France's looming demographic and military problems. The decline of the French birthrate, especially in comparison with Germany's, preoccupied many political and military leaders, and France was already having difficulty raising enough troops to defend itself in Europe. Employing African soldiers in the colonies would free French soldiers for service at home, or the *tirailleurs* might provide even more direct assistance by serving in Europe. West Africa was an "inexhaustible reservoir of men," which could provide 10,000 volunteers per year, if not many more.[18]

Mangin's vision of expanded recruitment in West Africa did not include conscription. He was sure that these "natural warriors" would be only too happy to volunteer, given the right incentives. The governor-general of the AOF concurred with Mangin's optimistic outlook, though he cautioned against doing damage to the economy by making soldiers of too many productive young men.[19] Mangin's enthusiasm was of course more pronounced, and after a 1910 mission to the AOF to assess the possibilities for recruitment, he announced that the army could easily recruit many thousands of willing volunteers in short order.[20]

Yet despite such enthusiasm, it was clear to most officials that more rigorous methods would be necessary to field a large force of *tirailleurs*. Recruiting efforts in 1910 and 1911 fell well short of the army's needs, and so in 1912, the government issued a decree organizing the recruitment of 8,000 men per year by conscription. Mangin disapproved, but he could not argue with the results: more than 16,000 new soldiers over the course of 1912 and 1913. Despite this success, administrative difficulties and changed circumstances brought an end to the draft in 1914.[21] Nevertheless, the French had established the mechanisms of conscription in the AOF, and this would have important implications for recruitment during the war.

In Algeria, the prewar introduction of conscription also established a foundation upon which French officials would build after 1914. In 1903, reduction of the benefits to which soldiers were entitled led to fewer voluntary enlistments during the following years and depleted the ranks of *troupes indigènes* in the Armée d'Afrique.[22] Early attempts to rectify this situation with plans for conscription came to naught, but in 1911, with French forces in Morocco facing popular unrest and threats from Germany destabilizing the international situation, the matter became more urgent.[23] In early 1912, a new decree set the terms for the draft, which included a special bonus, equal to that for men who enlisted voluntarily.[24]

This last measure was immediately controversial. Algerians, especially the assimilated and politically conscious among them, rightly interpreted it as a way to buy off the indigenous population and avoid treating native Algerians as citizens with the obligation of military service, a circumstance that nonetheless pleased Europeans in the colony.[25] The new soldiers would simultaneously be conscripts and mercenaries. In response to complaints about this and other aspects of the new system, the government made several political concessions to benefit veterans. This muted some criticism and helped ensure that the incorporation of the new draftees proceeded fairly smoothly.[26] In 1913, the army incorporated a second contingent of conscripts, but the late date at which the draft began and the small number of men incorporated (fewer than 2,500 per year) meant that when war broke out in Europe, the French Army could not rely heavily upon conscripts to fill its ranks in North Africa. Yet, even though fewer than 12 percent of *tirailleurs algériens* were draftees on 1 August 1914, conscription in Algeria would take on increased importance when France turned to its colonies for help in defending the metropole in the following years.[27]

By that time, French officials had instituted more or less effective systems to obtain indigenous soldiers in the colonies, but they still often encountered significant difficulties and occasional resistance from the subject populations. The nature of the difficulties and the forms of resistance in the prewar period established a pattern that would change only in scale between 1914 and 1918. Resistance to recruitment was minimal in Tunisia and Morocco: Moroccan soldiers were all volunteers, and while Tunisians were not always keen to enlist in the army of the conquerors, they did not offer much resistance to the draft—its precolonial existence had habituated them to obligatory military service and technically they were serving their titular ruler, the bey of Tunis. Difficulties were common in the other colonies, however, even before the introduction of conscription. In West Africa, the completion of conquest choked off the supply of enemy captives who could switch sides and fight for the French; slavery was in steep decline or eradicated in many areas, rendering scarce those recruits who would exchange their old masters for the French Army; and volunteers were hard to come by. In other colonies, *indigènes* preferred less dangerous or more lucrative employment, or shunned open collaboration with the colonial regime, and so volunteers were scarce. In addition, many Muslims considered military service corrosive of religious values, while elites rejected the manual labor and the servile status of service among former slaves and prisoners of war (in Africa), or merely among those lower-class men desperate enough to seek a career soldiering for the French.

Problems became worse when the French administration intensified its recruiting efforts, especially if this involved conscription. Abuses were common both in systems of conscription and of voluntary enlistments, because both methods often involved pressure and coercion on the part of indigenous auxiliaries trying to satisfy the demands of their colonial masters. Indigenous leaders, when they did not try to evade French demands altogether, often presented men who were physically unfit for service, either as "volunteers" or conscripts, in order to satisfy quotas set by colonial officials. Local notables frequently put forward members of their community who were the least wealthy, powerful, healthy, and suitable for military life, while exempting the potentially more militarily useful sons of the fortunate. Not only did this produce unfit candidates, but the inequity of the system provoked discontent, resentment, and social unrest. The widespread practice of allowing draftees to purchase substitutions further aggravated this situation, and substitutes most often came from the most desperate, most miserable, and least fit segment of the population. Such men, and others who entered the army because of conscription or other forms of coercion, made unwilling and unenthusiastic soldiers, many deserting at their first opportunity. For example, in Cochin China, the French use of conscription to form a permanent, standing army diverged from the precolonial indigenous rulers' practice of drafting men for short periods and specific circumstances. As a result, desertion rates ran as high as 16 percent.[28] Even draft by lottery did not always prevent abuses. In Algeria, local indigenous officials charged with administering the registration and the lottery that determined who would be drafted often arranged for the least powerful members of their communities to end up in the uniform of the *tirailleurs*. This, of course, was a large part of the reason that the draft boards saw so many potential recruits whose physical condition left a great deal to be desired.[29] Similar problems and abuses, along with resistance—ranging from the intentional undermining of French demands, to desertion or flight, to open rebellion—complicated recruiting efforts in many of the colonies.

These difficulties were really only a minor irritation for French political and military authorities in the colonies, but they established a pattern that would be repeated after 1914. During the prewar period, the French Army succeeded in instituting viable methods of recruitment and in fielding combat-ready units of *troupes indigènes*. Wartime demands would be unprecedented, and would put tremendous pressure on the French colonial administration and the subject peoples of the empire, with passive resistance occasionally flaring up into outright revolt. Nonetheless, practices set before 1914 allowed France to call upon its subject peoples to enter its military and fight the German invader on French soil. The unprecedented manpower needs of the war, along with republican notions of assimilation and the reciprocal duties of colonizers and colonized, spurred the French government to put hundreds of thousands of colonial subjects in uniform, while prevailing racial stereotypes determined patterns of recruitment both among and within the different colonies of the French empire.

## Wartime Recruitment in the Colonies

If France's colonial subjects were going to make a significant contribution to the defense of the metropole, then the army and colonial administration had to get more of these men into uniform, and quickly. In August 1914, France already had almost 90,000 *troupes indigènes* in the ranks.[30] However, the vast numbers of men engaged on the Western Front and elsewhere soon made it apparent that the French would have to employ new, or at least more intensive methods of recruitment. Conscription provided authorities with an effective way to exploit the manpower resources of several of the colonies, but new and urgent requirements necessitated some innovation. New approaches ranged from much more intensive and thorough conscription efforts to various incentives that attempted to encourage compliance with the draft and to attract volunteers. Powerful sentiments of entitlement and republican ideology added impetus to and justified a recruitment that was spurred by the need to make up for appalling losses at the front. Now that the *patrie* (fatherland) itself was in grave danger, republican France would demand that its colonial subjects pay the debt—the "blood tax"— they owed to the metropole for the supposed benefits of French colonial rule. Not only was this a fair price, many argued, for exposure to the French *mission civilisatrice,* but service in the army was a logical extension of this mission, because these soldiers would be both absorbing and upholding French values and culture. Republican rhetoric and ideology provided French political and military officials with the ideal justification for drawing on the resources of the empire.

The success of recruiting efforts depended upon cooperation among the military, the colonial administration, and the government in Paris, while subject peoples themselves influenced events through a range of actions: from open acceptance, to grudging compliance, to evasion, and even to armed resistance. Predominant ideas about race also determined the intensity of efforts to call *indigènes* to serve their "adopted fatherland." French authorities relied upon racial distinctions among the various subject peoples over whom they ruled in the colonies, distinguishing between what they called *races guerrières* (warlike races) and *races non-guerrières* (unwarlike races) in making decisions about where and how intensively to recruit. This could involve general comparisons among peoples in different colonies—Moroccans were allegedly more warlike than Tunisians, West Africans more than Indochinese—or among different "races" within single colonial possessions—the Sakalava people of Madagascar were supposedly more warlike than their Hova neighbors, and the Bambara more than the Fanti in West Africa. The unprecedented nature of wartime manpower needs made preferences for *races guerrières* over *races non-guerrières* more and more difficult to observe strictly, but such ideas and stereotypes still had a powerful influence on the nature and intensity of recruitment across the empire. Despite varying levels of intensity, the overall recruitment effort was quite successful, netting the French Army nearly 500,000 men between 1914 and 1918.

## Recruitment, 1914–1917

The history of the recruitment of *troupes indigènes* divides naturally into two parts, the first spanning the first three years of the war from 1914 through 1917, and the second from the end of 1917 to the end of the war in November 1918. The first period saw efforts to tap the resources of the empire to make up for the appalling losses the French Army was suffering in the fighting, though by the end of 1917, it appeared that the colonies had given nearly all they could to the war effort. The second period, however, saw a dramatic intensification of recruiting efforts in response to Clemenceau's determination to win victory at all costs.

By the end of 1914, after only five months of fighting, the French Army had suffered well over 500,000 casualties, with approximately 350,000 of those killed in action. By the end of the following year, France had lost at least half of the approximately 1.3 million men who would be killed before the fighting ended in 1918. Over three million more soldiers would be wounded, and again, more than half received their wounds before the end of 1915.[31] Clearly, French officials needed to find remedies, and quickly, for the resulting manpower crisis at the front. Political and military leaders turned to the nation's colonial populations, beginning their first concentrated efforts to recruit large masses of men in the colonies during the war's second year. Table 1 shows, in approximate round figures, the numbers of *troupes indigènes* recruited in each colony during each year of the war.[32] Not all of these men served in Europe, but a large majority did, and combined with the 90,000 *troupes indigènes* under arms when the war broke out, the colonies added about 500,000 soldiers to the more than eight million Frenchmen who were mobilized for war between 1914 and 1918.

As this accounting makes clear, the AOF provided more recruits than any other single colony. This was in part because it was a large and populous territory, but the intensity of recruitment there stemmed also from West Africans' reputation as, in Mangin's words, "natural warriors." Clearly evident, if not always clearly defined, ideas about race, with roots in the years before 1914, often determined the nature of recruitment efforts. First of all, there was a general consensus among many politicians and military men that West Africans were especially warlike. They had a reputation both as brave, disciplined, and loyal praetorians fighting gloriously for the French flag and as ruthless, bloodthirsty savages whose fury was fearsome to behold on the battlefield.[33] These attitudes had a long history in France, and stemmed from images of Africa as a dark, mysterious continent, whose people were primitive and ferocious, but at the same time exotic and childlike.[34] The result of such thinking was that West Africans stood highest in the martial hierarchy in which the French ranked their colonial subjects, and they often served outside the AOF, especially in Madagascar and Morocco, before 1914. Such precedents in

TABLE 1
Troupes indigènes *Recruited, 1914–1918*

| | West Africa | Madagascar | Indochina | Algeria | Tunisia | Morocco | Total |
|---|---|---|---|---|---|---|---|
| 1914 | 10,000 | 1,000 | — | 19,000 | 14,500 | 2,600 | 47,100 |
| 1915 | 22,000 | 1,000 | — | 14,500 | 4,250 | 5,000 | 46,750 |
| 1916 | 59,000 | 20,000 | 28,000 | 17,500 | 4,250 | 4,500 | 133,250 |
| 1917 | 12,000 | 20,000 | 22,000 | 33,500 | 11,000 | 4,500 | 103,000 |
| 1918 | 63,000 | 4,000 | — | 55,500 | 13,000 | 7,700 | 143,200 |
| Total | 166,000 | 46,000 | 50,000 | 140,000 | 47,000 | 24,300 | 473,300 |

both attitudes and practice guaranteed that efforts to expand recruitment in the colonies would focus carefully on the *tirailleurs sénégalais*.

The effects of ideas about race were not limited to such broad distinctions among the inhabitants of different regions of the colonial empire. French officers further divided the subject populations into groups within each colony or region, ranking them according to their alleged warlike natures. Such opinions were often based upon observation and the relative resistance to French conquest displayed by various groups, but they also often corresponded to political or ideological priorities that had nothing to do with warlike abilities. Such quasi-anthropological distinctions among various "races," or ethnic groups, were particularly important in West Africa. Mangin, who had always styled himself as an expert on the levels of martial ability among the ethnic groups in the AOF, made much of the militaristic past of West Africans in *La force noire*. Such views had become conventional wisdom in the French officer corps by the time of the Great War, and the High Command enshrined these ideas in a 1918 manual for officers new to West African units entitled *Notice sur les Sénégalais et leur emploi au combat*, which devoted several pages to evaluating the martial natures of the various "races" of the AOF. Men from ethnic groups residing in the interior, such as Bambara and Mossi, were *races guerrières*, while men from coastal areas, such as Fanti and Susu, were generally *races non-guerrières* and made "mediocre" soldiers.[35] These ideas influenced recruitment, and the French administration in the colonies often applied conscription selectively, with different quotas for different regions according to their ability to provide warlike recruits. The effects were dramatic: over 90 percent of West Africans recruited in Senegal during the First World War were from so-called *races guerrières*.[36]

Both the macro focus on West Africans in general as particularly warlike and the micro focus on certain "races" among them as even more so led French officials to demand soldiers from the AOF from the earliest stages of the war. Intensified recruitment in the colony began even before the extent of French losses and the length of the war became apparent. From August 1914 to October 1915, the colonial administration undertook several recruitment drives, bringing 32,000 more West Africans under the colors.[37] Even before the recruitment drives of 1915 were over, authorities were exploring ways of obtaining more men. Mangin, now a general, began once more to agitate actively for a more intensive exploitation of the manpower resources of the empire. On 2 August 1915, Mangin wrote to the minister of war arguing that the coming spring would likely prove to be the "the decisive phase of the European war," and that France ran the risk of being unprepared because of a shortage of new soldiers. He assessed the recruitment possibilities in each of the colonies (not including North Africa), claiming optimistically that France could raise an indigenous army of 700,000 men, 300,000 of whom would come from West Africa.[38]

General Pierre Famin, head of the Direction des troupes coloniales (DTC, which oversaw the administration of the Colonial Army outside North Africa) in the Ministry of War, was skeptical about Mangin's proposals, commenting that they "appear to me to be from the domain of the imagination," rather than from a realistic assessment of the resources available in the colonies.[39] Nevertheless, several of Mangin's allies in Parliament introduced legislation calling on the army and the colonial administration to intensify recruitment efforts. The law's sponsors amplified Mangin's ideas, arguing:

> We have the right to call on the aid of our colonial subjects. We have brought to our colonies prosperity and peace. We have delivered them from epidemics, raids, periodic famines, and civil wars. We have shed the most precious of our blood in order to spare them from powerful invaders and slave traders. Today, we struggle for them as well as for us. The yoke of the invader—they know it—would weigh as heavily, more heavily, on them than on us. France overseas fights for its own cause. We have the right to call on our colonies—and we have the duty.[40]

It was, they went on, merely a matter of equality of sacrifice: How could they stand by as 40 million Frenchmen provided millions of soldiers, while 40 million colonial subjects provided only "a few battalions"? The contribution of the AOF would make up a significant part of the whole, they emphasized, as the "recruitable" population *"exceeds the needs, great as they are."*[41]

There were few clearer statements during the war of how the republican ideology of assimilation (our cause is theirs too) and the civilizing mission (they owe us for all we have done for them) served as an ideal ideological justification for recruiting colonial subjects. Add to that the stereotypical image of West Africa as teeming with millions of ferocious and savage "born soldiers," and it was no surprise that the legislators focused in particular on the potential contribution of the AOF .

In the face of this pressure, the government preempted the proposed legislation on 9 October 1915 by issuing a decree governing recruitment in West Africa.[42] This decree would serve as the basis of recruitment for the coming year of 1916, during which the government demanded that the colonial administration in the AOF provide 50,000 new soldiers. Though the new drive was to be voluntary, the government did not renounce its right to apply conscription, in case of need, and the methods that French authorities employed to obtain "volunteers" did not exclude various forms of coercion. The governor-general himself estimated that only a little more than 13 percent were volunteers "in the real sense of the word."[43]

Coercion was an integral part of French methods, often channeled through regional colonial administrators and African intermediaries at the local level by the use of a quota system. Local auxiliaries were under pressure to provide a certain number bodies for the recruitment boards, but they were free to decide upon the means. Often, this meant that they provided men who were dispensable within the community: the poor, slaves, orphans, outcasts, or even younger sons. As one Senegalese veteran recalled, "In each family they took only one man, never two. And my father decided I should go into the army instead of my elder brother. Because, he told me, 'If I die, your elder brother could care for the family, but you are too young for that.'"[44] The physically infirm were also targets, helping to meet the quota but unlikely to pass the medical examination of the recruitment boards (though the standards of these boards were notoriously low).[45] Colonial officials fined or imprisoned reluctant chiefs, and even took hostage the parents or other relatives of potential recruits. Whole villages might suffer collective punishment, such as the destruction of crops, livestock, and other property, for noncompliance.[46] Such practices were well known enough to be ridiculed in the satirical French weekly *Le Canard Enchaîné*, which noted that recruiters obtained allegedly voluntary enlistments by stretching ropes across either end of a village and labeling all those between the ropes as volunteers and "presumptive heroes."[47]

During 1916, the colonial administration had another effective tool at its disposal, one that helps explain its success in exceeding the metropole's demand for 50,000 soldiers. As part of the October 1915 decree initiating the following year's recruiting drive, the government allocated 500,000 francs for the payment of "compensation" to chiefs, notables, and "recruiting agents," who received a bounty for each recruit they brought in. The incentive to commit abuses was obvious, and one official remarked that it would be more accurate to call recruits thus obtained "conscripts and not voluntary enlistees."[48] Such a system implied a large measure of institutional indifference to corrupt, exploitative, or even violent recruiting methods.[49] Some contemporaries recognized the dangers of the system, and a French senator criticized the colonial administration's methods, arguing that funds from the 500,000 francs should go directly to the recruits' families, not to larger communities, "the chiefs of which unscrupulously force enlistments to increase their share of the money."[50] African recruiting agents, working directly for the French administration, often conducted raids to capture and imprison young men, before presenting them as "volunteers." These methods were clearly reminiscent of the slave trade, despite the fact that the eradication of slavery was supposedly one of the proudest achievements of the French "civilizing mission" in the colonies.

West Africans were not any happier with the new demands of the war years than they had been with recruitment before 1914, and they resisted recruitment via methods ranging from the intentional presentation of candidates unfit for service to flight into the bush or neighboring areas not controlled by the French, to desertion, and even to outright armed revolt. This last form of resistance was rare, and often had its roots in longer-standing grievances against French colonial policies, but intensified recruitment clearly provoked a great deal of discontent.[51] Resistance caused the French authorities to rethink their policies, but changes developed slowly. Rather than renounce recruitment altogether, the army reduced its demands for 1917 to 12,000 men. Yet the new governor-general of the AOF, Joost van Vollenhoven, was an implacable foe of further recruitment in West Africa, believing that the exactions of African manpower were doing grave damage to the colonial economy and population, and that the AOF could better serve the metropole by pursuing a policy of economic exploitation (*mise en valeur*) to provide raw materials and agricultural products for the war effort.[52] By October 1917, Vollenhoven had persuaded officials in Paris to suspend recruitment in the colony. There would be no more aggressive efforts to recruit West Africans, and administrators would accept only truly voluntary enlistments.[53] Nonetheless, this suspension was short-lived, and 1918 would see yet another massive recruiting effort.

After West Africa, Algeria provided the largest number of recruits during the war. In all, North Africa contributed over a quarter of a million men to the war effort. This was not surprising, because North Africans in general had a fairly good reputation as soldiers. Though ethnic and racial distinctions were important in the overall French perception of the peoples of North Africa, internal political divisions and ideas about race were historically less important for recruitment there than in the AOF. In Algeria, the army first recruited auxiliaries among warlike tribes, such as the Zouaouas. During the nineteenth century, French officers developed a mythology around such peoples from Kabylia, which focused on the division between the predominantly Berber and largely sedentary people of this highland region, and the more nomadic Arabs who mainly inhabited the lowland plains. Such a dichotomy concealed a great deal of diversity in the colony, but it became the basis for French thinking about the ethnicity of indigenous Algerians.[54] Fighting against both groups convinced French officers that Kabyles were more solid, skillful, and disciplined, and less fired by religious fanaticism, than the Arabs.[55] Moreover, the blond-haired, light-skinned Kabyles of the Aurès led many French observers to conclude that these people were descendants of the Vandals and more like Europeans than other Algerians.[56] These qualities rendered the Kabyles preferable as recruits, but despite these well-developed ideas about ethnicity in Algeria, both Arabs and Kabyles served in the French Army, and ideas about *races guerrières* and *races non-guerrières* did not in the end play a prominent role in recruitment. After 1912, conscription helped to spread recruiting fairly evenly among the communes of the colony, mitigating against much of an ethnic imbalance in the ranks.

French perceptions also divided Morocco's population into Arabs and Berbers, but the effect on recruitment of ideas contrasting the two groups was equally doubtful. The extent of French penetration into the country clearly dictated early efforts to recruit Moroccans, as the first to serve in the French Army were Arabs from the coastal and lowland areas. More Berbers entered the ranks as the French extended their control, but Arabs remained an important part of the Moroccan forces.[57]

Ultimately, the most important distinctions the French military drew in North Africa were based upon political and ethnic differences among, and not within, the three colonies. Moroccans were the most desirable as soldiers, because they had a reputation as fierce warriors, but incomplete French control over the colony always limited recruitment there. Algerians were easier to recruit and had the reputation of being very good soldiers. Tunisians were the easiest to recruit, given the preexisting system of conscription in Tunisia, but the French doubted their warlike qualities, especially in comparison with their neighbors to the west.[58]

When the European war began, North African soldiers provided immediate help to the metropole, with units arriving from across the Mediterranean in August and September 1914. It was no surprise that North African units would make significant contributions to the defense of France from the earliest stages of the fighting, as the 19th Corps in which they served was integrated into the general mobilization plans for war in Europe as part of the metropolitan army.[59] In Algeria, authorities acted immediately to encourage voluntary enlistments, issuing a decree on 3 August 1914 outlining new terms and bonuses. A further increase in enlistment bonuses followed in October, attracting over 16,000 volunteers by the end of the year.[60] Senior military officials were pleased by the many "obvious and often touching confirmations that the indigenous population shares today our own aspirations and is deeply attached to us," proof that Algerians understood how much they owed to France for having undertaken its mission to civilize the colony's inhabitants.[61]

The cooperation of indigenous elites confirmed this impression, such as the participation of Captain Khaled, grandson of Abdelkader, legendary leader of resistance to the French conquest during the nineteenth century, in a cavalry unit dispatched to France in September. There could be no greater symbol of the army's assimilating role (and no greater propaganda tool) than a native Algerian whose family had been a symbol of resistance to French imperialism fighting in France with the rank of captain.[62] Other elites, assimilated Algerians, and religious figures also professed publicly their commitment to the cause of France, though this "loyalty" was most often more attributable to hope of reward or a desire to retain privileges than to a genuine French patriotism, and such sentiments certainly did not represent feelings among the masses.[63] It is not even clear that the many enlistments were truly voluntary, because the government-general of Algeria either promoted or sanctioned recruiting agents based upon their productivity and paid them a bonus for each "volunteer" they enlisted.[64]

Such methods still did not produce enough enlistments. It became clear that the war would continue into 1915, and though some French officials advocated intensified conscription in order to obtain the soldiers they needed, the government-general and Paris decided to call upon the class of 1915 at the usual time according to the customary procedures. Still, rumors of *tirailleurs* sacrificed in their thousands at the front added new fears to old resentments. Army officials noted that propaganda in the press, designed to fill Algerians with pride, actually frightened them and discouraged enlistment: "There is no battle in which our *tirailleurs* have not participated, not one assault on a trench in which they are not found in the first rank."[65] Algerians could easily deduce from this that if they entered the army and fought in France, they had a good chance of being killed. During the registration of candidates for the draft lottery in autumn 1914, there were some "surprises," as French military authorities delicately put it.[66] In October, in the commune of Mascara in Oran, a crowd, led by a marabout (Muslim holy man), threw rocks at and fired on the French official and gendarmes who had come to carry out the registration. A unit of indigenous cavalry called in to restore order was beaten back, with two of their number seriously wounded and two more missing. French soldiers sent immediately on a punitive expedition found the two missing soldiers the next day, beheaded, their faces mutilated, and their saddles lying nearby. Gruesome and disturbing though this rebellion was, by 9 October, the French had suppressed it and had registered the commune's young men for the draft.[67] Officials at the Ministry of War attributed such incidents, not to a larger political movement, but to traditional grievances, such as discontent over favoritism and injustice in the way indigenous officials administered the draft, and over the exemptions and replacements that allowed the sons of the wealthy to escape military service.[68]

In November, the French had another cause for worry: the Ottoman empire entered the war as an ally of Germany and soon declared it the holy obligation of all Muslims to fight for the victory of the Central Powers. Many feared that Algerians and other Muslims would see it as their religious duty to support their coreligionists, represented by the Ottoman regime, instead of their colonial masters, but as one Algerian religious leader put it, "The Muslims of North Africa have nothing in common with the Turks but their religion."[69] The prevailing quiescence among most of the population and continuing enlistments suggested that many other Algerians felt the same way. As one official remarked, "Voluntary enlistments, which have not ceased, are the best proof that our Muslims are not inflamed by the policies of the Young Turks [a secular nationalist party that had ruled the Ottoman empire since 1908]."[70]

Yet by the end of 1915, enlistments were waning, desertions were becoming a problem, and the manpower crisis at the front was growing more acute. Measures such as recalling retired soldiers and retaining soldiers who had arrived at the end of their term of service in the ranks "for the duration" had only a slight effect upon the total number of men under arms. Doubling to 5,000 the number of conscripts inducted in 1916 hardly had a dramatic effect either, in a war where armies (and casualties) numbered in the millions. These circumstances troubled army officials, who offered various explanations for the increasing difficulties they were having in attracting volunteers: the pool of men most desirous of becoming soldiers was drying up, as nearly 30,000 men had signed up in the first sixteen months of the war; news of the fatigue of men already in the army, tired of the long war, discouraged young men, who regarded a long stay at the front, waiting for an increasingly remote peace, with little relish; and there were more lucrative prospects outside the army, because wages had increased in Algeria (due to the labor shortage provoked by the departure of so many men for France) and many even higher-paying jobs were available in war industries in France.[71] Racial stereotypes played a role too. Officers opined that Algerians found trench warfare especially frustrating, because it did not correspond to their "penchant . . . for the war of movement."[72] Visions of glorious cavalry charges across the sand dunes of North Africa may have danced tantalizingly before the eyes of some young Algerians, but such fantasies were probably much more important in shaping the way French officials evaluated the psychology of their Algerian subjects.

Despite these concerns, the army believed that Algeria could furnish many more troops, so 1917 would see an expanded and early draft and more aggressive recruiting of volunteers in the colony.[73] This created an "explosive situation" among the Algerian population.[74] Revolts broke out in the southern part of the *département* of Constantine before the end of September and expanded to troubling dimensions as the autumn wore on. Authorities recognized that conscription lay behind the unrest.[75] The army had to devote thousands of troops, both European units and *tirailleurs sénégalais*, to putting down the uprisings, which they had largely done by February 1917.[76]

The unrest resonated among the Algerian soldiers and workers in France, and the postal censors noted many expressions of unhappiness about recruitment operations and much discussion of the revolts in letters between the metropole and North Africa.[77] One Algerian wrote in March 1917 that his three brothers had been "forcibly recruited by the state," adding that, "Our entire country is in great misfortune because of conscription. May

God change this unfortunate situation for Muslims into a better situation: Amen!"[78]

Unrest compelled the government to send the class of 1917 to France as soon as possible after their incorporation, to prevent desertion and to keep the new recruits from being influenced by the general climate of rebellion.[79] In spite of these problems and a dramatic decrease in voluntary enlistments, conscription ensured that recruitment for the year yielded the highest totals of the war up to that point. Over 52,000 Algerians entered the French Army, and by the end of 1917, well over 100,000 were helping to defend the metropole.[80] Still, given the difficulties that arose during the year, the colonial administration concluded that Algeria had reached the maximum potential that it could offer to the war effort.

Recruitment in Tunisia and Morocco followed a similar path, with officials there concluding by 1917 that they had offered what soldiers they could for the front. At the very beginning of the war, Tunisia provided immediate help by calling up the many reservists who were an integral part of that colony's long-standing system of obligatory service. There were 14,100 of these, while 11,900 men were already in the ranks at the outset of the conflict, and many of these 26,000 soldiers went immediately to fight in France.[81] Unfortunately, a number of these reservists were none too happy to be recalled for the war in Europe, and many deserted before they could be shipped out.[82] Worse yet, discontented reservists and some conscripts proved unreliable at the front. One battalion faltered during an attack in November 1914, while in another incident, a company flatly refused to march when ordered to attack. In the latter case, the divisional commander had the unit decimated the following day: every tenth soldier in the unit, a total of ten men, was executed by firing squad.[83]

By the end of 1915, the army had sent many reservists back to the colony. They were only causing trouble in France, and many officers felt that Tunisians possessed a "less warlike nature" than other North African troops anyway. The reluctance Tunisians showed about volunteering for service in the French Army only confirmed this stereotype. However, the vast majority of Tunisians were conscripts (almost 90 percent during the four years of war),[84] and so they probably served unwillingly, which could also easily explain their poor performance at the front. Moreover, even the army admitted that the long-standing system of conscription had led many Tunisians to the not unreasonable conclusion that submission to the draft fulfilled their duty to the French administration.[85] Still, many French officers preferred to see in Tunisians' behavior confirmation of a racial stereotype that placed them firmly behind Algerians in the hierarchy of martial worth.

Army policy on leave for Tunisian soldiers serving in France also damp-ened the enthusiasm of potential volunteers. From the earliest days of the war, colonial officials in Tunis were particularly adamant in restricting *indigènes'* ability to return home, whether on leave or convalescing from wounds. Resident-general Gabriel Alapetite reported that sending home wounded men, especially men with terrible wounds (*grands blessés*), de-moralized their families and friends by exposing them firsthand the terrible nature of combat in France. Soldiers home for leave or convalescence were no better, because they told frightening stories about the fighting, often por-traying the German artillery as vastly superior to the French guns, with some going so far as to predict France's imminent defeat. Even the most reliable soldiers could frighten their comrades with stories innocently told: "they like to give terrifying speeches recounting, with oriental exaggeration, the dangers they have run." These men included the cold weather in France in their tales of hardship at the front, adding "a new element of panic."[86] This racialized view of Tunisians as children given to fear, demoralization, ("oriental") exaggeration, and panic had real consequences, because both the wounded and soldiers on leave found it almost impossible to visit their families and homes during the first two years of the war. That the policy seemed to be aimed exclusively at Muslims only made the administration's discriminatory motives clearer. When pressed by the minister of war, who argued that the resident-general's insistence on such a restrictive leave pol-icy was hurting recruitment efforts in the colony, Alapetite responded by dis-missing any notion that republican ideals of universalism and egalitarianism should be applied to the Tunisian population. "It would be dangerous," he argued, "to make of this affair a question of principle or sentiment."[87] The special mentality of Tunisian Muslims was not like that of French people, who could be treated as adults and enjoy more liberal treatment, so it was necessary to proceed cautiously. Metropolitan officials recognized, however, that the policy was, as a parliamentary commission studying the question put it, both "unjust and dangerous." The French seemed to be saying to North African families: "Christian or Jewish mother, you will see your son, you will take care of him, you will embrace him. Muslim mother, you will not see your son, you will not take care of him, you will not embrace him." Such and attitude could only hinder recruitment, and officials eventually relaxed the policy somewhat.[88]

In 1917, officials decided to intensify conscription in Tunisia, but as in Algeria, this provoked reactions that called into question the government's ability to continue to make demands of the colony's indigenous population. To raise more troops, administrators increased the number of eligible candidates to be inducted and restricted to one third of the contingent the number of those chosen who could legally purchase exemptions from service (previously, the number of men allowed to purchase such exemptions had been unlimited). The new, larger class was inducted in the spring, but all of the men eligible to purchase their release from duty availed themselves of the opportunity. As the colonial administration fixed the price for 1917 at the not inconsiderable sum of 1,500 francs, some men clearly went to great lengths to procure their freedom from the army.[89] Many *tirailleurs* serving in France wrote home to urge their families to sell everything they had in order to purchase the freedom of their brothers or fathers. One wrote simply, "My brother must never come."[90] Writing to his father, Mohammed ben el Hadj of the 8th Regiment lamented the fact that his brother had been drafted, remarking that "[military] service is a painful thing, [and] he will not be able to bear the strains . . . it would be better to be reduced to poverty than to become a soldier."[91] When unable to buy an exemption, conscripts often deserted. By July, the Section d'Afrique (SA, responsible for overseeing the Armée d'Afrique in North Africa) of the Ministry of War noted that desertions in Tunisia were becoming "troubling," and the colonial administration advocated expediting the embarkation for France of new recruits, just as the army had done in Algeria.[92] Recruitment in Tunisia provided France with a considerable number of soldiers: by the end of 1917, more than 45,000 Tunisians had served in the wartime army.[93] But, as in other colonies, this came at a price. Increasing discontent among Tunisians both in and out of uniform, though it stopped short of the open rebellions that erupted in Algeria and West Africa, rendered the future of recruitment in the colony unclear.

In Morocco, several circumstances converged at the very beginning of the conflict to ensure that recruitment would be an important issue for political and military authorities in the colony. There were many French troops in the colony, as conquest was still under way, but the defense of the metropole took precedence, and the government immediately began to transfer these soldiers to France in 1914. Resident-general Hubert Lyautey, however, never ceased to uphold the importance of security needs in Morocco vigorously. Part of his strategy to minimize the weakening of French authority in the colony was to offer *tirailleurs marocains* as part of the forces he sent to France, allowing him to retain elements of the Foreign Legion and other French units.[94] The five battalions of *tirailleurs* Lyautey sent to France arrived on 17 August and took heavy casualties in the early campaigns, losing all but 800 men by the end of September (an appalling casualty rate of over 80 percent, though that was not uncommon in front-line units during those disastrous opening weeks of the war).[95] Such losses, along with Lyautey's desire to send *tirailleurs* rather than European soldiers to fight in France, led to concerted recruitment efforts in the colony.

Since Morocco was a protectorate, in which the sultan retained nominal power, and was not entirely pacified, the French authorities did not attempt to conscript indigenous men during the war. Enlistment was voluntary, and at first Lyautey sought to encourage volunteers by publicizing the actions and accomplishments of *tirailleurs* in France. Throughout the first months of the war, he urged officials in France to provide him with news of the troops at the front so that he could stimulate the pride of the populace by demonstrating the important role Moroccans were playing in the defense of the metropole. Yet by the middle of 1915, Lyautey was arguing that Moroccan units should be spared too much heavy combat, and that news of their prominent place in bloody combats frightened off potential volunteers.[96] By autumn, he was signaling problems with desertion and difficulties in obtaining volunteers, a situation that the minister of war characterized as a "crisis" of recruitment.[97] Restrictive leave policies and retention in the ranks "for the duration" of *tirailleurs* who had come to the end of their enlistment period only added to the disinclination of many Moroccans to volunteer. The colonial administration thus undertook more aggressive recruiting, putting pressure on Moroccan notables to provide the army with recruits. These notables, as in other colonies, met French demands by dubious methods: one officer reported that some recruits arriving in France complained that "they were forcibly recruited by their *caïds* (local chieftains), who promised their families sums of money, which were never paid."[98] Lyautey himself acknowledged that supplying France with soldiers had led to hasty recruitment, "under great pressure," and that such methods "were not without serious disadvantages."[99]

The number of Moroccan volunteers progressively diminished over the first three years of the war. Lyautey had resorted to accepting enlistments of shorter duration, and had persuaded the government to rotate units between France and Morocco each year in order to keep up morale and encourage others to volunteer, so there were only about 12,000 *tirailleurs marocains* under arms in April 1917, 4,700 of whom were in Europe.[100] Despite intensified recruitment efforts in 1917, enlistments increased by a grand total of 59.[101] Lyautey cited the higher bonuses paid to those who volunteered to go to France as workers and numerous revolts among the as yet unpacified tribes in the interior of the colony as factors preventing him from exploiting more fully the manpower resources available, and as the war entered its fourth year, it seemed that recruitment in Morocco was not going to provide many more soldiers for the front.[102]

Outside of West and North Africa, the French looked to Madagascar and Indochina for substantial numbers of troops. Prevailing racial stereotypes denigrated the military potential of men from these areas, so the decision to recruit intensively came relatively late in both places, but eventually each would contribute about 50,000 soldiers to the war effort. In 1914, the *tirailleurs malgaches* were a small force, and not a very highly valued one. Such attitudes had deep roots in the prewar period, when the French had used West African soldiers in Madagascar in large part because the allegedly more robust and warlike West Africans would strengthen units comprised of Madagascans, whose lack of military ardor supposedly reflected their easy life.[103] A 1904 manual for French officers serving in Madagascar summed up the general attitude: "Most of our tribes of *la Grande Île* have no conception of obedience, no notion of military esprit or discipline, the most important reason being that they do not have any traditions, laws, rules, [or] hierarchy whatsoever."[104]

Still, the French Army was eager to make use of whatever military value certain "races" on the island did have, and attitudes toward Madagascans also showed most clearly the powerful effect that quasi-anthropological ideas about *races guerrières* and *race non-guerrières* could have upon recruitment. From the earliest days of conquest, officers were keen to divide ethnic groups into these two categories. The *races guerrières* were composed of the coastal groups, especially the Sakalava peoples of the west coast, while the *races non-guerrières* consisted of peoples of the interior, such as the Merina (then known as Hova) whose kingdom had been the target of the French invasion of 1895. Officers and military doctors developed what one historian has called a "military ethnology," which allowed them to identify both worthwhile areas of recruitment and good soldiers.[105] This kind of control through classification and supposed knowledge was a salient feature of the emerging modern state apparatus throughout Europe during the nineteenth and twentieth centuries, and the military was integral to this process, as were ideas about race.[106] Colonies often served as "laboratories of modernity," where such practices could be employed and perfected, and the military ethnology of Madagascar was an excellent example of this phenomenon.[107]

The same 1904 manual that denigrated the military capacities of Madagascans in general summarized the racial characteristics of the various ethnicities in the region, ranking tribes "according to their military aptitudes." Topping the list were men from Zanzibar and the Comoros islands, and filling out the rest of the "very good" and "good" rankings were other coastal peoples, including the Sakalava. Hova and Betsileo (another group from the interior, neighboring the Hova) ranked dead last.[108] Yet from very early on, Madagascan units did not contain a majority of men from the coastal *races guerrières*. The very first experiments with these troops revealed them to be difficult to discipline, too independent, and insufficiently knowledgeable of the French language. To the dismay of French officers, many would not serve under the authority of anyone but their own local rulers.[109] As for the *races non-guerrières*, the French attitude was unambiguous. The Hova, for example, were "vain, proud, dishonest, sly, false, secretive, always ready to scheme, and even to plot, deceitful, treacherous, cowardly and greedy," according to the 1904 manual; "the Hova is as obsequious, even servile with superiors, as he is proud, arrogant, haughty, despotic, tyrannical with his subordinates."[110]

Still, manpower needs often overrode these beliefs, and stubborn demographic, geographical, and political realities limited the army's ability to recruit according to its ethnological predilections: the ethnic groups of the interior made up nearly 50 percent of the population of the island; they were more concentrated and linked together by a more extensive infrastructure than were the coastal tribes, and thus more accessible to recruiting agents; and they were less resistant to French authority.[111] In fact, though official preference set the maximum of Hova and Betsileo at one-fifth of the total indigenous force, these groups represented between 40 and 80 percent of *tirailleurs malgaches* during much of the prewar period.[112] This meant that the highly valued *races guerrières* were never as predominant in the ranks as the French command would have liked.

Though officers in immediate contact with Madagascan soldiers were satisfied with them, they "were relegated to the last rank of colonial indigenous soldiers" by the conventional wisdom of French military ethnology.[113] Thus France did not immediately call upon Madagascan troops in 1914, as it did with West and North Africans. Despite the enthusiasm of the new governor-general of Madagascar, Hubert Garbit, who offered to send troops to help defend the metropole, military authorities intended most of the over

7,500 *tirailleurs malgaches* then under arms strictly for defense of the island. The belief that the war would be short and the generally poor opinion of Madagascan soldiers meant that Paris was not eager to call on Madagascar for help. General Joseph Joffre, commander-in-chief of the French Army, doubted the value of indigenous troops in general, and Madagascans in particular.[114]

It was not until 3 May 1915, that the minister of the colonies asked Garbit to form a battalion of *tirailleurs* and ready them for European service.[115] Garbit recruited these men from among the best soldiers in the colony, and in September, the minister of war assented to the deployment of the battalion. However, these troops spent many months on garrison duty in Tunisia, then embarked for Salonika (Thessaloníki in northern Greece), where they served in noncombat roles.[116] This was an inauspicious beginning for Madagascan participation in the war, to be sure, and despite the enthusiasm of men like Garbit and Charles Mangin (who argued that Madagascar could provide 60,000 recruits), authorities were skeptical of their military value in a European setting.[117] General Famin's response to Mangin's 1915 colonial recruitment proposal singled out his confidence in the value of Madagascans for special criticism. Famin wrote that he had consulted many officers who had commanded Madagascan soldiers, all of whom had "denied that they had the least military value." These same officers had even opposed employing Madagascans as stretcher-bearers, claiming that they lacked sufficient courage to retrieve the wounded on the battlefield.[118] The Section d'Afrique voiced the same kinds of concerns about the usefulness of *tirailleurs malgaches*, arguing that they would have "no military value." Madagascans, along with Indochinese soldiers, were "troops of the lowest grade."[119]

Politicians shared this low opinion of the value of Madagascans. Senator Bérenger's report on recruitment in the colonies stated, for example, that "tropical races" such as those of Madagascar "do not always have the physical strength and endurance that accords with a warlike temperament." At best, he argued, such men might serve as workers to support the war effort.[120] In fact, the army, pressed by the increasingly acute shortage of manpower at the front, had already come around to this point of view. On 1 November 1915, the minister of war asked for another battalion of Malagasy soldiers, this time explicitly to serve in France as support troops, performing manual labor.[121] On 12 December, the government issued a decree extending to the other colonies the recruiting measures it had applied earlier to the AOF (in the decree of 9 October), including bonuses and family allocations to attract volunteers.[122] Still, negative racial stereotypes ensured that all but a few Madagascan soldiers who served in Europe would in fact serve as *troupes d'étapes*, staging troops employed as manual laborers.

Between December 1915 and March 1916, nearly 6,000 Madagascans volunteered for service in the French Army, 80 percent of them from the Hova and Betsileo populations in the interior—in other words, *races non-guerrières*.[123] It was not as if the army had abandoned prewar ideas about the relative martial natures of the various ethnic groups on the island, but the factors that had caused the French Army to recruit more heavily among the supposedly less martial peoples of the interior, in spite of the dictates of military ethnography, were at work during the war as well: these ethnic groups made up a substantial part of the overall population, the interior of the island possessed better infrastructure and a higher population density, and the level of resistance among coastal peoples to French domination remained higher than among those farther inland. Moreover, recruiting centers were located in the interior.[124]

In the meantime, the new recruiting efforts immediately ran into trouble. First, the arrest of members of a secret anticolonial society known as the VVS worried French officials enough to call a halt to recruitment in early 1916.[125] In the spring, once officials had the situation under control and resumed recruitment, much of the initial enthusiasm for enlistment had dried up. Results over the next few months were disappointing, but Paris began to make ever greater and more urgent demands for manpower to compensate for the terrible losses at the battle of Verdun, which dragged on for most of 1916. In his patriotic enthusiasm to contribute to the defense of the metropole, Governor-general Garbit waged a propaganda campaign throughout the island, soliciting patriotic *kabarys*, or discourses, from indigenous chiefs, colonial administrators, and even the governor-general himself; holding military ceremonies such as reviews and parades; and staging patriotic performances.[126] However, more aggressive measures also led to the increasing possibility of coercion, because the administration paid a bounty to local recruiting agents for each "volunteer" they brought in, sent mobile recruiting boards into more remote areas, and restored an old custom among the tribes of the island known as *tsondrano*, a gift that a village or group of families would offer to royal soldiers when they departed on an expedition. Recruiting agents demanded this "gift" to attract recruits, and prices soon escalated to several hundred francs, so notables resorted to taxing their fellow villagers to raise the funds. In short, recruiting methods were evolving toward the purchase of a mercenary force.[127]

At the end of the war, Garbit claimed to have taken measures to ensure that the colony sent "only volunteers" to France, and that "not one [soldier], to my knowledge, ever argued that he had not come [to France] voluntarily!"[128] In truth, however, the intensified efforts of late 1916 and 1917 evolved toward the kind of coercion that existed in West Africa, and at least some Madagascans did indeed claim to have come to France involuntarily. In September 1917, a Madagascan working in France wrote to his *tirailleur* father that the recruitment in Tananarive was forced, not voluntary, and that he had enlisted as a laborer to avoid this coercion.[129] Intense pressure from above and monetary inducements gave administrators and local recruiting agents a great deal of incentive to produce bodies for the boards to examine, regardless of the willingness of Madagascans to serve in the French Army.

Nevertheless, the French administration's intensified efforts achieved dramatic results: from October 1916 through February 1917, recruiters enlisted 22,500 men for service in France.[130] As with earlier efforts, recruitment was concentrated among the supposedly "less vigorous" peoples of the interior. In 1916, only about 2 percent of the men came from areas along the west coast, while six provinces in the interior provided 88 percent of the new recruits , and this disequilibrium was even more pronounced in 1917.[131] Still, the overall results were nothing short of spectacular, even exceeding the capacity of French shipping to transport the recruits to Europe. In fact, this became the primary problem facing officials trying to send soldiers to France, along with an economic downturn on the island caused by an acute labor shortage that military recruitment had provoked. By the latter part of 1917, recruitment had slowed to a trickle.[132] There were also signs that people were increasingly unwilling to submit to the recruiters' levies. In the Comoros islands, young men told the administration, "If the whites need us as *tirailleurs*, they will have to take us by force."[133] Thus, by the end of the year, as was the case in many other colonies, recruitment had all but ceased, and Madagascar seemed unlikely to contribute many more soldiers to the war effort.[134]

Official conventional wisdom about Indochinese troops was similar to views of Madagascans, and attitudes were similarly rooted in the prewar period. From the late nineteenth century right up to the eve of the Great War, many officials and journalists advocated garrisoning Indochina with *tirailleurs sénégalais*, claiming that native Indochinese troops lacked the requisite warlike nature.[135] This never happened, but such attitudes stemmed from a general perception that Indochinese men were feminine, too small and delicate to withstand the rigors of combat. As was the case with Madagascans, such ideas about the Indochinese would delay their recruitment and deployment in Europe during the war, where cold weather and the techniques of modern warfare, many argued, would overwhelm their limited capacities.

If the general stereotypes were similar, attitudes toward the different "races" within French possessions in southeast Asia followed a different trajectory than they did in Madagascar. Though military authorities were particularly keen to make use of the supposedly more warlike peoples in Tonkin and eventually made them the foundation of their indigenous forces in Indochina, there does not seem to have been the same kind of intense quasi-anthropological speculation about the relative martial worth of the various ethnicities in the region. Ideas about "race" did not play as large a role in determining the intensity and methods of recruitment as did political and administrative divisions among the five provinces that made up the colony. But if the French did not seek explicitly to recruit soldiers based upon a racial hierarchy of military abilities, they did exploit ethnic and cultural divisions among the Indochinese, though even this effort was not very intensive.[136]

French authorities engaged in only limited recruitment among the peoples of Cambodia, Laos, and Annam, preferring to exploit the more developed infrastructure and administration of Tonkin and Cochin China. The army did make a special effort to recruit from among the *montagnards*, or dark-skinned peoples of mixed ethnicity living in the highlands of the colony. These men, who enlisted voluntarily, had always resisted submission to the Annamese emperor, and soldiers recruited in these regions would go on to become valuable auxiliaries of both French and American armies through much of the twentieth century.[137] Even though some French officers did value the alleged warlike qualities of *montagnards*, the pursuit of soldiers outside of Tonkin and Cochin China was not so much an approach dictated by the varying levels of martial worth found among the ethnicities in southeast Asia as it was, in the words of a 1912 army study, a limited effort to "exploit racial particularisms, or, failing that, regional particularisms."[138] In other words, the French sought to take advantage of antipathies and rivalries among the different "races" in forming units to police various areas of the colony, rather than exploiting innate differences in their warlike qualities.

When war came to Europe in 1914, most French military officials doubted the utility of employing *tirailleurs indochinois*. The army rejected the suggestion of General Théophile Pennequin, who had served before the war as commander of all troops in Indochina, that France could make greater use of Indochinese troops, and it likewise declined offers from the civilian administration in the colony to send workers and soldiers to the metropole.[139] Negative stereotypes prevalent among French officers about the value of Indochinese soldiers meant that even the first steps toward deploying *tirailleurs indochinois* outside the colony, taken in the face of the increasingly acute manpower shortage the army faced in 1915, were hesitant. One battalion was sent to the French Concession in Tientsin (modern Tianjin) in China, and another embarked for garrison duty in Djibouti in September.[140]

In the meantime, though, momentum was gathering in France for an extensive recruitment effort in Indochina, spurred in part by General Mangin's characteristically optimistic estimate that the French could count on 300,000 recruits from that colony, a number equal to what he expected from West Africa.[141] Only slightly less optimistic, Pennequin also wrote to the minister of war, claiming that he could quickly raise an army of 200,000 in Indochina.[142] Such ideas also found expression among French parliamentarians: the legislative proposal of 16 September 1915 and Senator Bérenger's November report both deplored the failure to tap the potential for recruitment in Indochina.[143]

There was still considerable resistance to the idea of extensive recruitment in Indochina, based primarily upon negative racial stereotypes. General Famin's response to Mangin's proposals argued that Indochinese lacked "the physical strength necessary to endure the strains of this difficult campaign" and were not "solid" enough "to be able to face this terrible ordeal." He claimed that many officers with colonial experience shared this view, including Joffre and Lyautey.[144]

Responses to the parliamentary legislation were no more positive. When the measure's main sponsor, Deputy Pierre Masse, discussed his ideas in the Chamber's Army Commission, along with the minister of war and the minister of the colonies, the ministers argued that men from Indochina could not withstand the physical demands of soldiering in Europe, and would be useless in cold weather. After the ministers left the meeting, Masse himself expressed doubt about the prospect of extensive recruitment outside West Africa.[145] Joffre added his considerable authority to those skeptical of the value of recruitment in Indochina, writing to the minister of war: "The Indochinese, the Sakalava [from Madagascar], and the Malabars of India do not possess the physical qualities of vigor and endurance necessary to be employed usefully in European warfare." Hence, he added: "The effort to make, with regard to the *troupes indigènes* M. Masse has in mind, should thus focus exclusively on the recruitment and organization of black troops [from West Africa]."[146] Joffre's opinions carried great weight, not only because of his position as supreme commander, but also because he had long experience serving as an officer in the colonies.

Despite these hostile opinions, public and parliamentary pressure to confront the growing manpower crisis at the front finally compelled government action, and the 12 December decree expanding recruitment throughout the colonial empire included Indochina.[147] So despite continuing official reluctance, an intensive recruitment drive began in 1916, bringing some 28,000 *tirailleurs* into the army by the end of the year.[148] At first, preparation and oversight were so poor that indigenous authorities were able to present many unqualified candidates to the recruiting boards: in some areas as many as 60 percent to 90 percent were unfit for military service.[149] Moreover, the available camps and equipment were totally insufficient for the unprecedented number of recruits. By the beginning of the summer, however, conditions had improved, and the French authorities made a concerted effort to involve local notables in a concerted propaganda campaign, which included posters, postcards, publication of letters from men already in France, speeches by indigenous notables, and even a touring cinema showing the benefits of life and work for *indigènes* in the metropole.[150]

As was the case in other colonies, despite the nominally voluntary nature of these enlistments, there was a real blurring of the line between enlistment and conscription or coercion. Thousands of the *tirailleurs* sent to France were men already on active duty or recalled reservists, some of whom were conscripts under procedures in place before the war. Indigenous elites also applied a good deal of pressure to obtain the "volunteers" that the French authorities required of them. Local community leaders coerced men, mostly poor peasants, into joining the war effort to enable these notables to prove their worth and curry favor with the French administration. Letters to officials from mothers and wives complained of forced enlistments, as did letters that soldiers and workers in France sent home. As had been the case in the past, the sons of the wealthy and influential rarely had to serve.[151]

Despite postwar claims that, "recruitment operations were carried out in the greatest order," there was some significant resistance to French demands.[152] In both Cambodia and Cochin China, popular discontent and lack of cooperation significantly reduced contributions. The minister of war attributed Cambodians' lack of enthusiasm to the fact that they were "absolutely devoid of the sentiments and mentality necessary for a patriotic *élan*."[153] This was in large part because French influence there was weak, and colonial control also proved weak in Cochin China, despite a longer-standing French presence. Indigenous institutions were enfeebled, because the French had broken down local political structures without replacing them with viable institutions of their own. As a result, in neither province did the French find many recruits, and the colonizers ultimately relied heavily for recruits upon Tonkin and Annam, where they could exploit the relative coherence of the indigenous administration.[154] Thus, "race" played a smaller role in determining the ethnic distribution of recruitment in Indochina than did practical administrative and political realities.

Success in Indochina during 1916 led the government to make a similar effort in 1917, which brought over 20,000 more men into the French Army. However, as was the case in Madagascar, the number of recruits began to exceed shipping capacity, leading the colony's administration to slow, then suspend, the recruiting campaign before the end of the year.[155] Though officials could be pleased with the results thus far, Indochina was no different from most other areas of the French empire that had provided troops for the war effort, in that it was not clear there would be the means or the will to exploit the human resources of the colony further as France entered yet another year of war in 1918. In short, by the end of 1917, tapping these "reservoirs of men" had put tremendous strains upon the administrative structures, the economies, and the peoples of the empire. Recruitment had slowed or stopped in many areas, and it seemed that the colonies had given all they could to the metropole.

## Recruitment in 1918

The situation would change during that last year of war, primarily because of the arrival of new leadership in Paris. Georges Clemenceau, the new prime minister and minister of war (he held both portfolios simultaneously), provided the will to recommence intensive recruitment operations in the colonies, and he made it clear that his subordinates would be responsible for finding the means. Though the history of recruitment in the colonies in 1918 is necessarily briefer than that covering the first three years of the war, the final stage in the process saw some of the most dramatic developments.

"The history of black troops during the World War falls into two main divisions: before 1918 and 1918 itself," an early historian of West African soldiers during the Great War wrote.[156] This was not only true of West Africans, and the division had mostly to do with the intensification of recruitment stimulated by the change of government in Paris. When Clemenceau came to power in November 1917, he declared his intention of waging "total war," and such an approach made short work of problems in the colonies.[157] When discussing the inevitable opposition the government would encounter from the French residing in the colonies, who would fear unrest that recruitment might provoke, he affirmed, "the front interests me more."[158] Clemenceau wanted soldiers, and he would have them.

Clemenceau turned to the foremost proponent of the use of *troupes indigènes*, asking General Charles Mangin for an assessment of the possibilities of intensified recruitment throughout the French colonial empire. Mangin dashed off a report claiming that the army could obtain 362,000 *tirailleurs* and 252,000 workers, but only if colonial administrators subordinated everything to the recruitment effort, "the sole means that they have to contribute to the national defense and the victorious peace." France would have to increase incentives to encourage enlistment and ease discontent over conscription, in addition to remaining firm in the face of any resistance that colonial populations might offer. It was, he declared, "necessary to show force in order not to have to make use of it."[159]

This was precisely what Clemenceau wanted to hear, and scarcely a week after receiving Mangin's report, he informed the minister of the colonies: "The conclusion of this general officer is very clear, a broad call-up of men can be made in our colonies, without compromising their security, if certain precautions are taken by the responsible authorities." Clemenceau directed the minister to order colonial administrators to begin intensive recruiting efforts, laying out the new government's position in characteristically strong terms: "It will not escape you that in this moment of supreme tension it is necessary that the colonies participate in the common effort. It will be sufficient that the colonial authorities, civil and military, devote to this task all of their energy and intelligence and consider it as the most urgent of their duties."[160]

Despite some resistance from colonial administrators, Clemenceau's forceful efforts yielded results. These results varied, however, from colony to colony. The great distances from the metropole and difficulties in obtaining sufficient transport hampered efforts to intensify recruitment in Indochina and Madagascar. In Indochina, the campaign to enlist volunteers both to work and to fight in France continued, but most of the 50,000 Indochinese who would serve as soldiers had already entered the army by the time Clemenceau came to power. The same was true of Madagascar, where continuing problems with shipping capacity limited the number of men who could embark for France. The resources available in Morocco were relatively meager, so intensified efforts there produced fewer than 8,000 new recruits.[161] As for Tunisia, the call-up of 12,000 conscripts in 1918 provoked the same discontent that had marked previous efforts. Postal censors reported that Tunisians serving in France urged their families to pay "any price to exempt their brothers or relatives from service."[162]

West Africa and Algeria, then, were the areas in which Clemenceau's policies had the most dramatic effects. This was not surprising, given the well-developed methods of recruitment in place in the two colonies and the good reputation of their men as soldiers. Administrators in Algeria and the Ministry of War had expected to incorporate about the same number of recruits into the army during 1918 as they had in the previous year, or a little more than 30,000 men. This was not enough for Clemenceau, who demanded 50,000, half conscripts and half volunteers, overriding concerns for security in the colony. The only security that mattered, in the end, was that of France.[163]

There was, predictably, opposition to the plan among some officers and colonial administrators. The idea of obtaining some 25,000 volunteers in Algeria—four times the previous year's total—was particularly controversial. One army officer pointed out that many of the "volunteers" who had entered the army over the past three years had done so in response to overt coercion, and indeed recruiters often brought these men to places of enlistment under armed escort.[164] Other officials were skeptical that much could be done to make voluntary enlistment more appealing to native Algerians, while the governor-general pointed out the dangers to colonial security of Clemenceau's ambitious plan.[165]

Nevertheless, a change in personnel (i.e., a new governor-general) and Clemenceau's determination combined to propel a newly intensified recruitment effort. This effort, plus new incentives, did indeed produce more volunteers, nearly 14,000 before the end of the year, making it the most successful recruitment by this means since the first five months of the war (which had produced over 16,000 volunteers).[166]

This number still fell short of the 25,000 that the government had demanded, and so authorities sought to make up the difference by intensifying conscription. The effort was a success, and incorporation proceeded with virtually no resistance or unrest among the populace—a mere .33 percent of those called up failed to present themselves for induction. By the middle of the year, the governor-general reported to Clemenceau that he was well on the way to meeting the goal of 50,000 total recruits.[167]

Of course, the administration had to adopt expedients to achieve these figures. Many men whose health would normally have disqualified them from service ended up in uniform, and many more who belonged in the auxiliary services ended up in the regular army. Inspectors in France observed that recruits were "of an entirely inferior physical condition," many weighing only 40 to 45 kilograms, and that recruiters had accepted numerous men under the age of 18. The army expected that it would have to release as many as one-fifth of the contingent for health reasons.[168]

The general commanding French forces in North Africa admitted that the imperative of raising 50,000 troops meant recruiters often accepted physically substandard candidates. He attributed their miserable state to the "deplorable way in which the *indigènes* feed themselves," arguing that once on an army diet, the health of these men would improve.[169] This officer was typical in attributing the ill-health of Algerians to their childlike inability to take care of themselves rather than to drought and poverty, much of the latter induced by colonial exploitation, which was widespread in Algeria at the time. So race continued to play a role in how French authorities viewed colonial subjects, even as the French nation demanded unprecedented sacrifices from these same subjects. And the sacrifice was significant, because despite some problems with the health of recruits, over 55,000 Algerians entered the French Army during 1918.

The success of recruitment was even more spectacular in West Africa, thanks to Blaise Diagne, the black African deputy who represented some of the citizens of the AOF. Diagne had earlier proven his zeal to contribute to the French war effort, using his position in parliament to promote the recruitment of his constituents in the urban areas of Dakar, Saint-Louis, Gorée, and Rufisque (known as the Four Communes, where African residents were known as *originaires*) in return for recognition of their historical claims to full French citizenship.[170] Now Clemenceau chose the Senegalese deputy to lead a special recruiting mission throughout all of the AOF, using his status and influence to inspire Africans' cooperation.

Diagne was at first reluctant, inasmuch as such open collaboration with the French colonial masters might alienate his fellow West Africans. He also worried about potential conflicts with the colonial administration, which would not welcome outside interference, especially led by a black African. Governor-general Vollenhoven's hostility to further recruitment in the colony was, moreover, well-known. Diagne and the government agreed he would travel to the AOF as a special "commissar of the Republic" (reminiscent of the "representatives on mission" sent out to stiffen the resolve of French armies during the French Revolution), with a rank equal to that of the governor-general and the right to correspond directly with the government. Vollenhoven resigned in protest in January 1918, going to the front to serve as a soldier, where he died in a charge on German lines six months later.[171]

Diagne was the very embodiment of the republican and assimilationist justifications underwriting French demands that colonial subjects come to the aid of the metropole in its hour of need. An elected representative of the government, he represented the republican will of the people more perfectly than the seemingly arbitrary authority of the colonial administration. More important, as a black man, he represented the return Africans could allegedly expect for their loyal service: assimilation and acceptance by white French people as equals, with attendant rights and responsibilities.

In order to help Diagne avoid the charge of crass collaborationism and allow him to claim credibly that he had obtained concrete rewards for African cooperation, the government passed a decree outlining new incentives and rewards for veterans, their families, and the colony as a whole.[172] With such concessions, the government hoped to mitigate the hostility and resistance that had marked the earlier recruitment efforts of 1915 and 1916. Officials at the Ministry of War noted that many "volunteers" had been coerced in the past, but that Diagne's mission would employ persuasion.[173] The government hoped that the new commissar's status and race would inspire his fellow Africans to make sacrifices for France, and one journalist wrote that Diagne was sure to succeed "where certain failure awaited a white administrator or officer, whatever his merit, whatever his knowledge of the peoples of the AOF."[174] This comment was prescient, because the results of the mission surpassed even the government's expectations. In January, Clemenceau had ordered Diagne to recruit 47,000 men in the AOF, but by the beginning of the summer, he had signed up nearly 60,000.[175] By the time the recruitment drive ended in August, Diagne and the colonial administration had provided the French Army with 63,000 new recruits.

Historians have disagreed about the reasons for Diagne's success, but Diagne himself judged his presence to have been decisive.[176] Only three days after he arrived in Dakar in February 1918, he wrote to the minister of the colonies that Africans had welcomed him warmly and offered to enlist, because it was the first time, many told him, that "such an appeal was made for their voluntary collaboration and trust."[177] A month later, he reported that Africans whom he met viewed the government sending him on this mission as a "new symbol [of a] policy of justice and [a] demonstration [of consideration] toward the black race,"[178] Indeed, it was Diagne's ability to convince Africans all over the AOF that France would reward military service with expanded rights in the future that caused so many West Africans to rally to the same French cause that many had rejected during previous recruiting drives.[179] Diagne's entourage included several white officers and three African officers, whose presence and status as veterans of the fighting in Europe inspired others and proved that it was possible to return from France not only alive, but with enhanced rank and prestige. One can easily imagine the powerful effect upon the populace of the sight of a fellow African invested with so much authority, even over whites.

It is admittedly difficult to know just how many West Africans who enlisted did so voluntarily. One official estimate put the proportion of volunteers at about 25 percent.[180] This figure was undoubtedly too high, and a later scholar's figure of 14 percent is more realistic, though how truly voluntary even these enlistments were is open to serious doubt. Clearly, notables and chiefs used coercion to obtain the cooperation of members of their communities. Even so, the overall popular response was largely positive, and the proportion of truly voluntary enlistments was higher than in earlier recruitment drives.[181] Many chiefs offered their own sons to the French Army, even elder sons, and the absence of major revolts or of mass flight vindicated Diagne's approach. The absence of resistance indicated most clearly the new spirit of cooperation that Diagne fostered. In direct contradiction to the claims of Vollenhoven, who had feared unrest and economic disruption from renewed recruitment, his replacement as governor-general wrote: "Recruiting operations are reaching their completion amidst a perfect political tranquility and a continually increasing productive activity."[182]

No doubt many Africans retained a healthy suspicion of the motives behind their colonial masters', and Diagne's, demands and promises, but the fact that the French could recruit over 63,000 men in six months without encountering the kind of resistance and revolt that marked earlier, less intensive recruiting efforts showed that the new approach had struck a chord within the African population. The salience of race in this process was clear.

Diagne's African identity allowed him, and the government, to highlight the republican and assimilationist ideals of egalitarianism and universalism that justified their appeal for sacrifice from colonial subjects in the name of French patriotism.

The intensified recruitment of 1918 was the most successful of the war, especially in Algeria and West Africa. Those two areas alone provided almost 120,000 new recruits. The ultimate irony of this success, and of Clemenceau's aggressive push to recruit soldiers in the colonies, was that the urgent need for these soldiers passed with the ending of the war before the army could train most of them and transport them to Europe. They were valuable, however, for maintaining security in the colonies, and as occupation troops after the war, they allowed the government to demobilize European soldiers more quickly. The successes of 1918 also justified military policy toward the colonies in the eyes of metropolitan authorities, affirming the spread of French republican ideals overseas and the value of France's civilizing mission.

Diagne's mission in particular seemed to confirm claims about the progress of civilizing work in the colonies, and the intention of assimilating colonial subjects into the nation regardless of racial differences. Senator Bérenger's claim that "*la France coloniale* is no longer separated from *la France d'Europe*," and Diagne's assertion that France was united "above any question of origin or race," demonstrated the power of the rhetoric of universalism and egalitarianism that allowed French officials to demand sacrifices of their colonial subjects without, at least in their own minds, violating liberal republican principles.[185] According to this way of thinking, it was an honor for colonial subjects to enlist in the army or to submit to conscription, and they would thus be defending the interests they held in common with the white French citizens of the metropole.

This ignored the inherently exploitative nature of the colonial relationship, as well as more specific contradictions in the nature of military service for colonial subjects. The conditions of service for *troupes indigènes* most often placed them in an ambiguous position, somewhere between hired mercenaries and full French citizens. They were paid and supposedly volunteered like mercenaries, but were also sometimes subject to conscription and were supposed to be fired by patriotism and a sense of obligation. Yet neither conscription nor patriotism conferred upon them the rights and duties of citizens. This paradox, which would provoke at least some soul-searching before the war was over, revealed the importance of racial and cultural differences in the minds of even those ostensibly committed to the concept of the equality and universal humanity of all people. This is not surprising when one considers the important role that racial thinking and stereotypes played even in decisions about which colonial subjects to recruit. Discourse about *races guerrières* and *races non-guerrières*, whether to recruit soldiers from among this colonial population or that, and why or why not, demonstrated that race was as decisive as idealism in stimulating recruitment in the French empire.

After they had recruited large numbers of these colonial subjects, French military authorities were faced with decisions about how best to make use of the new soldiers on the battlefields of Europe. The following chapter examines these decisions about deployment. What precise role men from the various colonies would play in the French war effort depended to a large extent upon their racial identity. Prevailing stereotypes about the varying military capacities of the different "races" in the ranks determined the specific tasks they would undertake, and also shaped French perceptions of how well the *indigènes* performed their duties.

# CHAPTER TWO

# Race and the Deployment of Troupes indigènes

❖

Our *indigènes* are animated by a warlike spirit, but . . . [in the war in France] cold stoicism is, more than fiery passion, the primordial quality of the soldier.

—*Officier interprète Reymond, on Algerian soldiers, 1917*

[A]s much as possible, it is necessary to employ our Moroccans according to their aptitudes and their character. Service in the trenches, daily chores, [and] carrying supplies are not to their tastes. Ask them to work here and there, [and] they will do it with the greatest fervor; what is repugnant to these big children is the daily grind; ask them above all to fight [ *faire parler la poudre*], and today, as they have already done in the past, they will conduct themselves heroically. . . . We must take them as they are, with their character, their qualities, and their faults.

—*Colonel Vrenière, commander, 96th Brigade,*
*on the Régiment marocain 1915*

In saying that, notwithstanding Algerian troops' "warlike spirit," they lacked the "cold stoicism" of the native French, which was essential in the long attrition of the Great War, Officier interprète Reymond was expressing a common, racialized view of *troupes indigènes*. Officers often characterized soldiers from the colonies as aggressive and savage, even heroic warriors who loved "above all to fight," but also as "big children," impetuous, primitive, easily discouraged and bored with the mundane details of modern soldiering. This contrasted with their allegedly more solid and impassive French counterparts, animated by a patriotic sense of calm self-sacrifice. The practical roots of this contrast, these same officers admitted, lay in the undeniable fact that these men were fighting, not for their own homes and freedom, but for those of their colonial masters.

Official French rhetoric held that this was in theory not true. Rather, the *indigènes* should have been glad to repay France for the benefits of its imperial rule, and French citizens and colonial subjects were supposed to struggle together against German tyranny. A more pragmatic view, however, recognized that these men could have little enthusiasm for the fight in Europe, and that their performance in combat might therefore suffer. Yet there was an even more important reason French officers doubted the military capabilities of *troupes indigènes*, and this had more to do with their racial identity than with the natural reticence of the oppressed and exploited. Many French military and political officials thought that members of these supposedly inferior races would be ill suited to modern European warfare, despite the primitive and savage qualities that made some of them fierce warriors. French soldiers not only had the advantage of fighting for their homes and their freedom, and of knowing that appeals to their patriotism were more than rhetorical, but they were also assumed to be naturally capable of "cold abnegation," the higher sense of duty, sacrifice, and honor allegedly inherent in white men and necessary to fight this new kind of war. However warlike members of these inferior races were, they lacked this "essential quality."[1] So in order to render their aid militarily effective, the French Army took special care in the organization and deployment of *troupes indigènes*, trying to match their use to their presumed specific racial characteristics, to take them as they were, "with their character, their qualities, and their faults."

An examination of the expectations, perceptions, deployment, and evaluations of soldiers from different colonies highlights the distinct ideas about race prevalent among French military commanders during World War I. These preconceptions joined with accumulated experience and other factors in shaping the ways in which the army used *troupes indigènes*. Together, these elements also influenced perceptions of how well those troops ultimately carried out their duties. This is clear not only from the nature of military policy, but also from the words of French officers. Though officers' reports on military value and combat effectiveness have limitations, for it is difficult to distinguish between outright prejudices and actual (though not necessarily objective) reporting of experience, it is evident from the language they used that French officers made their judgments within the parameters of preexisting stereotypes based upon race. Even when actual experience modified the view of the usefulness or capabilities of a certain group, officers merely fitted the new realities neatly into racial categories they had already defined. In a very real way, race ordered the use of *troupes indigènes*.

This had very specific consequences. Though they had a reputation as loyal and skilled warriors, the performance of some West African and North African units during the earliest stages of the war in 1914 received mixed reviews, and similarly ambivalent perceptions of their military worth continued throughout the war. Still, the predominant view that they were well suited to combat, especially offensive combat, ensured that they would play a conspicuously active role at the front. On the other hand, authorities did not consider Indochinese and Madagascan troops at all appropriate for combat in Europe, and so it was not until 1916, when France faced severe manpower shortages stemming from the devastating campaigns of 1914–15 and from the massive bloodletting at Verdun, that any men from these colonies served as combatants. Even then, their use was limited. Perceptions could change— due to, say, the surprising ability of Indochinese and Madagascan troops to withstand European winters and to perform specialized duties that were normally reserved for French personnel, or the ability of some West and North Africans to adapt to European warfare—but views on the relative and absolute martial value of the various "races" remained remarkably stable.

Concerns related to the use and perception of *troupes indigènes* fell into four broad categories: the need for European personnel, the optimal organization for the deployment of various "races," the importance of distinguishing between *races guerrières* and *races non-guerrières,* and the effect of winter weather upon combat effectiveness. In all of these areas, racial stereotypes played a decisive role in determining the specific form that indigenous troops' duties would take.

The first set of concerns focused on the necessary presence of European personnel in indigenous units. There was a general consensus among French officers that childlike, unpredictable, and unreliable *indigenes* needed close supervision and leadership from their white superiors in order to maintain discipline and effectiveness under fire. The presence of metropolitan French

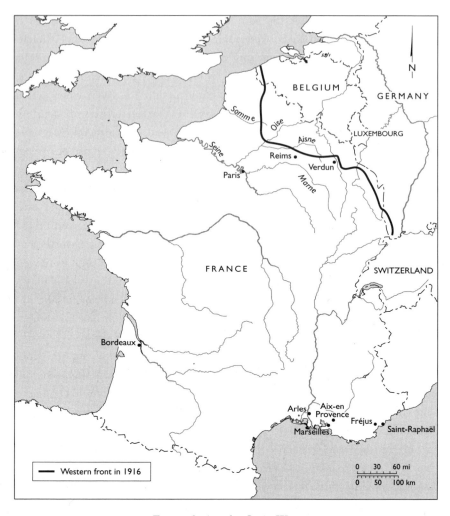

France during the Great War

soldiers was also necessary even in the lower ranks, as commanders almost always relied upon white soldiers to perform technical or specialized duties, such as manning machine guns, serving as a signaler or messenger (which required not only dependability but a reliable knowledge of French), driving, and performing clerical staff work and other tasks essential to the overall functioning of a military unit.

A second and related issue was how best to organize *troupes indigènes*. In most cases this boiled down to the need to link units of *indigènes* at the company, battalion, or even regimental level with corresponding units composed of native Frenchmen. With West African troops, this issue assumed particular importance as the war continued and the French Army deployed more and more units of *tirailleurs sénégalais* in combat.

A third issue that concerned military authorities was the warlike character of the *troupes indigènes*, a quality linked closely with their racial identity. French officers and the tactics they employed had to take full advantage of the martial qualities of each of the "races" fighting under the French flag. As they did when recruiting soldiers from the colonies, officers made distinctions between *races guerrières* and *races non-guerrières*. The latter, such as Indochinese and Madagascans, often found themselves relegated to non-combat duty, laboring as *troupes d'étapes*, or staging troops. Their allegedly more warlike compatriots, most West Africans and North Africans, served in combat at the front.

French tactical doctrines sought to take advantage of racial characteristics in specific ways. Members of "races" that French officers considered particularly warlike and aggressive found themselves used almost exclusively in the attack as *troupes de choc*, or shock troops, which, of course, increased their chances of injury or death in comparison with members of supposedly less warlike races. Nonetheless, many French officers questioned the suitability of even supposedly warlike *indigènes* for use in European warfare, revealing the durability of assumptions about the inferiority of nonwhites.

A final, but certainly not the least important, consideration for military authorities was the varying ability of soldiers from warm climates to adapt to the cold European winters. This factor had a great deal of influence over the ways in which commanders could use these troops. The common issue that united all four of these concerns was the overriding importance of the racial identity of these men, and how that identity influenced opinions about their abilities and usefulness as soldiers.

## European Personnel

The need for native French soldiers in indigenous units went beyond the necessary presence of white officers to command and control the rank and file.[2] French personnel were necessary at lower ranks as well, from noncommissioned officers to simple soldiers. French commanders believed that the mere presence of such men assured a greater level of security. White men, with their preeminent quality of calm self-sacrifice, were supposed to shore up their less reliable comrades under fire and help sustain their morale.

French officers clearly believed that nonwhites, even if certain of them were savage warriors, did not possess the inherent virtues of honor, dignity, and virility that would allow them to be effective soldiers on their own.

Military men were especially wedded to this concept of an internalized value system that esteemed the masculine virtues of unbending courage and stoicism in the defense of personal and national honor above all else. The overriding importance of the concept of honor had particular salience after 1870, as Frenchmen struggled to confront the implications of the humiliating defeat of the Second Empire at the hands of the Germans, and the emasculating effects of modern industrial civilization. In this failure of Frenchmen to prevail upon the field of battle, and in their growing "softness" in a world in which the Darwinian struggle for survival was largely absent, or at least attenuated, many men saw the origins of the feminist movement that was beginning to challenge the exclusivity of male domains such as the professions and politics.[3]

Over the course of the nineteenth century, bourgeois men had adapted aristocratic notions of honor to a more egalitarian context, especially under the Third Republic, and this chivalrous code thoroughly permeated the dominant social class by 1914. In the prewar period, one of the most salient indicators of the importance of the male code of honor was the prevalence of dueling as a means to resolve personal and public disputes between men. War, which for many was a duel writ large, provided an opportunity for Frenchmen to play a strictly defined cultural role that would preserve their predominance and their important self-image as courageous protectors of Frenchwomen and national honor.[4] These ideas animated many of the men who flooded into the army in 1914 to join career officers who, as professionals, were even more steeped in notions of honor and self-sacrifice.

One can discern a racial component to this code, in addition to its well-established ties to notions of masculinity and gender. The search for new fields upon which to establish the honor of the army and of France is apparent in French colonial expansion after 1870, and the supposed lack of the civilized and honorable qualities of Frenchmen among non-European peoples often served as an important justification for subjugating them. However, calling upon colonial subjects to defend France and prevent another humiliating defeat at the hands of the Germans threatened French notions of superiority and virility. One way to maintain the difference upon which the self-image of French officers rested was to deny that *indigènes* could display that essential quality of stoic courage necessary to fight effectively on a

European battlefield, even though they were capable of defending France by serving in the army. Not coincidentally, these same qualities were necessary in a duel: to stand alone on the field of honor in the face of imminent and grave personal danger. Hence, the presence of French soldiers in the ranks of the *troupes indigènes* was necessary for moral reasons and served to preserve the notion that Frenchmen were critical to the defense of the nation.

There were also practical reasons for the presence of French soldiers in indigenous units. For one thing, French soldiers could police the behavior of potentially unreliable *indigènes*. A rash of desertions of front-line Algerian troops in April 1915, inspired by their disillusionment with France and a feeling of solidarity with the Muslim troops of the Ottoman empire, Germany's ally, prompted the High Command to order an increase in the overall number of French soldiers in each company of *tirailleurs algériens*. These men would help the French officers keep a close watch over Muslim soldiers, preventing them from deserting their posts and making a break for the German trenches.[5]

But more technical reasons argued for the presence of French soldiers among the *troupes indigènes*. According to the conventional wisdom prevalent in the French Army, *indigènes* were incapable of performing, or even being trained to perform, the specialized tasks crucial to the overall effectiveness of units larger than small squads of riflemen. There were, of course, pragmatic reasons for this belief. Language barriers did prevent most *indigènes* from serving as liaisons with other units, or as signalers, messengers, or clerical personnel, whose jobs entailed reading, writing, or speaking French fluently. But officers also made arguments about the unsuitability of *indigènes* for specialized tasks that reveal more about racial stereotypes and prejudices than about the purportedly limited abilities of the *indigènes*. Paradoxically, even when certain "races" revealed themselves to be capable of performing some technical duties, such as Indochinese nurses and drivers, officials linked this very ability to supposedly inherent racial characteristics.

Political and psychological reasons for the absence of indigenous soldiers in roles requiring specialized or technical skill were evident before the war. Military officials in Indochina did not even trust long-serving professionals among the *troupes indigènes* and avoided "incorporating them into artillery or engineering units, branches that mark[ed] the technical superiority of the conqueror."[6] During the Great War, French officers rarely invoked this consideration of white racial prestige explicitly. More common was the argument that *indigènes* were incapable of performing such complex tasks.

In one sense, this was objectively true. In addition to problems caused by language barriers, most did not have the mathematical or technical training necessary to hold certain positions in an artillery battery. *Indigènes* also found themselves largely excluded from machine-gun companies, due to the higher complexity and delicacy of the guns, which were more susceptible than rifles to jamming or otherwise malfunctioning due to overheating or dirt clogging the parts.

Yet in many ways the incapacity of indigenous troops to serve in specialized roles stemmed from the racial prejudices of their white French commanders. *Indigènes* did not possess many of the necessary abilities because they did not receive the proper training, and they did not receive the proper training because officers did not consider them capable even of learning the requisite skills. Nonwhites could not serve in important positions in machine-gun companies because they were ignorant of duties that no one had adequately trained them to perform. French officers made their distrust of the *indigènes* on moral grounds even more clear when they argued that commanders had to consider that these men might abandon their valuable weapons to the attacking enemy, raising the prospect of Germans turning a captured machine gun on French troops in the trenches and subjecting them to murderous enfilading fire. As for language problems, authorities often did not even bother to teach *indigènes* proper French, condoning and supporting the spread of a pidgin form of French that marked colonial subjects and maintained the gulf that separated them from native French-speakers. This inability to speak proper French then barred these men from certain employments.[7]

Most French officers regarded *troupes indigènes* as little suited to the more complicated tasks of soldiering, and thought that they would therefore serve most effectively as attacking "shock troops," which required the least amount of complex training and maneuver. This would be the best use of the indigenous personnel in each unit, while white French personnel would provide the necessary moral and technical support. An inspection report on North African troops destined to serve in France in 1915 noted that "specialties" (machine gunners, telephone operators, liaison agents, and others) absorbed so many of the French personnel in the companies that there was a need for more whites in many units. In response to this observation, the Ministry of War promised to increase the proportion of the "French element" in each company to 20 percent of the total number of men.[8]

Early in the war, some indigenous units lacked even specialized equipment, let alone the French personnel to operate it. The five battalions of

Moroccans sent to France in August 1914 did not even have machine guns, and this posed a potential tactical problem, because the metropolitan units alongside whom they were to fight did have them.[9] Of course, this equipment was probably not often strictly necessary in Morocco, or really crucial in colonial warfare in general. The French Army as a whole, moreover, was not well supplied with machine guns, the importance of which in the new conflict many had yet to grasp.[10] Almost two years later, however, the commander of the Moroccan Regiment complained that regulations guiding the attribution of soldiers to his unit contained no provision for French personnel under the rank of officer for "special positions" that only Frenchmen could fill because of the "lack of ability of the Moroccans."[11] A similar disadvantage plagued West African battalions, which in 1916 had to be "bracketed" by European regiments, because the West African units had neither machine-gun sections nor telephone teams.[12]

This situation was especially problematic because, as the war went on and new and more complex weapons played an increasingly prominent role on the battlefield, technical skills became progressively more important. A December 1916 report noted that the High Command had to increase the proportion of French soldiers in Algerian units "because of the numerous specialties required by the current war, machine gunners, telephonists, liaison agents, etc." The author of the report did admit, however, that the *tirailleurs* made good grenade-throwers.[13] Grenade-throwing hardly represented the most technical of the new skills demanded by modern warfare, and the army put the vast majority of "special devices," such as machine guns, automatic rifles, field cannons, and others, at the disposition of white French soldiers.[14]

In light of the supposedly inherent inability of *indigènes* to carry out complex tasks, French authorities viewed the performance of specialized functions in indigenous units as a particular problem. In March 1916, a divisional commander cited the inferior value of Algerians for "delicate tasks" and "the impossibility of training telephonists, artillerymen, etc., among them" as proof that units of *tirailleurs algériens* needed more French personnel than army regulations specified.[15] Another officer was even more blunt: "The effectiveness in combat of our *tirailleurs indigènes* is not directly proportional to the power of the numerous devices with which they have been progressively equipped." In fact, he continued, the *indigènes* quickly lost faith in the machines put at their disposal because of their "absolute inability to use them." In battle, they often threw away unfamiliar weapons such as automatic rifles and picked up simple breech-loaders. One could train *tirail-*

*leurs* to use more complex weapons, but it would take much longer than to train Frenchmen, and the urgent need to get men to the front quickly did not allow such indulgence of the *indigènes'* weaknesses. The officer advocated increasing the proportion of French soldiers in his regiment to over 37 percent, so that indigenous units would be "comparable to good French regiments" and could "carry out the same missions with a useful result."[16]

Many officers attributed *indigènes'* inability to master the specialized tasks of modern warfare to their inherent mental inferiority. Responding to a request to allow North African soldiers to become officers in the artillery, the head of the Section d'Afrique at the Ministry of War maintained that, with rare exceptions, these men were unsuited to tasks that required meticulous accuracy, and were useful to artillery units only as drivers of animal-drawn carriages transporting supplies. The proof? In the infantry, North Africans were rarely good marksmen because, he argued, they lacked "notions of precision, indispensable to soldiers in specialized branches," and most of them were even ignorant of the concepts of parallel and perpendicular.[17]

Given such attitudes, the army deemed it necessary to maintain a significant proportion of French soldiers in indigenous units, above the necessary complement of officers, to ensure the combat effectiveness of *troupes indigènes.* By the middle of 1917, the High Command settled on the proportion of 30 percent, up from 20 percent, in units of North African soldiers.[18] A similar ratio prevailed in combat units from other areas of the empire.[19]

There was, however, one important difference among the various "races" that came to serve in France during the war. Military authorities regarded certain of these groups, specifically Indochinese and Madagascans, as more suitable for some specialized roles. This was the flip side of attitudes that denigrated the usefulness of these men as combat infantrymen. For example, while over 134,000 West Africans served as *tirailleurs* in Europe, Algeria, and Tunisia between mobilization in August 1914 and the end of the war, only an additional 133 served as nurses. Over 29,000 Madagascans served as *tirailleurs,* while another 1,907 were nurses; and 30,425 Indochinese served as *tirailleurs,* while 9,019 were nurses. In addition, Madagascar and Indochina provided, respectively, 2,054 and 5,339 *commis et ouvriers d'administration* (COA). These were, literally, administrative clerks and workers, a category that included clerical assistants, mechanics, butchers, lumberjacks, and other ancillary personnel who performed the myriad tasks on which the smooth administrative functioning of a wartime army depended. No West Africans served as COA.[20]

At the end of the war, summing up the advantages of employing Madagascans in France, Hubert Garbit—former governor-general of Madagascar, now serving in France as a colonel in the artillery, and principal propagandist for their use—cited their ability to serve as specialists as one of the factors that set them apart from other indigenous troops. This quality would allow Madagascans to form largely autonomous units, less dependent on the presence of European personnel to perform under fire. Not only could Madagascans serve in either the infantry or artillery, and in the services as secretaries, telephone and telegraph operators, automobile drivers, tailors, and butchers, among other jobs, some among them could even serve as doctors.[21] Another officer concurred with Garbit's assessment, noting the "astonishment and even admiration" of several regimental commanders in whose metropolitan units several Madagascan observers and signalers had served in August and September 1917.[22]

Stereotypes of Madagascans and Indochinese were similar—physical frailty, lack of a warrior spirit, intelligence combined with a lack of independent initiative, and *douceur*, a term difficult to translate in this context, but literally meaning gentleness or softness—and Indochinese soldiers also surprised observers with their ability to fulfill specialized duties.[23] The use of Indochinese as truck drivers to transport men and supplies at and near the front began in June 1916, in response to the rapidly expanding importance of automobile transport and the corresponding heightened need for drivers, and the skillful performance of the Indochinese during the offensive that summer on the Somme convinced the High Command of the utility of continuing and expanding the experiment. By the end of the war at least 4,000 Indochinese were serving as drivers.[24]

One official argued that qualities of endurance, supposedly stemming from a vegetarian diet, which also prevented more intense, brief exertions, and concentration, rendered these men particularly well prepared for grueling periods of driving under dangerous conditions. In fact, during the Battle of the Somme, Indochinese drivers remained at the wheel for thirty-six hours straight without displaying any more fatigue than did their French counterparts.[25] Europeans were the constant benchmark in evaluating any of the *troupes indigènes*, and this observer invoked the comparison in another report when he noted that after having received equal training, Indochinese drivers were as skilled as an average Frenchman. Even more positively, Indochinese drivers were easier on the machinery than their French colleagues (precisely how is not clear, though perhaps this was attributable to the Indochinese reputation for *douceur*), and the upkeep of trucks driven by the former cost less than a quarter of that for vehicles driven by French soldiers. The *indigènes* also drove safely, having successfully avoided any fatal accidents.[26]

The stereotypes that led to the use of Indochinese soldiers as drivers were clear: "intelligence, calmness, skill, aptitude for precise tasks, which are the chief qualities of the Indochinese." Moreover, "these same qualities of intelligence, *douceur*, and devotion, characteristic of the Annamite race" (though Annam was only one of the areas that made up the Indochinese federation, the French often used the term "Annamite" refer to Indochinese in general) decisively influenced the decision to use so many Indochinese as nurses.[27]

Many Indochinese served as drivers in the occupied Rhineland after the war, allowing the French to demobilize French troops more quickly. General Charles Mangin helped inspire this deployment, and he envisioned numerous possibilities for using Indochinese soldiers in the future because of their "subtle intelligence," and because they were "nimble, quick to learn, endowed with a remarkable gift for imitation, having a love and respect for intellectual culture." This "first cousin of the Japanese" could serve in all capacities, "everywhere where military technique requires manual skill, dexterity, precision, sang-froid, [and] orderliness."[28] Mangin expressed similar sentiments about soldiers from Madagascar, and when commanding troops during the occupation of the Rhineland, he asked for both Indochinese and Madagascan troops, who could serve as drivers, nurses, secretaries, cooks, tailors, bootmakers, and even draftsmen, in order to "reduce French recruitment."[29]

## Organization

Staffing units of *troupes indigènes* with European personnel and specialists caused particular concern for military authorities, but an even more pressing organizational consideration was how to distribute these units within the overall force structure of the army. Should commanders break larger indigenous units down into companies, mixing them with "white" companies to form mixed battalions?[30] Or should indigenous battalions remain whole, serving alongside white battalions in mixed regiments? Or perhaps *indigènes* should serve in regiments or even divisions of their own.[31] This was an important issue, because it pertained directly to the combat effectiveness of *troupes indigènes*. How they would operate in larger units at the front had a direct impact upon other units in their vicinity and upon the overall strategy of the High Command. If they failed to sustain an attack on their section of the front, or, worse, if they broke under the pressure of a German attack, this would threaten the lives of other soldiers and the integrity of French offensive and defensive power. Given prevailing racial stereotypes about the dubious reliability of nonwhite soldiers, this was a worrisome problem for French commanders. As a result, there was lively debate throughout the war about the best way to organize and utilize these troops in combat.

Debate over this issue focused primarily on North and West Africans, because so few Indochinese and Madagascan units served in front-line infantry combat. Just two battalions and one company of *tirailleurs indochinois* participated in operations on the Western Front (two more did so on the Salonika Front), while only one battalion of *tirailleurs malgaches* took part in combat in France. For the most part, commanders broke these units down and integrated them into larger units of white French soldiers, or combined them with other units of *troupes indigènes.* Splitting these battalions into separate companies, sometimes even sections, disrupted the organization and command structure of the units, and often placed *indigènes* under the command of officers who were unfamiliar with them. For example, during its service in the Vosges region in 1917, the 7th Bataillon de tirailleurs indochinois (BTI) was spread out within the 12th Division, with one divided company attached to the 3rd Battalion of the 54th Regiment (one section attached to each company); a whole company attached to the 1st Battalion of the same regiment; another whole company attached to the 67th Regiment; and a machine-gun company split into two sections, one serving with the 54th Regiment, and the other serving with the 67th. Such piecemeal deployment was disruptive enough, but frequent reassignment made the situation even worse. The second Indochinese battalion to serve on the Western Front, the 21st, found itself moved from one sector or division to another eleven times between April 1917 and November 1918.[32] The situation was similar for the 12th Bataillon de tirailleurs malgaches (BTM), the only Madagascan combat unit on the Western Front. The companies of this battalion often served separately, and the unit as a whole changed location repeatedly during 1917 and 1918.[33]

North Africans often served in larger, autonomous units, both battalions and regiments. This was primarily due to the well-defined structure even before the war of the Armée d'Afrique, which had grouped Algerian and Tunisian soldiers into nine regiments. Moroccan soldiers at first served in battalions alongside other units of colonial infantry, but from December 1914, they formed an autonomous regiment, with a second forming in 1918.[34] The army did, however, attempt to ensure the solidity of North African units by mixing them with white soldiers in several different ways. First of all, several Algerian and Tunisian battalions formed part of five "mixed regiments" that served on the Western Front, the other component of these regiments being Zouaves (mostly Europeans living in Algeria). Even regiments composed entirely of *indigènes* (except, of course, for the usual 20–30 percent European complement of officers, specialists, and regular soldiers deemed essential to the proper functioning of the indigenous units) usually combined with at least one French regiment in brigades during an attack.[35] An Algerian interviewed sixty years after his service in the Great War indicated a final possible method of mixing French and indigenous elements, at least during an attack. According to this former *tirailleur,* French officers would arrange the ranks in such a way that one French soldier stood behind every three *indigènes* in an attempt to ensure that they carried out their duties.[36]

Despite this concern with the organization of North African units, the greater part of attention to the matter of organizing units of *troupes in-digènes* focused on West Africans. After the initial deployment of several battalions to counter the German invasion in the summer and autumn of 1914, the *tirailleurs sénégalais* withdrew to the south of France and to North Africa to sit out the winter weather, which severely compromised their utility at the front. Previewing their redeployment in the summer of 1915, the Direction des troupes coloniales (DTC) drafted a plan to divide sixteen *ba-taillons de tirailleurs sénégalais* (BTS) between two *divisions mixtes,* which would include eight regiments each. These regiments would consist of two BTS and one battalion of white soldiers. However, the decision of the minis-ter of war to send West Africans to participate in the Franco-British invasion of Turkey in the spring of 1915 prevented the DTC from carrying out the experiment of mixed divisions. In the Dardanelles, local commanders split the BTS into companies, forming mixed battalions with two African and two white companies.[37]

Yet the army did not automatically transfer this system to Europe when the *tirailleurs sénégalais* returned to the Western Front in the spring and summer of 1916. In fact, their exact organization remained in flux through-out the war, varying considerably according to time, place, circumstances, and the preferences of local commanders. The one constant was a concern to find a system that would take advantage of Africans' allegedly aggressive

instincts, while units of white soldiers accompanied them to stiffen their resolve and provide guidance. In January 1916, the initial plan of the Ministry
of War was to deploy the BTS in mixed regiments, including two or three
BTS and one battalion of whites, formed together into mixed divisions.[38]

General Joffre did not approve of the mixed divisions, however, instead
preferring, in some cases, to integrate autonomous BTS into larger army
corps or, in others, to insert one or two mixed regiments into divisions made
up of white soldiers.[39] Joffre probably preferred this organization in part because it promised to cause less disruption upon the inevitable withdrawal
of the West Africans during the winter: a mixed division depending on the
presence of several African battalions would be useless once they withdrew.
However, opinions of the overall utility of the West Africans in combat,
opinions based upon their racial identity, also played a role. In a proposal
outlining the specific organization of the BTS during 1916, the High Command declared that because West African units were of a "warlike temperament, but slow in training," they were utilizable on the Western Front only
if they were composed of experienced soldiers and "amalgamated with
white troops" in a proportion of about 1:3. So during 1916, West Africans
would be distributed by battalion among several larger units of the French
Colonial Army, but these would be combined with two white battalions in
order to take proper advantage of the "real fighting value of *sénégalais* supported [*encadrés*, literally, bracketed side by side] by Europeans."[40] In other
words, only proper organization—supporting potentially ferocious fighters
with a scaffolding of more reliable and steady white units—could render
the *tirailleurs sénégalais* useful in Europe.

Despite the High Command's intention of leaving the structure of the
BTS intact, local commanders had considerable leeway in organizing their
forces. During the Somme offensive that summer, several battalions were
broken into companies, and some companies broken into sections, and mixed
with white units of the same size, while BTS assigned to other corps or divisions fought as battalions or were even combined to form all–West African regiments.[41] Many judged the performance of the West Africans on the
Somme a failure, but General Mangin, in a new position of influence helping his friend and recently appointed supreme commander of the French
Army General Robert-Georges Nivelle plan the massive offensive on the
Chemin des Dames ridge in the Aisne region for the spring of 1917, now
wanted to make even greater use of West African troops. In February 1917,
Chef de bataillon [Major] Arnaud, commander of the 64th BTS, offered

a detailed plan for organizing the West Africans that was designed better to suit their distinctive qualities. According to most observers, commanders should not break up battalions, because this ran the risk of placing the *tirailleurs* under the command of officers who were unfamiliar with them. These officers would not know how best to use their new charges, and the Africans would be less effective fighting for leaders whom they did not know or trust completely.[42] Arnaud's scheme addressed this concern, even while preserving some mixing of black and white companies. His plan called for the pairing of West African battalions with white battalions, combined with the *panachage*, or variegation, of one company from each.[43] This simply meant that two neighboring battalions swapped companies, but the *tirailleurs* remained closely linked with their battalions and thus more effective in combat. Specifically, *panachage* addressed what many regarded as a serious shortcoming of the West African units. Commanders could not position them on the wings of an attack, the complex maneuvers of which were "tricky to carry out and difficult to make understood to units of a rustic intelligence." The flexibility of variegated units, however, would allow battalion commanders to position white units, "better qualified than the blacks to deal with the unexpected," on the most dangerous wings of an attack.[44]

Arnaud's carefully presented plans did not become official army policy. The High Command never gave a definitive indication of exactly how local commanders were to deploy the BTS during the offensive on the Chemin des Dames ridge, which began on 16 April, generally leaving the specific form of their deployment up to the commanders of the larger formations to which the BTS were attached. The term many used to describe the tactical deployment of the West Africans was *accoler*, a verb meaning to place side by side or to bracket, vividly evoking the role white units played in shoring up, containing, and even policing their African comrades. In some cases, policy dictated placing white units behind, rather than side by side with, West African units: a 1918 guide for officers commanding West Africans warned its readers that "behind the black battalions one must always have in support a French unit."[45] Rather late, on 3 May, the High Command reminded commanders of metropolitan units, who were unfamiliar with the *tirailleurs* and how to deploy them, that each BTS should form the fourth battalion of a regiment.[46]

Meanwhile, different commanders used their West Africans in different ways, some forming regiments from three BTS, some deploying the battalions autonomously or in predominantly white regiments, and some employing *panachage* by exchanging companies between black and white battalions (though this was often at the last minute before an attack, resulting in un-familiarity between companies that would depend upon each other under fire, and a lack of overall unit cohesion).[47] One general argued that the system in place in his corps, combining one company of *tirailleurs* with three companies of white soldiers, was best suited to the special characteristics of the Africans. Grouped together in battalions, the West Africans were unable to stand firm and hold defensive lines, and such an organization left them virtually alone on large sections of the front. Mixed in with companies of white soldiers, the West Africans would be more reliable.[48] General Philippe Pétain, who replaced the disgraced leader of the failed "Nivelle Offensive" as supreme commander of the army, confirmed that the "amalgamation" of one West African company to three white companies should be the rule at the front, but that the BTS should remain intact when training or resting in rear areas.[49]

That did not settle the issue, however. The failure on the Chemin des Dames, on which Nivelle and Mangin had staked both hopes of an ultimate French victory and the reputation of the effectiveness of *troupes indigènes* in a European war, further complicated the debate. While some officers advocated forming mixed companies, others adhered to the notion of mixed battalions, and proponents of *la force noire* maintained their faith in West Africans fighting as whole battalions or even regiments. In preparation for the redeployment of *tirailleurs sénégalais* in the spring of 1918, the High Command ordered West African battalions broken down into companies for use at the front. An officer who commanded West Africans vigorously protested this policy, which he termed "wrong, ineffective, contrary to national interests," insisting that the army should use the BTS "in an intensive fashion and not by small packets." "The Algerian is more intelligent, more civilized than the *sénégalais*," the officer admitted, but he argued that the main concern was to ensure that the BTS were "well-supported," with a proportion of European personnel equal to the 20 to 30 percent that was the rule in Algerian battalions. "The BTS thus augmented," he wrote, "will be as good as an Algerian battalion and will be able to be employed in the same manner."[50] Even Arnaud, previously an advocate of *panachage*, had come around to this opinion after the experiences of 1917, recommending that West African battalions remain intact, with more white personnel added to ensure effective performance in combat.[51]

Despite these opinions, there was still no consistent rule for the tactical deployment of West African units during the campaigns of 1918. Some commanders variegated the BTS with white battalions, while others used intact West African units as powerful offensive spearheads. There was, however, an indication that the idea of mixed battalions would eventually have become the general rule in the French Army had the war continued into 1919. By the summer of 1918, both Clemenceau and Supreme Allied Commander Ferdinand Foch had given their full approval to an ambitious plan to deploy "a shock Colonial Army" composed of "mixed divisions." The battalions that made up these divisions would contain both white and black companies, and the resulting force of uniformly mixed African and European troops would have constituted the most coherent policy on the organization of the West African troops utilized during the whole war.[52] Despite the stillbirth of the plan for mixed divisions, it revealed the final judgment of high-ranking military officials about the best organization for the *tirailleurs sénégalais*. As with the insistence that the proportion of European personnel in units of *troupes indigènes* be no less than 20–30 percent, the imperative of mixing, or "bracketing," African units with white units revealed French officers' fears that nonwhites, even those with a warlike spirit, were incapable of withstanding the rigors of European warfare on their own, lacking as they did the sense of calm self-sacrifice that sustained white Europeans.

## Races guerrières and Races non-guerrières

Clearly, in deciding how to employ *troupes indigènes* and in assessing their potential and actual performance in combat and in other necessary military tasks, the French Army made great use of racial concepts that assigned values to groups based upon their "warlike" qualities. Military officials placed a great deal of emphasis upon the supposed differences among various ethnic groups both among and within each of the colonies, preferring *races guerrières* to *races non-guerrières* for combat duty. In the end, ideas about *races guerrières* and *races non-guerrières* within certain colonies were less important in decisions about deployment during the war than broader distinctions among larger groups of soldiers from different colonies. These distinctions had a profound impact upon the specific duties assigned to the *troupes indigènes* and the danger they faced (and thus their chances of being killed or wounded), and revealed a great deal about the specificities of French racial ideas. Allegedly less warlike Madagascan and Indochinese men did not often serve in combat, while "warlike" men from West and North Africa served most often as combat troops.

Attitudes toward men from Madagascar and Indochina differed, but the similarities were striking and led to men from these colonies performing similar roles within the French Army. Both groups stood at the bottom of the racial hierarchy of martial worth that guided French officers during the war, and at first the High Command hesitated to bring Madagascans or Indochinese soldiers to France. In November 1914, the Ministry of War expressed its doubts about a proposal to send two battalions of Madagascans to Djibouti for garrison duty, skeptical of the value of using *tirailleurs malgaches* outside their home island at all, let alone in France. These soldiers, officials argued, had never proven their worth against enemies other than their own fellow Madagascans, and that they were "notably inferior" to West African troops was clear from experience during the French conquest of the island in 1895.[53] A year later, another officer at the Ministry of War expressed similar doubts about sending Madagascans to police restive areas of southern Tunisia. The head of the French forces in North Africa did not even want to use West African troops against such skilled adversaries, so there was no question of using "Madagascans, who do not have the military and warlike value of the *sénégalais*."[54] Madagascans did eventually serve in Tunisia, but many nonetheless doubted that they would be as useful as West Africans in the all-important European theater.[55]

Opinions about the utility of Indochinese soldiers outside southeast Asia were, if anything, even more negative. After the war, one general remarked, "*no one*—including ourselves, colonials who knew them best—thought that Indochinese could be used at the front."[56] Indeed, in 1915 an officer with long experience commanding *tirailleurs indochinois* argued vehemently against employing them in Europe, because the vast majority of Indochinese did not make good soldiers. Even those few who did—some, he admitted, had served the French well, fighting to the death rather than retreating during battles in Indochina—would be useless on the Western Front, where "one requires exactly the opposite from the '*poilus*,' that is, to advance without getting killed" (the term *poilu* was slang for a French soldier of the First World War). Though some Indochinese had been effective in helping the French conquer Indochina by fighting against other Asians, they were simply not the answer to France's "manpower crisis."[57] Even after the government began recruiting soldiers in Indochina, Joffre had no intention of using them in France.[58]

Nevertheless, thousands of *tirailleurs malgaches* and *indochinois* eventually did serve in France, and as it turned out, some French officers gave them qualified approval. Yet for the most part, these men served as *troupes d'étapes*, doing guard duty behind the lines or performing labor such as repairing roads and railroads, delivering supplies, driving trucks, digging trenches, unloading ships, and other essential noncombat work. In Senator Henry Bérenger's November 1915 call for increased recruitment in the colonies, in which he admitted that Madagascan and Indochinese men did not always have the physical attributes necessary for a true warlike nature, he lauded the "native qualities of flexibility, touch, [and] skill," which would make them good laborers.[59]

The army ultimately agreed with Bérenger, and by the end of 1917, fourteen Indochinese and twenty-two Madagascan battalions were serving as staging troops in France (plus three more of the latter with the Armée d'Orient in Salonika).[60] As Senator Bérenger's comments indicated, it was not only because Madagascans and Indochinese lacked warlike qualities that they were better suited to manual labor, but also because they possessed the distinctive racial characteristics of "flexibility, touch, [and] skill." In February 1916, the Ministry of War issued instructions relative to the use of Indochinese labor, leaving no doubt as to the specific racial characteristics that the army valued: a natural ability to perform technical work and a quick grasp of tasks requiring precision; nimble and flexible fingers and joints; and an agility that was only partly compromised by a lack of power and endurance.[61]

Despite their status as *troupes non-combattantes*, even staging troops often faced mortal peril when repairing roads and trenches under enemy shell fire or delivering supplies to the front lines. One company of the 16th BTI, working on the railroad in the spring of 1918, withstood artillery fire and frequent bombings from German planes, while German soldiers took prisoner several men from the 14th BTI during an attack in the Aisne region.[62] A Madagascan battalion in this same region, constructing artillery emplacements not far from the front lines in the summer of 1917, suffered significant losses.[63] In the end, given these sacrifices and the quality of their work, French authorities were pleased with the performance of the *troupes d'étapes*.

Evaluations of the few combat units from Madagascar and Indochina were also positive, though in the end somewhat ambiguous. One of the few early proponents of using Indochinese troops for fighting in Europe wrote in November 1915 that although they did not have the "drive" of the West Africans and thus were not dependable for assaults, the Indochinese would display great resistance in the trenches, fighting to the death to beat back enemy attacks.[64] Though the High Command did not agree completely with this assessment, a company of the 6th BTI did take part in the assault on Fort Douaumont at Verdun in October 1916, and reports on the action remarked that the Indochinese fought well, with no breakdowns in discipline under murderous fire that left 16 killed, 22 wounded, and 12 missing.[65] In 1917, the 7th BTI fought in various engagements, including the disastrous Nivelle offensive, in which the unit suffered almost 200 casualties. A second combat unit, the 21st BTI, fought in the Aisne and in the defense of Reims. French officers voiced no complaints about the performance of these units, and a censor's report of October 1917 noted that, not only were officers of the 7th BTI fully satisfied with their men, but the Indochinese had comported themselves "like real '*poilus*.'"[66]

This was the ultimate compliment, because white French soldiers stood at the top of the racial hierarchy of martial worth and were the universal standard against which French observers judged all *troupes indigènes*. Nonetheless, in spite of what one postwar report characterized as the "brilliant" performance of these two battalions, and the numerous decorations they won (an estimated average of thirty *croix de guerre* per company), the overall reputation of Indochinese soldiers remained undistinguished. In fact, even the glowing postwar report seemed to attribute the success of the two combat battalions to their ability to transcend the faults of their countrymen, noting that the soldiers displayed "a simple and natural ease that fortunately contrasts with the humble servility of certain Indochinese countryfolk."[67]

This remained conventional wisdom long after the war. "The Annamite was, in the past, a warrior by force," one observer wrote 1931. "But it does not seem that he is one by temperament."[68] (It is probably not too much to suppose that this attitude, which dismissed Indochinese men as having no particular natural proclivity for war, as members of a *race non-guerrière*, played a large part in the disastrous defeat of French forces thirty-six years after the end of the Great War by Vietnamese Communist troops at Dien Bien Phu, where French commanders grossly underestimated the capabilities of their enemies and placed themselves in a militarily untenable position.) From this and numerous other statements that spoke of a specific "temperament" necessary in order to make good soldiers, it was evident that many French authorities considered martial inclinations and skills to be an inherent quality, and thus varying among different "races."

The military reputation of the one combat battalion of Madagascans corresponded in large part with that of the two BTI. The army formed the

12th BTM in October 1916, and the unit entered the front lines in April of the following year. Ironically, this elite fighting force drew two-thirds of its personnel from the Hova and Betsileo populations of the island.[69] Such a large proportion of members of *races non-guerrières* bore witness to the contradictions in French policy on this issue. At first used as *troupes d'étapes* during the Nivelle offensive, the 12th BTM soon engaged in fierce fighting in the Aisne region. In a pattern that would repeat itself throughout their participation in the war, the Madagascans performed well under fire and lost considerable numbers of men. In their first engagement, 74 *indigènes* and 13 Europeans were killed. Consigned to labor for the winter of 1917–18, the 12th BTM took up positions on the front line again in Champagne in the spring of 1918. In one week of intense defensive battles against the massive German offensive of that spring, the battalion lost 9 of 19 European officers, including the *chef de bataillon*, 66 other European personnel, and 489 Madagascans. Despite these losses, half its strength, the 12th BTM took part in the French counteroffensives of July, losing 2 officers and 184 French and Madagascan troops in four days of fighting near Soissons. A bloody two-week period in September followed, during which the battalion lost another 8 officers and 479 French and Madagascan soldiers.[70]

The Madagascans won much praise and many decorations for these sacrifices. In 1919, the new commander of the 1st Régiment de chasseurs malgaches, a unit created from an expanded 12th BTM, described the performance of the Madagascans as "a veritable revelation," and cited their many individual and collective decorations as proof of their bravery and effectiveness in combat.[71] The commander of the Moroccan Division, with which the 12th BTM had fought on several occasions, admitted that he had been apprehensive at first when using Madagascans alongside such experienced fighters as the Moroccans in his division. But from the very first day he deployed them in combat, they had won a place of honor in the division through their "brilliant conduct" and discipline. He too had found their performance "a revelation," especially given the number of Hova among them.[72]

This praise was not without ambiguity, however. First of all, the term "revelation" merely confirms that the consensus in the army was that Madagascans were poor soldiers. Moreover, the commander of the Moroccan Division still insisted upon the importance of European personnel, especially officers, within this and other indigenous units, while the commander of the new Madagascan regiment admitted that Madagascan soldiers did not, in general, have a "warlike temperament," but noted that they were intelligent and possessed a highly developed sense of duty. Even Colonel Garbit, the foremost proponent of the effectiveness of *tirailleurs malgaches,* made an identical observation, saying: "The Madagascan is not a warrior by tempera-ment. He is receptive, on the other hand, to the sentiment of duty."[73]

If such qualified praise was common in the evaluations of the men who knew the Madagascans best, even though these officers had an interest in vaunting their soldiers' worth, it is not surprising that the opinion of the army as a whole remained largely unchanged by the performance of the 12th BTM. In fact, as one historian has put it, the Great War constituted a "parenthesis" in the image of the *tirailleur malgache,* and no more. After the war, one general cited the lack of a "sentiment of duty" among the Hova, precisely the quality that their commanders had praised in Madagas-can soldiers, as a primary reason to deny them access to the rank of officer. And in 1926, while serving in Syria, a demoralized column of Madagascan soldiers failed to defend themselves against a rebel attack, helping to recon-firm the low opinion that many in the army had of the *tirailleurs malgaches* in general.[74]

North Africans stood much higher than either Madagascan or Indochi-nese soldiers in the estimation of French officers. One indication of this was that the vast majority of North African soldiers served as combat troops. Of course, the perceptions of these officers were still filtered through racial ste-reotypes, and no North Africans enjoyed a reputation as the equals of white French soldiers. Conventional wisdom dictated that these colonial subjects were still in need of firm guidance from their French officers and support from other crucial French personnel. Most of the concerns about North Af-ricans' combat performance in Europe focused on their suitability for Eu-ropean warfare. In brief, if these men were formidable and fierce in the cavalry raids of intertribal warfare in the open desert and mountains of the Maghreb, there remained grave doubts about their adaptability to modern forms of warfare in Europe and their effectiveness in the face of a racially superior European enemy.

These doubts cut across the lines that differentiated men from the three French colonies in North Africa, but army policies and the comments of officers reveal specific attitudes toward each group. To some extent, the French absorbed these attitudes from the images they believed North Af-ricans had of themselves. In October, a government official reported that, on the evidence of his visit with North African troops stationed at Aix-en-Province and Arles, there was a great deal of antipathy between Moroccans, on the one hand, and Algerians and Tunisians on the other. This stemmed, he said, from attitudes reflected in a classic Arabic saying that divided North Africans into three distinct categories: "Moroccans are warriors, Algerians men, and Tunisians women."[75] These three classifications corresponded neatly with French perceptions during the war.

Moroccans, the only true warriors according to the saying, did indeed enjoy a reputation as fearless and savage fighters, and as an elite force among the *troupes indigènes*. For one thing, they were all volunteers, because there was no conscription in Morocco. The Moroccans were true mercenaries, and the French considered them professionals to be deployed when circumstances required speed, ferocity, and decisiveness in the attack. The contrast with their immediate neighbors in North Africa was clear. In 1916, the High Command characterized the Moroccans an "exception" among North African troops: they were volunteers, more intelligent, and of a "more warlike" temperament than conscripted Algerians, and were "superb attacking troops." After attacks, commanders would remove the *tirailleurs marocains* from the line, because they disliked long periods of defensive duty in the trenches.[76]

This reputation was well established before 1916. Five battalions of Moroccans were among the very first *troupes indigènes* to arrive on French soil, in August 1914, to take part in the fight against the Germans, and both Resident-general Lyautey and the minister of war felt it politically important not to disappoint such ardent warriors (and, of course, their French officers) by keeping them in Morocco while much of the rest of the French Army was engaged.[77]

These first units played a prominent role in the French retreats in the opening weeks of the campaign, in the Battle of the Marne, and in the French offensives that followed. One senior commander under whom they served praised the performance of these troops, noting that they did not give ground or panic even under heavy artillery fire, and that in a costly attack on the plateau of the northern bank of the Aisne River, the Moroccans displayed the "drive" and endurance one could expect from such natural warriors.[78] Even before the Moroccans began fighting, the Ministry of War informed officers who would be commanding them that these men were "intelligent, maneuverable, courageous, passionately warlike . . . tough, sober, and good marchers." Furthermore, Moroccans were better marksmen than Algerians, and that certain among them, "of the Berber race," shot very well indeed. In short, these were elite troops, of which commanders could make very effective use in offensive actions.[79]

Their reputation as fierce warriors cost the Moroccans dearly. The original five infantry battalions that arrived in France in August 1914 had lost over 80 percent of their men by the end of September. Later engagements over the next four years were also costly. Such sacrifices served to sustain the reputation of Moroccans as dedicated and fierce fighters, not least among the Germans, who called them "swallows of death."[80] Resident-general Lyautey, worried early on about the effect this would have on recruitment and the political outlook of *indigènes* in Morocco, complained in 1915 that "the regiment of *tirailleurs marocains*, because of its value, has been, if I may express myself thus, 'put in all the sauces,' and [is] always deployed in the front line, at all points on the front."[81]

The extensive use of the *tirailleurs marocains* throughout the war revealed the High Command's faith in their effectiveness, but this confidence was not unambiguous. If the Moroccans occupied a high place in the hierarchy of martial worth that was conventional wisdom in the French Army, they still did not rank as high as native Frenchmen. For one thing, they were more difficult to train. As one officer remarked in 1916, one could not form a Moroccan regiment as easily as a French one, because even the youngest French recruits—fired by patriotism, motivated to do well, better educated, and learning from instructors speaking their language—completed their training more quickly than did the *tirailleurs*.[82]

Moroccan soldiers' inferiority stemmed not only from the difficulty in training them, however, but also from other aspects of their mentality. Even as some French officers viewed them as particularly well suited to rapid, aggressive, and violent offensive action, these same officers also regarded them as particularly ill suited to many aspects of European warfare, especially as it developed after 1914. The Ministry of War's initial notice on the use of Moroccan troops, which praised their many soldierly qualities, warned against using them for certain tasks. Inasmuch as they did not know the French language or the uniforms of the various branches of the French Army and those of allied armies, they would not be useful on patrols or reconnaissance missions, where French supervision would be weaker and independent action would be necessary. Nor could their commanders leave them on their own, because of their "instinct for piracy." In warfare in North Africa, they were accustomed to the slaughter of noncombatants, rape, and pillage, and this occurred even among allied tribes. Such behavior, if left unchecked, would harm the French cause in the eyes of its allies, while presenting a danger even to the French population.[83] These comments, made before Moroccan troops had begun to fight, were, of course, not based upon the behavior of these men in France. However, they reveal a concern that the Moroccans would introduce the "uncivilized" methods of primitive tribal warfare they practiced in North Africa into Europe.

Officers' comments made after the fighting had begun struck similar themes. In the summer of 1915, an interpreter noted that morale was beginning to suffer at the depot for Moroccan soldiers in Arles. Their initial enthusiasm had disappeared, and none lined up anymore at headquarters to request a combat assignment, as they had done earlier in the war.[84] This was, no doubt, in large part a sensible reaction to the horrendous casualties the Moroccan units had suffered, but some saw in this decrease in martial ardor an indication of the Moroccans' unsuitability for European warfare. In short, their fiery impulsiveness, typical of primitive races, served them well in the wide-open warfare they enjoyed in North Africa, out on the *bled*, but they lacked the selfless stoicism that enabled white French soldiers to endure such a long and terrible conflict. Such perceptions prompted one senior commander to stress that though the Moroccans were great warriors, the current war was not what they had dreamed it would be. Unable to "hunt the enemy" in the open, these childlike *tirailleurs* detested the everyday chores of soldiering on the Western Front.[85] Another officer noted that "the simplistic mind of the Moroccans" had difficulty making sense of the form that the current war had taken.[86]

Although Algerians were "men" according to the Arabic saying, and not "warriors" like the Moroccans, they did have a reputation for being warlike and fairly good soldiers. This stemmed in part from the difficulty the French had had in conquering Algeria, which required over thirty years of hard fighting. Military, political, and colonial officials routinely referred to Algerians' "naturally warlike" sentiments or natures. These men, with the proper training and leadership, could be of great service to the French Army. The origins of Algerians' natural tendencies for war lay in their culture, history, and mentality: "The Arab and Berber races constitute, like the French, warlike peoples," a report noted. "War for them is not an accident, something unexpected and fearsome. They accept it as a normal event, chronically recurring. They can, it is true, meet their deaths in it, but who can ever escape that? Sooner or later, it must happen. Fatalism makes good soldiers."[87]

A report on conscription in Algeria made much the same argument, praising Algerians' intrepidity, bravery, endurance, and disregard of danger, and recalling the legendary exploits of the *turcos* in France during the

Franco-Prussian War. Noting their value as attacking "shock troops," the report claimed that an additional 300,000 Algerians in the ranks in 1914 would have turned the balance against the Germans, transforming the battle of Charleroi into a French victory and preventing the invasion of the northern *départements*.[88]

Not all evaluations of Algerian soldiers were this enthusiastic, especially when it came to the quality of conscripts from that colony, but the army did view them primarily as "shock troops" and for the most part as fierce fighters. However, as was the case with Moroccan troops, many officers were doubtful about the suitability of Algerians to the conduct of modern war in Europe. Doubts likely arose from the popular image of North Africa, especially Algeria, and of the kind of warfare the French Army had encountered there during the period of conquest. The wide-open spaces, alternating with rugged mountains, constituted terrain particularly well suited to quick cavalry raids, hit-and-run tactics, and aggressive frontal assaults. Combined with this was a prevailing stereotype of Arab fighters as duplicitous, undisciplined, and prone to pillage.[89] As early as October 1914, officials at the Ministry of War noted problems with the performance of Algerians in combat in France: "If the bellicose affinities of the Algerian *indigène* are admirably adapted to the mode of combat in Morocco, where he struggles against an enemy placed in approximately identical conditions, the blows that rain down on them today and decimate them, without them even being able to see an enemy, discourage and terrify them."[90]

The primitive aggression that the army believed made Algerians effective fighters in North Africa was of little use against a sophisticated European enemy who used modern tactics and technology, such as artillery bombardment. This attitude persisted throughout the war. Near the end of 1917, an officer wrote that Algerians were indeed animated by a warlike spirit, but the kind of colonial warfare they had known in North Africa, with expeditionary columns, lightning raids, and pursuit of the enemy, was not what they found in Europe. Here they found a stationary war, where stubborn, principled endurance was more important than impetuous zeal.[91] Quite simply, *indigènes* lacked the higher moral and intellectual qualities of white French soldiers, qualities essential to waging modern war. The High Command, though praising Algerian troops as "fiery" and "suited to the attack," qualified this praise by noting that the *tirailleurs algériens* were less suited for defensive duty digging or manning trenches. It was necessary to move them frequently, "to stave off boredom."[92]

Like the simple and childlike Moroccans, Algerians supposedly craved the kind of wide-open action they could not find on the Western Front unless on the offensive. As was the case with other troops, this translated into fairly high casualty rates. It is difficult to determine precisely how many Algerians saw combat in Europe or how many lost their lives there, but it is likely that from about 120,000 to 125,000 fought in France, and approximately 25,000 were killed. This mortality rate of around 20 percent is roughly comparable to that among other *troupes indigènes* and among native French soldiers.[93]

If conventional wisdom in the French Army held that Algerians and Moroccans were not necessarily perfectly suited to European warfare, most officers at least believed they had redeeming value as soldiers, given their essentially warlike natures. The same was not always true of Tunisians. Though *tirailleurs tunisiens* served alongside and even within Algerian units, and some officials spoke of the "naturally warlike sentiments" the two groups possessed in common, most regarded men from the smaller colony as decidedly inferior. As neither warriors nor men, but "women" according to the Arabic saying, Tunisians made unlikely candidates for participation in the war in Europe. Integrated, however, into the overall structure of the Armée d'Afrique for occupation duty in North Africa long before the war began, Tunisians continued to serve primarily as combatants alongside their Algerian compatriots. Yet officers often singled Tunisians out as deficient in comparison with other soldiers. Even positive remarks often came as backhanded compliments. In January 1915, the minister of war wrote to Joffre to inform him that the reports of officers serving with Tunisian soldiers in France indicated that their men had a good attitude, "despite their not very military nature."[94]

Whenever difficulties arose with Tunisian troops, officials made similar comments, portraying the *indigènes'* lack of martial fervor as the result of a natural, inherent aversion to warlike pursuits. Early in the war, when some Tunisian reservists committed acts of indiscipline and deserted before embarking for France, one officer attributed the problems in part to German propaganda, which affected Tunisians particularly because of their "indolent" nature and "less warlike instincts."[95] In January 1915, commenting on the effect that the Ottoman sultan's declaration of Holy War on the Triple Entente powers was having on the loyalty of France's North African troops, the minister of war claimed that Moroccan soldiers were more committed to France than they had been at the beginning of the war, and Algerians' sentiments had given no cause for concern. However, he expressed less certainty about the loyalty of the *tirailleurs tunisiens.* Censors' reports had indeed revealed some grumbling about having to serve outside Tunisia, but Resident-general Alapetite did not attribute this to either sympathy for Turkey or hostility to France, but to "a lack of bravery." With the Arabic saying portraying Tunisians as "women" and not warriors in mind, the minister of war noted that this assessment conformed to opinions about Tunisians in the Muslim world, so it was probably correct, if regrettable.[96] Even earlier in the war, in November 1914, the Ministry of War informed the High Command that, among North African troops in France, only the morale of Tunisians left something to be desired. This was due in part to the presence of reservists who were reluctant to serve outside Tunisia, but also to the Tunisians' "less warlike nature than that of their Algerian and Moroccans coreligionists."[97]

Soldiers from West Africa had a reputation as the elite fighters among *troupes indigènes*. The idea that West Africans were mentally primitive and savage, but aggressively so, as well as loyal, hardy, and dependable, if properly led, determined the French Army's decision to use large numbers of these troops on the Western Front, and to use them specifically as attacking "shock troops." However, when these men faltered in battle, or suffered serious defeats, or when French officers simply found them deficient in certain tasks, it was again supposedly due to immutable racial characteristics that rendered them inferior to native French soldiers.

Opinions on the value of West African soldiers displayed such ambiguity from the very beginning of the war. Between September and November 1914, various units of *tirailleurs sénégalais* fought in several areas along the rapidly forming Western Front. The French High Command demonstrated its confidence in their abilities by using them extensively in the continual flanking movements that comprised the "Race to the Sea" during that autumn, and this proved costly to the West Africans. For example, the 12th BTS, engaged in Picardy between 20 September and 11 October, lost 328 men killed, wounded, or missing out of an original complement of 832. Later in October, Joffre employed a regiment of *tirailleurs sénégalais* in operations in Champagne. These attacks not only failed and caused heavy casualties, but some units panicked under fire, leading to their removal from the front.[98]

In November, three battalions of West Africans fought on the Yser River, near Dixmude in Belgium. This time, they maintained better discipline in combat. Yet losses were appalling, and soon the cold, wet weather incapacitated the West Africans, who were used to a tropical climate. On the Yser, as in other places along the front where West Africans fought, the use of these troops appeared to be a costly failure. From the four battalions that made up the regiment in which the West Africans served at Dixmude (three BTS and one European battalion), French commanders could only scrape together one reconstituted battalion when survivors gathered at a camp in the southern French city of Fréjus. Ultimately, only 3,728 of the 5,300 *tirailleurs* who had come that autumn from their posts in North Africa to fight in France remained to make the return trip for the winter.[99]

The difficulties of these early campaigns contributed to the ambiguous reputation of West African soldiers. On the one hand, the fighting on the Yser prompted two observers to dedicate a book to describing "the sublime heroism" of "these fine, brutal forces of nature and instinct . . . images of primitive humanity, proud athletes of bronze."[100] On the other hand, there had been clear problems with their performance. It did not matter that these were not entirely their fault. As one historian has noted, they were "badly judged, badly used, and even badly led."[101] One could say the same of white French troops, who had also suffered repeated defeats and heavy casualties in the opening months of the conflict, but many military officials were particularly skeptical about the value of the *tirailleurs sénégalais*, and even when the need for troops overcame this reticence and led to the more extensive use of West Africans on the battlefield, some commanders regarded these soldiers with decidedly mixed feelings.

Nonetheless, the West Africans did have their partisans, and even the terrible losses of the initial battles of 1914 did not dampen the enthusiasm of some of their officers. A captain in the 2nd BTS, which in the opening weeks of the war had lost 350 men and 13 officers out of an original complement of 800 men, reported that morale in the unit was high despite heavy casualties. He praised the bravery of the West Africans, who were "very superior" to Algerian troops and, but for the effects of cold weather, were the equals of any other soldiers. He even paid them the ultimate compliment, noting that as shock troops they were "incomparable, even to many white troops." The West Africans, simultaneously brave and childlike, even overcame their fear of heavy artillery bombardments, which now "made them laugh."[102] Another officer with experience commanding *tirailleurs sénégalais* considered them "equal in quality to the best troops that we have in France." Best used, he wrote, as shock troops, the West Africans were born warriors, and this officer too claimed that some were even better than certain French troops.[103] Of course, General Mangin was foremost among those who vaunted the utility of West African troops. Urging what he believed to be their proper use early in the war, he noted that they were "troops of an essentially offensive temperament," so it was necessary to keep them in reserve until the moment of a sustained attack.[104]

Mangin had an unyielding predilection for the offensive, regardless of the cost: after the war he wrote simply, "To make war is to attack."[105] But this attitude conformed to the dominant current of thought within the military on the use of West Africans in battle. Even reports that pointed out problems with their use on the Western Front noted that they had value as "shock troops." In some senses, this term applied to all combatant *troupes indigènes,* either because officers considered them particularly warlike (Moroccans and Algerians qualified as shock troops for this reason) or because a straightforward frontal assault did not require complex maneuvers beyond the capabilities of such supposedly simple-minded men. However, West Africans were clearly considered the elite among offensive troops, and this had a great deal to do with their supposed racial characteristics, savagery foremost among them. This idea had wide currency among the general French public as well as within the French Army. One West African soldier recalled that upon the arrival of his unit in France, crowds of people cheered him and his comrades as they paraded through the streets, with some of the spectators shouting to the Africans, "Cut off the Germans' heads!"[106]

Many Germans shared this belief in the fundamental savagery of West Africans fighting for France. French officers noted that "an almost irrational fear of our black units" afflicted German soldiers in the field, while the Kaiser's government made alleged atrocities—ranging from rape, to the summary execution of prisoners, to the mutilation of corpses—the primary focus of an international diplomatic and propaganda campaign to protest French violation of the rules of war by introducing such an uncivilized element into civilized Europe.[107]

But it was the prevalence of the vision of black Africans as bloodthirsty and savage warriors within the French Army that would have the greatest impact upon the West Africans themselves, because it led to their deployment as shock troops. A clear indication of this came in the autumn of 1916, when a senior commander gathered together the testimony of numerous officers in his corps who had commanded *tirailleurs sénégalais* directly during combat on the Somme during the previous summer. Though opinions varied on the overall degree to which the West Africans were useful in the current conflict, a general consensus emerged about the nature of their strengths and weaknesses. One divisional commander wrote that negative opinions often resulted from officers making an unfair comparison between black and white troops, a "comparison that leads them inevitably to regret the absence among the *sénégalais* of certain essential qualities of the European soldier, leading to a decrease of confidence in the unit entrusted to them." The real question, he argued, was whether the West Africans could be useful in modern combat, and he thought that they could be if used as shock troops. West Africans, "naturally warlike and ready to fight," had the essential qualities for offensive warfare: "bravery, *élan*, quickness in action."[108]

A battalion commander summed up the racial stereotypes that shaped the attitudes of many French officers toward the *tirailleurs sénégalais*, commenting that the West African soldier was brave and "a good marcher," who loved to fight, preferred hand-to-hand combat, and was disciplined, but who was capable only of short bursts of violence and needed prompt rest after an effort, who feared "what he did not know," and who reacted reflexively to events, being dominated by his animal instincts and not "by will or reflection."[109] Other officers cited West Africans' limited intellectual capacities, their complete lack of initiative, their susceptibility to cold weather, and their childlike fear of bombardments, making it clear that black troops, with all of these deficiencies, could not replace white troops. However, with the proper leadership, a sufficient number of Europeans to perform specialized tasks beyond the capacity of the West Africans, and essential support from neighboring units of white soldiers, West Africans could make "a contribution [by] allowing [us] to spare a certain number of European lives during assaults."[110]

This blunt statement shows the dangerous implications for the *tirailleurs sénégalais* of these racial stereotypes and the tactical doctrines that resulted from them. Fighting primarily during offensive operations exposed the West Africans to an increased probability of death. Whether or not West Africans served as "cannon fodder," as critics of their exploitation by the French have charged, has been the subject of some scholarly debate. Recent research has suggested that in some ways West Africans did indeed suffer a higher proportional casualty rate than did white troops.[111] In fact, if one compares the number of West Africans killed to the number of Frenchmen killed as a proportion of combatant troops, *tirailleurs sénégalais* sustained losses 20 percent higher than their French counterparts. Moreover, West African casualty rates increased as the war went on, while French casualty rates decreased, suggesting that commanders really were seeking to "spare" French lives at the expense of African lives. Lastly, French ideas about the relative martial worth of the various "races" that made up the population of West Africa caused commanders to employ so-called *races guerrières* in more dangerous offensive missions, causing members of these groups to suffer particularly disproportionate casualty rates.[112]

These facts were the logical outcome of the long-standing racial stereotypes that shaped tactical doctrine. In 1916, policy in the 10th Colonial Division called for the use of West African troops in attacks and counterattacks, especially those "to be launched immediately, without lengthy preparation." Commanders would send them on "energetic and risky missions, not those [demanding] tenacity." In other words, they were good for taking enemy trenches, not for defending their own; not for "any meticulous action that does not require offensive audacity, shock force, and contempt for losses."[113] That these attitudes prevailed in the army throughout the war was evident from the *Notice sur les Sénégalais et leur emploi au combat* (Notice on the Senegalese and Their Use in Combat) that the High Command published in October 1918 in order to educate officers down to the company commander level in the best use of West African soldiers. This manual sought to familiarize its readers with issues such as the characteristics of the various "races" of West Africa, *races guerrières* and *races non-guerrières*, their medical problems, religious beliefs, languages, and the principles that guided their deployment. In addition to stressing the vital role of white officers in the combat effectiveness of *tirailleur* units, the pamphlet stressed the "highly developed warrior instinct" of West Africans, their bravery, their spiritedness upon entering combat and launching an attack, their inability to undertake complicated operations involving liaison with artillery or military aviation, and their inability to prepare defensive positions.[114] In short, after four years of war, perceptions of the West Africans had changed little. Valued for their primitive aggression, they were seen as primarily useful for quick, uncomplicated attacks that would neither demand too much of their allegedly limited mental capacities nor require them to endure long periods under artillery fire.

## Winter Weather and Combat Effectiveness

Inasmuch as all *troupes indigènes* came from hot climates, their ability to withstand European winters was a serious concern, and this in turn had an impact upon their effectiveness as soldiers. When colder weather arrived on the Western Front in 1914, there were some indications that North Africans suffered from frostbite and increased respiratory illnesses, but it eventually became clear that for the most part these men could still serve at the front during the winter. Commanders were careful to avoid leaving them exposed in the trenches for too long during this season, and kept a careful watch on their health and hygiene, but no dramatic measures became necessary.

The same was not true of West Africans. By November 1914, it was obvious that the West Africans could not remain at the front during the coming winter. Demoralized by the cold, unable to carry out their duties effectively, and thus threatening the security of any place along the front where they manned the trenches, their health was deteriorating rapidly, to the point where the vast majority of them would soon be literally incapacitated. The 2nd and 3rd BTS reported losing almost four hundred men to the cold alone over a five-day period in mid-November.[115] Most of these cases were frostbite, but soon pulmonary illnesses like bronchitis and pneumonia added to the misery of the *tirailleurs sénégalais,* and the High Command had to pull them from the front lines and send them to encampments in the south of France and North Africa until the spring.[116]

The army repeated this procedure each winter, a practice known as *hivernage* (literally, "wintering"). Problems still arose, however, even in the relatively warm areas of southern France, and when commanders either failed to remove the West Africans early enough in the autumn, or brought them back too early in the spring. Mangin would do this in 1917, eager to begin the disastrous offensive of that April, and the misery of West Africans suffering in the cold rain on the Chemin des Dames, only to march into near-certain death in the face of murderous German artillery and machine-gun fire, became legendary.

The inability of the army to employ West African units for several months each year influenced opinions about their usefulness. Some commanders argued that these troops were ultimately of limited effectiveness in a war outside tropical climates. Defenders of the *tirailleurs sénégalais* countered that they could in fact serve during the winter after a period of acclimatization and if commanders properly looked after their men. Nonetheless, the withdrawal of West African battalions for the winter months continued to cause controversy and did indeed limit the ways in which the army could make use of them.

French officials at first believed the same would be true of Indochinese and Madagascan troops, but that turned out not to be the case. Indochinese soldiers did suffer from the cold, as did all men from hot climates, and those from the southern province of Cochin China seemed to be more vulnerable than those from more northerly Tonkin, so the former spent their winters in the south of France.[117] Yet authorities were pleased to learn that many battalions of *troupes d'étapes* and the two Indochinese combat units could remain at the front during the winter, as long as their commanders attended carefully to their clothing and living conditions.[118]

Madagascans, though, provided the most dramatic example of how resistance to winter weather could influence decisions about deployment and perceptions of the effectiveness· of *troupes indigènes.* As with many of the Indochinese units, Madagascan *troupes d'étapes* and the 12th BTM proved able to withstand the winter weather and remained within the combat zone in northeastern France year-round. At the outset of the war, it was not clear that this would be the case. In November 1914, the minister of war wrote that he would probably not deploy Madagascan troops in Europe because their ability to stand up to "a climate so different from that of the Grande Île is not known."[119]

By the summer of 1917, however, the Madagascans' unexpected ability to bear the rigors of the French climate led the High Command to experiment with redeploying several thousand *tirailleurs* from *bataillons d'étapes* to batteries of the heavy artillery. Admittedly, much of the impetus for this experiment came from the rapid and unprecedented expansion of the heavy artillery during the war of attrition, and from the efforts of the former governor-general and current artillery officer Hubert Garbit.[120] Yet it was the Madagascans' ability to serve throughout the winter that first recommended them for this duty, even if the army decided to send them to the heavy artillery because they would enjoy less exposure to the elements in that branch's more stable and comfortable accommodations and less frequent movements than they would working with the smaller pieces and more mobile batteries of the field artillery.[121]

In October 1917, the minister of war ordered 5,000 Madagascans, selected for their physical health and stamina from among the six battalions of staging troops then serving at the front, to begin integrating into batteries of the heavy artillery.[122] He stressed to officers in this service that they were to consider their new soldiers as combatants, not as simple laborers, though they would not serve in the sensitive technical position of *pointeur*, aiming the guns. In addition, thirty Madagascans (thirty-five for the heaviest pieces, the 220 and 280 millimeter cannons) would be needed to replace twenty Europeans.[123]

The deployment was a success, and by the end of the war, 15,000 Madagascans had served in the artillery. In March 1918, the Ministry of War urged the minister of the colonies to resume recruitment in Madagascar, because men from that island had surpassed all expectations in their service in the artillery. They had "withstood perfectly the rigors of the winter," and by their "docility" and "good will," they had performed their technical duties well, astonishing the officers who commanded them.[124] One of these officers wrote that Madagascans had acted heroically under fire and performed their duties without difficulty, concluding: "They are very useful to us and have no cause to envy the courage of our French gunners . . . the test is complete. We are confident in our Madagascans."[125]

Advocates of expanding the use of Madagascan troops touted their performance in the artillery and their ability to serve during European winters as conclusive proof of their value. It would be wrong, however, to exaggerate the transformation this experiment in the heavy artillery wrought in the image of the Madagascan soldier. A July 1918 report on the performance of Madagascans in the artillery, while positive and even enthusiastic about the results up to that point, still regretted that "The intelligence of the average Madagascan is low" and foresaw limiting their duty to the more basic operations of the batteries.

Of course, a lack of education really did make it impossible for Madagascans to serve in technical positions such as that of *pointeur,* but this comment cited an inherent lack of intelligence, not instruction. Such perceived shortcomings undoubtedly lay behind the implication that thirty *indigènes* were required to do the work of twenty Frenchmen. Even Malagasy gunners' positive attributes were filtered through racial stereotypes, because it was their "very mild and very cheerful" character that rendered their relations with their white comrades so easy.[126] Though some officers considered it a "revelation," the year-round service of Madagascans in the artillery, as with the good performance of the 12th BTM in infantry combat, did not decisively alter the overall racial stereotypes that dominated thinking within the French military.

## Experiences of Combat

Examining the role of European personnel in units of *troupes indigènes,* the ways in which the military structured these units for optimal effectiveness, the varying military tasks men performed depending on their racial identity, and the salience of winter weather as a concern for both the soldiers and their commanders can allow for a reasonable reconstruction of what the experience of soldiering in Europe was like for different groups of *indigènes.*

Of course, this still obscures the wartime experience of individuals and makes it difficult to answer the question, which those who have not been to war frequently pose so urgently and insistently to those who have, "What was it like?" It is never easy to access, in particular, the incommunicable experience of combat itself, what it is like "out there," where the shooting is, at "the sharp end."[127]

This is even truer of the experience of *troupes indigènes,* who left fewer memoirs of their experiences than did their European counterparts, for reasons of illiteracy, language barriers, or lack of opportunity or audience. The work of some historians, who collected the oral testimonies of soldiers many years after the events they describe, can provide a sense of what these experiences might have been like, but the military archives are relatively silent on the question, because for officers in the midst of fighting a war, combat effectiveness was more important than how soldiers felt while they were fighting.[128] This is true even of postal censorship records, which focused on matters of morale—the quality and quantity of food, the regularity of mail, issues of military discipline—or of political significance to the censors themselves—loss of faith in the French cause, disillusionment with the colonial relationship, sex and love across the color line.[129] However, these records are not completely silent, and attentive researchers can catch occasional glimpses, even if frustratingly brief, into the combat experience of *troupes indigènes.*

Though the attention of postal censors usually focused on other matters, a report on Indochinese correspondence sent in late winter 1916 contains several revealing extracts from soldiers' letters. This was the period during which a company of the 6th BTI fought for the first time at Verdun, and the censors and their superiors were curious to see what effect the experience had had. The extracts the censors provided are consistent with the comments one can find scattered, widely though infrequently, throughout other sources, so these soldiers' comments can serve as a representative (if quite small) sample of the reactions of many *troupes indigènes* to combat.

Not surprisingly, one soldier began his description of his circumstances by noting, "It is very cold here," while another wrote of "suffering from the cold . . . the rigor of the temperature." Soldiers often wrote of suffering from the cold of autumn in northeastern France, and any consideration of the experience of *troupes indigènes* soldiering in the Great War must keep this physical discomfort in mind. Soldiers often linked their personal suffering in the war, from cold and other discomforts, to the seemingly unending nature of the war. It had lasted two years already, one wrote, and there was no end in sight, "the two nations [France and Germany] fight constantly day and night and there is a great deal of misery, we suffer." This writer hinted at what others made more explicit: the stupendous nature of the struggle they were witnessing and in which they were taking part. As one *tirailleur* put it, summing up the unprecedented character of much of the fighting in this first truly industrialized war, "The French fight in all ways, with terrible explosives, airplanes, submarines, barbed wire, mines, gas."

Similarly, Corporal Ham wrote of the trench warfare and artillery fire that defined the experience of fighting on the Western Front, "The war is made in the air, under the ground; trenches are dug, from which enormous projectiles are fired, which fall like rain on the enemy trench."[130] In this sense, the experience of these Indochinese, and of all *troupes indigènes* who fought in combat (or even those who performed their duties near the front in harm's way), would not have been all that different from that of the average French soldier in the trenches on the Western Front.[131]

Despite these horrors, the Indochinese soldiers who wrote these letters generally displayed both confidence and eagerness, qualities that pleased their commanders. One *tirailleur* claimed that, "Here among us, many request to go fight." Some of this eagerness, and certainly some of the confidence the soldiers expressed, resulted from success on the battlefield. *Tirailleur* Hoc described combat he had seen as a success: his unit had taken 4,000 prisoners without suffering any losses. Sergeant Am's positive outlook may have been typical of a noncommissioned officer (hence, perhaps a career soldier); the constant artillery fire one always heard at the front prompted him to write: "The war is truly very amusing." However, he noted that war was "made under strange conditions," and that even though the Germans would be defeated "in three years," they were nonetheless "very solid."

This expression of confidence in an ultimate French victory was typical. Even a soldier who called the conflict "a war of extermination between the two countries," fought with new and terrible weapons day and night, causing many people to die, finished by asserting, "but we will conquer." Corporal Ham conceded that both adversaries in the conflict were "skillful," and neither was giving way, "but the French side is the strongest." Yet such confidence could not conceal the terrible nature of combat, a subject on which some writers were more forthcoming than others. One soldier's description was particularly vivid, "Here, battle howls like a devil, one fights in all ways with bullets that blaze; the Westerners leave many houses in ruins, and as for us, we must fight and it is truly frightening: in a recent combat, we lost more than seventy men, the Westerners *push* us to fight."

This last statement indicates that not all soldiers were always so eager for combat, especially after they had previously experienced it. Perhaps the most eloquent summary of the experience was one of the most straightforward, laconic, and understated: "We are in the midst of the French soldiers and we attack with them. There are Annamites dead and many wounded in the course of our fighting; it's not fun, far from it."[132]

In 1916, a lengthy Ministry of War report systematically reviewed the various strengths and weaknesses of the ethnic groups available to serve as workers in France. Indochinese workers were, the author argued, "in general mild and submissive," but needed close supervision and were best suited to work that required concentration and patience, not great force or endurance. Madagascans were similarly intelligent and good for technical work. West Africans, with few technical skills and little education or intelligence, combined with an inability to withstand European winters, were not worth using as workers. Moroccans were good for hard, difficult work requiring endurance and toughness, but needed firm guidance from their superiors, while Tunisians too were good workers, and also "mild" and capable of improvement through instruction. The assessment of Algerians was steeped in the "Kabyle myth," which contrasted honest and industrious men from the Kabylia region with their Arab countrymen, but many of the characteristics that made Kabyles good workers were similar to those that made Algerians in general good soldiers.[133] Though this report focused on workers, not soldiers, its judgments and the language it employs reveal the common set of racial stereotypes that shaped official policy toward all colonial subjects who came to France to contribute to the war effort.

That these stereotypes survived the war unchanged in any fundamental way, and that they applied to soldiers as well as workers, was clear from a report written by General Mangin in 1920. As part of his efforts to persuade the political and military authorities to expand the role of *troupes indigènes* in French security both in Europe and in the colonies, Mangin summarized the principal characteristics of each "race" that made up France's non-European colonial forces. The document represented the primary qualities that French officers sought in these troops, as well as the accumulated wisdom gained from wartime experience. Treating Tunisians and Algerians together (which was logical from an organizational point of view, because they often served together), but apparently focusing on Algerians, Mangin claimed that these men were particularly suited for combat duty, being "very robust, very good marchers, and very brave, endowed with a remarkable visual acuity." Best deployed in infantry or cavalry units, they could only perform elementary tasks in the artillery and were almost entirely unqualified for specialized duties or services, such as the engineering corps, aviation, automobile or liaison services, and as COA, nurses, and so on. The "atavistic" qualities of the Arab and Berber "races" meant that they could adapt to and fight in a wide variety of climates. Much the same, Mangin argued, was true of Moroccans, though they perhaps possessed "a sharper intelligence," greater technical aptitudes, and more resistance to the cold. Their conduct in the war had been "irreproachable."

Predictably, Mangin devoted most attention to West African soldiers, and his ideas were much the same as during the prewar debate over *La force noire*. He did, however, concede that it was not wise to pay too much attention to the differences between *races guerrières* and *races non-guerrières*, because military service in units that mixed both types tended to even out the differences among these groups. Like Algerians, West African soldiers were best deployed in the front lines, where they would display their signature characteristics of endurance, hardiness, and loyalty. West Africans were little suited to specialties or to positions of authority, and he typically attributed these shortcomings to both inherent qualities and external circumstances, their "lower degree of intelligence, and their lack of instruction." Obstinately, Mangin clung to his belief that, with the proper precautions, "the *Sénégalais* is fit to serve everywhere" except for the very coldest regions (which, he argued, did not include France or Germany). As for Madagascans, Mangin repeated the now standard comment that their service had been a "revelation," and he praised their ability to serve in diverse services and specialties, their relatively high level of education, and their ability to serve in all but the coldest climates. Above all, the Madagascan soldier was valuable for his discipline and loyalty, and his "simple spirit . . . devoid of duplicity." Mangin made similar comments about the Indochinese, praising their technical abilities and industriousness.[134]

That Mangin would stress the positive qualities of each of these groups and their suitability for military service is not surprising, considering that he devoted a large part of his life before, during, and after the war to promoting the use of *troupes indigènes*. Yet his comments are revealing, for they reemphasize the fundamental importance and resilience of racial stereotypes in determining how the French Army assessed both the aptitudes and the performance of these troops, which in turn determined how they would be deployed. Observers like Mangin attributed even the unexpected strengths of various groups to well-known and widely accepted ideas about racial characteristics. Indochinese and Madagascans were capable of serving as secretaries, signalers, or nurses, for example, because of their supposed affinity for technical tasks, an affinity that rendered them unfit for tasks requiring brute force or great strength. These men also allegedly possessed an elevated level of culture and intelligence in comparison with more rustic and primitive peoples such as West Africans.

The Ministry of War's 1916 assessment of workers and Mangin's postwar evaluation of soldiers drew from a fairly coherent and consistent body of racial ideas that molded the images and expectations many French people had of nonwhites. These ideas were behind the army's construction of a hierarchy of military worth that shaped perceptions of the utility and performance of indigenous soldiers, often with profound consequences for how the army employed these troops. Ideas about race were equally influential on thinking about hierarchy and rank. In fact, as the next chapter shows, notions of a hierarchy based on race, with whites at the top, had a profound effect upon the way the army constructed a more purely military hierarchy based upon rank.

CHAPTER THREE

# *Hierarchies of Rank, Hierarchies of Race*

❖

It is especially in speaking of these troops that it is true to say:
like leader, like troops.
> —*General Antoine Dessort, commander of the 16th Division of
> colonial infantry, on West African troops,* 1916

What rank, then, do we hold?
> —*Algerian* officier indigène, *1915*

In 1915, Lieutenant indigène Boukabouya Rabah of the 7th Regiment of *ti-railleurs algériens,* the only indigenous officer to desert to the Germans from the front lines in France, published a brochure entitled *L'Islam dans l'armée française* (Islam in the French Army) in Istanbul. Boukabouya, who now worked actively for the German and Ottoman governments to incite his former comrades in arms to desert the French Army and join in a holy crusade against their colonial masters, railed against the French military's use of North Africans to fight in the European war. He was particularly outraged by what he saw as the misbehavior of the "hierarchy of French officers who are responsible for leading men into action."[1] Not only was he concerned with effect of "contempt and racial hatred . . . among a manifestly ambitious Arabophobic officer corps"[2] on all North Africans, but he also indicted French treatment of the few *indigènes* allowed into the officer corps. These *officiers indigènes,* merely a "'dead letter' compared to French officers," faced discrimination and derision from their French colleagues, as well as insurmountable obstacles to advancement and a distinct lack of authority over their subordinates, he argued.[3]

Boukabouya's pamphlet, a polemical attack on the French military for propaganda purposes, focused on two of the most important issues involved in staffing all units of *troupes indigènes:* the respective roles of white and nonwhite soldiers in the command hierarchy of these units. First of all, the army had very clear ideas about the qualities white officers would have to possess in order to command indigenous troops, though officials encountered very real problems finding Frenchmen who conformed to this ideal. These problems were especially troubling given the conventional wisdom that in units of *troupes indigènes,* "Tel chefs, telle troupe" (Like leader, like troops), a modification of the axiom "Tel père, tel fils" (Like father, like son), and the paternal analogy was no accident. Secondly, French policy toward the few *indigènes* who rose to positions of authority—either as noncommissioned officers (NCOs) or, more rarely, as commissioned officers—was often contradictory. It was hardly surprising that these policies would inspire an *officier indigène* to wonder, "What rank do we hold?" Of course, French authorities would dispute Boukabouya's claim that "contempt and racial hatred" was the foundation of their policies, but stereotypes and racial thinking often played as large a role in shaping these policies as did concrete, pragmatic military concerns. The role of hierarchy, both racial and military, in these units provided important insights into the attitudes among white French officers and other French officials responsible for establishing policy in these areas.

White commissioned and noncommissioned officers were crucial in the army's plans to deploy *troupes indigènes* on European battlefields. Ideally, military authorities sought French soldiers who had experience serving in the colonies with *indigènes,* and perhaps even some knowledge of their languages, to staff (or *encadrer,* a French verb meaning literally to frame or to surround, which evokes more vividly the position and responsibilities of these French soldiers than the English verb "to staff") indigenous units. The prevailing attitude of these French personnel was to be paternal, guiding and caring for their childlike charges. Yet this ideal was increasingly difficult to maintain as the war continued and casualties among experienced French officers mounted, and the quality of officers in indigenous units often fell short of expectations.

The decisive role of racial prejudice was even more evident in army policy toward *officiers indigènes.* Even this term, which divided the officer corps into two distinct parts, French and indigenous, implied that distinctions based on race remained operative even when *indigènes* ascended in the military hierarchy. There were opportunities for these men to rise in rank, and army policy often focused on promoting those of an elevated social status within indigenous societies—notables or sons of chiefs—thus transferring a pre-existing social hierarchy into the military. Yet despite real opportunities for advancement for some *indigènes,* racism placed significant restraints on how quickly and how far they could rise. Most military officials considered non-whites unsuited for positions of real authority, particularly over white soldiers, and even the highest-ranking indigenous officers did not find acceptance as colleagues or equals among their French counterparts. Ultimately, in this as in other areas, racial prejudices interfered with and often negated republican ideals of egalitarianism and advancement based solely on merit, particularly important in the French Army since the days of the Revolution of 1789 and Napoleon.

## White Officers and Nonwhite Soldiers

Military authorities considered the role of white officers as decisive in all in-digenous units. In fact, they argued, the quality of the white French personnel entirely determined the value of such units. Axioms in wide use among those who claimed expertise or experience with these soldiers encapsulated the con-ventional wisdom that said, "Like leaders, like troops," "Troops are only as good as their officers" ("Tant vaut le gradé, tant vaut la troupe"), and "*Troupes indigènes* are what the officers and NCOs who command them are" ("Troupes indigènes sont ce que sont les officiers et les sous-officiers qui les comman-dent"). These pithy slogans remained unchallenged orthodoxy throughout the war. Of course, officers were decisive in determining the value of any military unit, French or indigenous. Like all armies, the French army during the Great War naturally relied on good leadership. Yet officials repeatedly went out of their way to stress that the quality of indigenous units was entirely dependent upon the quality of their officers, largely because one could not depend on any inherent qualities among the *indigènes* themselves.

Given this attitude, it was logical that the army wished officers leading *troupes indigènes* to possess certain characteristics. "It is necessary that the *sénégalais* be staffed by brave, energetic European officers and soldiers *who have already served with black troops* and know their mentality, their cus toms, *and* their language," a 1916 report on the combat performance of West African troops asserted.[4] This single sentence sums up virtually all the major points made in countless other reports and communiqués during the war. Though bravery and energy were important for officers serving in all units of the army, these qualities were particularly important for the proper leadership of colonial subjects, without which their natural, primitive warlike potential would lack direction and would be wasted. Above all, experience commanding *troupes indigènes*, who were so in need of specialized attention, was critical. "This factor cannot possibly be overlooked," General Mangin declared.[5]

*Troupes indigènes* needed leaders who "knew" them. Officers would get the most out of their troops if they were acquainted with what the French perceived as the special mentality of *indigènes*. This included the ability to understand and respect the cultural differences that made daily life in such units very different from that in metropolitan units. Communication, and thus linguistic ability, was of critical importance. Armies rely heavily on the ability to communicate quickly and clearly up and down the military hierarchy. At the very least, an officer in an indigenous unit confronted the difficulty of communicating with men whose first language was not French. In many cases, indigenous soldiers had acquired only the most rudimentary knowledge of French during training, and the troops often spoke many different languages among themselves. Thus it is unsurprising that the authorities placed particular emphasis on the linguistic capabilities of the officers called to serve with *indigènes*. "They are, generally speaking, perfectly devoted to their leaders, who speak their language and have been on campaign with them for a long time," the minister of war noted of Moroccan infantry in August 1914.[6]

The most qualified officers were those who had already served with *troupes indigènes* in the colonies. As the mobilization effort for the European war was of unprecedented scale, such experienced officers were not plentiful enough to staff all indigenous units, so the army called on mobilized white French residents of the colonies, and even students and scholars who had studied foreign languages. Such men were not always brought into indigenous units directly as officers, but sometimes as common soldiers, who would gain experience serving with nonwhite troops before being promoted. As early as 15 November 1914, Joffre was asking the minister of war for "a few French soldiers, as much to allow recruitment of clerks and officers on the spot as to render the troop more manageable and maneuverable under fire. . . . Voluntary enlistees and French draftees from Morocco and Algeria who have a little knowledge of Arabic would be particularly appropriate."[7] One important pool of such men served in the Zouaves, recruited mostly from among white French settlers and indigenous Jews in Algeria. The army drew extensively on the Zouaves from the beginning of the war to staff and reinforce North African units, and mixed regiments of Zouaves-*tirailleurs* were eventually created.[8]

According to French authorities, the need for white officers arose from the special nature of indigenous soldiers themselves. One senior officer claimed that among the "native qualities" of *indigènes,* their devotion to "leaders whom they knew well" stood out.[9] *Indigènes* had, as another officer put it, a real "repugnance" for serving with officers whom they did not know, which allegedly stemmed from the primitiveness and immaturity of the soldiers.[10] This belief in the primitiveness of *indigènes* was evident in one general's assertion that Tunisians' profound attachment to their tribes was transferred to the companies and battalions in which they served, causing them to cling to officers whom they knew.[11] Given this attachment, French officials presented the ideal relationship between officers and their men as one of paternal devotion. Édouard Montet, a professor specializing in the study of Islam at the University of Geneva in Switzerland who served the French government as a propagandist and liaison with Muslim soldiers during the war, reinforced this ideal in a pamphlet responding to Boukabouya's charges that *troupes indigènes* served under "leaders imbued with a manifestly hostile attitude . . . staunch enemies of the Arab."[12] After visiting with North African troops, Montet claimed that "the rapport between French officers and Muslim soldiers was inspired simultaneously by a stern but fair discipline and by a benevolence and kindness to which the soldiers responded with a touching attachment and an absolute devotion to their officers."[13]

This image of officers as fathers and *indigènes* as children best characterized the ideal situation in indigenous units. Just as children needed their parents, indigenous soldiers were supposedly more comfortable with and developed better under the familiar paternal discipline and leadership provided by officers whom they knew well. In fact, officers repeatedly referred to their men as "children." "If your leaders are fathers to you, you must behave toward them as affectionate and docile children and show them, in everything, a limitless confidence," a government representative told a group of West African soldiers.[14] The army held up as a shining example of this paternalism the officers who had conquered the interior regions of West Africa, "at the head of their blacks, who followed them everywhere, surrounded them, shielded them when necessary from assailants, and gave them their complete devotion on days of combat in exchange for care received, for a paternal and provident command."[15]

Of course, the idea that officers should behave paternally toward their men was not limited to those serving with *troupes indigènes*. The notion has had a long history in many nations' armed forces, and in 1891, a famous article in the *Revue des Deux Mondes* by Hubert Lyautey, "Du rôle social de l'officier," outlined a distinctly paternal and educative capacity for the entire French officer corps under a regime of universal obligatory military service.[16] Still, the idea of paternalism was a particularly good fit with the overall project of French colonialism under the Third Republic, which promoted the view of Frenchmen bringing education and other benefits to the "children" of the French Empire. As the influential writer Gabriel Hanotaux put it after the war, the French were engaged in "true colonization, which is the mother country offering itself to these young peoples, these children," and France had "saved the black, educated him, hovered over him and presented this child with civilization."[17] The imagery here is more maternal than paternal, but the relationship between adults and children remains the operative idea. Lyautey, perhaps France's most famous colonial soldier, argued for the decisive role of the army in this paternal civilizing project, following up his earlier article with one entitled, "Du rôle colonial de l'armée."[18] Thus, within the overall imperial context under France's Third Republic, and especially within the army, indigenous soldiers were children and more profoundly in need of adult guidance than were native Frenchmen serving in the ranks.

Given the nature of the service of *troupes indigènes*, many authorities considered surveillance to be one of the most important duties of white officers. Though republican assimilationist rhetoric stressed that the *indigènes* were actually fighting for their *patrie*, inasmuch as all subjects and citizens of the empire were in theory at least potentially French, some observers pointed out the tenuousness of the *indigènes'* emotional links to the French nation. As one general put it, "The principle factor for Algerian *troupes indigènes* is not patriotism, but personal attachment to the leader; the selection of leaders is thus of particular importance."[19] This was especially true of North Africans, called on to fight an enemy coalition that included fellow Muslims from the Ottoman empire. One corps commander, writing in April 1915, noted that he needed more French corporals to carry out a "discrete, but nevertheless close and attentive surveillance" on Algerian troops because of "the propaganda of the enemy facing our *tirailleurs*, which incites them to desertion."[20] A subordinate earlier wrote to this same corps commander that it was necessary to have in each section of *tirailleurs algériens* at least one white French soldier from Algeria who had "extensive knowledge of the Arabic language," so that "surveillance would be effective."[21]

Lower-level officers had the most immediate effect on their men, because they had the most intimate daily contact. A consensus that captains were the most important officers commanding nonwhite troops prevailed. This was primarily because the captain was the highest-ranking officer at the level of the company, the unit considered most fundamental and inviolable among indigenous units. In a further refinement of the axiom that, in units of *troupes indigènes*, the worth of the officers determined the worth of the troops, a manual for officers serving with West Africans asserted that "like company, like captain *and vice versa*, is a fact, a truth and it cannot be otherwise, [because] the captain is the head of the family, the father of his *indigènes*. . . . Even more than in French units, the company is the base of the organization of *indigènes*, because it is the unit in which the commander can know each of his men, his character, his faculties, his needs, his faults."[22] In May 1918, when the High Command wanted to reinforce the officer corps in all indigenous combat units, it began by increasing the maximum number of captains.[23] When one general suggested keeping some officers serving in West African units at the front while their men withdrew to the rear for the winter, he still recommended extreme caution in removing captains, "who, for the blacks, embody authority, family, *patrie*."[24] In a postwar work with the revealing title *Peaux noires, cœurs blancs* (Black Skins, White Hearts), a former officer who served with West Africans asserted, "Among the *tirailleurs sénégalais* of yesteryear, the captain was the essential leader." Other officers, he maintained, were too high up and far removed to become close to their men, but the captain was "truly the father," ensuring care and equal justice in the unit.[25]

For captains, as well as other officers and NCOs serving with West Africans, firmness was paramount, because "for the black, to command is to know how to enforce obedience." Paternalism was no less important, and officers had to be solicitous of their men's well-being, food, clothing, and quarters. Also, officers owed their men protection, both on the battlefield and off, and had to prevent their men from being "bullied" by native French soldiers who did not know them or regarded them as "material to be consumed." Officers had to treat their men as "little brothers," all the more so because they were less able to defend themselves, and had to uphold France's civilizing mission among West Africans: "Their moral education is a duty for us; it must be constant, and it is easy, by carefully chosen examples, to make the blacks understand the benefits of our protection in exchange for the burdens we impose upon them."[26] This sense of superiority was not merely paternal, but was rooted firmly in ideas about the racial superiority of whites. The West African soldier was brave and had confidence in his officers, willing to follow them anywhere, because he was convinced that "where the captain and the white Frenchman are, one is sure of victory."[27] Even black Africans' inherent quality of bravery depended upon the leadership of whites in order for it to be focused and effective.

These attitudes applied to other *troupes indigènes* as well as West African soldiers. Because West African and North African (especially Algerian) men constituted the majority of indigenous troops recruited during the war, and certainly a majority of those serving as combatants, issues and problems surrounding their staffing by white officers generated the most commentary. However, it is clear that attitudes toward all indigenous soldiers placed them in a dependent position vis-à-vis their white officers, and for similar reasons. When it came to command and staffing (unlike recruitment and deployment), distinctions among soldiers from different areas and of different ethnicities were more a matter of degree than of fundamental importance. For example, Colonel Garbit stressed that Madagascan soldiers ought to be commanded by officers who were acquainted with such troops. If this was not possible, it would be necessary to "carefully introduce their European officers *to all the particularities of their character and their temperament.*"[28] Another officer remarked that the Madagascans were brave and performed well in combat, but "as with all indigenous formations, officers must be very numerous, very reliable, and know well the men whom they have the honor of commanding."[29] Officials considered the value of all indigenous units to be directly proportional to the quality of their officers. In 1916, the Ministry of War stipulated that recently arrived battalions of Indochinese, Madagascan, and Somali soldiers, who were to be used as staging troops in combat zones, should be "grouped under the command of leaders who, knowing them, will obtain from them the best results."[30]

This ideal became increasingly difficult to live up to as the war progressed. When the war began, many units of *troupes indigènes* were staffed with white officers largely according to the ideal: with men who had already served with indigenous troops, knew the language of their men, and had most or all of the particular attributes deemed necessary to get the most out of their charges. For example, several units of Moroccan cavalry that Resident-General Lyautey readied for service in France in August 1914 were

"staffed with a majority of French officers, so that they can be of real service." In addition, each squadron counted thirty French officers who spoke
Arabic.[31] However, given the particularly high casualty rate among French
officers and the increasing numbers of *indigènes* entering the army, this
ideal situation did not last long. The High Command had to replace dead or
wounded officers as best it could, and often these replacements did not have
experience with *troupes indigènes*. Unsurprisingly, complaints soon surfaced
about the quality of those officers. One commander's problems showed how
far the situation had degenerated after only four months of fighting. This
general noted that only ten French officers were left in one of his North
African regiments, and only one of them had served in North Africa before.
Several companies no longer had any officers or noncommissioned officers
who spoke Arabic, and a "wall" thus separated officers and men. This development was more troubling for *troupes indigènes* than for native Frenchmen, he believed, because the personal connection between men and their
officers was more important for *indigènes*.[32]

The reasons for the dearth of officers in these and other units were clear:
casualty rates were higher among front-line officers than among their men.
Some estimates put their chances of being killed at double those of enlisted
men, in large part because officers led by example, often exposing themselves
to enemy fire when in combat. This ideal was reinforced by the prevalent
masculine military code of honor. Exposing oneself to danger, in short, was
heroic. Thus, early in the war, an official at the Ministry of War informed
regional commanders that word had arrived in Paris "repeatedly that, on
the battlefield, some officers remained standing" when their units had taken
cover, "with the very honorable goal of setting a courageous example for
their men." However, "This way of doing things presents grave problems,"
because it offered enemy artillery and rifle fire easy targets and led to useless
losses that compromised the integrity of command, which was particularly
grave because troops without their officers lost much of their value. The
official instructed commanders to tell their field officers to take more cover.[33]
French officers' devotion to honor cost them dearly—the officer corps lost 50
percent of its original strength during the first two years of the war—and
also deprived the army of its most qualified leaders.[34]

The loss of officers was particularly damaging because their role was
critical to the functioning of the army, and because a great deal of time
and effort went into their training. The army could not replace them over-
night, and this was especially true of officers in indigenous units, who were

required to possess extensive knowledge of the special nature of their men. Replacing losses both in terms of quantity and quality proved impossible. After less than two months of war, General Mangin reported that losses in his division had exceeded the total of its initial strength, so it had been renewed nearly completely, and there remained in each regiment only three or four officers of the active army (the others being reservists and men called out of retirement).[35]

In April 1915, Mangin observed that total French losses in officers at the front were at least equal to the number in service on the first day of mobilization.[36] The commander of the 6th mixed colonial regiment, which contained two white French battalions and one West African battalion (the 3rd BTS), also reported dramatic losses during the 1915 invasion of Turkey. The division of which his regiment was a part had left France with a total strength of 14,000, and soon lost 200 officers and 9,000 men in ten days of battle. His regiment had begun with 54 officers and 3,000 men on 4 March; by 9 May, only 4 officers (he himself was wounded twice) and 900 men were left in action. The 3rd BTS had only 250 men left out of an original 1,000.[37] Officers felt that such losses had a particularly deleterious effect upon *troupes indigènes*. An interpreter noted in July 1915 that Moroccans fighting in France had lost a good deal of their initial enthusiasm, because "the officers with whom they left Morocco have for the most part disappeared." The Moroccans had suffered "enormous" losses and, "deprived of their usual leaders, they are bewildered."[38]

Since officers in indigenous units were required to be more active in leading their men, who were allegedly incapable of directing their own energies or of showing initiative, exposure to danger was correspondingly high. As one regimental commander put it, "The task of the European officer is arduous; he must keep a close eye on each *tirailleur*, fix him constantly on his mission, his role, and he cannot take in his whole unit with a single glance; it is for this reason that the losses among European officers are always high during combat."[39] Another officer offered an even more remarkably pragmatic and blunt assessment of the role of white officers: "Officers will have to be able, *before falling*, to indicate to each *tirailleur* his job—the battalion, once in place, will leave directly, straight toward the goal, so as to stop only at the enemy positions to be taken: the role of officers and European specialists in the initial assault, once movement is launched, is limited to setting an example."[40] This comment assumed that French officers would fall as a matter of course, and that they had better do their job and set an example

early, while still alive and unwounded. The casualties among French officers resulting from such attitudes soon exhausted the capacity of the army to
replace the fallen. A general inspecting North African troops summed up the
predicament in 1915: "Now, Frenchmen, officers or not, constitute the back-
bone of the company; this observation has moreover been made at the front;
unfortunately, the depots do not have sufficient numbers of them to satisfy
the requirements of the armies in the field."[41]

Aggressive recruitment in the colonies only compounded the problem: as
the number of *troupes indigènes* grew, the number of French officers who
had gained experience leading them during tours of duty in the colonies
decreased due to casualties. The new officers who served with *indigènes* in
France acquired experience only slowly, or not at all if they quickly became
casualties themselves. This situation had clear consequences in the life of
these units and at the front. Reports on the performance of West African
troops on the Somme during the summer of 1916 revealed near unanimous
agreement among superior officers that the lower-ranking officers under
whom these troops served left much to be desired in terms of both quantity and quality. Many were cavalry officers who had no experience leading
West African infantry, and many others were simply unsuited to their jobs.
Numerous officers had never served in West Africa and lacked the requisite
"moral ascendancy" over their men. This situation resulted in low morale
and poor performance. One battalion commander observed that the European officers in his unit did not know their men well and "appear to have
the conviction that a black would march only if he was beaten, see only their
faults, recognize in them no quality." In short, these officers lacked "confidence in the tool that has been given to them," and they failed in their basic
duty to "raise the performance" of these troops "by an intelligent action and
a ceaseless and always alert activity."[42]

Such officers tended to misuse their men on the battlefield, leading to
mistakes or heavy losses, and even to abuse of their men off of it. In November 1917, Blaise Diagne wrote to the minister of war to complain about
an incident of such abuse. Diagne charged that when a *tirailleur* had complained to an officer about the rough treatment he had received at the hands
of a corporal, the superior officer had threatened him with a revolver. The
accusation was vague, and the commander of the 6th Army, in which the
incident allegedly took place, protested vehemently against Diagne's letter
for accusing "officers as a whole of a lack of conscience, a sense of duty, and
candor."[43]

Ever the tireless defender of the rights of *troupes indigènes*, Diagne again wrote to the minister of war about another incident in August 1918. Late one morning, he wrote, a lieutenant in the 49th BTS had come across one of his men who had become lost the night before while driving a mule and had only just returned. The officer bitterly reproached the *tirailleur*, slapped him several times, and finally threw him down from a height of seven meters, breaking the unfortunate soldier's left leg. Diagne noted that it was not the first time this particular officer had committed such brutalities either.[44]

Whatever the precise truth of these accounts, it was clear that there were problems between officers and their men in these units, and that at least some of them resulted from the inexperience of the former. The problems were not limited to West African units. An inspector reviewing the Algerian conscript class of 1917, recently arrived in their camps around France, reported serious shortcomings among the officers in charge of these troops. Several commanders had not even thought to take special measures to protect these men, so recently arrived from the warmer climate of North Africa, from the winter cold. In sum, he noted, "Certain camp commanders appear to me clearly not up to their task."[45]

Even when the army took care to equip indigenous units with supposedly experienced and knowledgeable white officers, such as Zouaves, the results were not always satisfactory. Lieutenant Boukabouya argued in his propaganda tracts that in many ways the Zouaves were the worst possible men to serve with *indigènes*. The majority of Zouaves were Frenchmen living in Algeria, and it was these racist settlers who despised the native Algerians most. Boukabouya called them "Neo-French-cosmopolitan-Arabophobes," in order to emphasize their essentially foreign and urban or Jewish origins (many French citizens in Algeria were of Italian, Maltese, Spanish, Jewish Algerian, or of other descent) and recently acquired French citizenship. He criticized their role in the surveillance of *indigènes*, even claiming that the Zouaves had received the "criminal order—always secret—to blow out the brains of any Muslims who dared to show the least gesture of kindness toward the Turks or the Germans."[46] Boukabouya also asserted that these settlers spread false stories about Algerian soldiers and infected the French metropolitan population, both military and civilian, with their racist notions.[47] In sum, these "neo-Frenchmen," with the characteristic zeal of new converts, consciously behaved as though they were "more French than the French," so to speak, lording it over the Algerians at the front, just as the settlers did in North Africa.

Boukabouya made these charges for propaganda purposes, and his claims were no doubt exaggerated (in particular, it seems unlikely that Zouaves were ordered to "blow out the brains" of *indigènes* who failed to show the proper hostility toward the enemy). Still, his criticisms provide an indication of how some Algerian soldiers might have viewed the white personnel who were supposed to make indigenous units operate more efficiently by virtue of their special knowledge of the men. Boukabouya also pointed out another problem that did in fact plague the administration and command of *troupes indigènes:* many officers did not speak the language of their men. The use of settlers from the colonies was supposed to address this very problem, but Boukabouya scoffed at so-called *vieux connaisseurs* (old hands) who had served with *indigènes* for as long as thirty years and retired after having learned only fewer than thirty words of Arabic.[48]

In fact, authorities sometimes abandoned the linguistic requirement altogether. In June 1915, an officer asking that twenty to twenty-four more French soldiers be assigned to each company of North African infantry said, "[I]t is not absolutely necessary that these men speak Arabic."[49] Another officer put it even more bluntly: he needed French officers to ensure the training of his men, and "The question of speaking Arabic or not has no importance."[50] In fact, policy on this question was never entirely clear or consistent, given the chaos and exigencies of war. One officer called to serve with workers from the colonies commented ironically on this confusion, which could leave men without superiors whom they could clearly understand: "Because I speak Arabic, I have been assigned to supervise Chinese workers. . . . Every man in his place!"[51]

The obstacles to communication that resulted from these situations could have serious effects besides an inability to give or receive clear orders. Failure to be able to understand and look after the "moral" needs of the men, as well as to carry out effective supervision could lead to lower morale and even desertion. In the aftermath of several desertions among Algerian soldiers in the spring of 1915 (one of whom was Lieutenant Boukabouya), the commanders of the units in question agreed that the lack of officers knowing the *indigènes,* in particular, knowing their language, had reduced the effectiveness of command and supervision and contributed to the rash of desertions.[52]

Poor, indifferent, or hostile officers could also no doubt provide the motivation, not just the opportunity, for desertions. At the German prison camp at Zossen, where he worked for the German government urging his coreligionists to volunteer to fight for the Ottoman empire, Boukabouya told a fellow Algerian that he had deserted "because of the ill treatment he had seen inflicted on his men by French officers and he was unable to tolerate it."[53] Boukabouya was undoubtedly an extreme case, but it is not unlikely that others among his fellow deserters were similarly disillusioned with their white French leaders.

The effects of having poor or inexperienced officers serving with *troupes indigènes* went beyond problems with desertion. In May 1917, the minister of the colonies wrote to General Ferdinand Foch to relay complaints by *indigènes* about their officers, specifically alerting the military to problems this was causing with recruitment. Tales of incompetence or abuse made their way back to North Africa, and it was becoming more difficult to entice *indigènes* to volunteer for service in France.[54]

Poor leadership could lead to discipline problems. In December 1917, a group of 163 soldiers, men from Martinique and *originaires* from the Four Communes of Senegal, refused to go on exercises because, they said, it was too cold and they had just arrived from the front and wanted to go on leave. Later, the men tried to liberate one of their comrades who had been imprisoned for disciplinary reasons, and in the ensuing melee, a noncommissioned officer suffered a bayonet wound and a civilian was shot. An investigation into the matter found that the European officers in charge were insufficiently attentive and too distant from their men. The officers came in for sharp criticism for how they had handled affairs both during and after the incidents.[55]

In a similar incident in March 1917, a violent fight broke out between the men of the Somali Battalion and those of the 12th Madagascan Battalion, in which six Somalis were killed and seven wounded. The commandant of the camp at Fréjus–Saint-Raphaël, where the incident occurred, placed all responsibility for the blood spilled upon the European officers. They had lost their heads, he charged, and despite their claims to have fired only blanks during the fracas, the dead and wounded Somalis indicated otherwise. He recommended that several officers be punished, and that two officers in the Somali Battalion be removed as "unfit to serve in an indigenous unit."[56]

Ultimately, from the army's point of view, the worst effect that unsatisfactory officers could have on an indigenous unit was to compromise its performance in combat, and there is evidence that this did indeed happen. Reports on the combat effectiveness of *troupes indigènes* cited the crucial role of white officers, and they received a large share of the blame for poor combat performance. This was only logical, if, as the saying went, "The troops are only as good as the officer." Reports on the performance of West African units on the Somme in 1916 were especially explicit on this point, observing that many officers were inadequate to their tasks, because they had so little knowledge of their troops.[57]

Similar problems led one officer to criticize the dispersal of *tirailleur* companies among regiments of French infantry, a practice that had placed West Africans in battalions under the command of officers "not specialized in black troops, uninterested in having them and using them." These officers often used their new companies as mere labor and had a low opinion of their effectiveness.[58] This would hardly enhance West African troops' combat readiness or their ultimate performance under fire.

Despite these problems, not all of the officers who served in indigenous units failed to live up to the expectations of the army and of the *indigènes* themselves. Authorities often expressed satisfaction with the job that the officers were doing. An October 1914 inspection of North African units in France praised French officers for ensuring that the Ottoman empire's partnership with Germany did not compromise the loyalty of French Muslim soldiers. The inspector remarked that "it is for me certain that if we have retained over our Muslim troops sufficient authority to get them to fight for us without weakening, we owe it solely to our officers, whose valor is the object of admiration and enthusiasm among their soldiers."[59]

One report on West African troops singled out a section that was able to perform night work more efficiently than others because it was commanded by an *adjudant* who knew his men and who was well known to them.[60] The commander of French forces in West Africa claimed in 1918 that colonels, majors, and many captains had a profound knowledge of their West African soldiers and, though this was less true of lower-ranking white personnel, many of the latter had served in Africa. Moreover, he added, he did not hesitate to "withdraw personnel who, for whatever reason, are reported to me as unfit to serve with *troupes indigènes*."[61]

Thus, although many officers assigned to indigenous units as the war went on were ignorant of the language, manners, and characteristics of the men whom they commanded, this was certainly not always the case. The authorities often did their best to ensure that officers spoke the language of their men, even as extensive recruitment drives stretched resources quite thin. For instance, despite some problems with the use of Zouaves to serve in North African units, these men did often have at least some familiarity with Arabic. And it was clear even to the *indigènes* that officers were sometimes solicitous of the cultural observances of their men. One Tunisian *tirailleur* serving in France wrote home that his captain had taken measures to ensure the proper celebration of a religious holiday, supplementing the ordinary rations, to the great happiness of the men: "Though the celebration was not like in our country, it gave us great pleasure."[62] Such actions were important for morale, and were exactly what the army desired when it searched for officers who had experience with *indigènes* and could take measures to ease the dislocation and hardships of service in France.

Sometimes merely establishing cordial relations was enough to win the affection of the soldiers and to perform the social and paternal role outlined for French officers. A Madagascan soldier expressed real satisfaction with the solicitude his captain showed for the *indigènes* under his command: "He says to us: How are you? What do you need? Is anything bothering you? Know that in me you will find a father and a mother. When he left us, he added: Do not be sad, I will be happy. When he was finished, tears ran from our eyes." Another expressed much the same sentiments toward his sergeant: "The *vazahas* [Europeans] behave well toward us. The sergeant who leads us is very kind; we are all fond of him."[63]

No doubt there were many officers who inspired such positive feelings, though the evidence is admittedly not abundant. This is partly because problems and difficulties were much more likely to generate comment and reaction, thus leaving more archival traces. Officers merely doing their jobs ably were unlikely to attract much attention. But indications are numerous that not all officers in indigenous units conformed to the ideal set by the army for men called to such special duty. The stresses of war—heavy losses and the increasing need for more troops from the colonies—often combined with racism to lower the quality of leadership in indigenous units. This situation was alleviated somewhat by the presence of noncommissioned and even some commissioned indigenous officers who could act as intermediaries between the men and their white superiors. However, even this role was frequently undermined by racial prejudice.

## Indigènes in the Hierarchy

Lieutenant Boukabouya's 1915 pamphlet was critical, not only of the poor quality of white officers in indigenous units, but of the institutionalized racism in the French Army that prevented *indigènes* from ascending the military hierarchy and obtaining high rank. In a direct reply to these charges,

Mokrani Boumezraq el-Ouennoughi and Katrandji Abderrahmane, Algerian functionaries attached to hospitals for sick and wounded North Africans in Paris, published a pamphlet designed to refute Boukabouya's "lies." This government-sponsored propaganda tract disputed Boukabouya's claim that the army unfairly denied most *indigènes* access to higher ranks and discriminated against those few who became officers. The authors asserted that all *indigènes* who desired to attend French military schools were admitted, and pointed to Lieutenant-Colonel Cadi, who served in the artillery, and Captain Khaled, a graduate of the elite military academy Saint-Cyr, as examples of the heights to which *indigènes* could rise in the French officer corps.[64] In sum, the authors claimed, "Officers, French as well as *indigènes,* have done their duty magnificently, side by side, and if anything ought to be regretted, it can only be their insane fearlessness."[65]

This official response to his first pamphlet induced Boukabouya to publish a second edition in 1917. In it, he ridiculed his critics, continuing and expanding his criticism of the army's treatment of indigenous NCOs and corporals (or *gradés*) and officers.[66] Indigenous noncommissioned officers saw their authority "systematically trampled" by their superiors, he said. French officers often did this in front of the other *tirailleurs,* treating them with mistrust, hostility, or contempt, as when, at the moment of an attack, the officers ordered *gradés indigènes* to take up places in the ranks as simple soldiers, while Frenchmen gave the orders. Not only was this humiliating, but it undermined the position of these *gradés* in the eyes of their subordinates. For *officiers indigènes,* the situation was similar. Boukabouya derided the French policy of limiting promotions for *indigènes* to the rank of captain, and further limiting these captains to "seconds," who would yield to the authority of a French lieutenant in the direct administration of a unit. He characterized this inversion of military hierarchy as a "burlesque," unheard of in any other army of the world.[67]

"The Muslim officer, *gradé,* and soldier, who know how to die for France, should know how to require the respect that is due under arms to their pride; that is part of the dignity of a man, even if he is a subject of French domination," Boukabouya concluded.[68] He evidently felt that the only way he could gain respect and preserve his dignity was to desert the French Army. Just before he himself had done so, the captain of his company had been killed and the commander of his regiment had refused to promote Boukabouya to the dead man's place, instead elevating a French lieutenant who was less experienced. As galling as this apparently was to Boukabouya, his commander followed proper procedure, which stipulated that promotions for *indigènes* were at the discretion of senior officers.[69]

Boukabouya's case notwithstanding, among lower-ranking *indigènes,* especially noncommissioned officers, there were opportunities to advance in rank. Racial prejudice always limited advancement and undercut the authority *indigènes* might otherwise possess due to their rank, but French officers often relied heavily upon their indigenous subordinates to train, administer, and control their units. In choosing and promoting *indigènes,* the army usually made a conscious effort to recruit men who possessed "natural authority" in indigenous societies, even going so far as to form special schools for the sons of notables and "chiefs." Boukabouya's charges of French racism toward *indigènes,* even those who became officers, nonetheless had substance. Both entrenched attitudes among white French officers and official army policy allowed notions of racial hierarchy to interfere with and sometimes undermine the purely military hierarchy based upon rank.

Some of the opportunities for advancement that did exist arose in combat situations. In 1916, a French battalion commander reported that during his first experience with West African troops, a company assigned to fight alongside his men had lost all of its French officers during an attack. The West Africans would not have been able to maintain the trench that they had captured, then, had it not been for a French lieutenant from another company and a West African sergeant. For his actions, the latter was promoted to *adjudant* (a top noncommissioned rank, between sergeant and lieutenant).[70] The role of indigenous *gradés* was crucial. They acted as intermediaries between French commanders and their men. This was often necessary for linguistic reasons, but also because the military authorities regarded the *indigènes* as uniquely equipped to sustain the morale of their *frères de race.* In fact, one battalion commander argued that, since Frenchmen who had experience with West African troops were scarce or unavailable, it was best to entrust some low-level command responsibilities to indigenous sergeants, because they were more likely to get the most from their men.[71]

Army policy on West Africans emphasized the importance of *gradés,* asserting that they were "assistants to French noncommissioned officers, [who were] incapable of making themselves understood and, one can say, of doing anything without [them]." It was important for French officers to choose the best of their men to fill this role, to teach them French, to educate them, and to wean them from their "superstitions" and reliance on traditional native culture, in a word, to "win their confidence and raise them above the other *tirailleurs.*"[72]

The ideal relationship between French officers and their indigenous subordinates was one of close cooperation and collaboration. In all tasks, the indigenous *gradé* was to be an "auxiliary" to his French superior, and though French subordinates were also supposed to be auxiliaries to their officers, the special nature of indigenous troops made the relationship in those units even more essential. French officers could exercise their command much more effectively if they could rely upon a dependable liaison with their men, not least to translate orders. This intermediate role was explicit in descriptions of particularly effective *gradés indigènes*. A citation for bravery described a Madagascan *adjudant* as an "invaluable auxiliary" to his company commander, assuring communication during violent combat and asking to remain at his post even after being seriously wounded.

Given the French Army's belief that indigenous soldiers were ineffective without their French officers, indigenous subordinates who could continue to fight effectively and lead their comrades in the absence of killed or wounded French officers attracted special notice. Thus a Madagascan corporal was cited for bravery for his skill in directing his artillery battery by himself during heavy bombardments over several days.[73] No doubt these citations were well-deserved, and white soldiers also attracted praise and honors for rising above their rank and taking initiative. Yet *indigènes*, who were perceived to be useless without good French officers, earned distinction, not only for conspicuous bravery, but for rising above the low expectations for nonwhite soldiers and fulfilling their duties without the direct guidance of their French superiors.

Another indication of the important role of *gradés indigènes* was the decision to send those among them recovering from wounds in France to their colonies of origin to mentor new recruits just beginning their training. These wounded men would be able to pass along the experience they had gained at the front, and their example would bring out the natural warlike qualities thought to be dormant or misdirected among their fellow *indigènes*. This was especially true of North Africans. This policy not only helped alleviate resentment over the very restrictive leave policy for these soldiers, and attested to the manpower crisis the French very quickly faced, but also points to the important role that indigenous *gradés* played in helping French commanders train their men.

As for recruiting indigenous officers and *gradés* themselves, French officers sometimes applied the principle of merit, choosing the brightest, most motivated, and most competent of their men. Still, French military officials often attempted to transfer the existing social order of the colonies into the ranks. In 1915, a general who had commanded Indochinese troops before the war and now supported their use in Europe wrote in support of a plan to "make a generous place in the officer corps for the Annamite part of the ruling classes, to give lieutenant's stripes to the sons of mandarins and the educated."[74] Similarly, legislators seeking to intensify recruitment throughout the empire advocated recruiting on a broad basis in order to obtain men from all social levels. Thus the existing indigenous social order would be reflected in the new units. "This civilian life will carry with it its hierarchies already constituted and solid. It will suffice for us to militarize them." Societies like those in West Africa were strictly hierarchical, according to French experts, and former methods of recruitment mostly obtained men from the bottom of the social ladder, such as prisoners, mercenaries, the poor, and the desperate. The army needed men such as the sons of tribal chiefs to enter the ranks and exercise their natural authority over other *indigènes*. In Indochina, furthermore, many members of the indigenous elite were likely to be literate and to speak enough French to bridge the linguistic gap between French officers and their men. In short, "Officered [*encadrés*] by the best of their men, commanded by Frenchmen, we believe that France, in the future as in the past, can count on the youthful ardor of its *indigènes*."[75]

Broadly based recruitment was designed to ease problems of staffing and command, and the higher pay and enhanced status of a *gradé* or officer were intended to attract members of the higher levels of indigenous society. During the aggressive recruiting drive in West Africa in 1918, the French administration sought the help and acquiescence of tribal chiefs by offering to assign older chiefs who enlisted to service in the AOF or in Algeria; by facilitating the rapid promotion of influential chiefs to the rank of *adjudant-chef,* and then even to *sous-lieutenant;* and by creating special training platoons for young chiefs and sons of chiefs so that they might enter the ranks as corporals or sergeants.[76]

Despite this effort, the High Command admitted, most of the men who entered the army were not members of the elite, and in fact many were slaves. It was thus important for the French officers in West African units to identify the few free men and sons of chiefs, to educate and train them, and to place them in positions of authority over their comrades. This might seem to conflict republican principles and be "contrary to our egalitarian ideas," but primitive social mores would take time to change. In the meantime, the army would make the social inequalities of West African society work to its advantage.[77]

Recommendations for the promotion of indigenous soldiers, listing the specific characteristics of the candidate that qualified him for such consideration, indicated the criteria by which the army chose its officers and *gradés*. One such recommendation, submitted in April 1918 for Sheikh Mademba, one of the sons of the *fama*, ruler of Sansanding in the French Sudan (Mali), noted that he was intelligent, active, the son of a prominent figure who had rendered "precious services to France," and from a family of proven loyalty to the French. He also had a great deal of influence over his fellow *tirailleurs*, belonged to one of the most warlike races in the interior region of West Africa, and served *au titre français* (meaning he was probably naturalized). Other nominations submitted along with Mademba's make clear that social status was as important as military ability—nearly all were sons of chiefs. All spoke French well, and though this knowledge was helpful, along with proving oneself under fire, social status outside the military helped many *indigènes* move up in the military hierarchy to a position that corresponded to their place in their own civilian social hierarchy.[78]

The importance of this practice was evident in the fear that French authorities had of promoting a soldier to a rank beyond his social station. The experience of Sous-lieutenant Abdelmoumen was illustrative. An Algerian who accompanied and acted as an interpreter for an important religious figure, Lieutenant Si Brahim, on a propaganda tour among Algerian soldiers stationed in depots and hospitals in France, Abdelmoumen turned out to be a poor candidate for such responsibility and seemed to confirm French fears about the risks of transgressing the indigenous social hierarchy. This soldier was promoted to *sous-lieutenant* because of his knowledge of the French language, and he accompanied Si Brahim in part because he was his brother-in-law. Algeria's Governor-General Lutaud worried, however, that the newly minted *sous-lieutenant* was socially and mentally unfit to hold that rank. In February 1915, Lutaud wrote to the minister of war that Abdelmoumen was a "schemer" who had been fired from his job in the colonial administration for "deplorable manners." His poor reputation was unlikely to raise Si Brahim's mission in the eyes of Algerian soldiers, and the governor-general hoped that promotions to the rank of officer would in the future be cleared with him in advance.[79]

In response to these observations, the Ministry of War admitted that "like every Arab," Abdelmoumen "was intoxicated by the title of *sous-lieutenant*," but that his behavior had improved after he had been advised to show more discretion. In fact, he seemed to be a good candidate for promotion, because he was "very resourceful" and politically well connected.[80] Yet when Si Brahim repeatedly requested that he himself be admitted to the Legion of Honor for his services, Lutaud raised the issue again, refusing to support the award primarily because Abdelmoumen's behavior had discredited the whole initiative. Upon his return to Algeria, he had quarreled with his brother-in-law and had even come to blows with him. Abdelmoumen had been imprisoned for eight days for this incident. Subsequently, too, he had continued to wear his uniform, with its officer's insignia, for some time after being told to be more discrete. This caused great astonishment among his fellow Algerians, who knew his "bad, very bad reputation," and who would have less respect for the French and the army for having honored such a miscreant by making him a *sous-lieutenant*.[81] The whole incident indicated the trouble that could result from promoting a soldier beyond his social rank, Lutaud argued. The governor-general's comments made clear his belief that respecting and reproducing the indigenous social hierarchy within the army was important for preserving order both in colonial society and in the military.

Despite the unfortunate example of Abdelmoumen, many officials believed that North African societies offered particularly good opportunities to take advantage of preexisting social hierarchies by grafting them onto the military hierarchy. Units of Moroccan and Algerian cavalry were often composed of prominent tribesmen, sometimes organized and outfitted at the expense of a powerful chief. Such units contained enough chiefs, sons of chiefs, and members of prominent families that staffing them with indigenous officers and *gradés* was relatively easy. *Tirailleur* units were less exclusively recruited, and the practice of substitution among conscripts in Tunisia and Algeria reduced the number of prominent and wealthy men in French uniform, but the army still often promoted soldiers on the basis of education and social status.

The experience of Algerian soldiers provided a particularly good example of this practice. At the beginning of the war, the army claimed that it lacked the raw material it deemed necessary to form indigenous officers and *gradés* in its Algerian units. Officers had, one Ministry of War official explained in 1916, searched unsuccessfully for viable candidates. Educated and assimilated Algerians were unenthusiastic about military service, and few of them joined the army, while sons of chiefs or prominent families ("sons of the great tents") did not want to serve as simple soldiers. They wanted a guarantee that they would be *gradés* or officers and would not have to perform common labor and march alongside other men whom they regarded as beneath their station. Many Algerians considered soldiers as by definition uncouth and irreligious. In fact, the men attracted to service in the army were often from the lowest levels of indigenous society, and the army was hardly eager to recruit officers from these men. Even if knowledge of the French language was the criterion for advancement, the official argued, the result would be elevating the "floating population of the cities." To solve this problem, the Ministry of War had proposed back in 1913 to establish special schools in which to train future officers, hoping thereby to attract the better elements of society. The plan was scuttled at the time, however, by the objections of colonial administrators.[82]

During the war, the idea of special schools for *officiers indigènes* resurfaced. Paris made increasing demands upon the Algerian administration for recruits, and part of the government's plan to ease the resentment caused by expanding the scope of conscription was to end the privilege of replacement. The cost of a substitute to serve in a conscripted man's place had risen as high as 10,000 francs in 1916, and though the governor-general still thought replacement was a valuable way to preserve the loyalty of important *indigènes,* he finally agreed to end the practice. As a condition for its elimination, however, he demanded that a special school at Miliana, designed to recognize the elevated social status of certain recruits, accommodate the sons of indigenous notables. This would mollify these families, who "feared above all the contact of their children with the *tirailleurs.*" The young men who attended the school would be promoted quickly to noncommissioned and commissioned ranks and would thus be able to "do their service in a position that will conserve their pride and their social station."[83]

The school at Miliana had, in fact, opened well before the authorities suppressed replacement in January 1918. By the end of 1916, three such schools—at Miliana, at Constantine, and at Bizerte in Tunisia—were functioning. The schools at Constantine and Bizerte primarily trained educated *indigènes* to be corporals and sergeants, while the Miliana school received only those of higher social status destined for both noncommissioned and higher ranks. These elite conscripts had their own separate barracks, were exempt from general work details, and were required to take care only of their weapons and uniforms, which were well made and of fine material. Instruction was intensive, and promotions were fairly rapid.[84]

These special schools produced mediocre results, according to the Ministry of War. The well-born sons of the notables unfortunately turned out to be "the poorest students," and very few of them possessed the "perseverance in work permitting them to rise to the rank of officer."[85] Still, the army believed that there was a political interest in continuing with the instruction there, and even in attracting more students.[86] Ultimately, whatever the value or level of competence of the officers and *gradés* who graduated from these schools, their existence attested, not only to a determination to mollify indigenous notables, but to a strong commitment to reproduce the indigenous social structure in the military hierarchy.[87]

## Officiers indigènes

That this policy contradicted republican rhetoric about social equality and positions open to the talents did not go unnoticed even by the army, but officials justified the decision to promote soldiers based upon social standing as a pragmatic approach to recruitment and staffing. Yet policy in general toward indigenous soldiers, and especially the officers and *gradés* among them, allowed the issue of race itself to undermine the ideal of a purely merit-based military hierarchy. Though the situation was often far from the ideal even for white soldiers, republican egalitarianism and the Napoleonic model held that each man in the French Army, from common soldiers to members of the officer corps, had the opportunity to rise as far as his abilities would take him. Hence the cliché that "every soldier carried a marshal's baton in his knapsack." This ideal was not only just, it would act as an incentive for the entire army. However, this was manifestly not true of nonwhite soldiers, and their situation in the army is a particularly striking example of the triumph of racism over republican egalitarianism.

Nonetheless, there were limited attempts to place indigenous soldiers on an equal footing with their white comrades, and to open up many of the same paths to advancement to them, at least in theory. "The rank of *officier indigène* is much too difficult to reach; the training of noncommissioned officers must be pushed in a way that enables the appointment of a larger number of officers and thus encourages all the troops," a report on West African soldiers noted.[88] A circular on policy involving all *troupes indigènes* stipulated that the conditions for their advancement to the ranks of corporal and noncommissioned officer were the same as those for French soldiers.[89]

When, by the later part of the war, many Madagascans served in the artillery, the army was careful to specify that they were to be treated exactly like their French comrades, and that the rules of advancement were to be the same.[90] In early 1918, when the government was taking steps to boost morale and encourage recruitment of Algerians, the minister of war announced that he was not only ending the practice of replacement but would ensure that *indigènes* had access to all ranks, subject to the same requirements as their French comrades.[91]

It was apparent that the army was concerned there be ample opportunities for advancement in order to sustain morale and to provide incentive in all units of indigenous troops. The authorities took complaints seriously, like those that surfaced at the end of the war in the 7th BTI, that opportunities were lacking.[92] When Mangin wrote his 1920 proposal for a large army recruited in the colonies, he noted that the war had proven that *indigènes* were increasingly able to serve as officers and *gradés,* thus reducing the need for European personnel.[93] Yet Mangin was characteristically optimistic in this regard, and many of his colleagues did not share his high opinion of the ability of *indigènes* to serve as more than simple soldiers. In fact, racial prejudice rendered equality of opportunity meaningless, because many officers regarded *indigènes* as by definition less qualified than Frenchmen for positions of authority.

Nonetheless, the theory of equality of opportunity, even if its application was imperfect, made advancement a real goal for many *indigènes.* The main attractions were, of course, higher pay and enhanced prestige, but another important incentive was authority over white Frenchmen. Long after the war, a West African corporal remembered with pride that he "was ranked . . . among the 'white' men. I was even giving orders to some 'white' men [in France]." Moreover, many West Africans found to their satisfaction that white officers usually punished Frenchmen who disregarded the authority of their nonwhite superiors.[94]

Yet this was certainly not always the case. When a legislator noted that "the white corporal is an element of discord because of his racial authority, which is [properly] contested, according to a precise military point of view, by the black sergeant," he pointed out the fundamental conflict that existed between racial hierarchy, in which whites were by definition superior to blacks, and military hierarchy, in which rank determined superiority and subordination.[95] The racial prejudices of white Frenchmen thus interfered with the strictly military hierarchy essential for clear chains of command and efficient operation. In fact, even measures that ensured the advancement of *indigènes* often placed significant limits upon these opportunities by setting maximum numbers for indigenous *gradés* and officers in units and by insisting upon the iron rule governing indigenous authority: in cases involving a Frenchmen and an *indigène* of equal rank, the white's authority always prevailed.

In fact, indigenous officers often faced outright discrimination in many forms. If, by the end of the war, *indigènes* received the same pay and bonuses as Frenchmen of equal rank, they were nevertheless denied family allocations, because their families lived in the colonies, where daily burdens of existence were allegedly "much less onerous than those of the metropole."[96] The provision was inconsistent, because the army did pay allocations to the families of *indigènes* who served *au titre français* (in the French capacity), that is, to those who were naturalized, whose families in the colonies faced the same conditions as officers who served *au titre indigène* (in the indigenous capacity). Moreover, conditions in the colonies were actually usually worse for impoverished families whose main breadwinner was away at war, despite inexplicable claims that this absence did not "modify the conditions of existence" for those left to fend for themselves at home in the colonies.[97] Officials also claimed that because *indigènes* received bonuses when they volunteered or were conscripted for military service, while Frenchmen were simply called up with no special bonus, this meant that *indigènes* were technically paid more than their French counterparts, so that indigenous families were already provided for.[98]

Army policy on leave directly discriminated against indigenous *gradés* and officers. Unlike their French comrades, very few *indigènes* were able to visit their families and homes during their wartime service. The government placed severe restrictions upon permissions for all *indigènes,* and it must have been especially galling to indigenous officers to see their French subordinates benefit from privileges of which the *indigènes,* for the most part, could only dream. Some were able to return home when wounded and then subsequently assigned to staff new units training in the colonies, and restrictions did loosen somewhat as the war wore on, but permissions remained very limited throughout the war for the great majority of *indigènes.* One indigenous officer, who was denied leave to visit his family in Algeria after recovering from wounds, complained bitterly: "I cannot believe that as an *officier indigène*, having served seventeen years in the French ranks, I am not accorded this privilege. I came here to France like all my indigenous comrades, with a smile on my lips to defend our mother *la patrie*. And there should not be, especially at the current time, any distinction between a French officer and an indigenous officer."[99]

To add insult to injury, North African NCOs recovering from wounds at hospitals in France were not allowed to leave the facilities alone, but only in groups and under the guard of a French *gradé.* The *indigènes* complained about this discriminatory treatment, especially humiliating because some-times veteran and decorated NCOs found themselves escorted by junior French *grades*. To alleviate the problem, the Ministry of War ordered that special individual afternoon or day passes be given to those *indigènes* worthy of such a privilege, but such treatment remained exceptional.[100] These and other small, daily humiliations marked the service of indigenous officers, and betrayed French racial prejudices and fears about the trustworthiness of their colonial subjects, regardless of rank.

The French authorities were in fact much more concerned about preserv-ing the status of their white personnel than in protecting their nonwhite officers from humiliation. At the very beginning of the war, the minister of war objected to a plan to attribute a *khalifa* (a sort of deputy indigenous officer who would facilitate religious observances among the *indigènes*) with the insignia and pay of a captain to squadrons of the Algerian cavalry. This would put French lieutenants "in a difficult situation."[101] The army often voiced its concern over this problem of white prestige, and was careful, if at all possible, to avoid situations where the racial sensibilities of white Frenchmen would be upset by the presence of a nonwhite superior. Many white French officers did not welcome their nonwhite colleagues. During his inspection of two Tunisian regiments, one general noted that certain commanders did not "appear to desire the presence of these [indigenous] officers." Arguing that the influence of indigenous officers on their men was "useful," he suggested that their number be increased, but he admitted that the military aptitudes of the *indigènes* sometimes left something to be desired and agreed with the commanders of the units that the French per-sonnel constituted "an element of strength and confidence" and should be augmented.[102]

Indigenous officers were well aware of the discrimination they faced. Boukabouya was particularly critical of the lack of respect and racist insults that he and his fellow colonial subjects endured, but deserters and propagan-dists were not the only ones who expressed frustration with such treatment. An Algerian, noting that "an indigenous officer returning from the hospital to his depot is called *tu* like a dog [*tutoyé comme un chien*]," instead of be-ing addressed with the formal and respectful *vous*, wondered what rank it was that he actually held.[103] *Indigènes* often did not receive the respect due to their rank and status as participants in the defense of France, making a mockery of strict notions of military hierarchy. In the end, race often came before rank; racial hierarchy trumped military hierarchy.

This was true of *officiers indigènes*' relationships with their colleagues. There were many indications that white officers never really treated *indigènes* as true colleagues. The fear that a racial inferior would possibly have the authority to give orders to a lower-ranking white soldier rankled many Frenchmen, and the stipulation that the white officer prevailed in cases of equal rank prevented any true sense of respect or equality from developing.

Such attitudes, in evidence in Indochina before the war, prompted one colonial official to remark, "The army is the last fortress to open to the Annamites." Meanwhile, Indochinese NCOs traveled in third class, while their French equals in rank traveled in second, and lower-ranking French soldiers from the metropole refused to address their *adjudants* as "Mon *adjudant*," as they would a white soldier of that rank.[104] In 1915, the resident-general of Tunisia wrote to the minister of foreign affairs that many Tunisian officers did not want to be naturalized because they were "kept at arm's length" by French officers.[105] Such discriminatory and disrespectful behavior was hardly calculated to instill the *indigènes* with a sense of the dignity of their rank.

The French authorities claimed that their treatment of the indigenous officers grew out of and corresponded to the attitudes of indigenous soldiers themselves. In response to a 1917 legislative proposal to reduce the number of lower-ranking French personnel in Algerian units, the Ministry of War asserted that French *gradés* and officers commanded more respect than did *indigènes* and were thus essential to the operation of the units. Exceeding the current proportion of one indigenous lieutenant, four sergeants, and eight corporals per regiment risked compromising the morale and effective command of Algerian troops.[106] The army's position was simple: the moral authority of white officers, which stemmed directly from their racial identity, gave them, and only them, the crucial ability to inspire the confidence of their men. One officer argued that indigenous officers could not be depended upon to sustain the morale of their men, a task where the officer must "find his influence in the elevation of his character and his sentiments." Moreover, even in cases "of equal merit, a *gradé indigène* will not have on the *tirailleurs* the moral effect that a French *gradé* will draw from the very fact that he is French by race."[107] This same officer returned to the theme in another report, maintaining that though French personnel might not be crucial for operations in North Africa, where enemies were inferior in arms, discipline, and tactics, the situation was different in the European war, "where numerous examples have shown that when all European officers disappear, indigenous soldiers do not want to place themselves under the command of their indigenous officers or NCOs, but gather around French soldiers, even those without rank. Racial superiority? Probably."[108] Another officer commanding West African troops summed up the argument most succinctly: "In difficult moments, in fact, even the bravest have their eyes fixed on the white leader."[109] Countless other officers made precisely the same observation about indigenous soldiers from all different parts of the empire: these soldiers themselves trusted the authority of whites more than that of their own peers. French officers, however, never seemed to have asked themselves if their own obvious mistrust and discrimination, and not the *indigènes'* inherent racial inferiority, was decisive in undermining the status and influence of indigenous *gradés* and officers in the eyes of their men.

Ultimately, whites deemed nonwhites morally and intellectually below the tasks of leadership. "The *indigène* cannot yet make a good officer, such as we understand it, when he is not under the constant surveillance of a superior," one officer observed. "His mentality is still too distant from ours. For him this is an axiom: to obtain authority is to make use of it for personal gain. Hence bribes, corruption, arbitrariness."[110] Many French officers believed that these alleged character flaws, stemming from racial inferiority, not only prevented *indigènes* from gaining the respect of their men, but also impeded their performance in combat. One report advised that West Africans not be employed in occupying and defending captured enemy trenches, because their indigenous *gradés* were unable to focus their men's efforts effectively. Such duty called for "tenacity in the face of incoming artillery fire, quickness, intelligence, and initiative, individual qualities that are totally absent" in these men. The author of the report admitted that part of the problem with the *gradés indigènes* was their inexperience, but their inherent inferiority was at the root of their weaknesses.[111]

There were nonetheless practical reasons why it was difficult to integrate *indigènes* fully into the French officer corps. A lack of education and language skills, essential for efficient communication, and thus for operations both in and out of combat, was the main problem. In response to a parliamentary initiative to open up access to higher ranks for North Africans, the Ministry of War observed that, in applying the same rights and obligations to both colonial subjects and Frenchmen in the name of egalitarianism, the proposition would actually put the *indigènes* at a grave disadvantage. Nearly all of the indigenous *gradés* and even officers were nearly completely illiterate in both Arabic and French, and current army policy allowed *indigènes* to rise to the rank of officer after passing an examination that was scarcely equivalent to a French certificate of primary studies. Had they been sub-jected to the same standards in a French unit, the Ministry of War argued, the majority of indigenous lieutenants would not even have risen to the rank of corporal.[112] Education and language barriers were very real and had an effect on indigenous performance of their duties. For example, many ob-servers remarked upon the difficulty West African *gradés* had in translating orders from French for their men, thus severely reducing the value of the units in which they served.

Yet even these pragmatic assertions about the shortcomings of indige-nous *gradés* and officers had racial components. Thus, the argument that *in-digènes* lacked the education necessary to fulfill their duties as effectively as Frenchmen begged the question of whether this was actually a failing of the part of the French, a key component of whose "civilizing mission" in the colonies was supposed to be the education of indigenous peoples.[113] More-over, the army, which was one of the institutions that was to undertake this civilizing and educative role, should conceivably share some of the blame for this failure. "It seems impossible, when the duty of France is to educate the *indigènes*, that the means has not been found—and this is a question of a warrior race—to modify their mentality in the curriculum of the army," one observer wryly noted.[114] More concretely, the criticisms of *indigènes'* in-ability to communicate effectively in French were most evident in matters where it was less technical linguistic ability that was in question than the obstructive role of the *indigènes'* "mentality." Hence, the French authorities accused indigenous superiors of being unable to communicate the complex ideas of their French commanders to the men, thus endangering morale and loyalty.[115]

Though technically *indigènes* from all parts of the empire could advance to the rank of officer, the promotion of North Africans generated the most discussion. The army considered West Africans too primitive and uneducated to make good officers, and so these men rarely rose above the rank of NCO. *Originaires* from the Four Communes of Senegal had greater opportunities in theory, because of their status as French citizens, but in practice their ser-vice in French metropolitan units put them in direct competition with na-tive Frenchmen for promotions, and thus at a distinct disadvantage. Mada-gascans and Indochinese were also eligible to serve as officers, but they faced obstacles and restricted opportunities, and their relatively small number, es-pecially in combat units, made the issue of promotions less pressing. The ad-vancement of North Africans presented a much more visible problem. More of them served in the army than any other group of *indigènes*, and their loyalty was particularly important in light of the alliance of the Muslim Ottoman empire with the German enemy. Thus, despite racial prejudices, many French political and military authorities were concerned throughout the war with presenting opportunities for advancement in the army both as an incentive for recruitment and as a demonstration of trust and gratitude for Muslims' fidelity.

This was the context in which the Commission interministérielle des affaires musulmanes (Interministerial Commission on Muslim Affairs, or CIAM, a group that included officials from the Ministries of War, Foreign Affairs, the Interior, and the Colonies) took up the question of indigenous officers in North African units in January 1916. The sustained defense of the army's restrictive practices by Colonel Hamelin, who represented the Ministry of War on the commission, clearly reveals the attitudes that shaped official policy in this area and the limitations and discrimination that *indigènes* faced in the French military. The initial question was whether or not the government should take steps to equalize the opportunities and requirements for advancement between North Africans and native French soldiers.

Colonel Hamelin began by arguing that not even the *indigènes* themselves would want to be subject to the same regulations as French soldiers. A naturalized *indigène* could serve *au titre français* and then would have access to all ranks in the hierarchy, providing that he demonstrated the same aptitudes as his French comrades. But the vast majority of colonial subjects served *au titre indigène* in order to benefit from special cash bonuses for enlistment. Beyond this, *indigènes* from the better classes did not see military service as compatible with religious observance or with their social status, and so the French recruited indigenous soldiers "from the least healthy part of the population," and it was from among these men that officers and *gradés* were chosen. Despite this, the army was able to obtain excellent NCOs. "The natural military qualities of our *indigènes* lend themselves to the exercise of this rank," Hamelin observed. However, it was not the same when it came to training commissioned officers. Repeating the common argument that other *indigènes* had no respect for their comrades once they became officers, he maintained that men in the ranks looked to whites for real leadership. Not only did *indigènes'* limited education and training fail to equip them to handle the responsibilities of power, he argued, but their inherent "mentality" was lacking, and not even instruction or training could change that entirely. The result was that *indigènes* were so unqualified for command that if one were to ask indigenous soldiers to elect their corporals, NCOs, and officers, they would choose Frenchmen rather than their own comrades.[116]

These failings were also clear to French soldiers, and Hamelin noted that it was "painful" for French officers or NCOs to be under the orders of an *indigène,* particularly because they knew that the requirements for the *indigène* to arrive at his rank were scarcely equal to those required of a Frenchman. For Hamelin and other officers, the race of the *indigène,* and his corresponding "mentality," were the real problems. Observing that the army had recently created the rank of *capitaine indigène,* Hamelin explained the essentially hollow nature of even this measure, ostensibly designed to open up higher positions to *indigènes.* These captains were not allowed to take command of companies or exercise direct command over a unit of any size, merely serving as "assistants" to their superiors. "The indigenous mentality is actually incompatible with the exercise of the administrative command of a company or squadron," according to army policy.[117] In fact, the rank was primarily a way of rewarding especially prominent *indigènes* for joining the French Army, and it was an exceedingly rare honor.[118]

Hamelin's remarks hit upon one of the most striking paradoxes that characterized the promotion of *indigènes* to higher ranks when he pointed out that indigenous officers did not exercise direct command over units. The most basic purpose of rank in a military hierarchy is to confer authority upon those of higher rank over their subordinates, yet *indigènes* found that they their real authority was limited and undermined in many ways. The stipulation that in cases of equal rank, a white soldier prevailed over an in-digène was dramatic proof that the fundamental question at issue was one of race. The army went even further to ensure that the direct authority of indigenous officers over native Frenchmen would be limited by making them "assistants" to French commanders. In order to demonstrate how little disposed the army was to open up advancement to higher ranks to *indigènes,* Hamelin cited the recent introduction of legislation to create the rank of *adjudant indigène* to fill vacancies left by lieutenants who had been wounded or killed. Through an odd administrative oversight, prewar legislation governing the staffing of Algerian units had allowed for indigenous sergeants to be promoted to *sous-lieutenant,* but not to the intermediate rank of *adjudant.* Once the war accelerated the number of vacancies among the ranks of lieutenants, the army realized that promoting sergeants directly to *sous-lieutenant,* and thus from noncommissioned to commissioned officer, was un-desirable. The proposal sought to end this anomalous situation, a measure no doubt justified from a strictly military point of view, because the situation led to unpromoted sergeants filling roles that higher-ranking NCOs normally filled, or to *indigènes* in effect skipping a rank as they were promoted up the hierarchy. Still, the commentary surrounding the legislation made it clear that most were skeptical that *indigènes* had the proper education and mentality to enter the officer corps and felt that they were better off as *adjudants* leading their comrades in sections or platoons.[119] Moreover, keeping nonwhite soldiers primarily in the ranks of common soldiers and NCOs reduced the chances that there would be conflict between the status of the *indigènes* and white French soldiers' feelings of racial superiority.

Responses to Hamelin's remarks by his colleagues reveal the paradoxical nature of the military's policy on promotion of *indigènes*. One observed that it seemed illogical to have two different categories of officers, especially if one of them had no real authority. Another pointed out that in the Foreign Legion, it was easier for non-French soldiers to attain the rank of officer than it was for *indigènes*, who were after all French subjects (if not citizens), to attain the same rank in the French Army. Finally, one member asserted that if the French did not more actively address the problems that *indigènes* had in obtaining advancement, discontent and resulting problems with recruitment and staffing would remain insoluble.[120]

Such comments were clearly justified, but given the prevailing racial prejudices and corresponding doubts about the competence of *indigènes*, the situation was unlikely to change. This was evident when the issue came up again almost two years later. In response to a request to expand opportunities for promotion of North Africans in the artillery, Hamelin again articulated the reasons behind the army's restrictive policies. He argued that only very rarely were *indigènes* suitable for tasks that required precision. They were useful as drivers of the horse teams that transported artillery, but positions requiring technical knowledge or ability were beyond their limited capacities. Hamelin claimed that *indigènes* did not do well in the special schools set up to train officers, noting that even those naturalized *indigènes* who were admitted to French military academies usually dropped out after a few months, because they were incapable of "forcing themselves to do the intensive work" required in such institutions.[121]

Later in the war, under pressure to improve the conditions of service as part of the new Clemenceau government's push to stimulate recruitment in North Africa, Hamelin finally produced a plan to address the criticisms many had leveled against the army's unwillingness to promote *indigènes*.

Parliament began to consider Hamelin's plan in the first months of 1918, but it quickly became apparent that it preserved some of the worst inequities of the system already in place. *Officiers indigènes* would serve *au titre indigène*, which meant that they could only serve in indigenous units, a stipulation clearly designed to minimize the chances that a colonial subject would outrank a white Frenchman in his own unit.[122] The new regulations would set maximum numbers of *indigènes* for each rank, thus placing an arbitrary and rigid limit on promotions. These promotions would continue to be left to the discretion of French commanders, a less concrete limit, but no less arbitrary. Finally, white prestige and the racial hierarchy would remain intact, because *indigènes* would continue to have to defer to French soldiers of equal rank. *Indigènes* recognized this "reform" for what it was, and they objected especially to the injustice of deferring to a Frenchmen of equal rank. "Equality in dangers, equality in responsibilities," one Algerian political activist protested, and the Ministry of War eventually submitted a new, more liberal plan at the end of 1919. The CIAM adopted it, but the plan got tied up in the legislature and never became law. Another plan in 1920 had a similar fate, and senators allied with settler interests blocked a final effort in 1923. In the end, then, France decided against rewarding the wartime service of Algerian *indigènes* with increased access to promotion.[123]

Ultimately, the scarcity of *officiers indigènes* is the clearest evidence of the failure of reforms and of the reluctance of military and political officials to elevate colonial subjects to equality with their French comrades. The highest rank an *indigène* could hope to attain was captain; "their marshal's baton had to stop there," the historian Belkacem Recham observes.[124] Moreover, the army awarded this rank only rarely and as compensation for extraordinary service, and the position still came without any real command authority. In 1921, there were only three *capitaines indigènes* in all of the North African infantry, all promoted in 1919. Lieutenants were more numerous: 70 in 1921, 15 promoted before 1914, 39 during the war, and the rest in the months immediately following the armistice. There were 76 *sous-lieutenants*, 14 promoted before 1914, 52 during the war, and the rest in 1918–19. Adding those in the cavalry, there were 229 *officiers indigènes* in the Armée d'Afrique three years after the war ended.[125]

These figures do not, of course, include those who left the army or who were killed, but they indicate the limited opportunities available for rising in the ranks. In fact, if the 3rd Regiment, with 24 *officiers indigènes* serving during the war, was typical of the ten indigenous regiments that served in

France, then the numbers for 1921 may very well reflect the general situation between 1914 and 1918.[126] Even expansion of the French forces, the gaps opened in the officer corps when members were killed or wounded, and the opportunity for *indigènes* to prove themselves under fire failed significantly to alter the overall position of inferiority, both in race and rank, of North Africans.

The same was true of *indigènes* from other colonies. Before the war, there were only 52 *officiers indigènes* in the entire Colonial Army, plus three Indochinese officers who served, *au titre étranger*, in the Foreign Legion.[127] In Madagascar, all 326 officers serving with French forces were French, as were over 75 percent of the NCOs.[128] Given the perception that Madagascans in general were members of a *race non-guerrière*, this was perhaps to be expected, but among the *races guerrières* of West Africa, the army promoted only 28 *indigènes* to the rank of officer between 1862 and 1914.[129] Only a few more became *sous-lieutenants* or lieutenants before 1918, and despite a concerted effort by the government and senior officers to encourage the promotion of West Africans, only about a dozen more became officers during that year.[130] Madagascans and Indochinese, with far fewer *tirailleurs* engaged, especially in combat, faced even more limited opportunities to rise above the rank of noncommissioned officer. In 1920, General Mangin headed a Commission interministérielle des troupes indigènes (Interministerial Commission on Indigenous Troops), or CITI, which devoted a large part of its attention to expanding the number of *officiers indigènes* in France's colonial forces. Mangin argued that there were military, political, and moral reasons for doing so: the army would require 1,000 new *officiers indigènes* to staff the 300,000 *troupes indigènes* he expected to be part of France's postwar army; such a gesture of justice and magnanimity would improve the political climate in the colonies; and, finally, France had an obligation to show its appreciation for the loyalty of its colonial subjects.[131] As one report generated by the CITI put it, contrasting France's liberal republican and military tradition with that which prevailed in Britain's colonial army: "The welcoming generosity of our military tradition cannot condone British restrictions on the indigenous officer in our military institutions."[132]

Yet the liberal ideals embodied in Mangin's plans ultimately foundered on the opposition of his fellow officers, colonial administrators, and politicians, and the prewar status quo underwent only minor changes. Military officials in particular opposed any diminution of the racial prestige of white French officers, which an expansion of the ranks of *officiers indigènes* would allegedly entail. Officers consulted on the issue insisted that white French officers continue to have explicit authority over *indigènes* of equal rank, and that "one must absolutely avoid placing French soldiers under the orders of indigenous soldiers."[133] One indication of the importance many officers placed upon maintaining the all-important racial hierarchy, even at the price of a technical violation of the military hierarchy, was an insistence that white French soldiers not be required to salute *indigènes* of equal rank. Even more remarkable, in some cases, white French soldiers were not expected to salute, or even necessarily to obey, *indigènes* of superior rank. As one officer put it, "one cannot subordinate the authority of the '*master*' to *that of the pupil.*"[134]

Evidently, maintaining the white racial superiority that underpinned France's colonial empire was, for most officers, more important than offering real opportunities for advancement to colonial subjects. The efforts of Mangin and others stemmed from a genuine desire to expand the role of France's colonial subjects in the military and to elevate the status of *indigènes* who contributed so much to the defense of France during the war. Yet more representative of the postwar attitude was a Ministry of War official who criticized "inopportune demonstrations of enthusiasm toward the indigènes" and argued that Mangin's proposal for increasing the number of *officiers indigènes* was unnecessary. The experience in the army in North Africa was conclusive: most French officers in regiments of *tirailleurs* viewed indigenous officers "as useless auxiliaries."[135]

Race was a primary consideration in officering units of *troupes indigènes*. Of course, the kinds of practical factors that influenced the selection of officers in any unit were also important: competence and leadership abilities, level of experience, and ability to communicate effectively. Yet when it came to *troupes indigènes*, the army sought leaders in men who also had experience in the colonies and who knew the "mentality," and perhaps a little of the language, of the specific group they would command. Thus, though the ideal relationship between officers and men in all sections of the army was paternal, there was a specific ethnic and racial cast to the paternalism with which white French officers were to treat the colonial subjects whom they led. This paternalism was predicated upon the prestige and superiority of these officers, conferred not just by their rank, but by their race. In many cases, however, shortages of officers who could live up to this ideal resulted in many *troupes indigènes* serving under officers who possessed none of the special qualifications to serve with colonial subjects, with the exception of white skin.

That competence, authority, and whiteness were inextricably linked is clear from the position of the *indigènes* themselves in the hierarchy. Thinking about rank and promotion rested soundly on notions of the racial inferiority of nonwhites. Despite real but limited opportunities for *indigènes* to work their way up in the ranks and to exercise a measure of authority within the French Army, a racial hierarchy that placed them firmly below white Europeans in intelligence, competence, and authority was replicated in a military hierarchy that carefully preserved the principle of white supremacy. This produced tensions and contradictory situations: officers who did not actually command the units in which they served; equals in rank who were unequal in authority based upon their ethnicity or the color of their skin; opportunities for advancement that ended abruptly at the rank of lieutenant, or at most captain, for the unnaturalized, whatever the proven abilities or experience of the indigenous candidate; the de jure ability of naturalized *indigènes* to progress to all ranks compromised by de facto biases and discrimination. These situations were the result of the ideals of republican universalism and egalitarianism clashing with racial prejudice. The republican ideal of "La carrière est ouverte aux talents" (The career is open to the talents), a saying attributed to Napoleon, highlights the supposed importance of merit alone in propelling soldiers up through the ranks in the French military. Yet ideas about the racial inferiority of colonial subjects prevented the French Army from living up to France's lofty republican rhetoric of equality, even when engaged in a desperate attempt to defend the Third Republic and its ideals. This was evident, not only in policy toward officers and promotion in units of *troupes indigènes*, but also in the approach of military officials to the problem of language in these units. As the next chapter shows, racial stereotypes and prejudices played a decisive role in shaping the army's linguistic policies.

Maurice Romberg's depiction of an Algerian soldier on horseback in a poster
advertising a war loan in 1918. The dramatic and highly stylized image reflects
stereotypes of Algerians as exotic and aggressive desert warriors.
Library of Congress, POS-Fr .R65, no. 3.

Lucien Jonas's advertisement for the 1917 Journée de l'Armée d'Afrique et des
troupes coloniales, perhaps the best-known wartime poster to feature *troupes
indigènes*, drew on stereotypes of black West Africans as savage
and primitive warriors.
Library of Congress, POS-Fr .J65, no. 9.

West African soldiers working on a trench in the Somme region, 1916. In addition to fighting, many *troupes indigènes* performed such heavy manual labor.

Établissement de communication et de production audiovisuelle de la défense [ECPAD]/Ivry-sur-Seine, France/Édouard Famechon.

Photo taken in 1916 of a graveyard by a shell-damaged church in Woesten, Belgium, featuring grave markers for French Muslim soldiers. These headstones were part of the French army's efforts to maintain morale by interring its North African soldiers in accordance with Muslim burial customs.
ECPAD/France/M. Baguet.

Algerian cavalry soldiers gambling and drinking tea at a "Moorish café" behind the Western Front in northern France in 1916. The French army provided such establishments in an effort to assuage homesickness and sustain the morale of their North African troops. The Arabic inscription on the wall reads: "May Allah grant victory to the young Frenchmen."
ECPAD/France/M. Baguet.

Moroccan troops on maneuvers in northern France in 1916, under a typical command arrangement: an indigenous noncommissioned officer (*left*) and a French officer (*right*). *Troupes indigènes* from all areas of the French empire found it difficult to ascend the military hierarchy into the officer corps, despite the French Army's, and the Third Republic's, nominal commitment to meritocracy and egalitarianism.

ECPAD/France/Emmanuel Mas.

Portrait of Prince Dinah Sali-Fou, son of the king of Nalou in lower Guinea, taken in Paris, 1916. French authorities sought to promote such indigenous elites into the officer corps, with significant restrictions. He rose to be second lieutenant by 1920.

ECPAD/France/Gabriel Boussuge.

A West African soldier in the Somme region, 1916, equipped for "trench-cleaning" duty with the distinctive knife known as the *coupe-coupe*. The knife and such images promoted the stereotype of West Africans as savage warriors who would mutilate and behead their German opponents.

ECPAD/France/Louis Vigier.

A West African soldier talks with young French girls in northern France in 1916.
Such interracial contacts often went beyond conversation, and they caused
French officials considerable consternation.
ECPAD/France/Emmanuel Mas.

Indochinese soldiers in the Marne region, 1918. Though neither Indochinese nor Madagascan soldiers served in combat on the Western Front in large numbers, the relatively few who did endured miserable conditions typical of trench warfare, compounded by exposure to the cold and wet weather of northern France.

Agence Roger-Viollet, Paris, France; 1294-1.

# Race and Language in the French Army

Every colonized people—in other words, every people in
whose soul an inferiority complex has been created by the
death and burial of its local cultural originality—finds itself
face to face with the language of the civilizing nation; that is,
with the culture of the mother country. The colonized is elevated above his jungle status in proportion to his adoption of
the mother country's cultural standards. He becomes whiter as
he renounces his blackness, his jungle.

> —*Frantz Fanon*, Black Skin, White Masks

And it is thus that knowing better our language, the sentiments that unite us will only be strengthened.

> —*French Foreign Ministry, 1916*

. . . we did not speak a common language . . .

> —*West African soldier, recalling wartime interactions*
> *with French civilians*

Y'a bon!

> —*Advertising slogan for the popular breakfast drink*
> *Banania, 1915*

One of the most prominent issues involving the use of *troupes indigènes* in the
French Army during the First World War was language. The vast majority
of these men spoke French imperfectly or not at all, and this presented the

army with a serious problem. Not only could language barriers and misunderstandings be inconvenient during training, but they could also be lethal in combat. Moreover, language had a tremendous importance in French culture, an importance that carried over into the colonial arena in a particular way. Republican colonial ideology held that educating *indigènes*, particularly in the use of the French language, was part of France's "civilizing mission" to uplift subject populations. As Frantz Fanon, one of the most incisive critics of French colonialism, recognized long after the war, to speak French, especially to speak it well, was to leave "the jungle" behind, to lighten one's "blackness." Official French propaganda concurred, if in more elliptical terms, envisioning language raising the "sentiments" of the colonized to the elevated level of those of the colonizers.

Despite these imperatives—military necessity and ideological vocation—racist assumptions on the part of French authorities, not ignorance or incomprehension on the part of *indigènes*, often hampered attempts to teach these soldiers French. This state of affairs led at least one soldier to regret that he could find no "common language" with the citizens of the nation for which he was fighting. Indeed, the speech for which *troupes indigènes* became best known during the war was an impoverished and fractured form of pidgin French most often associated with West African soldiers. In 1915, advertising for the hot breakfast drink Banania began to feature the image of a *tirailleur sénégalais* grinning widely over the slogan "Y'a bon!" (Is good!), a popular advertising campaign that lasted decades beyond the First World War. The use of the *tirailleur*'s image capitalized upon the popularity of these troops among the French public, as well as exploiting the racial stereotype of the simple, fun-loving, good-natured child, while the slogan was emblematic of the broken French many of these men spoke.[1] The slogan was also emblematic of official language policy within the military. This policy not only failed to correct such imperfect phrasing; in many ways officials actually encouraged and perpetuated *troupes indigènes*' linguistic ignorance and pidgin French.

To be sure, linguistic policy in the French Army was never consistent or rationally planned. It evolved primarily in response to changing circumstances and the use of more and more colonial subjects as soldiers in Europe. Yet two general conditions informed the army's approach to the issue of language among *troupes indigènes:* on the one hand, practical military considerations and the undeniable unfamiliarity of most of these soldiers with the French language, and on the other, racist assumptions about the limited capacity of *indigènes* to learn proper French. The use of French interpreters (*officiers interprètes*) was not an adequate solution to language problems in indigenous units, as the number of these men was fairly low and their duties were extensive. The army's response to these challenges was to train indigenous soldiers in the practical use of the French language within the constraints imposed by limited time and opportunity. In other words, the unprecedented manpower demands of the war necessitated rapid language instruction for non-French-speaking troops, an instruction that focused on basic commands and the immediate requirements of military life.

But racial attitudes played as much a part as expediency in determining the nature of this instruction. Ultimately, linguistic policy toward nonwhite soldiers in France during the Great War was the result of the interplay of racial prejudices, military necessity, and republican colonial ideology. The best example of this contradictory mix of motives was an attempt to teach West African soldiers a simplified and purely utilitarian form of communication that reflected and reinforced racial stereotypes. Indigenous soldiers themselves realized the value of learning French, mostly for practical reasons, but West Africans also recognized the poverty of the language they were being taught and how it prevented them from communicating with other French people on an equal basis. Thus language, a tool that ought to have enhanced the integration of these men into the French nation for which they were fighting and dying, actually served to isolate them, retarding or preventing their full participation in French life.

## The Importance of Language

In Benedict Anderson's famous formulation, modern nations are "imagined communities," and members of those communities do much of that imagining in particular languages. In other words, language gives shape to and reinforces national identity—"generating imagined communities, building in effect *particular solidarities*"—and is one of its most important constituent parts.[2] As such, language defines boundaries of inclusion in and exclusion from the national community. Ideally, language is inclusive because, "in principle, anyone can learn any language," and language carries with it national cultures, customs, ways of seeing and acting in the world.[3] In short, as Fanon recognized, "To speak means to be in a position to use a certain syntax, to grasp the morphology of this or that language, but it means above all to assume a culture, to support the weight of a civilization."[4]

In France, language and national identity have been especially closely aligned throughout modern history. To speak French is to have unique access to the greatness of the culture, to share in its achievements. To speak the language well is to gain a certain measure of cultural acceptance, and fluency in French has become one of the most important prerequisites for membership in the national community. Since the Revolution of 1789, the French language has become closely tied to republican values and ideals, while retaining older associations with geographical space, historical destiny, and ethnic belonging. Membership in the national community is contingent, in the words of Dennis Ager, upon acceptance of "the strength of the French identity structure, based on and around the myth of territory (the geometrical hexagon), of individual acceptance by the citizen of his role in defending the universal values of human rights, of the specific French contribution to humanism, and of the special role of the French language in representing these values."[5]

The Third Republic played an instrumental role in fusing the values of the Revolution with the French language. Since these values—embodied in the Declaration of the Rights of Man and Citizen, and the fundamental principles of "Liberty, Equality, and Fraternity"—are universal, applying to all humanity, it followed that the French language belonged to humanity, Ager reasons. Thus, the inclusiveness of the French political community, grounded in universal values and rights, is embedded in the very language in which these values and rights are expressed. This tradition of national belonging has formed "a cultural space" in France "in which values such as Liberty, Equality, and Fraternity, the secular state, and human rights are regarded as both French and universal, and make Frenchness available to all people."[6] The governments of the Third Republic worked very hard after 1870 to create this cultural space, forging a nation unified around republican principles by dispatching instructors to all corners of France to teach the nation's children French and civic belonging in secular schools. France at this time was by no means a modern, unified nation, and as much as half the population still did not speak standard French.[7] The state, with its army of village schoolteachers, waged war on the various regional dialects and patois of rural France. That this was a war had been clear since the Revolution, when the former abbé Henri Grégoire had advertised the linguistic and ideological program of the new order in his *Rapport sur la nécessité & les moyens d'anéantir le patois, & d'universaliser l'usage de la langue française* (On the Necessity and Means of Annihilating Patois and Universalizing Usage of the French Language) (1794). The Third Republic revived this campaign against regional cultures and clerical influence, drilling pupils in proper French vocabulary and grammar and inculcating the civic virtues proper to a nation founded on secular liberal principles and natural rights.[8]

There was more than a hint of imperialism in this process. The government in the center reached out from Paris to the provincial peripheries and taught standard, that is, Parisian, French, conquering these territories politically and culturally and bringing about "the end of a profound division of the mind."[9] This was a "civilizing" process analogous to the *mission civilisatrice* that the Third Republic was beginning to undertake simultaneously much farther afield, in Africa and Asia, as the modern French colonial empire emerged. Educational officials made the connection explicit, one noting that methods for teaching French were "as applicable to little Flemings, little Basques, little Bretons, as to little Arabs and little Berbers."[10]

Teaching French, whether in Brittany or in Algeria, involved more than just enforcing linguistic unity upon subject populations and thereby rendering administration more efficient and rational. The messages that instructors sent to their students via the medium of French were equally, if not more, important: allegiance to the state, gratitude for the benefits of its enlightened rule, and a civic commitment to the principles of the Republic (whether or not those principles applied to the student personally, in the case of colonial subjects outside France). And in an essential way, the medium was the message. The French language itself carried within it the greatness of liberal French ideals. Learning French was to transform the learner, creating a new human being. As Ernest Renan, an accomplished scholar and linguist, and one of the preeminent commentators on the French language and French national identity during the early Third Republic, put it, "It [the French language] will say quite diverse things, but always liberal things. . . . It will never be a reactionary language, either. . . . This language improves [those who learn it]; it is a school; it has naturalness, good-naturedness, it can laugh, it conveys an agreeable skepticism mingled with goodness. . . . Fanaticism is impossible in French. . . . A Muslim who knows French will never be a dangerous Muslim."[11]

Politicians and colonial officials made the connection between language and imperialism even more explicit. The great socialist politician Jean Jaurès asserted in 1884 that "our colonies will only be French in their understanding and their feelings when they understand French. . . . For France above all, language is the necessary instrument of colonization."[12] In French West Africa, Governor-General Amédée William Merlaud-Ponty expressed great confidence in the ability of instruction in the French language to inculcate

"uplifting notions" in Africans, ideas "that are our own and whose use en-
dows us with our moral, social and economic superiority," which would
"little by little transform these barbarians of yesterday into disciples and
auxiliaries." Via the French language, French "influence will insinuate itself among the masses, penetrate and envelop them like a thin web of new
affinities," so that Africans would have "a more and more exact comprehension of the French mentality and the colonizing concepts that are the honor
of the government of the Republic." Echoing Renan, Ponty also maintained
that knowledge of French would counter Islamic fanaticism, "for experience
has taught us that Muslims who know French are less prejudiced."[13]

The preeminence of the French language in Third Republican political
culture and in the process of French imperialism was thus well established
by 1914. Once the war began and the French Army began to bring thousands
of colonial subjects to France to serve as soldiers, practical considerations
mixed with ideological imperatives to make language, and language instruction, a major concern for officials. It quickly became apparent, however, that
despite all the rhetoric extolling the virtues of French-speaking colonial
subjects, very few were to be found. Solutions to this problem eventually
revealed a profound paradox that undermined claims about the French language serving as a vehicle for transmitting the sublime essence of French
culture and values. These soldiers were fighting to preserve that culture and
those values, yet racist preconceptions about the inability of *indigènes'* primitive mentality to grasp the complexities of French and internalize modern liberal ideals produced policies that kept colonial subjects ignorant of
French and outside the national community.

Nevertheless, there was no question that language was an important preoccupation for French authorities charged with administering indigenous
troops. In January 1918, the secretary-general of the Mission laïque française, a secular organization with a mission to teach both the French language and republican principles to foreigners in the colonies and elsewhere,
wrote to Premier and Minister of War Georges Clemenceau to suggest the
establishment of "Colonial clubs [*Foyers coloniaux*] and French classes" for
colonial and foreign workers in France.[14] He justified the need for such an
initiative in terms that could easily, and even more strongly, have applied to
colonial soldiers serving in France, worrying that the presence of "workers
ignorant of our language, our ways, our customs, could lead to conflicts."
Such conflicts, some of them serious, had in fact already occurred, having "no other cause than misunderstandings stemming from ignorance."

A knowledge of French among the *indigènes* would improve relations and obviate the need for interpreters.[15] Misunderstandings could certainly be inconvenient, or even worse, among workers, but communication problems were potentially much more serious in military units. In a time of war, and especially on the battlefield, the army's reliance upon clear and rapid communication was particularly urgent, and miscommunication could be fatal. Ideally, indigenous soldiers should learn French. Yet the demands of war were urgent, and language training for soldiers was often cursory.

Even if some *indigènes* did know how to speak French, many more did not, and the practical problems associated with this ignorance could greatly inhibit the smooth operation of the French military machine. Groups like the Indochinese and Madagascans on the whole possessed greater facility in French than men from West or North Africa, and thus could fill positions that men from these other regions of the empire could not. In his 1920 report on the military value of the various ethnic groups represented among the *troupes indigènes*, General Mangin remarked that it was because "numerous" Indochinese knew French that they could serve as secretaries, while the progress of French education in Madagascar had qualified many men from that colony to serve as nurses, secretaries, telegraph operators, and even doctors. Language skills also enabled both Madagascans and Indochinese soldiers to undertake the technical training necessary for employment in the engineering corps, aviation, the automobile service, and liaison services.[16] Another general, commenting on his experience commanding Madagascan troops, reported that he was able to "train secretaries, telephone operators, and even about fifteen radio operators from among those who speak enough French (there are a great number of them)." This knowledge of French rendered Madagascans superior to many other indigenous soldiers, he wrote, because so many could "fill positions generally reserved for Frenchmen."[17]

Still, French commanders had to be careful even when employing Indochinese and Madagascan troops in positions where knowledge of French was important, despite their relatively elevated level of French education, and not all observers were so impressed by the linguistic ability of these men. In August 1917, an inspector charged with monitoring the activities of Indochinese soldiers and workers in France, reported that Indochinese nurses in the hospital at Amélie-les-Bains "suffer from their ignorance of French," and one could scarcely communicate with them.[18] A July 1918 report on the performance of Madagascan troops serving in the artillery voiced similar concerns. Madagascans' education and intelligence were supposed to have qualified them for the more technical demands of service in this branch of the army, but this report asserted that "The intelligence of most Madagascans is low," and that "the possibilities for training are very limited, despite the evident good will demonstrated by all." Specifically, "Their comprehension of the language, even with an interpreter, is very difficult as soon as one stops giving familiar orders and tackles new subjects."[19]

Troops whose European education and exposure to French was yet more limited had even greater difficulties. In August 1914, the Ministry of War warned that the use of Moroccan soldiers for infantry patrols and reconnaissance was inappropriate in Europe, where they were "entirely ignorant of the language and customs of the country," while Moroccan cavalrymen could not report or transmit information because they were "naturally ignorant of the French language."[20] French authorities still had concerns about these soldiers' knowledge of French at the end of the war, when one commander of Moroccan troops advised against using his men for occupation duty in the recently reconquered provinces of Alsace and Lorraine (which, though claimed by France, had belonged to Germany between 1870 and 1918 and possessed a distinctive culture and language that was a blend of French and German influences). This officer feared that "the education of our men does not enable them to understand that the inhabitants of our recovered provinces have nothing in common with the Boches [Germans]. Hearing the Alsatians speak their patois will arouse the suspicions of the Moroccans, and regrettable misunderstandings could follow."[21] It was not that Moroccans would specifically perceive the differences between French and the Germanic Alsatian patois, but that they would know Germanic speech when they heard it and would know that it did not resemble the little French they knew. Moreover, French officers' ability to explain the difference to their men was limited.

The same kinds of considerations ruled out the use of many *troupes indigènes* in technical or specialized positions. For instance, the commander of an Algerian regiment reported in 1917 that at least one Frenchman had to serve on all teams of stretcher-bearers in his unit. Citing a racial stereotype about Algerians' indifference to the suffering of others, he claimed that Frenchmen were needed for this duty, because *indigènes* lacked the "pity and compassion" to risk their own safety to ensure that no other soldiers were left wounded on the battlefield and to carry the wounded with "swiftness, intelligence, devotion." But on a more practical level, he claimed that the Algerians' lack of proficiency in French meant that men were often left to die because stretcher-bearers became lost and the *indigènes* did not know how to ask for directions or how to read signs.[22] In the same spirit, part of the reason why the army insisted that the proportion of native French soldiers serving in indigenous units should be at least 20–30 percent was that knowledge of French was necessary to fill specialized positions. As a report on the effectiveness of West African soldiers put it, their "limited intellectual faculties" and inability to speak French meant that there was "no question" of training them to fill such specialized positions. It was especially important that there be enough men in the units who spoke French so that orders could be relayed quickly and effectively.[23]

To some extent, the solution to this problem was to employ French officers who knew the language of their men. At the beginning of the war, the French Army made a concerted effort to provide indigenous units with officers who had previous experience serving with nonwhite troops and who spoke the particular language of the men they led. Yet few qualified French officers spoke Arabic, Indochinese, Malagasy, or one of the numerous West African dialects, and these disappeared quickly as casualties took their toll.[24] As the author of a report on the North African soldiers of the 38th Division noted in December 1914, many companies lacked an officer who spoke Arabic. As most of the men did not speak French, command was difficult, and "an insurmountable wall" separated the officers from their men.[25] This lack of multilingual officers persisted and grew worse as the war lengthened. The Ministry of War's objections to Mangin's ambitious proposal to raise 700,000 *troupes indigènes* in 1916 centered on the difficulty of staffing the new units with thousands of French officers who spoke the languages of these colonial subjects.[26] The challenge was to prevent "an insurmountable wall" from forming between French officers and *troupes indigènes*. One way of doing so was to use multilingual Frenchman and *indigènes* who knew enough French for military purposes as interpreters.

## Officiers interprètes

Candidates to serve specifically as interpreters were not always much more plentiful than multilingual field officers. One report on West African soldiers noted that the soldiers hardly ever corresponded with their families because there was no one to help them with writing.[27] The same shortage had the opposite effect upon the censorship of the correspondence of Indochinese and North African soldiers. Officials often complained that they lacked enough qualified personnel to read all the letters that passed through their offices.[28]

Moreover, the few translators who were available tended to be employed in ways that limited their efficacy. In July 1917, one of these *officiers interprètes* argued that interpreters were not close enough to their Tunisian and Algerian men, being stationed at divisional headquarters.[29] In a March 1918 report to the minister of the colonies, an inspector noted with approval that the elimination of the divisional interpreter and the attribution of one interpreter to each regiment had rectified the problem in one division.[30] Yet one interpreter per regiment was hardly an effective way to address everyday communication problems, because a full-strength regiment contained several thousand men.

If the number of European interpreters was fairly restricted, the number of *indigènes* who held the position was even more so: very few became *interprètes*, at either commissioned or noncommissioned rank. First of all, most *indigènes* did not know French well enough to translate orders from French to their own language and pass this information on to their comrades. Nurses and administrative personnel (*commis et ouvriers d'administration*, or COA) were the main exception. Many of these men attained positions as COA precisely because they already possessed a relatively elevated level of education and training, and further specialized instruction in the army could only improve their proficiency in French.[31] In other units, some *indigènes* had learned enough French to gain promotion to a noncommissioned rank, and these men were in fact the principal, if largely informal, interpreters in most indigenous units. Yet an incomplete understanding of French and mistrust on the part of their white superiors often hampered their service in this capacity.

This mistrust arose out of two related concerns: the distinctive nature of interpreters' wide-ranging duties, and the presumed inability of *indigènes,* even if they spoke French, to perform these duties. The role of interpreters among *troupes indigènes* went far beyond mere translation and facilitation of communication. In fact, this fundamental role often seemed subordinate to the more important function of carrying out surveillance and dispensing propaganda. *Officiers interprètes'* primary function was policing language as a means of control. Concern over the inadequacy of interpreters stationed at divisional headquarters stemmed from the fear that these interpreters would be too far away from their men to exercise effective "moral action," a term used to describe moral guidance and the preservation of French authority through propaganda, as well as work intended to maintain good morale in the ranks. Reforms attributing one interpreter to each regiment had the most positive effect on the morale of *indigènes,* because these officers headed *sections des œuvres morales* that organized social and religious life.[32]

North African troops appear to have received much greater attention from interpreters than did soldiers from other areas of the French empire. In May 1917, an *officier interprète* voiced a concern that not all hospitals separated North Africans from West Africans. He believed that West African soldiers might become jealous and resentful when they observed the "special considerations" North Africans received, among them "frequent visits from an *officier interprète* inquiring after their needs, recording and passing on their complaints."[33] North Africans' religious and cultural identity was, of course, the reason they received more attention from interpreters concerned about their material and moral well-being than did West Africans (or Indochinese or Madagascans, for that matter).[34] Even before the Ottoman empire formally entered the war as an enemy of France at the end of October 1914, the Ottoman government's sympathies were clear and were a cause for concern among the nations of the Triple Entente. France, with so many Muslim soldiers fighting under its flag, was in an especially awkward position, asking these men to fight against the allies of the Ottoman empire, whose sultan was simultaneously the caliph of the Islamic Umma, or global community of all Muslims.[35] Morale among Algerians, Tunisians, and Moroccans was thus a particular preoccupation of the French authorities, and interpreters were assigned to ensure the continued loyalty of France's Muslim soldiers (though many West Africans were also Muslims, they lacked the historical and cultural ties that linked North Africa to the Ottoman empire).

On 23 November 1914, three weeks after war officially began between the Ottoman empire and the nations of the Triple Entente, the French Ministry of War issued a confidential instruction outlining the importance of the propaganda role that interpreters would play in units containing North African soldiers. The directive began by outlining the ways in which interpreters were to sustain morale:

> They must therefore maintain constant and close contact with these troops, from the officer to the simple soldier, join daily in their conversations and, without interfering in purely military questions, be attentive to their needs, not hesitate to inform the competent authority [about those needs], help them with advice, speak to them of their country and keep them up to date about what is happening there, in a word show them that in France they are neither isolated, nor, even less, abandoned.[36]

Interpreters were also to mention often the loyal attitude demonstrated by the bey of Tunis, the sultan of Morocco and the religious confraternities of

Algeria; to explain that the Ottoman empire's alliance with the Germans was contrary to the interests of Islam; and to carry out a "discrete but active surveillance" of the soldiers' mail. This last function was particularly important. The Ministry of War reminded the *officiers interprètes* that they were called "to contribute, to the greatest extent, to assuring for us the loyalty of our indigenous soldiers and of their correspondents in North Africa."[37] This censorship could often be even more intrusive and direct than a simple reading of soldiers' mail. A September 1915 instruction on this issue noted that indigenous soldiers were often illiterate, so they prevailed upon others to write letters home for them. Since such third parties might be suspect in the eyes of the French authorities, the interpreters were advised to make themselves available to write letters for the soldiers. The *officier interprète* would thus be in a position to make sure that *indigènes* sent home news that was "reassuring, from a general point of view as from a personal point of view" and to suggest that the letter writer use "expressions likely to serve our cause."[38]

Instructions to interpreters emphasized the importance of their task in light of the Ottoman declaration of holy war, which sought to rally all Muslims against the Triple Entente, and attempts by the Germans to provoke rebellion among the populations of North Africa and desertion among the North African soldiers fighting in France.[39] The situation became even more delicate when Britain and France invaded Turkey in the spring of 1915. The minister of war feared that news of the invasion might provoke resentment and Muslim solidarity, so on 12 March, the ministry drew up a document outlining the arguments interpreters were to use when questioned by Muslim soldiers about the actions and motives of the Entente. The text stressed the subjugation of the Ottoman government to the "criminal aspirations" of the Germans; professed the enduring friendship that France felt for the people of Turkey, who had been so disastrously and unwillingly led into war by their unscrupulous government; and challenged the legitimacy of the declaration of holy war.[40] Other similar instructions ordered interpreters to emphasize that the Young Turk government in Istanbul had "no regard for the interests of Islam," and that the deliverance of the Turkish people from the dominance of Germany (and this was precisely the aim of the Entente) would contribute "to the salvation of Islam."[41]

Clearly, the tasks of interpreters went far beyond mere communication and translation, and their propaganda role continued to be of the highest importance as long as the Ottoman empire remained in the war. When, in 1916, the sharif of Mecca declared his open opposition to the Ottomans and their identification of the interests of Islam with those of Germany, the Ministry of War instructed *officiers interprètes* to make much of these events in the Middle East in their conversations with Muslim soldiers.[42] Later, in 1917, interpreters were to publicize the sharif's criticism of the Turks for desecrating the tomb of Muhammad at Medina, and to contrast this with the respectful attitude toward Muslim holy places displayed by France's British allies when they occupied Baghdad.[43]

Interpreters also sustained morale in ways other than spreading official propaganda. They organized "Moorish cafés" (i.e., in the style common in North Africa, serving mint tea and other drinks popular with North Africans), with diversions such as lotteries, dominos, and card games, in order to ease the soldiers' disorientation and homesickness.[44] Perhaps the most important arenas in which the interpreters acted were hospitals, where they served as essential intermediaries between medical staff and patients ignorant of French. In fact, the attribution of interpreters was most systematic in hospitals, and it was there that *indigènes* were most likely to have significant interaction with these officers. The *officier interprète* who worried that West African soldiers would become jealous of their North African comrades because of the special attention Muslims received from interpreters may have had reason to fear such resentment. In a December 1914 meeting of the Interministerial Commission on Muslim Affairs (Commission interministérielle des affaires musulmanes, or CIAM), Colonel Hamelin, representing the Ministry of War, assured his colleagues that *officiers interprètes* visited the wounded daily and took great care to facilitate the practice of Muslim religious observances.[45]

It is not at all clear that other *troupes indigènes* benefited from such conscientious attention. Nonetheless, visits from *officiers interprètes* were probably a genuine relief to the soldiers who received them. Being wounded was bad enough in itself, and a stay in a hospital could be quite confusing and frightening for *indigènes*. One member of the staff at the Scottish Women's Hospital at Royaumont observed that for wounded West African and North African soldiers, "the agony of their wounds was as nothing to the terror of their minds when they realized that a visit to the operating theatre often meant the loss of a mangled or gangrenous limb." Ignorance of French only accentuated the fear: "They spoke only a few words of pigeon [sic] French, and the horrible legend spread among them that the first visit to the theatre meant incisions—mere senseless slashings of the surgeon's knife, to their unsophisticated intelligences; the second, amputation; and the third the slitting of their throats. It was days before the terror subsided."[46] In French hospitals, interpreters often intervened to alleviate these kinds of fears. The French authorities explicitly instructed *officiers interprètes* attached to hospitals, not only to act as intermediaries between the *indigènes* and their doctors and to work to boost the soldiers' morale, but also to "bring an end to the resistance that, in their ignorance, the Muslims put up, in general, to surgical operations."[47]

Despite the authorities' concerns about the suitability of colonial subjects to carry out these and other delicate tasks related to "moral influence," *indigènes* sometimes acted as interpreters. This was often the case on a more or less informal basis, when men whose French was a little better than that of their comrades served to relay orders between French officers and their men, but *indigènes* also could fill the formal post of *interprète indigène*. Both arrangements had clear advantages, because it was often difficult to find qualified French candidates who could speak and read even one of the various languages spoken among the *troupes indigènes*. As interpreters often helped write letters for the soldiers, writing was also a desired skill, and even a French interpreter's expert technical knowledge of the language in question was not always adequate. This became apparent when in October 1914, Resident-General Lyautey wrote from Morocco to the minister of foreign affairs to express his appreciation of the efforts that interpreters had made to send postcards from Moroccan soldiers to their families. Despite the value of such initiatives, though, he wrote that it would be a good idea to employ interpreters who knew "colloquial Arabic," because letters written by interpreters were often "written with terms and phrases that are not customary among the Muslims of Algeria or Morocco." In this same spirit, Resident-General Alapetite wrote from Tunisia at about the same time that families would find such postcards more convincing if they actually carried the signature of the soldier.[48]

Some *indigènes* did in fact serve as interpreters, helping to mitigate such problems, though fairly few colonial subjects served formally in this capacity. Not only was finding linguistically qualified candidates difficult but, more important for French authorities, *indigènes* lacked the "moral" qualifications necessary for the role. Most French officers regarded the job of interpreter as beyond the capabilities of *indigènes,* and a rare report by one *interprète indigène* only emphasized the difficulty the army had finding acceptable candidates. Soulah Mohammed was university-educated, an exceedingly unusual circumstance among colonial subjects, and his report on

"Our [North] African Troops and Germany" makes clear his high level of assimilation to French culture, the values of which he seems to have shared fairly completely. Even so, he was not an *officier interprète*, but a *sergent interprète auxiliaire*, a title that emphasized the exceptional and subordinate nature of his position.[49] In reality, this was only logical, given the propaganda role assigned to interpreters. As the High Command noted in July 1918, West Africans could not translate the "general notions" expressed by French officers "likely to act upon the morale of the *indigènes*." The men the army was looking for were "reliable interpreters, with a well-developed general culture and of a proven moral worth," and these were difficult, often impossible, to find.[50]

The same was true in North African units, where officers considered propaganda and moral influence much more critical. For instance, religious or political conviction, or social convention, would probably have prevented an indigenous interpreter from giving the official French version of recent events concerning the sharif of Mecca to an imam, then watching over him as he gave a speech based upon it to the troops, as Officier interprète Mercier did at a hospital in Aix-en-Province in May 1917.[51] Indeed, the Ministry of War directed that interpreters keep imams under "discreet surveillance."[52]

These tasks, and related ones, such as choosing acceptable candidates to travel home to North Africa for a short period of leave before helping to staff and train units of new recruits, called upon interpreters to exercise moral influence upon and judgment over other soldiers, which the French did not feel *indigènes* could do.[53] And it went without saying, no doubt, that the French authorities could not expect indigenous interpreters to inform female nurses of the "quite special mentality" of North African soldiers, putting the nurses on guard against problems that could result from being too friendly or too intimate with their Muslim patients, as the Service de santé militaire (Military Medical Service) directed French *officiers interprètes* to do in 1915.[54]

French officers' racial prejudices frequently prevented *indigènes* from acting as interpreters, but certain inescapable realities also rendered these men unsuitable to serve as intermediaries between their comrades and the French officer corps. As one French officer noted, many West African non-commissioned officers did not know French well enough to relay orders accurately to their men.[55] Moreover, not all members of the same unit spoke the same language, because there were often several different dialects or languages even within the same colony. The multitude of tongues spoken in

West Africa, for example, virtually ensured that no interpreter could communicate with all the West African soldiers in larger units. There were other, less obvious problems as well. Interpreters, like other officers, were supposed to possess and inspire a spirit of calm self-sacrifice and stoic solidity, innate qualities that the *indigènes* allegedly lacked and that the current war demanded. As Minister of the Colonies André Maginot, who had served as a combat soldier earlier in the war, asserted in 1917, *indigènes* lacked the "notion of moral duty" necessary for a full commitment to the French cause.[56] This supposed lack of a sense of moral duty often precluded *indigènes* from becoming interpreters. Of course, this same logic often prevented *indigènes* from becoming field officers, which would have helped solve language problems and reduced the need for interpreters.

To some extent, claims that *indigènes* lacked the necessary elevated intellectual, emotional, and moral qualities rested on a pragmatic foundation: one could not expect men from hundreds or even thousands of miles away to feel that they were defending their homes and families by fighting on the Western Front, despite the claims of republican colonial ideology that *indigènes* fought alongside native Frenchmen for a common *patrie*. Yet assertions about the lack of an innate sense of patriotism and commitment on the part of *indigènes* also stemmed from racist assumptions about nonwhite soldiers. In 1918, the army advised officers serving in West African units to accompany all verbal instructions with material demonstrations, to be sure the African soldier understood completely, and to "take carefully into account his pride and his mentality." The French officer could not completely trust an *indigène* to explain instructions to his fellow soldiers: "Very proud to be an interpreter, allied thus to the authority of the white, he gloats over his comrades and if one is not constantly on guard, for the smallest things, he will translate or say anything." The instructions warned especially about having orders or questions relayed through an interpreter, recommending that officers always confirm that both interpreters and soldiers understood everything, lest the interpreter convey what he thought the commander wanted rather than what the officer actually said.[57] The problem here, according to the army, was clearly not only ignorance, but mental and emotional inadequacy stemming from African interpreters' race.

French authorities believed overdeveloped "pride" and a distinctive "mentality" rendered North Africans unreliable as interpreters as well. In 1917, the Ministry of War outlined the principal duties of interpreters serving with North Africans. Interpreters were to "facilitate relations between our North African subjects and the French administration; and to guide them in their present participation in our national life, the complexity of which could disconcert their primitive mentality."[58] The practical and objectively justifiable condition that interpreters be familiar with and able to negotiate the administrative complexities of life in France was allied to the assertion that interpreters be able to help mitigate the problems that *indigènes'* innate "primitive mentality" caused. It followed necessarily from this that the interpreter be French, because no matter how well an indigenous interpreter spoke French, or even how well he understood the complexities of French life, he still shared the "primitive mentality" of his fellow *indigènes*. Distrust of this mentality was a strong element in shaping the view that *indigènes* were unsuitable as intermediaries between French officers and their men. One report on North African officers argued that indigenous lieutenants were superfluous when the French captain of the company spoke Arabic, and even worse when the captain did not, because in that case "the French officer is 'in the hand' of the *indigène*, whose hidden influence can be felt over the company, sometimes to the detriment of discipline, [and] in any case, without possible supervision."[59] To prevent such a state of affairs, and to address the linguistic problem among *troupes indigènes* more squarely, the ideal approach to the army's linguistic problem was to have *indigènes* learn French. Yet moves in this direction were equally fraught with problems.

## Learning French

Aside from the use of interpreters, a second way the French Army attempted to alleviate linguistic difficulties in indigenous units was to introduce French instruction. As the head of the Mission laïque pointed out to Clemenceau in 1918, such instruction would render the use of interpreters unnecessary. Beyond this and other practical benefits—increased efficiency in transmitting orders, improved and more rapid instruction, fewer misunderstandings—many observers added important political, ideological, or moral reasons for the teaching and use of French in these units. In the text of a legislative proposal it submitted to the Chamber of Deputies in June 1915, the government argued that West African recruits from the Four Communes of Senegal should not be allowed to enter units of the regular French Army unless they knew French, despite Blaise Diagne's attempts to have all *originaires* enrolled in the metropolitan army by virtue of their status as electors. These men, the government asserted, were not only ignorant of the French language, but had retained the "the dress, the customs, and the mentality" of Africans. They would have to be instructed in Wolof (the dominant language in the Four Communes), and their presence would disturb the efficient training and functioning of the French units. That the proposal envisioned the incorporation of these West Africans into white units only once they had learned French demonstrated the government's faith in the assimilating power of knowledge of the French language, as well as of French military instruction. Learning French would render West Africans easier to instruct and would begin to change their "mentality."[60] The same was true of Algerians, according to Governor-general Lutaud. Europeans needed to be on their guard against "sudden eruptions of Muslim fanaticism and nationalism." Only when French instruction was widespread, "civilization leading to a more complete fusion of aspirations and a coming together of ideals," would the danger subside.[61]

As the spread of French culture, and of the French language in particular, was a principal pillar of republican colonial ideology in France, it was ironic that French authorities often denigrated those *indigènes* who knew French. One military official argued that it was generally a bad idea to recruit indigenous corporals from among those who spoke French well, because these French-speakers were often politically unreliable city-dwellers.[62] In reality, though, it was not just members of an unstable urban proletariat who caused the most trouble for French authorities, but a well-educated and politically conscious younger generation of colonial subjects. Assimilated, politically active *indigènes*—such as those belonging to political groups like the Young Algerians or Young Tunisians, or *évolués* in West Africa—had learned the French language and adopted much of French culture, and used their education and status as minor civil servants in the colonial administration to demand greater political rights.

This was clearly not what colonial officials had in mind when they envisioned a melding of interests between France and its newly French-educated colonial subjects. The Ministry of War demonstrated its preference for a pragmatic policy of association over an idealistic and uncertain assimilation when it opposed a plan to naturalize indigenous Algerian and Moroccan veterans partly on the grounds that those who knew French were generally "those who have the worst attitude and the least loyalty." These men were also parvenus, seeking social and political advancement outside the conventional hierarchies of their societies and through assimilation into the new colonial order. Promoting and rewarding them with citizenship would upset the traditional social order that French authorities exploited to rule the colonies. As the army had gone to great lengths to graft this social order onto its own military hierarchy, often promoting traditional chiefs and notables to positions of authority in their units, giving these upstart, assimilated *indigènes* enhanced status could harm morale in indigenous units.[63]

Still, the view of the French language as an indispensable civilizing tool, and the goal of assimilation, remained strong among some authorities. One political official cited the progress of the French language among men from the Kabyle region of Algeria and their corresponding "rapid evolution" as a reason to consider offering naturalization or political rights to those Kabyles who had served in France during the war.[64] In September 1918, a French censor noted that a Madagascan doctor had written in "very pure French" of his strong enmity toward the Germans, thus indicating that he was coming to share the values of the Frenchmen with whom he was serving. By linking the language the Madagascan used with the sentiments he expressed, the censor made a logical connection between these two indications of assimilation: a command of proper French and a correspondingly proper "mentality." The content of the letter and the way in which it was expressed were equally important.[65] Similarly the author of a postwar report on the experiences of Indochinese workers and soldiers who served in France noted that many of these men had learned new skills and had even been able to learn French. Admittedly, he wrote, this might mean that many would return home with new ideas, and perhaps would shed their traditional discipline and be less submissive in the future. Still, there was little to worry about, because these newly transformed men would recognize the beneficence of their "protective *patrie*," which had treated them so well while they were contributing to the national defense, and they would be valuable auxiliaries in France's civilizing mission in Indochina.[66] Learning French, for some, was linked with a greater understanding between France and its colonial subjects.

As the report made clear, there were opportunities for *indigènes* to learn French while they were serving in France. Because of their location in population centers, colonial workers often would have had more opportunities to take French classes offered by organizations like the Alliance française, though scant free time and segregated living and working environments would necessarily limit these opportunities. But some soldiers could also pursue language study when stationed behind the front, recovering from wounds in hospital, or spending time in camp. West African and some Indochinese troops, who spent the winter in camps in the south of France and in North Africa, probably had the greatest access of all combat troops to French instruction. Language classes were part of the daily routine for many in these camps, along with military training and work details. Other soldiers were able to study French while in hospital, and they eagerly took advantage of the opportunity. The hospital at the Jardin colonial, just outside Paris in the Bois de Vincennes, housed many wounded North Africans, and a French propaganda release claimed that "Muslims take a keen interest in" the French courses offered to convalescents, saying, "they compete with the passion, industry, and emulation that reign there." This interest proved "how many of our *tirailleurs* attach a high price to education." The release went on to note the value of this education to France: "And it is thus that [by their] knowing our language better, the sentiments that unite us will only be strengthened."[67]

Even if French officials made these claims for the purposes of propaganda, other sources confirmed the eagerness of hospitalized *indigènes* to make use of their convalescence to learn French. In March 1918, the minister of foreign affairs wrote to other cabinet officials and colonial administrators in North Africa about the success of efforts to "propagate our language" among North African troops. Civilian teachers had volunteered to teach courses in hospitals, and the foreign minister urged his colleague at the Ministry of War to continue and expand the efforts, remarking, "The interest that we have in teaching our language to our African subjects is too obvious for it to be necessary to insist upon the importance of opening French classes in all health facilities specially reserved for *tirailleurs,* as well as in their transit camps in Aix, Arles, and Alais." For his part, the minister of public instruction concurred on the importance of these courses and called the instruction an "eminently patriotic task."[68] Reports from the teachers involved confirmed the minister's claim that many *tirailleurs* "have demonstrated a truly good will to learn French." One instructor reported that his students became dissatisfied with the class time allotted to them at night and requested exercises to do in the hospital during the day, while another wrote that his students were "very industrious, very attentive" and learned a great deal. A Tunisian sergeant who had begun with only the most rudimentary knowledge of the French alphabet was soon able to read any book he liked. The teacher declared that the soldier's reading ability would soon be perfected, and his writing was already fairly good.[69]

Indochinese soldiers were no less enthusiastic about opportunities to learn French. Frenchwomen who volunteered to correspond with soldiers at the front, sending them packages of food and clothing, and providing them with friendship were called *marraines de guerre* (literally, "war godmothers"), and one report remarked that for front-line Indochinese soldiers, the Alliance française was their *marraine*. The Paris chapter organized French lessons, social gatherings, and football matches for troops on leave or stationed in Paris, and the Alliance sent textbooks and paper, along with milk and chocolate, to Indochinese troops serving in Greece with the Armée d'Orient.[70] Such efforts inspired one soldier to write home about the warm welcome he received at the Alliance, expressing the wish that he could continue his studies there, despite the expense of Paris.[71]

One *interprète indigène*, a corporal in the cavalry named Le Van Nghiep, was so proud of his achievements, which included placing second out of sixty candidates in the exam for an elementary certificate in French, that he wrote to a friend in Hanoi and asked him to have an article about these successes printed in a local paper, along with his picture. As encouraging as such enthusiasm was, the corporal's behavior pointed to the possible dangers some saw in overeducating colonial subjects. The censor dryly noted that Nghiep was pushing his studies "rather far," and that his "modesty is fading."[72] At least two other Indochinese corporals, in separate units, knew enough French to write letters home for other members of their units and used this ability to extract money from their comrades.[73] This caused fierce resentment, and it is not unlikely that men in these units would have been particularly enthusiastic about learning French for themselves, if only so as not to have to pay.

Eagerness to learn French and pride in having begun to master the language was not limited to Indochinese soldiers. Although the censor noted that many of the letters Madagascan soldiers sent home were written in a French that he characterized as "most often very clumsy or even absolutely deformed," some were so proud to use the language that they claimed no longer to know their mother tongue. Thus, Benoit, of the 18th Madagascan Battalion, sent to his family a long letter written in a French that was "more than rudimentary," to which he added the following note to his wife: "You will request that the schoolteacher translate this letter for you; I no longer know Malagasy."[74] As Frantz Fanon would later note, this was a not uncommon attitude for colonial subjects to take after spending time in the mother country: "he answers only in French, and often he no longer understands Creole . . . since the Negro is appraised in terms of the extent of his assimilation, it is also understandable why the newcomer expresses himself only in French. It is because he wants to emphasize the rupture that has now occurred.

He is incarnating a new type of man."[75] Some *troupes indigènes* realized that knowledge of French was useful for interacting socially with native French people. Rakoto Tokalala informed a friend back in Madagascar that in France, "the biggest oafs have at least four women," and that Madagascans "who know French and have good manners are even more sought after."[76]

Many *indigènes* sought practical benefits from learning French, from increased opportunities for advancement in the French Army to success with Frenchwomen or simply acceptance into French society, which was what so gratified Khamaci Mohamed, a Tunisian soldier recovering in a hospital at Troyes. Khamaci wrote to a friend in Tunis that he had recently received an invitation from a French friend to his parents' house for dinner. After the meal, listening to singing and music until midnight, it became clear that "[e]veryone takes me for a Frenchman and is astonished to learn that I am an Arab . . . they think that I know their language better than they themselves." He wrote the letter for his Tunisian friend in Arabic, in the middle of the French family's drawing room. His knowledge of both languages further surprised his hosts, and he instructed his friend to inform his mother "that I would be better off nowhere else than here, that I am considered as a true child of the family."[77]

Language was not only a passport to acceptance into French society, but also a means of advancing in colonial society once the soldiers returned home. Many looked forward to the advantages that new skills learned in the army and in France, including knowledge of the French language, and their status as veterans would give them when they reentered civilian life. For some, it took exposure to life in France to be able finally to recognize the fundamental and inescapable reality of life under their French colonial masters. As Bang, an Indochinese soldier stationed in France, put it in a letter to his wife: "It's very good that our son is going to school, but tell him to learn French if he does not want to remain an ignoramus all his life. I myself spent years learning Vietnamese, and it has been of no use to me."[78] The dominance of French culture, expressed in the French language, was as real as colonial political supremacy. The indispensable key to civilization and advancement was a knowledge of French, not the indigenous language.

## West Africans and the Langue-tirailleur

Given the importance of learning French both to military and political authorities and to the *indigènes* themselves, it is not surprising that the army incorporated some language instruction into the basic training of *troupes indigènes*. Though the teaching and use of French was clearly important in all units of *troupes indigènes*, French authorities focused a great deal of their efforts to teach French on West African soldiers. This was because so many West Africans served in combat units (rather than labor battalions), where language barriers and misunderstandings could be most dangerous or even fatal, and because the vast majority of soldiers from France's West African colonies lacked formal instruction, especially in French—in 1913, less than 1 percent of school-age children in the AOF were enrolled in French schools.[79] It is true that North Africans were just as likely to serve in combat as their West African counterparts, and that most Algerians, Moroccans and Tunisians also lacked formal instruction in French. Yet the most numerous North African soldiers, those from Algeria, had experienced French rule for a comparatively long time (since 1830) and had lived in close proximity to a large French-speaking population. The service of white Algerian settlers in the ranks and the experience of day-to-day contacts between French people and Algerians had contributed to at least some linguistic understanding between French and Arabic speakers.[80] Moreover, the majority of North Africans spoke a common language, Arabic, that some French officers knew, or at least could learn.

This was not true in the vast, diverse, and populous territories of West Africa, where colonial penetration had not made the deep impression for which administrators consistently hoped. Though perfect linguistic unity did not exist among soldiers from any of the colonies, the situation among West Africans was most complex, because of the existence of dozens of different dialects. While a European officer who spoke a little Arabic could find a way to communicate with most of his North African troops, no European, even with extensive linguistic training and experience in Africa, could speak the languages of all West African troops, and even many of the men themselves could not understand each other. In this situation, a common language was essential. Over the last decades of the nineteenth century and the first years of the twentieth, the number of West Africans serving in the French military was fairly low, and most of these men spoke either Wolof or Bambara, keeping linguistic difficulties to a minimum. Before the war, Charles Mangin had described Bambara as the "military language" of French West Africa. But with the expansion of recruitment in 1912, and then its acceleration after war broke out in 1914, many men came into the ranks who spoke neither Bambara nor Wolof, in addition to being ignorant of French.[81] With the dramatic expansion of the *force noire* and the beginning of a large-scale, modern war in Europe, communication became even more important. At the same time, the number of European officers with at least some knowledge of African languages decreased proportionally—both because of the larger number of *tirailleurs,* necessitating more officers to staff the new units, and because experienced officers were being killed in battle at an alarming rate. Efforts to teach French to the *tirailleurs* thus intensified.

The 1916 publication of a 35-page manual for teaching French to West African soldiers is particularly revealing of the intertwining of racial and linguistic concerns among the military hierarchy. The anonymous author (or authors) of *Le français tel que le parlent nos tirailleurs sénégalais* (The French Our *Tirailleurs Sénégalais* Speak) addressed an audience of commissioned and noncommissioned officers serving in West African units, particularly NCOs who would undertake the initial training of new recruits.[82] The manual provides a striking example of the blending of a pragmatic approach to the military problem of effective communication with racist preconceptions about the inability of *indigènes* to learn proper French. The simplified and purely utilitarian form of communication that resulted both reflected and reinforced racial stereotypes.

The manual begins by setting forth the two most important rules in teaching French to the *tirailleurs.* First, "Always refer to the same object or express the same idea by the same word"; and, second, "Always give the French sentence the very simple form that the sentence has in all the primitive dialects of our West Africa."[83] These rules betrayed both subtle and not-so-subtle racialist prejudices. The first was predicated upon the unspoken assumption that the soldiers' limited minds would be unable to grasp variations in vocabulary, while the second rule clearly assumed the essential intellectual simplicity of West Africans, whose languages were correspondingly "primitive." The brochure reinforced the importance of the first rule by pointing out to the reader "the words and expressions that common usage has established because of their ease of pronunciation and that it would be advantageous to adopt definitively, to the exclusion of other words or expressions having the same meaning."[84] In other words, the pamphlet advocated teaching West Africans a simplified form of French that would serve the immediate needs of the military.

The first part of *Le français . . .* is devoted to outlining the specificities of this simplified grammar. The author describes this process in a striking metaphor: the altered rules of grammar will serve to create the "mold" in which the French sentence is to be "cast" in order to render it intelligible to *tirailleurs* who have begun to learn a few words of French.[85] The rules fall under ten headings, which denote various elements of grammar. First, the pamphlet insists upon the suppression of articles before nouns, which simply confuse men used to speaking African languages that do not use articles. The only exception to this rule was for certain words that *tirailleurs* learned along with the article, such as parts of the body; they then regarded the article and the word together as one word. Thus, *tête* (head) became *latête* (thehead).[86] Gender was reduced to the masculine for all inanimate objects—*ma maison* became *mon case*. The use of *case* (hut) for *maison* (house) also indicates the dual nature of such simplified language instruction. Perhaps *case* was a more familiar term for *tirailleurs,* many of whom lived in rural areas, but such a substitution may also have implied a subtle stereotype by betraying a belief that *maison* was a concept more suited to civilized white Frenchmen than to primitive black Africans. In any case, the normally feminine noun *case* now took the masculine possessive adjective *mon.* For feminine animate beings, whose gender was not so easily disregarded, soldiers and officers would add the word *femme* (woman) to the noun. As for number, words would always be in the singular. To indicate many or only a few, one would add *trop* (too many) or *peu* (not many), incorrectly pronounced as *trope* and *pé,* but in the interests of accuracy, especially important for practical reasons in the military, commanders would encourage soldiers to use specific numbers as often as possible.

The manual claimed that its recommended rules for qualifying adjectives were not arbitrary, because in Bambara and other West African dialects, qualifying adjectives were formed with the equivalent of the verb *être* (to be), so the same approach in forming French adjectives would facilitate quick apprehension by the *tirailleurs.* Demonstrative adjectives were reduced to *ça* (that), eliminating the need to distinguish number or gender with *ce, cet, cette, ces,* and so forth, or the more descriptive *y en a là* (essentially, "that there"). The soldiers would use possessive adjectives only in the masculine, and only to indicate *mon* (my), and less frequently *ton* (your). Otherwise, they would employ *pour* (for), as in *case pour lui/nous/eux* (hut for him/us/them). Possessive pronouns also employed *pour,* as *le mien* (mine) became *ça y en a pour moi* (that there for me), while personal pronouns were also simplified, as *je* (I) became *moi* (me), *tu* (you) became *toi* (a distinction not operative in English), *il/elle/on* (he/she/it) became *lui* (him/her/it), and *ils/elles* (masculine and feminine for "they") became *eux* (masculine for "them," even for the feminine, which ought to have been *elles*). As for verbs, the foundation of West Africans' vocabulary was *y'a* (an abbreviated version of *il y'a*, "there is"), used in place of the verb *être:* "Je suis malade" (I am sick) became "Moi y'a maladi" (Me [there] is sick; translation into English of constructions using *y'a* are inexact and fail to convey how truly awkward such phrasing was). They would also employ *y en a* when the verb *être* was preceded by *que* or *qui* ("that" or "who"), and for qualifying adjectives. For example, "Le tirailleur malade [le tirailleur qui est malade] est arrivé" (The sick *tirailleur* [the *tirailleur* who is sick] has arrived) became "Tirailleur y en a maladi y'a venir" (Tirailleur that there is sick is come). The expressions "Y'a bon" ("There is good" or "Is good") or "Y'a pas bon" (Is no good) became emblematic of the *tirailleurs sénégalais* among the wider French public, as the popular "Y'a bon!" slogan of Banania shows. *Gagner* ("to gain," "to earn," or "to win") replaced the second most important verb in French vocabulary, *avoir* (to have). Thus, "Moi y'a gagné cheval" (Me got horse) would mean "J'ai reçu / on m'a donné / j'ai un cheval" (I have received / have been given / have a horse). For other verbs, West Africans would dispense with conjugation, using the infinitive for the present indicative.

Though General Mangin claimed elsewhere that the teaching methods that officers used to teach simplified French to West Africans "do not necessitate the knowledge of the various idioms of West Africa,"[87] *Le français . . .* informed its readers that in some ways, the modifications to French grammar were explicitly designed to render the rules of French more like those of West African languages, particularly Bambara, which many *tirailleurs sénégalais* spoke. This was particularly apparent in the rules for certain parts of speech. Since prepositions and conjunctions were often rare in West African dialects, the *langue-tirailleur* (*tirailleur*-language) did not make use of them either. Speakers would indicate possession merely by juxtaposing the noun and its possessor in reverse order from correct French usage, dispensing with *de, du* (of, of the), and so on: *le fusil du soldat* (the soldier's rifle) thus became *soldassi marfa*. The modification of the vocabulary itself, evident here, was the result of incorporating West African forms and words into the military argot, and the reversal of word order was to accommodate the order common in West African languages. Rather than have the *tirailleurs* make the mental effort to invert the words each time they heard them, French officers would alter their own language to make themselves more readily understood. This clearly had advantages when one wanted to teach French to soldiers quickly, and to avoid delays or misunderstandings during either exercises or combat, but also addressed the supposed intellectual inferiority of West Africans.

This same approach characterized syntax. Since "[a]ll the languages of the AOF have great simplicity with regard to syntax," their simple and straightforward progression—subject, verb, predicate, with no inversion—would be preserved, along with the suppression of articles and prepositions. This was "the primitive sentence," which was in fact the "the very simple mold" into which the thought of the *tirailleur* was "poured."[88] Yet this striving after familiarity and simplicity often led to complications, at least from the point of view of the native French speaker. When asking a question of a soldier, commanders were not to resort to the common French technique of inversion of the subject and verb. Thus, "As-tu mangé le riz?" (Have you eaten the rice?) had to be phrased "Toi y'a mangé riz?" (You is eaten rice?), with the interrogative implied only by inflection of the tone of voice. This rule was perhaps not too difficult to remember, but the same probably could not be said of the fundamentally important and seemingly straightforward use of *oui* and *non*. For questions phrased in the affirmative, the use of "yes" and "no" conformed to the same rules as in normal French. To the question "Toi y en a gagné fusil?" (You there got a rifle?), the soldier would reply "Oui" or "Non," according to whether or not he in fact had a rifle. But for questions asked in the negative form, the rules of French were reversed. In reply to the question "Toi y en a pas gagné fusil?" (You there not got a rifle?), "Oui" meant that the soldier did not have a rifle, while "Non" meant that he in fact did have one. The brochure recommended that officers serving with West Africans completely avoid phrasing their questions in the negative form, but this cannot have been easy or automatic for many Frenchmen, especially those who had only recently joined their units or who had served there for only a short time. The potential here for confusion, or outright bewilderment, is obvious.

The two guiding principles of language instruction were to be simplicity and the avoidance of a confusing amount of variety in vocabulary. To observe this second imperative of reducing as much as possible the number of words used, and avoiding the use of different words to refer to the same idea, *Le français . . .* provides several helpful examples. For instance, the concept embodied in the noun *rapidité* (speed) was expressed by the adverb *vite* (quickly), which was easier to pronounce. It followed from this that *vite* also replaced the adjective *rapide* (rapid) and the adverb *rapidement* (rapidly), while the concepts of *lent* (slow) and *lentement* (slowly) became *pas vite* (not quickly). One would also have to remember not to order West Africans to *accélérer* (speed up), but to *marcher plus vite* (march more quickly), and so on. In addition to choosing words that would be easier to pronounce for the soldiers themselves, their commanders were also to avoid using terms that sounded similar to others having different meanings.

The second part of the pamphlet provides specific examples of French sentences that might be needed in training a West African soldier, along with translations into language that he could understand, following the rules outlined in the first section. These translations provide the best evidence of the grammatical contortions that the *langue-tirailleur* required of its speakers. Every single translation into this pidgin French is longer than the original French instruction or command, and the correct French versions are more direct and less cumbersome. To be sure, the examples avoided a confusing variety of vocabulary and took a form that West Africans could easily understand, but this was probably because these forms were all West Africans had been taught. When outlining instructions for a soldier assigned to sentry duty, the French officer was not to say, "Elle doit voir et entendre tout" (He must see and hear everything), but, "Sentinelle y'a besoin faire manière mirer, lui y'a besoin faire manière entendé tout" (Sentry needs try hard to gaze, him needs try hard hear everything).[89] It is hard to see how this awkward substitution contributed to the ease and efficiency of command or instruction.

The manual concluded by emphasizing the importance of accompanying speech with gestures and actions to reinforce the meaning of unfamiliar terms, and offered a word of caution to white French officers in units of *tirailleurs sénégalais:* it was important not to transmit these grammatical rules to the men by way of their West African NCOs, because these NCOs had already distorted the French words when they themselves learned them, and "it would be deplorable to allow [this distortion] to become more pronounced by a succession of defective transmissions." Of course, the French that white officers were using and teaching was already quite deformed, and the author completed the irony by adding, "From distortion to distortion, one would quickly end up with absolutely incomprehensible terms."[90]

As anyone who has learned French as a second language can probably affirm, dispensing with pesky grammatical details such as gendered nouns, adjectival agreement, the finer points of pronunciation, and verb conjugation would seem a blessing and would make French a much less difficult language to learn. But learning such a deformed and simplistic form of pidgin language did not serve the soldiers well in their dealings with native French people, who found in the *tirailleurs'* speech both amusement and a confirmation of their ideas about Africans' intellectual inferiority. Officers taught soldiers a simplified version of French because of their supposedly limited mental capacity, and this caricature of proper French only served further to reinforce their reputation as savage, childlike innocents.

There are, however, indications that at least some French people realized how unfair to West Africans such a characterization was. A 1918 cartoon in the satirical newspaper *La Baïonette* depicted a bourgeois family addressing a West African soldier, caricatured with oversized lips and the distinctive uniform of the *tirailleurs sénégalais*. The father calls out to the soldier and compliments him exaggeratedly in the very fractured and incorrect (not to say nonsensical) French that *Le français . . .* advocated teaching to the *tirailleurs:* "Eh! bien, Bamboula: li brave poilu, macache bono; y'a bon!" (Well! Bamboula: zee brave *poilu*, not at all; is good!) In response, the *tirailleur* says, in perfectly correct French, "Excusez-moi, monsieur, mais je ne comprend que le français!" (I'm sorry sir, but I understand only French!).[91] Aside from expressing a critical view of the fractured French of the "*tirailleur*-language," the author of the cartoon no doubt wished to ridicule French people who could not conceive of a West African who could speak French well. The periodical *Annales coloniales* even noted that the brochure *Le français . . .* was more indicative of "Senegalese as the French speak it" than of how the *tirailleurs* spoke French.[92] Moreover, it is probably unlikely that all prospective officers in West African units memorized the grammatical rules outlined in the pamphlet, even if it did inform the approach that some of them took in speaking to their subordinates.

Still, it is clear from other sources that the kind of *langue-tirailleur* embodied in the pamphlet was widespread in units of West African soldiers, and that it shaped the way these men expressed themselves in French. Their expression "Y'a bon" did not become famous, as in the Banania advertising campaign, for no reason at all, and the teaching suggested in *Le français . . .* would only have reinforced this unorthodox mode of expression. In the memoir of Lucie Cousturier, a writer who lived near the camp at Fréjus in southern France where West Africans spent their winters, and who on her own initiative taught (proper) French to many soldiers during the war, most of the West African soldiers she meets speak the same kind of pidgin French described in the pamphlet.[93] Moreover, superior officers who led West African troops advocated teaching them this "simplified French." Mangin even remarked, "This instruction is given by the direct method (the Berlitz method)...," though it is not at all clear what instructors of French in Berlitz schools would have made of *Le français*....[94]

During 1918, the issue of language among the *tirailleurs sénégalais* gained renewed prominence for two reasons. First, Monsignor LeMaître, a Catholic missionary who had been active in West Africa, undertook an inspection mission of all West African battalions stationed in France, with instructions to report to Prime Minister and Minister of War Georges Clemenceau. Second, the great recruitment drive of 1917–18, the largest yet undertaken in West Africa, promised to bring even larger numbers of raw West African recruits to France, with corresponding linguistic difficulties. Both of these developments provided ample evidence that the kind of pidgin French described in *Le français*... was indeed widespread among the *tirailleurs sénégalais*.

LeMaître's mission provoked a great deal of discussion about language, because he cited the lack of interpreters to act as intermediaries between the soldiers and their French commanders as the major problem he found in West African units. His recommendation for the formation of a special corps of interpreters provoked great resistance among the officers who commanded West Africans and demonstrated the officers' commitment to maintaining the distinctive *langue-tirailleur*. "Because of the multiplicity of dialects spoken in the black battalions, the unity of language can be usefully and easily pursued only by the teaching of simplified French, already spoken by all the *gradés indigènes* and by a great number of *tirailleurs*," a top military aide to Clemenceau wrote, adding that the army would intensify efforts to teach this simplified French.[95] General Mangin himself noted that linguistic diversity among the *tirailleurs* necessitated the use of a common language for military purposes and argued that that common language could only be French. Moreover, the acquisition of French was more than just a military necessity. Mangin maintained that through the knowledge of French, "at first simplified," the young *tirailleur* would "succeed in drawing closer to us ... and in sharing all of our sentiments."[96]

Mangin's vision of the power of language to assimilate Africans closer to their colonial masters corresponded well with the French ideal of an imperial obligation to carry out a civilizing mission among savage peoples, but the reality was more prosaic. Most *tirailleurs* never had the opportunity to progress beyond the "simplified French" that constituted their preliminary language instruction in the army. Though one senior officer claimed that the soldiers learned the necessary vocabulary quickly and "themselves devise the pidgin [*petit-nègre*, literally, "little negro," which remains a synonym in French for pidgin and clearly betrays racial prejudice] language that they use with us and among themselves," it was clear that French officers helped create and perpetuate this pidgin language.[97]

In fact, the belief that Africans themselves developed this *petit-nègre* form of French because their primitive minds could not comprehend the complex, sublime, and sophisticated language of their colonial masters was in evidence well before the war. Thus, in a 1904 study of West African languages, the colonial administrator Maurice Delafosse asked how one could expect "that a black, whose language is of a rudimentary simplicity and of a nearly always absolute logic, assimilate himself rapidly to an idiom as refined and as illogical as ours?" Answering his own question, Delafosse claimed, "It is well and truly the black—or, more generally speaking, the primitive—who has forged the *petit-nègre*, by adopting French to his state of mind."[98]

Even the "logic" of African languages was evidence of their crude, child-like simplicity, while the "illogical" nature of French only served to prove that it and its speakers were more highly evolved and civilized. This was precisely the attitude that stimulated *Le français . . .* and was typical of the opinions French officers expressed when explaining the role of language in training *tirailleurs*. As one regimental commander put it, "For the Senegalese, in particular, good military training is all the more necessary because he is generally of a coarse and limited intelligence, acquiring a vocabulary sufficient for understanding what is expected of him only after long months, and, finally, one really must admit he is naturally clumsy."[99]

Attitudes like this were institutionalized, not only in the brochure *Le français . . .*, but also in other publications emanating directly from the High Command, such as the 1918 *Notice sur les Sénégalais et leur emploi au combat* (Notice on the Senegalese and Their Use in Combat), prepared for officers in West African units, which informed its readers that only "very simple, very common ideas" could be expressed in native African dialects, so one had to define French terms in ways that Africans could easily grasp. Above all, it was important to "materialize" instruction, always accompanying words with movements, demonstrations, and concrete examples, as if one were teaching a child. The reasons for this were explicit: "If the black is sensitive, proud, often intelligent, durable, always devoted, appreciating good treatment and praise, one must also know that he is lazy above anything a European can conceive of, even more from the intellectual point of view than the physical, and he will learn nothing unless constrained and forced by regular repetitions, which will create in him habits akin to instinct."[100] In fact, this stress on the dull, instinctual nature of Africans' intelligence seemed to evoke animals rather than children, or even human beings at all. On the whole, the pamphlet is a revealing example of the mix of pragmatism and racism that characterized the army's approach to teaching French to *tirailleurs sénégalais:* simplicity, repetition, and concrete examples served the need for quick and accurate instruction in the necessary tasks of military life, while the same attributes also addressed the supposed intellectual and racial inferiority of black Africans.

Of course, black Africans were not the only men to whom the French Army taught French. Nothing like *Le français* . . . existed for the instruction of other *troupes indigènes,* but there were other more or less systematic attempts to teach some French to *indigènes* in the army. These efforts echoed many of the same themes that guided French instruction in West African units, though without precisely the same emphases. In the spring of 1918, the Ministry of War gave its explicit support to the efforts of the Mission laïque to offer French courses to North Africans in hospitals and depots behind the front. As the head of the Service de santé noted in a letter instructing his subordinates to support these efforts, "Most North African soldiers have acquired, by a prolonged stay in the metropole, a practical use, definitely limited and incorrect but useful, of spoken French." He went on to explain that the courses would offer "methodical language exercises, from which all grammatical complications will be banished." Reading and writing exercises were to be "extremely simple, and aiming at immediately useful goals: writing letters, complete and correct addresses."[101] The "practical use, definitely limited and incorrect but useful" of French no doubt referred to a fractured French like the distinctive pidgin spoken among the West African soldiers, and the emphasis on expediency and utility was similar to the tone of *Le français.* . . . Even the political cartoons of the satirical newspaper *Le Canard Enchaîné* tended to conflate the *petit-nègre* spoken by West Africans with soldiers from other colonies, such as Morocco and Madagascar, putting the same kind of fractured French in all these men's mouths.[102] In the eyes of these cartoonists (who, despite antiracist and anticolonial convictions, still viewed the inhabitants of the colonies through a haze of stereotypes) and many other French observers, the pidgin language of all colonial subjects in uniform was of a piece, the best speech one could expect from limited, primitive intelligences.

Nonetheless, it is important to remember that military authorities had every reason to require that expediency govern language instruction provided to their soldiers. The exigencies of command and military life necessitated this approach, and even writing letters and addressing envelopes was important for sustaining the morale of men in the army and their families at home in the colonies. The Mission laïque, allied to the military for the purposes of teaching soldiers during the war, emphasized a utilitarian approach. This was even true of the instruction given to workers, whose needs were not as urgent as those who would have to follow orders under fire, and whose free time for learning French (though certainly not abundant) was potentially greater than that of soldiers. In a brief document that outlined the Mission's principal teaching methods in classes offered to North African workers, an official of the organization cautioned teachers: "Do not study grammar in itself, nor for itself; the exposition of the rules will be, for the most part, useless. The student can be led to use them without knowing them: the procedure will depend, above all, upon the culture and the intelligence of the audience; for most of them, it will suffice to give them the habits of language." Thus, teachers were not to confuse the simple minds of their students with the intricacies of the rules of grammar. The best they could do was to memorize the forms of the language, to develop a shallow and instinctive sense for the right words and syntax. As was the case with the army's training of West Africans, in which officers were to materialize the instruction of *indigènes* through frequent demonstrations, the Mission's teachers were to "put into action every new notion," and each lesson would begin by showing the students a concrete object and then naming it, before moving to more complex allocutions from this solid foundation. Vocabulary would focus on terms that would be immediately useful in the everyday life of the workers. Yet the Mission teachers' approach differed from the approach advocated for West Africans in *Le français* . . . in one important respect: sentences that the instructor taught were to be "simple, but correct."[103]

In this sense, North African workers (and it is not unlikely that North Africans in the army received similar training, because the Mission laïque also played a role in the instruction of these soldiers) were better served than West African soldiers, whose instruction was often deliberately incorrect. Part of the explanation no doubt lies in the independent status of the Mission, which did not face the same requirements as did army instructors, who had a great deal to accomplish in military training without also having to teach correct French grammar and vocabulary. The emphasis on simplicity and usefulness, as well as on rendering instruction in concrete terms, owed something to the time constraints under which everyone involved with the war effort in France labored, but it also stemmed from racial assumptions about the limited capacities of nonwhites. Moreover, dispensing with the rules of grammar was perhaps more characteristic of the training West African soldiers received because many French people regarded them as more "primitive" than their North African counterparts.

Unsurprisingly, colonial subjects resented these attitudes and the instruction that resulted from them, knowing how their imperfect speech set them apart, especially in a culture so proud of its language. As Frantz Fanon noted, it didn't take long for the colonial subject who came to France to understand the importance of mastering the language: "Yes, I must take great pains with my speech, because I shall be more or less judged by it. With great contempt they will say of me, 'He doesn't even know how to speak French.'"[104] West African soldiers found their experiences dealing with French people frustrating because of their linguistic disability. Taught a form of speech that only served to make them look and feel foolish in the eyes of their interlocutors, the *tirailleurs* were keenly aware of how their broken French marked them. Lucie Cousturier noted that the *tirailleurs* knew from their French listeners' laughter that their language caused them to look ridiculous: "'[I]t is French only for *tirailleurs*,' they recognize sadly." One even said, "[T]hese are words found by the Europeans to make asses of the Senegalese."[105] The awareness of their handicap made avid students out of the *tirailleurs*. When some West Africans had the opportunity to take French courses during a winter of factory labor in 1916–17, their commanders noted that they were "very assiduous" and demonstrated their aptitude for learning "rather quickly."[106] Lucie Cousturier soon found her French classes overflowing her small rooms, and her students showed a remarkable eagerness to learn and capacity for work.[107]

One historian has argued that the insufficient instruction "was intended to ensure" that the *tirailleurs'* grasp of the French language remained rudimentary, in order to inhibit contact between French civilians and West African soldiers, but it is more likely that racial preconceptions led military authorities to believe that West Africans were incapable of anything but *petit-nègre*.[108] And though women like Lucie Cousturier did help some *tirailleurs* to refine their French skills, and though the few soldiers who were destined to become NCOs or to handle specialized weapons did receive better language training within the army, instruction such as that exemplified by *Le français . . .* was, as Marc Michel has observed, "without doubt more a factor of 'subculture' than of acculturation."[109] When one *tirailleur* explained the lack of meaningful contact between the French populace and West Africans in part because "we did not speak a common language," he could just as likely have been referring to the difference between the pidgin French of the *tirailleurs* and proper French as to the difference between Bambara and French.[110]

Language policy vis-à-vis *troupes indigènes* in the French Army during the Great War combined elements of pragmatism, republican colonial ideology, and racial prejudices. The practical aspects of this policy were fundamental: officers had to meet the basic need of communication in order to carry out their duties and contribute to the war effort. A linguistic gulf separated most French officers from their men, because the majority of colonial subjects did not speak French, rendering training and communication on the battlefield difficult. The army intended *officiers interprètes* to fill this gap. Yet officials valued interpreters more for their propaganda and "moral" roles than for their translation of day-to-day communication between officers and men, indicating the importance of colonial politics in guiding linguistic policy.

Likewise, the practical necessity of facilitating communication in the ranks, combined with republican beliefs about the power of the French language to "civilize" colonial subjects and assimilate them to French culture, stimulated efforts to teach French to indigenous soldiers. Yet even republican beliefs were not strong enough to overcome racial attitudes that characterized nonwhite peoples as intellectually inferior to whites. A striking example of this was the effort to teach West African soldiers an incorrect and impoverished form of French that only served to maintain the distance between colonizers and colonized, not a form of the language that would "civilize" them, or lift them up to the cultural level of their French colonial masters. It was this "*tirailleur*-language," and not proper French, that served as the common language in West African units. Republican rhetoric identified language as a ladder to assimilation and acceptance. As Mangin put it, knowledge of French was to help the *tirailleur* "succeed in drawing closer to us . . . and in sharing all of our sentiments." Yet the *langue-tirailleur* that the army perpetuated did not perform this unifying function. Instead, it impeded the integration of *troupes indigènes* into the nation for which they were fighting.

Perhaps this should not really be surprising. Fanon noted that "to speak is to exist absolutely for the other," and for the colonized to speak in proper French to the colonizers would have forced an acknowledgment of coexistence within the French national community, an acknowledgment of the *troupes indigènes* as men fighting for the liberty of France on an equal basis with their white metropolitan comrades.[111] To be sure, military necessity forced a certain amount of expediency on official policy, and wartime was hardly the most propitious moment to undertake an idealistic crusade to teach the French language to soldiers needed at the front. Yet even before the war, colonial officials in West Africa, despite their claims to be using French as a civilizing and uplifting tool, sought primarily to render Africans "useful men" through language instruction that focused on practical, concrete, not to say mundane realities of everyday life. In other words, the goal was to make Africans practically useful and productive colonial subjects in the fields and in other economic enterprises that would benefit the metropole, not to transform them and then welcome them into the national community.[112] In this light, the (allegedly) utilitarian pidgin French described in the manual *Le français tel que le parlent nos tirailleurs sénégalais* was in a certain sense consistent with prewar official colonial policy. Perhaps equally consistent are contemporary French policies giving some support to immigrants' languages, not to give them a status alongside French, but to maintain "links with their original languages and cultures, in the expectation that they might return 'home.'"[113] French officials during the Great War expected *troupes indigènes* to return home and to subordinate status as colonial subjects outside the core body of the national community.

In the end, the poor French of *troupes indigènes* meant that they did not "exist absolutely" for most native French people. The soldiers themselves recognized this impediment for what it was, some clearly feeling their exclusion acutely. Religious beliefs among some of these soldiers were another such mark of difference and exclusion, at least in the view of French officials. In short, religious diversity seemed as much a problem as linguistic diversity. The Islamic beliefs of North Africans were a particular concern, and the next chapter examines the ways in which French authorities attempted to come to terms with religious diversity in the ranks.

# CHAPTER FIVE

# Islam in the French Army

I continue to observe the strict rules imposed upon us by our
holy religion, which is for me a source of internal joy and
resignation, during the sad days that we are in the process of
going through. Ah, "may we all make ardent vows that the
atrocious hostilities end soon."

       *—Djilani ben Smail, a Tunisian tirailleur, 1917*

. . . the Arabized *indigène* becomes more conscious of his Muslim mentality, and of the distance that separates him from us.

       *—Charles Lutaud, governor-general of Algeria, 1915*

As these statements make clear, *troupes indigènes* and French officials held
contrasting views about the implications and utility of religious beliefs, particularly those associated with Islam. For Muslim soldiers, their faith was "a
source of internal joy and resignation" in the midst of a terrible war in a
foreign land. For the authorities, this same faith raised Muslims' consciousness of the gulf that lay between colonized and colonizers, and as such, it
presented an obstacle, even a threat, to the goals of "civilizing" and obtaining cooperation from colonial subjects. Nonetheless, the soldiers and officials
did agree that religious belief was an important issue in the lives of *troupes
indigènes*. Though Islam was of primary concern to the army and the government, there were other faiths represented among the various groups that
came from the colonies to fight for France, from the animistic beliefs of
some West Africans to Catholicism and Buddhism among the Indochinese
and the Protestantism of many Madagascans. Given the importance of these

beliefs to many soldiers and to their overall morale, the French Army strove to accommodate religious differences and the desire for the observance of worship, burial rights, and holy days.

Yet despite the obvious importance of making efforts to accommodate all of the different beliefs of the soldiers, the beliefs of Muslims received the most attention. This was in large part because the only truly independent, politically and militarily powerful Muslim state in the world, the Ottoman empire, whose sultan claimed the titles of Caliph of Islam, Commander of the Faithful and Successor of the Prophet, was allied with Germany. The problem became more acute when France and Britain invaded Ottoman territory in the Dardanelles campaign of 1915. Political and military officials worried about the dependability and loyalty of their Muslim soldiers, who might balk at fighting directly against fellow Muslims, or even the Turks' German allies. It did not help matters that Germany and Turkey made explicit appeals to the religious solidarity of North Africans, encouraging disloyalty and even desertion. In the end, fears about the loyalty of France's Muslim soldiers were misplaced, because religious solidarity did not move many of them to overt acts of hostility against their colonial masters, but the possibility was never very far from the minds of French authorities.

Yet it was not just the Ottoman alliance with the Central Powers that raised anxieties about the use of Muslim soldiers in the French Army. Traditional views of Islam and its followers as hostile to "civilization," and specifically to the enlightenment that supposedly reigned in Europe, dominated thinking in many French intellectual and political circles. These long-standing prejudices and stereotypes shaped French attitudes toward their Muslim soldiers, influencing military policy and revealing an entrenched suspicion that Islam itself prevented North African soldiers from serving as reliable defenders of the French cause. These two concerns—that religious solidarity with the enemy would undermine the loyalty of Muslim soldiers, and that Islam created an unbridgeable gulf between its followers and France—became the primary focus of French policy with regard to religion among *troupes indigènes*, because many West Africans and virtually all North Africans were Muslims, constituting a significant majority of the men who came from the colonies to fight in Europe.[1]

Recently, historians have come to a greater realization of the importance of religion in shaping the understanding of events during and after the Great War, some pointing to religious belief, especially among soldiers, as a critical element in understanding the war and the societies that fought it.

If, as they argue, religious belief was both a reflection and a formative part of the *culture de guerre* of the Great War, then one must examine not only Christianity and its French, German, British, and other European adherents, but also the other faiths represented among non-European soldiers who fought for those belligerents.[2] The religious beliefs of the *troupes indigènes* also helped determine the *culture de guerre*, not just because these soldiers often viewed their experiences through the prism of their faith, but because French officials took these beliefs into consideration when forming policy.[3]

The largest issue French authorities had to confront concerning religion and *troupes indigènes* was how to reconcile the Islamic faith with service in the French Army. Long after the war, the arrival in France of millions of Muslim immigrants, many of them from the same former colonies that provided so many soldiers during the Great War, has transformed the issue into how to reconcile Islam with French citizenship and national identity.[4] Many French people, along with the French state, have had a notoriously difficult time integrating Islam and its followers into their society and their conceptions of national identity, but if the presence of millions of Muslim immigrants has posed the problem in a particularly dramatic fashion, it is certainly not new.[5]

French perceptions of Islam over several centuries set the stage for this cultural confrontation, but the presence of several hundred thousand Muslims in the French Army and on French soil during the Great War confronted France with dilemmas similar to those it faces today, though of course these dilemmas differed in certain respects from those posed by the presence of millions of permanent residents and citizens. It is undoubtedly a distortion to present Islam as a "problem" that the French people and their government must solve, but this is the way many in France have seen the issue, and because they have, an investigation of their perspectives is worthwhile.[6] French authorities certainly saw things this way when formulating policy toward Muslims in the army over eight decades ago.

## Madagascans, Indochinese, and West Africans

If North Africans and Islam were the primary concerns for French authorities during the war, they were not the only ones. In all cases, officials called for the military to be careful to respect the *indigènes*' "liberty of conscience."[7] Madagascans presented perhaps the least problem in this regard. Most Madagascan soldiers were Protestants—there had been many English,

Swedish, and Norwegian missionaries on the island for years—and nearly all of them were baptized and had Christian first names.[8] Though France was predominantly Catholic, the secular republic had little trouble meeting the religious needs of Protestant Madagascans, because a common Christian heritage made respecting burial customs and other rituals relatively easy. In fact, this may have been a factor in the largely benign view many French people took of the *tirailleurs malgaches*, especially in contrast to soldiers professing Muslim belief, or seemingly more "exotic" and "primitive" animistic beliefs. The letters of Madagascan soldiers often reveal strong spiritual sentiments. Numerous extracts from censors' reports contain references to God, and one censor noted that "religious sentiment is demonstrated in nearly every letter," often combined with patriotic sentiments. Statements such as the *tirailleur* Rakotofotsay's "Ask God to give victory soon to our mother France" could only flatter the French and may have disposed military officials more favorably toward the Madagascans. Some soldiers were certainly pleased with the ways in which officials facilitated their worship. Sergent Rajasfera wrote, "We have a place to meet (church or temple). I, along with all the other soldiers here, often ask God to help us to defeat our enemies."[9]

The army attempted to facilitate the religious practices of other groups of *indigènes* as well. At the huge camp at Fréjus in southern France, where many *tirailleurs indochinois* spent some time during their service in France, the camp authorities erected a traditional pagoda for Buddhist soldiers. Indochinese Catholics, of course, had little trouble practicing their religion in France. It is not clear, however, that the depth of religious feeling among Indochinese soldiers, Catholic or not, impressed French officials. In January 1917, a censor's report noted a letter written by an apparently devout Catholic, but commented that it was only the second letter that the censors had read that had mentioned religion since formal censorship procedures were inaugurated in October 1916.[10] Later in 1917, another report observed that Maréchal des logis [a cavalry rank equivalent to an infantry sergeant] Chu Hao was perhaps the only one among his comrades to speak of a papal intervention to end the war. The censor, perhaps imbued with the anticlericalism so central to early Third Republican political culture, ridiculed this soldier's belief that the failure of the pope to halt the conflict would mean that the world was nearing its end, referring dismissively to his "weak intelligence" and "childish opinion."[11] However, during that particularly dark year of the war in France, it would be surprising if many native French Catholic soldiers did not feel the same way.

Some French people were, however, more enthusiastic about the spirituality of the Indochinese. In the summer of 1918, an inspection revealed that some Catholics were conducting "religious propaganda" among Indochinese workers and soldiers. There had been several conversions among workers in Toulouse and Montpellier, and there was even a Protestant organization that had hosted numerous Indochinese, as well as Madagascans. The conversions seemed sincere, the inspector wrote, but in view of the problems such conversions could cause within (not necessarily Christian) families once the men returned home, it would be a good idea to remind people who had contact with the *indigènes* that religious propaganda was strictly forbidden and that they were to have complete liberty of conscience and the freedom to practice their own faith with no interference.[12] Of course, workers would be more exposed to these influences than would soldiers, especially if they were serving away from population centers at the front, but many *troupes d'étapes*, as well as combat troops withdrawn for rest and reconstitution, may have encountered similar proselytism.

Not only were the authorities careful to respect the freedom of conscience of the *tirailleurs*, but the army took concrete steps to promote the observance of religious beliefs. Army medical personnel received special instructions about how to bury the deceased properly. Like Madagascan Protestants, Indochinese Catholics presented no special problem, but Buddhists were different. The Service de santé (Medical Service) gave specific instructions for the preparation of the body (fingernails clipped; dressed in comfortable clothes, traditional if possible, with no buttons or metallic objects attached; head wrapped in a white turban if the parents were living; hands at the sides of the corpse, not crossed upon the chest), the funeral procession (made up as much as possible of other Indochinese), and the headstone (which depicted a yin and yang symbol instead of a cross).[13] Unfortunately, those responsible did not always follow these instructions scrupulously. An inspector visiting a cemetery in Marseille reported that the regulation headstone appeared on only some of the graves, while others were merely marked by a number.[14] Officials must have followed the procedures reasonably often, though, because censors reported in April 1917 that many Indochinese letter writers praised the treatment they had received in hospitals and the honors rendered there to those who died.[15]

Like the Indochinese, with both Catholics and Buddhists present in the ranks, there were two main forms of religious belief represented among West African troops. The first was what the French called *fétichisme,* a broad term that covered various traditional and largely animist beliefs. The second was Islam, which had won many converts in West Africa and was firmly established in numerous areas by 1914. Muslim soldiers from this area received the same religion-specific burial treatment as did North Africans. There was also an Arabic-language interpreter stationed at Fréjus to censor the mail of the thousands of West African Muslims who spent the winter there, as well as to help them write letters and to tend to their special religious and moral needs.

Despite this solicitude on the part of French military authorities, there was some concern over potential problems that West Africans' Islamic faith might pose. For instance, a report on the state of a battalion of *tirailleurs sénégalais* who were stationed in Algeria during the winter of 1916–17 warned that the progress of Islam in West Africa had conferred upon all things Arab a certain aura of respect, and Muslim soldiers in this Arab land were under its spell. West Africans seemed to feel that "every civilized contribution, clothing, writing . . . art, etc., is of Arab origin" (especially galling, no doubt, inasmuch as colonial subjects were supposed to look to Europe, especially France, with such reverence), and some troops in North Africa began to display a greater consciousness of their identity as Muslims. The report noted that most of the Muslims in the battalion belonged to one company, and the members of this unit had begun to go about their religious observances, such as daily prayers, with great ostentation and a certain haughtiness, which disrupted discipline in the battalion.[16]

In 1918, Monseigneur LeMaître, the Catholic missionary active in West Africa, mentioned in Chapter 4, whom the government had sent on a special inspection mission among West African troops in France, also warned of the dangerous implications of Muslim consciousness among the *tirailleurs*. He believed that "the Muslim spirit, which lurks constantly like a threat" around the tribes of West Africa would provoke a spirit of resistance to French rule, doubly dangerous in men trained in the ways of modern war, who had "become aware of their worth as seasoned troops," and who would undoubtedly return to take leading positions in indigenous society. LeMaître urged the army to prevent Muslim soldiers from sending home money that would fall into the hands of anti-French marabouts (holy men).[17]

Yet such fears about the reliability of Muslim *tirailleurs sénégalais* were always in the minority. LeMaître's warnings of the perils of Islam were not unexpected from a Catholic missionary. Moreover, his ulterior motives were plain. His main purpose in citing problems in the army's West African forces was to gain a place for him and his fellow missionaries as interpreters in West African units and obtain the appointment of a Catholic chaplain to France's *troupes noires.* The Ministry of War responded negatively to the suggestion of a chaplain, noting that the camp at Fréjus had for some time been the object of a sort of competition among various religious figures for the hearts and souls of the *indigènes* there. If the army appointed a Catholic chaplain, then the Protestants would want one too, especially given that *troupes noires* at places like Fréjus might include Madagascans, and the presence among them of a Catholic cleric would constitute a direct threat to Protestant missionaries. Then both faiths would be closer to their goal of setting up "veritable missions" at the camp. The army had earlier designated a chaplain for the soldiers at the front, a West African cleric known as l'Abbé Sané, but he had been killed in action. In the end, the Ministry of War judged it unwise to encourage LeMaître's obvious attempts to extend his missionary work among the *tirailleurs,* all the more so because such a situation was certainly not what the government had intended in conferring the inspection mission on LeMaître in the first place. Numerous high-ranking officers who commanded West African units also judged LeMaître's true motives to be a transparent attempt to revitalize missionary work in the AOF, which had made little headway.[18]

LeMaître's warnings notwithstanding, the army did not consider the struggle against Islam among West Africans to be a high priority. This reflected recent developments in colonial policy within the AOF. Up to 1912, colonial officials had openly attacked Islam and local marabouts, whom the French considered agents of oppression and superstition, but a revolt against this policy on the part of some *indigènes* caused a shift in policy that sought a closer accommodation with Islam, rather than confrontation.[19] This combined with an overall fairly benevolent view among some French people of West African Muslims, especially in comparison with North Africans. Even the report that cited the heightened Muslim consciousness of West Africans stationed in Algeria admitted that Islam was not dramatically expanding in the AOF, because "it is faced with native ways and customs that are better suited to a not very demanding *fétichisme.*"[20] The stark contrast between this stereotype of relaxed West Africans practicing a relatively benign "Islam *noir*" and that of "fanatical" North African Muslims was decisive in shaping French military attitudes and policies.[21]

From very early in the war, it was clear that the army would take advantage of the *fétichisme* of some West Africans, and the allegedly less fanatical and more reliable Islamic faith of others, by employing them in situations where considerations of religious politics called for caution. In November 1914, the Ministry of War sent a battalion of West African troops to Djibouti, the small French possession on the Somali coast to reinforce the local militia there, who were surrounded by a population of "very fanatical Somali Muslims," liable to commit acts of rebellion inspired by Ottoman propaganda. The implication, of course, was that such disciplined soldiers with different religious beliefs, or at least a more "reasonable" attachment to Islam, would serve French interests better in such a delicate environment.[22]

News from the AOF itself only further encouraged French officials. Colonial administrators reported that the "Islamic situation" in West Africa was "excellent," with no major disturbances, no significant anti-French propaganda, and no indication that Muslims in that part of the world viewed the Ottoman sultan as leader of the Islamic world.[23] Declarations of loyalty from important religious figures all over the AOF came in by the dozens to the government-general, many of which condemned Ottoman actions. One proclaimed that the Ottoman sultan and his government had betrayed Islam, saying, "they have no right to involve or compromise the interests of religion in a conflict where the said interests are not in question."[24]

Of course, as gratifying as such declarations were, they came from notables who depended upon their good standing with the colonial administration for their positions of power in indigenous society, so they were not an objective indicator of the loyalty of the majority of Muslims in the colony. Still, there were no indications at any point in the conflict that religious feeling threatened to provoke unrest, rebellion, or even much resentment in the AOF, whose Muslims did not feel any affinity for the faraway Ottoman sultan and his declaration of holy war against the Entente.[25]

The extensive use of *tirailleurs sénégalais* in the Dardanelles campaign demonstrated the French military's trust in West Africans even in direct combat with fellow Muslims. This positive attitude toward West African Muslims in the army continued to the end of the war. In 1918, the High Command informed officers that in some ways, West African Muslims made better soldiers than *fétichistes*, who were allegedly hopelessly naïve, superstitious, and subject to the undue influence of "sorcerers" who exploited "the simple minds of the blacks." Islamicized tribes were actually more advanced, and Islamicization could constitute "a genuine benefit," provided that these Muslims did not consider "the hatred and contempt of all that is not Muslim" a religious duty. The High Command advised officers in units of *tirailleurs* not to combat the ideas and beliefs of religious figures like Muslim marabouts and even animist "sorcerers," but rather to "channel" their influence.[26]

Marc Michel argues that such attitudes and policies may have actually encouraged the spread of Islam among West African soldiers in France, often at the expense of animist beliefs. Not only did animist beliefs rely more on the West African environment and rituals that were more difficult to transport into such a radically different context, but official favor, concretized by the construction of mosques and the observance of Muslim burial rites, raised the prestige of Islam over that of *fétichisme* in the eyes of many soldiers. The colonial administration in Dakar expressed concern about this, but the army's immediate interest in accommodating the religious beliefs of its soldiers to keep up morale trumped the possible postwar social and political implications for the empire.[27]

Solicitude toward West African Muslims clearly stemmed from assumptions about the relatively unthreatening nature of Islam as practiced by them. Certainly, though they provided all Muslims with the means to observe their religious beliefs, French officials never showed themselves so unconcerned about the implications of the Islamic beliefs of North Africans. Experiences during the war only served to reinforce this perception among the authorities. After the war, many officials regarded West Africans as ideal occupation troops for North Africa, because their lack of Islamic "fanaticism" supposedly made them more reliable than North African soldiers. In December 1918, Deputy Blaise Diagne advocated using West African troops for garrison duty in both Morocco and Algeria, which would augment French forces in North Africa with "troops of absolute loyalty," immune from "all Muslim influence." Such a policy would also please colonists in Algeria who were worried about religiously inspired resistance among the indigenous population, Diagne argued.[28]

General Mangin made similar statements in his postwar proposals for the use of *troupes indigènes*, pointing out that "pan-Islamic propaganda" would have no effect upon West African troops. Mangin also cited the lack of "religious fanaticism" among Indochinese troops as proof of the utility of these two groups in places like North Africa and the Middle East.[29] When it came to religious belief, clearly, the biggest concern for French officials was the Islamic faith of North African soldiers.

## French Views of Islam, North Africans, and Muslim Identity

Prevailing French views of Islam combined with the strong sense of religious identity apparent among North Africans to shape French military and political policy during the war. The roots of these attitudes toward Muslims lay deep in the prewar past. French intellectuals had been keenly interested in "the Orient" and Islam for centuries. Montesquieu's 1721 *Persian Letters* presented an ostensibly positive view of the Near East, primarily with the goal of satirizing French society, but by the end of the century, dominant currents of thought in France no longer considered Islamic societies appropriate for such comparisons. Napoleon's invasion of Egypt in 1798 and the resulting prominence of academic and scientific studies of these societies gave rise to an "Orientalist" view of Islamic culture and history, premised on a kind of cultural fall from grace. Whatever the undeniably great accomplishments of past Islamic civilizations, with their achievements in science, philosophy, and even war and governance, in modern times these formerly great civilizations presented only a picture of decay and decadence.[30]

Under the Third Republic, a long-standing tendency to regard the Islamic world as inferior and benighted, and in need of transformation under the enlightened tutelage of France, intensified.[31] The last remaining great Islamic power, the Ottoman empire, displayed increasing political and military weakness. Several wars in the Balkans had dramatically demonstrated Ottoman frailty on the eve of the First World War, and this only emphasized the "fallen" state of Muslim societies in the modern world. In the years leading up to the war, other European powers had consistently jockeyed for position in order to gain the most out of what they regarded as the imminent carving up of Turkish territory, the once great Muslim empire and now the "Sick Man of Europe." Little had changed from the early nineteenth century, when, after a trip to the Middle East, Chateaubriand compared the region's inhabitants unfavorably with the native peoples of the New World. In Arabs, he conceded, one could "still see something of delicacy in their manners and customs: one feels they were born in this East from which came all the arts, all the sciences, all the religions . . . in the American, everything proclaims the savage who has not yet reached the level of civilization; in the Arab, everything shows the civilized man who has relapsed into savagery."[32]

According to Orientalist discourse, a large part of the reason for this alleged relapse was Islam. Of course, such an evaluation of the current state of the Muslim world defied chronology, because the great achievements of Arab civilization had come after, and in many ways because of, the spiritually and politically unifying force of Islam. Still, most observers either ignored this contradiction or explained it away by arguing that whatever the attainments of the past, Islam was incompatible with continued progress in the modern world. Such sentiments provoked Alexis de Tocqueville, for instance, to contrast the Koran, which contained "political maxims, civil and criminal laws, and scientific theories" in addition to spiritual principles, with the Gospels of the Christians, which addressed only "the general relations between man and God and among men," imposing no other teaching or belief. "This alone," he argued, "among a thousand other reasons, suffices to show that the first of these two religions could not long dominate in times of enlightenment and of democracy, while the second is destined to prevail in these as in all other areas."[33]

More than a half a century after the death of Tocqueville, whose travels in Algeria had inspired his observations on Islam, Algeria's Governor-general Lutaud demonstrated the continuing currency of such ideas. "Pure Islam always appears, in fact, as a bronze wall, which, despite the repeated assaults of civilization, has not yet been seriously weakened," Lutaud wrote at the end of 1915. Such obstinacy, along with superstition, had prevented Muslims from accepting or understanding the benefits of civilization that France had brought to its subject peoples. "Before this superb indifference," he maintained, "in the face of the wonders of the earth: steam, electricity, telegraphy, the telephone, hot air balloons, aviation; before the unshakeable resolve to see only the heavens and to attribute to them the results of human effort, there is only the negation of progress!" Inveterate fatalists, Muslims were not even effective working the land (an assertion that conveniently justified the massive dispossession of *indigènes* from millions of acres by colonists in Algeria) because they accepted with a "profound resignation, all the evils sent by the Almighty." Lutaud conceded that all hope was not lost for France's *mission civilisatrice* among Muslims. Some Berbers were imperfectly Islamicized, and the hardships of daily life in North Africa rendered too profound a fatalism impossible. Still, the colonizers' work could not be easy, given the importance of Islam in Algeria, "a religion of annihilation of the individual in a frenzy of mysticism, fanaticism and extinction of the finest faculties of man, a religion that literally pursues a work of destruction and death!"[34]

Lutaud's statements were dramatic, not to say extreme, examples of

French suspicion of and hostility toward Islam from one of the most important figures in the French colonial hierarchy, but there are many indications that these attitudes permeated both political and military policy-making circles during the war. The idea that Muslims had to evolve a more reasonable relationship between secular and religious law in order to join the modern world was an article of faith in these circles. In a June 1916 discussion of naturalizing Algerian soldiers in the Interministerial Commission on Muslim Affairs (CIAM), Octave Depont, the representative from the Algerian colonial administration, remarked that the French would be able to point to progress among Muslims when law and religion were distinct from each other. That this kind of evolution took time was evident from the example of the Jews, who had taken centuries "to separate Hebraic law from the religion." An official from the Foreign Ministry remarked upon "the profound difference that seems to exist between the Muhammadan religion and the Catholic religion: the latter adapts itself to all forms of law; it is sufficient to recall that our law comes from Roman law, which is of pagan origin."[35]

In a strong indication that these kinds of opinions were not limited to conservative, even reactionary, colonial figures like Lutaud, the moderately liberal Colonel Jules Hamelin of the Ministry of War noted: "the crux of the question [is]: Islam can adapt itself to no other law than Koranic law." Georges Bèze, the head of the Algerian department at the Ministry of the Interior, who was often at odds with the colonial administration and no friend of Lutaud or Depont, observed that the Catholic Church had long exercised public powers, notably with regard to civic registration (births, deaths, marriages), public assistance, and education, "but, little by little, an evolution occurred, and the Church was stripped of everything that concerned the social order, retaining only that which had to do with religious doctrine."[36]

Clearly, the ideal evolution for primitive and underdeveloped Islam and its adherents to follow was a clear separation between the legal system and the state, on the one hand, and religion on the other. This orthodox republican insistence upon the separation of spiritual and secular life was hardly surprising, given the battles over "clericalism" that were such a prominent part of political life during the first half of the Third Republic, but it also echoed traditional ideas about Islam such as those Tocqueville had voiced during the nineteenth century.

Another session of the CIAM, in October 1917, reveals the power of the vision of Muslims as members of a civilization that had decayed and left them ill-equipped to confront the realities of the modern world. Hamelin responded to a request to allow North African soldiers to become officers in the artillery by declaring that *indigènes* were simply unqualified, lacking "notions of precision." Many of them, he asserted, had even lost the concepts of parallel and perpendicular. Describing these as "lost," Hamelin's comments resonated with allusions to the great achievements of Arab mathematicians, who had made indispensable contributions to the field over the centuries. Challenged by Bèze to reconcile his statements with the precision and artistry still evident in Muslim architecture, Hamelin claimed that it was clear from the work of North African soldiers, when given tasks such as the construction of barracks and camps, that "they do not even have the sense of a straight line." Even the Foreign Ministry official Jean Goût, who admitted that education could remedy such deficiencies, showed his belief in the harmful effects of Islam, stating: "Arabs, like all peoples who have been gripped by Islam, appear to have suffered a sort of arrest. They are frozen, but this is not to say that this stagnation must be permanent."[37] The belief that education could cure this "stagnation" merely indicated Goût's faith in French superiority and in France's civilizing mission.

Perhaps the most common stereotype associated with Muslim troops, especially in the eyes of those who worked more or less directly with them, was the fatalism mentioned by Lutaud. There was no question in the minds of French officials that this fatalism was firmly linked to Islam, a faith that they believed stifled individualism and initiative. To a certain extent, the words and attitudes of *indigènes* themselves encouraged this perception. In October 1916, postal censors seized a "Chanson sur la guerre" (Song on the War) that a Tunisian soldier had sent home to his father. Among the complaints about the war and life in France, the author of the "Chanson" lamented the loss of so many of his comrades, but, he declared, "it is the will of God, we must resign ourselves to it."[38] Such statements only confirmed opinions that French officials already held about Muslim soldiers.

In some cases, Muslim fatalism seemed to be militarily useful. One officer attributed the legendary discipline of Moroccan soldiers to the "sentiment of absolute obedience that the Muslim religion requires of the believer toward his leader, who receives his power from God."[39] When Moroccans transferred this unconditional obedience to their French officers, the result was a particularly effective combat unit. In March 1917, censors in Tunis noted many laments, expressions of homesickness, sadness, and even hopelessness in letters from the front, but these were tempered by a "profound resignation, drawn from religious sentiment, which is the guide of their life."[40] If the trials these men faced were "the will of God," then their discontent was much less likely to develop into open resistance or acts of indiscipline. As a report written a year later put it: "They are resigned, like every good Muslim. God has decreed that they serve France during the hostilities; they bow, demanding simply of the Most High to permit them to return to their country as soon as possible."[41] In some ways, this discourse about the fatalism of North Africans was linked to a larger perception of non-Europeans as simple-minded, naïve, and superstitious: censors also noted that Madagascan soldiers accepted their lot "with the habitual passivity of the Madagascan who, in all difficulties, see the hand of destiny, against which it is vain to struggle."[42] Yet such comments about other *indigènes* were rare, and French officials viewed Muslims as especially given to sentiments of resignation in the face adversity.

Most observers clearly felt that the potential benefits of Muslims' fatalism did not outweigh the disadvantages Islamic faith brought with it. Even West African Muslims, despite French officials' more benign perception of them in comparison with North Africans, presented possible difficulties. In 1918, the High Command warned officers commanding *tirailleurs sénégalais* that though discipline was normally quite easy with these men, because they were above all obedient, one had to watch out for the few "Islamicized [men] who have developed a taste for squabbling over Koranic controversies."[43] Indeed, Muslims who displayed what French officials regarded as too great a consciousness of their religious identity seemed most dangerous, and indications are that this described a majority of North Africans serving in France. Soldiers often expressed this identity in terms that opposed Muslims to their Christian exploiters and oppressors. As the Tunisian author of the "Chanson sur la guerre" put it, "the Christian discounts our existence."[44] Another Tunisian complained of being "under the authority of Christians," while still another warned his friend at home that "Muslims are in the process of losing their way in the midst of unbelievers."[45]

Some evidence indicated that the actions of specific Christians may have provoked such sentiments. In August 1917, censors reported on a letter that featured a drawing of a man's head, complete with hair and a large beard. Underneath the illustration was a caption that read, "Here is the head of a priest; may God curse the religion of his beard, hair by hair! When he speaks, it is like a cannon that rumbles in the sky; may God curse the infidelity of his mother. Do not blame me if I insult religion; I do it because they behave toward me like unbelievers."[46]

Similar sentiments no doubt provoked the author of the "Chanson sur la

Guerre" to wish wistfully for the reestablishment of a distinct separation between religions, as had been the rule under the great caliphs of the past.[47] Such wishes were even more threatening when it was clear that Muslims were thinking, not of the past glories of Islam, but of a more contemporary political context. In March 1917, two Tunisians stationed near Nice with their artillery unit wrote to the head of their religious confraternity back in the colony, asking him to join them in praying that God "deliver us from this unfortunate situation we find ourselves in, along with all Muslims; may God give victory to the religion of Islam and to the sultan, and may he rout the infidels." The censors determined that the only sultan to whom the soldiers could be referring was the Ottoman sultan, then at war with France.[48]

## Accommodating Islam

Faced with clear evidence that North Africans were cognizant of their religious identity, and that many framed their experience in the French Army in terms of what it meant to them as Muslims, officials made special efforts to accommodate the religious beliefs of these soldiers. The army felt especially vulnerable to criticism on this issue, because it was crucial both to maintaining morale and to combating German and Ottoman propaganda that tried to expose as false France's claims to be acting in the true best interests of Islam. Many of the soldiers' complaints focused on the difficulties military service and the war created for the observance of Muslim customs. The Tunisian "Chanson sur la guerre" charged that the French and the bey of Tunis had forced men to serve, to leave their homes, to serve among infidels, and to die alone and miserable without a friend or family member to make proper burial arrangements. For an observant Muslim, the thought of being buried "in a tomb in a strange land, in a land of infidels," without a proper sepulcher, was particularly painful.[49]

Public criticism of France for failing adequately to respect the needs of its Muslim soldiers was even more dangerous. *L'Islam dans l'armée française* (Islam in the French Army), the propaganda tract written by the Algerian deserter Lieutenant indigène Boukabouya Rabah under German and Ottoman patronage, made much of the "desecration of Muslims' religion in the French ranks," which he claimed would certainly shock Muslims "in their most intimate convictions." Among the "religious assistance of which Muslim soldiers have been totally deprived during the war," he wrote, were the means to follow sacred customs such as burial procedures and rites; the opportunity to celebrate holy days and keep the fast of Ramadan; and the guidance of religious figures (curiously, he called them "priests"), present to minister to the spiritual needs of all French soldiers except Muslims.[50]

The French government and military sought to counter such charges and to facilitate the observance of the customs and tenets of Islam among Muslim soldiers. One important aspect of this, as the above criticisms make clear, was the burial of the dead. Even the Algerian author of a "Chant de guerre" ("War song") much more favorable to the French cause than the Tunisian "Chanson sur la guerre" lamented the interment of Muslims and "unbelievers" together in mass graves at the front.[51]

French officials recognized this as one of the most serious issues they faced in using Muslim soldiers. In 1916, an Arabic pamphlet entitled "Contempt for the Muslim Religion in the French Ranks" charged the French Army with neglecting the proper obsequies for the Muslim dead. This provoked Senator Étienne Flandin, head of the parliamentary Committee on Foreign Affairs, to warn the government that, given the attachment Muslims had to their faith and to the care of the body after death, "Our enemies could not find a subject more likely to overexcite Muslim fanaticism."[52]

Resident-general Lyautey had sounded a similar warning from Morocco earlier in the war. In October 1914, he wrote to the minister of foreign affairs to report the widespread impression in Morocco that Muslims were buried not according to Muslim traditions, but at the same time, in the same place, and with the same ceremonies as Christians. In order to counter such dangerous rumors, Lyautey suggested leaving the rituals and interment to fellow Muslims in the unit, and when that was not possible, to do nothing contrary to the religious beliefs of the deceased. This last situation, however, was not ideal, and unless the French wanted to face a very grave problem with public opinion in North Africa, the Ministry of War should make Muslim personnel readily available to help their comrades with funeral rites.[53]

Officials in Paris were aware of the problems Lyautey identified, and the minister of war had in fact already issued orders stipulating the procedures for burying Muslim soldiers a few days before Lyautey sent his warning. The order made many of the same points that the resident-general did, noting that it would be a good idea to avoid any "ceremony of a religious character" when fellow Muslims were not present to conduct the proceedings. The minister also reminded subordinates that, in accordance with Islamic custom, these soldiers were to be buried in a shroud, not a coffin.[54]

Yet these were hardly specific or complete guidelines, and the reliance on other Muslim soldiers to take care of their own dead was certainly not adequate once it became clear that the war would not end as quickly as many had initially believed. Hence, in December 1914, the minister of war expanded his previous instructions. The new order gave details on last rites, how to prepare the body of the deceased, and how to bury the corpse oriented southwest-northeast, on its side, with the face pointed toward Mecca. Muslims were also to have distinctive grave markers, not a cross, with inscriptions in both Arabic and French (a detailed illustration accompanied the order). The instructions ended by stating: "This memorial, which we owe to our Muslim soldiers who have died for France, is easily achievable."[55] This was probably the case in rear areas and hospitals, but it depended upon the goodwill of local commanders and administrators, and it is likely that at least some Muslims did not benefit from this scrupulous treatment when they died in the chaotic conditions of the front lines. Still, to maintain morale among Muslim troops and to counter propaganda claims to the contrary, French authorities were careful to institute policies that would demonstrate their respect for one of the most sacred rites associated with Islam.

There were also attempts to publicize this sensitivity to the religious beliefs of Muslims. Édouard Montet, a noted scholar of Islam, included the text of the Ministry of War circular outlining special burial procedures for Muslim soldiers in a pamphlet in which he addressed some of the criticisms Boukabouya had made.[56] That the policy itself could have a positive result was clear from the May 1917 report of an officer at the depot in Aix-en-Province, which noted that obsequies performed by an imam (a Muslim cleric similar to a priest or minister, but without the same hierarchical authority) there had made a "profound impression" upon a number of soldiers.[57]

The army also made attempts to facilitate the observance of Muslim holy days. From the opening months of the conflict, the Ministry of War instructed local commanders to give Muslim soldiers some respite from their daily duties on religious holidays and to allow them to pray together and to celebrate according to their customs. The motive for such solicitude was explicit. Allowing Muslims to observe the fast of Ramadan during the day, serving them their meals after sundown on those days, and informing them of the dates of holidays within the holy month so that they could celebrate them, would be "good policy," because the soldiers would see concrete proof of the "precautions that we are taking to respect their religion and their customs."[58] French officials understood the importance of Ramadan as one of the most sacred times in the Muslim calendar. As the Ministry of War observed in 1916, not without a snide reference to the lax attitude of Muslims outside the month of Ramadan: "If it happens frequently that the Muhammadans forget certain of the precepts of Koranic law, as when they too readily consume forbidden beverages, such as alcoholic drinks, it is very rare that they do not scrupulously observe the fast of Ramadan."[59]

As this last statement suggested, there was some ambivalence among French officials about Muslims' conscientious observance of the tenets of their religion. The length and importance of Ramadan posed a particular problem in this regard. On the one hand, heightened religious sensibilities during this time seemed to present potential difficulties, as when a general attributed the desertion of a Tunisian *tirailleur* during Ramadan to the fact that during this month that "Muslims are most especially subject to the religious influences of Mecca."[60] On the other hand, altering work and meal schedules for an entire month presented inconveniences for commanders trying to maintain a viable fighting force during wartime, and some officers even suspected the purity of the motives of Muslims who wanted to observe the fast and holidays of Ramadan. As the holy month approached in the summer of 1915, some Muslim soldiers wrote home to ask religious authorities whether or not they could break the fast of Ramadan while serving in France and still remain true to their religion. In response, two important religious figures in Tunis and Algiers issued fatwas, decrees concerning points of Islamic law, dispensing soldiers on campaign in a foreign land from keeping the daily fast. The Ministry of War translated these fatwas and distributed them among officers in all units containing Muslims, who would read them to their troops. Though this clearly indicated a hope that Muslim soldiers would not disrupt their units by demanding that their officers accommodate the strict observance of the requirements of Ramadan, the Ministry of War still maintained an official commitment to respecting the religious beliefs of its soldiers and cautioned that the interpretation of the fatwas "must be left to the judgment of indigenous soldiers."[61]

By the following year, however, officials demonstrated some impatience and skepticism toward some Muslims who expressed a desire to keep to their religious obligations during Ramadan. In July 1916, the Ministry of War judged a petition to this effect from Algerian soldiers to be motivated by "the desire to enjoy a long rest behind the front," and not the desire to remain true to the ideals of Islam. The army wanted to facilitate the observance of Muslim holy days, but was not above suggesting that soldiers might dispense with some of the observances that interfered with military imperatives. Of course, French officials had to do this carefully, and they recognized the necessity of obtaining the help of indigenous religious figures. The Ministry of War pointed out that the Koran and the hadiths (sayings of the Prophet) provided ample justification for breaking the fast of Ramadan in the kinds of circumstances in which Muslim soldiers from the colonies found themselves, but such an assertion meant very little coming from non-Muslim army officers, so officers were once again to read the fatwas of the previous summer to their Muslim troops.[62]

Boukabouya had criticized the French Army not only for failing to ensure the proper burial of dead Muslim soldiers and to facilitate the observance of Muslim holy days, but also for refusing to ensure the presence of qualified Islamic clergy to minister to the troops' spiritual needs. As with his other charges, this one was only partially true. As early as November 1914, Governor-general Lutaud praised the effect upon morale of the presence of Lieutenant Si Brahim, the brother of an important religious figure in Algeria, among Muslim troops in France. Si Brahim had carried out an effective propaganda campaign on behalf of French authorities, and Lutaud thought it a good idea for the lieutenant to carry out some of the functions of an imam as well, administering funeral rites to the deceased and otherwise acting as a comforting spiritual presence. The governor-general also advocated giving other influential *indigènes* missions of this sort.[63] Still, the Ministry of War took no immediate action to provide Muslim soldiers in France with imams, and some officials argued at the end of 1914 that such a measure was unnecessary.[64]

Yet the government soon changed course on this issue, and the only question remaining was how to choose the imams. The minister of war preferred to appoint persons without official titles, which essentially meant marabouts, or locally popular holy men. Lutaud argued that these men were often unreliable and leaders of anticolonial movements and uprisings, so that it was important to have at least some of the imams in France come from the ranks of the more pliable "official clergy," whom the French had sponsored and appointed to important positions in indigenous communities. Officials in Paris were skeptical on this point, arguing that members of the official clergy had no real stature among Algerians, but conceding that half of the imams should be appointed from among the official clergy and half from among marabouts.[65] Lutaud remained unconvinced, wishing to choose the imams at his own discretion from among the religious figures he considered reliable.[66] In the end, the governor-general prevailed, and in May 1915, the minister of war agreed to allow Lutaud to appoint seven imams to serve among Algerian soldiers in rear-area hospitals and depots, organizing places of worship, administering to the religious needs of the men, and supervising the burial of fellow Muslims.[67]

This was not enough to protect the army from criticism entirely, however, because even though there were imams in rear areas, none were present among the troops at the front after two years of war.[68] Responding to complaints along these lines, the Ministry of War asked colonial administrators in North Africa to appoint an imam from each colony to minister to soldiers at the front. Lutaud appointed one from among those already in France, moving the imam from the Paris region to the front as an army chaplain attached to a unit of stretcher-bearers. Resident-general Alapetite in Tunisia, who early in the war had already sent Muslim notaries to aid Tunisian soldiers and help with burial rites, had the greatest difficulty finding an imam, and the one willing candidate would only serve if he was not sent to the front and could return home when he wanted.[69] As for Morocco, Lyautey pointed out that the imams of Algeria were the creation of the French, and no equivalent religious figures existed in the newer colony for which he was responsible. Moreover, unlike Algeria and Tunisia, Morocco had never been under Ottoman rule, so the sultan of Morocco united all religious and political authority in his person; he was the "one and only Imam in Morocco." Appointing imams to Moroccan units would only seem ridiculous to the soldiers, and the proclamations that the Moroccan sultan had already sent to the troops in France were the best means of sustaining their morale.[70] In the end, the Ministry of War was able to provide only Algerian troops with an imam at the front.[71]

Nonetheless, French officials felt confident that the measures they had taken to provide Muslim troops with a clerical presence effectively refuted criticisms like Boukabouya's. Lutaud dismissed Boukabouya's complaint about the lack of religious figures among the troops, pointing out that, not only had the administration appointed imams, but they were much better paid than Christian chaplains or Jewish rabbis serving in the army, because imams received salaries from both the Algerian administration and the Ministry of War.[72]

Fittingly, two imams appointed to serve in hospitals in France, Mokrani Boumezraq el-Ouennoughi and Katrandji Abderrahmane, authored the official public reply to Boukabouya's charges. Their pamphlet informed readers that imams did in fact serve among Muslim troops in France to minister to the men and oversee burial procedures. The authors even went so far as to question whether Boukabouya was really a Muslim, because his complaint that Muslim soldiers did not have the services of "priests" in the ranks, as Christian soldiers did, indicated that he did not know that there was no ecclesiastical hierarchy in Islam equivalent to that of most Christian denominations.[73]

Boukabouya later responded to these countercharges, refuting the claim that he was not a Muslim, and even taking credit for the appointment of imams in the French Army. This policy, he wrote, was surely a direct result of his initial criticisms. Had he not himself had to serve as imam to dead and dying comrades on the front before he deserted? Was it not only with the arrival of a metropolitan doctor in his regiment that anyone began to observe the proper rituals when burying Muslim dead? In this sense, not only were his critics French stooges, but they owed their positions to the publication of his first pamphlet and the embarrassment it had caused the French Army.[74]

Boukabouya was, of course, wrong about the impetus for French efforts to accommodate the religious sensibilities of Muslim soldiers, but French officials did have an external motive. Policies on burial procedures, holy days, and imams, as well as the construction of mosques and the careful accommodation of dietary needs (no pork or wine, plenty of couscous, mint tea, and coffee), were designed to maintain the morale of Muslims fighting for the French, but authorities also worried about the loyalty of these soldiers as they faced the machinations and propaganda of Boukabouya's sponsors, the Germans and the Turks. Ultimately, these concerns over loyalty were most revealing of the difficulties that prejudices against Islam created for the use of North African Muslims in the war effort.

## Germany, the Ottoman Empire, and Islam in the French Army

Both editions of Boukabouya's *L'Islam dans l'armée française* culminated with chapters devoted to the much better treatment Islam and its followers allegedly received at the hands of the Germans. In the first edition, Boukabouya outlined the virtual life of luxury that Muslim prisoners of war lived at a German camp at Wünsdorf-Zossen, near Berlin, which was comfortably situated in an area of lush greenery and "bathed by a veritable climate of one of the best African locales," Boukabouya claimed. The barracks were spacious and clean, meals were culture-specific and ample, and amenities included "Moorish cafés" and "Moorish baths." Authorities encouraged health and exercise, as well as the study of the Koran, for which they provided facilities, books, and instructors. The crowning achievement of all this solicitude was the construction of a magnificent mosque, a picture of which Boukabouya included in the pamphlet.[75]

Of course, only the most gullible reader would believe assertions about the balmy weather of northeastern Germany, but there was indeed a camp there where the Germans gathered Muslims whom they had taken prisoner from the French, British, and Russian forces. These men did benefit from the ability to practice their religion in a specially built mosque, while also enduring a heavy dose of propaganda from German and Turkish officials (and Boukabouya himself, who worked at the camp) seeking to persuade them to change sides and join the fight against their colonial masters. The French government also undertook the construction of mosques for soldiers in France, as well as other measures designed to ensure their loyalty by demonstrating France's respect for Islam. In the second edition of his brochure, Boukabouya predictably claimed that such measures in France were merely reactions to more honest German overtures, but in fact the dual efforts to win the hearts and minds of Muslim soldiers reflected a larger struggle for legitimacy in the Muslim world.[76] Both sides in the war attempted to present themselves as the true guardians of Muslim interests: the Germans as allies of the Ottoman sultan, and the French as the guarantors of the integrity of an Islam that a selfish minority party in Turkey had hijacked, betrayed, and sold to serve Germany's international ambitions.

In the middle of this European power struggle stood Muslims from Morocco to India. German propaganda aimed at these populations in general, inasmuch as the colonial empires of its opponents contained millions of Muslims, but France's numerous North African soldiers were obviously specific targets. German efforts focused not only on turning prisoners of war into agents and soldiers for the Central Powers, but also on provoking resistance to conscription, indiscipline, and even desertions among enemy frontline troops. This began during the opening months of the war, before the Ottoman empire was an official ally of Germany. French reports indicated that the Germans were carrying out active propaganda among prisoners of war, trying to persuade them to change sides, as early as the beginning of October. Revealingly, French officials referred to this as *racolage,* or solicitation, a term that could refer, depending on the context, to the way military recruiters, salespeople, or prostitutes attracted clients.[77]

In November, after France was officially at war with the Ottoman empire and the sultan had declared jihad against the Triple Entente, officials at the Ministry of War were even more worried. One ministry report observed that the arguments made in the call to holy war were "irrefutable from the Muslim point of view." This promised to have a profound effect upon France's Muslim subjects, even the most loyal. "Our soldiers themselves," the report continued, "who are the most indifferent to the political and religious point of view, already appear anxious."[78] Others had already pointed out specific examples of this anxious attitude among the *tirailleurs* from North Africa. An inspector, touring depots in Aix and Arles in October 1914 to assess the morale of North African soldiers, reported that one soldier had asked him, "Is it true that our Sultan is going to declare war on France?" He was able to reassure the soldier on this point, because the encounter took place before the official Ottoman entry into the conflict. The inspector was also able to reassure Tunisians who said they had "often hesitated to fire on the Germans for fear of killing the friends of the Sultan of Constantinople."[79] The inspector's visit calmed the similar fears of another soldier, who later said, "I have not fired upon the Germans, because I believed them to be friends of the Sultan; but henceforth I will not fail to [shoot them]."[80] Yet, such changes of heart notwithstanding, the very fact that the soldiers made such statements indicate that the attitude of the Ottoman empire and its sultan was of great importance to at least some Muslim *tirailleurs*.

The Germans were quite active in attempting to exploit these circumstances, and not just among prisoners of war. One Algerian reported that when he was lying wounded on the battlefield, a German officer passed by close to him, looked at him with "commiseration," made sure he was not dead, and then spoke words that the *tirailleur* could not understand, but that indicated the German's pity for the Algerian's condition. After leaving the soldier with "gestures of friendship," the officer walked over to a French noncom lying wounded nearby, jerked him to his feet, showed him to the *tirailleur*, and shot the Frenchman in the head. "I understood," said the Algerian, "that the Germans act this way in order to demonstrate to us that they are not enemies of Muslims and that they are only after Frenchmen." Moroccan soldiers reported that Germans in the trenches opposite them cried out in Arabic, "Why are you fighting us? We are your brothers, we are Muslims like you."[81] Wounded Algerian and Tunisian soldiers testified from their hospital beds to similar incidents, the Germans claiming to be Muslims, "like you servants of the Caliph of Istanbul."[82]

French officers did not have much trouble combating such dubious claims, but the Germans made more sophisticated appeals as well, spread-ing leaflets in the French trenches that called for resistance and desertion in explicitly religious and nationalistic terms. One of these leaflets, written in Arabic, quoted from the Koran and claimed that by serving with the French, English, and Russian armies, Muslim soldiers were fighting alongside the "worst enemies of Islam," committing "a manifest impiety." The Entente powers were using their Muslim soldiers as cannon fodder, placing them "in the front lines and exposing you to death." The Ottoman sultan's declara-tion of jihad aimed at ridding the world of the authors of such abuses, and Turkey had allied with Germany to do so, so there remained "no excuse for a Muslim to abstain from holy war." The leaflet concluded by claiming that a warm welcome awaited those soldiers who deserted the French ranks. They would be sent to Istanbul for the rest of the war, and, if they so desired, the Ottoman government would train and equip them to help its army defeat the French and liberate other oppressed Muslims in the colonies.[83]

There was evidence that the German and Ottoman appeals were having an effect upon some soldiers. Resident-general Alapetite wrote from Tunis in December 1914 that although enemy propaganda had little effect upon the civilian population, the same was not true of Tunisian soldiers. This pro-paganda was wreaking "fearsome ravages" among the *tirailleurs,* "to whom it is said that the Commander of Believers forbids them to go and get them-selves killed for the infidels."[84]

Tunisians were a particular concern for French authorities. Of France's three North African colonies, Tunisia had the closest historical ties to the Ot-toman empire, whose sultan Tunisians still recognized as the spiritual leader of Islam. Moroccans, though they had never been under the authority of the Ottomans and did not consider the Ottoman sultan as the head of Islam, were also potentially troublesome, given the strong German commercial and political presence in Morocco during the prewar years. Algeria had weaker ties to either enemy power, but officials were nonetheless worried about the effect of calls to religious solidarity upon a population they considered rife with Islamic "fanaticism." In fact, fears about Turkish and German manipu-lation corresponded closely with French prejudices against Islam. Governor-general Lutaud made this clear when he claimed that "Islam, for a long time supported by Germany, clearly aims, despite its ethnographic variet-ies and divergent rites, at *a unified struggle* against European civilization."[85] Germany and Islam, in other words, were equally enemies of civilization, which the Entente powers were fighting to preserve.

Yet despite French fears of the machinations of their enemies, and of the larger hostility they believed to exist between Islam and the West, most Muslims outside the Ottoman empire were wary of appeals to religious solidarity. It soon became clear that though the French would have to work to counter enemy propaganda, French Muslim subjects easily perceived the self-interest and even deception evident in the appeals, rejecting German and Turkish claims to represent the Islamic faith. One Algerian soldier rejoiced over the murderous effects of French artillery upon "the enemies of Allah." The (admittedly assimilated) Algerian sergeant who translated this sentiment for his French superiors claimed that the struggle against the Germans was for Muslims "like a holy war," and that *tirailleurs* of the 2nd Regiment charged into battle crying, "Blessed be the Prophet, holy war to the infidels."[86] Lieutenant Si Brahim, during his tour of the depot for North African soldiers at Arles, told the *tirailleurs* that the war against Germany was "a holy war," and that "in taking up arms for our country [France], Muslims are defending the interests of their faith, the honor of their homes, and the integrity of the lands of Islam." Apparently, these exhortations were effective. After hearing Si Brahim, Tunisians who had earlier admitted that they had not shot at the Germans for fear of firing upon Muslim Turks who might be in their ranks, were now asking to return to the front, eager to fight the Germans and even fellow Muslims.[87]

Si Brahim's display of loyalty was not unusual. The French government and colonial officials received many declarations from indigenous notables professing continuing allegiance to France and condemnation of Ottoman and German actions, particularly for inappropriately bringing Islam into the struggle. The declarations, and proclamations by the same notables to troops from their countries, came from figures as exalted as the sultan in Morocco and the bey of Tunis, as well as from lesser religious and political figures of more local importance. Of course, self-interest inspired a good deal of the enthusiasm for the cause of the metropole, because *indigènes* who depended upon the colonial administration for their places in society were likely to offer their support to shore up their positions within the colonial order. French officials were aware of this. The minister of war told Lyautey in Morocco that "the counterproclamations [to the Ottoman proclamation of holy war] of our religious brotherhoods are themselves suspect in the eyes of *indigènes*."[88] Lutaud also wrote that, though he was "far from casting doubt upon their sincerity," Algerian elite protests against the Ottoman declaration of holy war were of limited influence, if only because "they emanate from leaders empowered by us or from marabouts outwardly rallied to our cause."[89]

Still, despite some continuing nervousness, French authorities soon found that they had little cause for immediate worry about the loyalty of the Muslim masses of the North African colonies. Officials at the Ministry of War reported no serious troubles, and many overt expressions of loyalty, among the populations of all three as early as November 1914, the very month in which the sultan proclaimed jihad.[90] Nonetheless, the French government sought to stave off potential trouble through its own counterpropaganda, which unambiguously distinguished between the government of the Ottoman empire and its peoples. Officials claimed that France was at war with the former, not the latter, and even the sultan was not necessarily the target of the Entente, because he was in reality a prisoner of the Germans and only able to do their bidding. The intended audience for such claims were France's Muslim subjects, both in the colonies and in the army. After the first few weeks of war with the Ottoman empire, French authorities decided that, though they could not take it for granted, the loyalty of North African soldiers was reasonably solid. By the end of December 1914, a senior Ministry of War official declared confidently that the worries generated by the declaration of holy war had disappeared.[91] This was not entirely true, but military and political officials were confident as they entered the new year.

Yet 1915 brought a new and dramatic challenge to France's continued use of Muslim soldiers when France joined Great Britain in the Gallipoli campaign of the spring of that year. Many thought that North African soldiers would withstand the climate of Asia Minor better than European forces and would be familiar with the kind of topography, style of warfare, and opponent they would encounter there, making them an ideal addition to the expeditionary force. This was the argument of "an important indigenous Algerian leader," who served with the French Army on the Western Front. He reported to his superiors that there was nothing to fear in deploying Algerians in Turkey or even Syria, and that these soldiers "would show their value there better than elsewhere, because they would find in this country the style of combat that suits them."[92]

Such comments were not surprising coming from a member of the Algerian elite, but he was not alone in his confidence. In March 1915, the Ministry of War informed the Ministry of Foreign Affairs that Entente operations in Asia Minor would not alienate France's North African subjects, who had proved that they were immune to appeals to religious solidarity and calls for jihad. The *indigènes* saw through the cynical manipulation of the Ottoman government, which had compromised "the Islamic cause" at the instigation of "its Christian protectors."[93] It was probably not entirely in the best interest of the French government to highlight this opposition between Christians and Muslims in its presentation of the political situation in the Ottoman empire, but the point was that France and Britain were fighting for the "Islamic cause," and that the loyalty of North Africans was assured. This prompted one general to observe that, "[t]he use of [North African] *indigènes* . . . against the Turks, who have also been [in the past] their enemies, can be contemplated without fear," except perhaps for Tunisians, who remained more closely tied to Istanbul than other North Africans. He cited the example of prewar French campaigns in Morocco as proof that the army could use North African soldiers against fellow Muslims without serious difficulty.[94]

Despite such expressions of confidence, many other officials felt that it was one thing to trust North Africans to man trenches in Europe opposite the Germans, allies of the Turks, and quite another to trust Muslims to fight against their coreligionists in an important Islamic country. Among those most vigorously opposing the use of North Africans in Asia Minor were colonial administrators. As was often the case, Algerian Governor-general Lutaud was the most forceful and eloquent voice advocating caution. As the invasion was beginning, he sent the minister of war a thirteen-page letter outlining in detail his "unfavorable opinion about sending *troupes indigènes* to the Orient." Among numerous objections, he cited the existence of a religious affinity that existed between the Ottoman empire and Muslims everywhere. French officials should not be fooled, he argued, by the numerous expressions of loyalty and rejections of the call to holy war coming from many quarters in indigenous society. Despite these, the Ottoman sultan remained an important spiritual leader to many North Africans. Moreover, fighting against fellow Muslims in a place like Morocco was totally different from fighting the Turks in a land many Muslims considered holy. Ottoman territory, even outside the seat of the caliphs in Istanbul, was a land "veiled in mystery: it is for the Islamite a sacred land, a land of holy places, which seems like something miraculous, [and] any hand foreign to Islam that falls on it is a sacrilegious hand." This comment was squarely in the tradition that viewed Islam as a faith rife with mystical superstition and irreconcilably hostile to Western civilization, and Lutaud made this second assumption even more explicit when he claimed that Islamic society was principally based upon "the Koran, which is fundamentally hostile, in its essence, to everything that is not Muslim." The governor-general also denied that North African soldiers were any more suited to the style of combat they would find in Asia Minor than they were to that they had found in Europe. In fact, he predicted that operations in Turkey would reproduce the conditions of trench warfare prevalent in Europe (in this he was remarkably prescient), and he was among those who felt that *indigènes'* performance under the conditions of modern warfare left a great deal to be desired.[95]

In the end, objections like these, especially as voiced by important officials such as Lutaud and Resident-general Alapetite in Tunisia, were decisive, and no North Africans participated in the Dardanelles campaign. Even after the Entente withdrew from it in failure at the end of 1915, and French troops moved from Turkey to reinforce the Armée d'Orient fighting in the Balkans, the army maintained its policy of excluding North Africans. By the autumn of 1916, though, the Ministry of War began to rethink this policy. Not only was the loyalty of the indigenous populations of North Africa more assured than ever, but the religious justification for keeping Muslims out of the ranks of the expeditionary force had disappeared. Fighting against the main enemy facing the Armée d'Orient, Orthodox Christian Bulgaria, "obviously cannot offend the Islamic sentiments of our Algerian or Tunisian *indigènes.*" Even if Ottoman forces eventually joined the Bulgarians, this was not a serious problem, because the Ottoman sultan was no longer the uncontested supreme religious authority in the Islamic world.

In June 1916, Hussein ibn 'Ali, sharif of Mecca and self-proclaimed king of the Hejaz and of all the Arabs, led a revolt against Ottoman rule, for which he received substantial British and French aid. Part of the French portion of this aid came in the form of troops, some of them North Africans, who fought alongside sharifian forces in Syria. Now that there was legitimate and significant resistance from within the Islamic world to the Ottomans and their call to holy war against the Entente, the French could call on their Muslim troops to fight against the troops of the sultan even in the heart of the Middle East.[96]

As a result of these considerations, the minister of war decided to send North Africans to reinforce the Armée d'Orient, mostly as labor and support troops. Some also served in the Middle East later in the war.[97] Despite this relaxation of French policy on the deployment of North African troops, the invasion of Turkey starkly highlighted the limits of French trust in the reliability of North African Muslim troops. Trust was forthcoming only when the sharif of Mecca had created conditions that would split the religious loyalties that French officials considered to be of overriding importance to their Muslim soldiers.

For some of these soldiers, these circumstances belied French claims of solidarity with the interests of Islam and, worse, claims that colonial subjects and French citizens were involved equally in a common struggle in the name of civilization. Indeed, the refusal to send North Africans to participate in the Dardanelles campaign, a policy designed to avoid the risk of confronting Muslims with the prospect of fighting fellow Muslims, actually carried with it the risk of alienating many *tirailleurs*. Instructions that the Ministry of War drew up to guide *officiers interprètes* when explaining France's intervention in Turkey betrayed French fears about the religious sensibilities of Muslim soldiers. The general thrust of these instructions was that the Ottoman empire was under the domination of the Germans, that the current Turkish rulers had sacrificed "the true interests of Islam to their ambition," and that the Entente powers wanted to help the Turkish people, who were the unwilling victims of the policies of their government and of the Germans. "All true Believers desirous of seeing the integrity of Islam and the independence of the caliph respected," the interpreters were to declare, "send their best wishes to the Allied forces and count on them to work toward the salvation of the Islamic world."[98]

Their best wishes were the most that Muslim soldiers—"true Believers" though they might be—would see sent from them to aid the forces of the Entente in the Dardanelles. The *indigènes* would certainly not be sent themselves to help "work toward the salvation of the Islamic world." Yet if anyone had an interest in assuring the integrity of Islam and the independence of the caliph, these men did. And official French propaganda itself raised a potentially awkward question: if France were representing the true interests of Islam, why then did its government not trust North Africans to help in this fight to save Islam from those who would pervert it in pursuit of their secular political ambitions?

Some officials pointed out the potential dangers of such a contradictory policy, noting that it might lead *indigènes* to conclude that France did not trust them, and that they would be humiliated by this. Lutaud had dismissed such fears as baseless, but in his anti-French propaganda, Boukabouya made much of France's evident mistrust of its Muslim soldiers, clearly believing that this would resonate with his audience. Boukabouya also told soldiers at the Wünsdorf camp that he had deserted because of his disgust over being left out of the invasion of Turkey.

Even before Boukabouya made these claims himself, officials at the Ministry of War had already guessed that exclusion of North Africans from the expeditionary force might have prompted bad feelings and a number of desertions, including Boukabouya's. On 29 April 1915, only four days after the first Entente troops had landed on Ottoman soil, the Ministry of War wrote of these suspicions to the High Command, reporting that many Algerians apparently considered "the fact of not having been called to contribute to the constitution" of the French contingent of the invasion force "as a measure of unjustified mistrust." The ministry suggested that Joffre send a battalion of *tirailleurs algériens* to Turkey as a gesture of faith in their loyalty, but the army could not spare a battalion from the Western Front, and officials like Lutaud did not drop their opposition to such a deployment, so the Algerians never went to Turkey.[99]

Some Algerians and other North Africans ended up in Asia Minor nevertheless, but on the side of the Central Powers. It was well known to French authorities that the Germans and Turks, along with agents such as Boukabouya, were trying to persuade Muslim prisoners of war at the Wünsdorf camp to fight in the Ottoman Army. Given prevailing ideas about the religious sensibilities of North Africans, this seemed to present a serious danger. As one officer put it, the Germans were exploiting the "religious fanaticism" of the prisoners by building mosques and promoting religious studies, and this risked inspiring "a Janissary spirit" (Janissaries were elite troops who had served the Ottoman empire in its heyday).[100]

By early 1916, rumors reached France that some of these men were actually in the Ottoman Army and fighting in the Middle East. This was true, but intelligence gathered from North Africans who had managed to escape the Turkish lines and desert to British forces indicated that the Germans had forced the vast majority of these men to join the Turks. Captured German documents corroborated the soldiers' claims, revealing that about one thousand men had been formed into a battalion of four companies and dispatched to Istanbul, from where they were sent to various locations in the Middle East.[101] Even with corroborating evidence that captured *tirailleurs* were being forced to serve France's enemies, some officials remained worried that their doing so indicated the susceptibility of North African soldiers to appeals to religious solidarity. A Moroccan soldier interrogated by French and British officers found such suspicions ridiculous, claiming that the Turks "distrust[ed] French Muslims" as reluctant soldiers who were "all ready to desert" at the first opportunity, and he made clear his dislike of the Germans, declaring, "Cursed be the Jews who nursed them."[102]

Notwithstanding this and much other evidence to the contrary, French military and political authorities never quite rid themselves of suspicions based upon the religious identity of North African soldiers. In July 1915, an officer reported from the depot at Arles that Tunisian soldiers never even spoke of Turkey or the operations of the Entente there, and "the rare echoes that reach them leave them indifferent."[103] If the Tunisians, with their supposedly stronger political, religious, and cultural links to the Ottomans, were indifferent, then surely one could safely assume that the loyalty to France of its North African *troupes indigènes* in general was fairly solid. This is not to underestimate the problems confronting French officials. They had every reason to be nervous about the willingness of members of a subject population to fight against an enemy with whom they had much more in common than with their current colonial masters. Moreover, there was ample evidence that Muslims took their religious identity very seriously; this was clear from the words and writings of many of the soldiers themselves. But French fears often appeared immune to repeated demonstrations that, though their Muslim subjects may not have had unqualified enthusiasm for the French cause in all circumstances (certainly an unrealistic hope anyway), the appeals that Germany and the Ottomans addressed to their sense of religious duty were not very effective. No matter what their religious sentiments, *indigènes* could easily discern the Central Powers' manipulation of the concept of Islamic brotherhood and recognize their own best self-interests and the realities of colonial power. Much official French suspicion and fear, then, had its roots in deeper misgivings about Islam itself, about its alleged incompatibility with European civilization and its inveterate hostility to the West. Despite the loyalty of hundreds of thousands of Muslim troops, and the deaths of thousands "pour la France," these suspicions and fears would survive well beyond the end of the war.

The French recognized from the beginning of the war that the deployment of hundreds of thousands of colonial subjects as soldiers in Europe would present numerous cultural challenges for both the soldiers and their hosts. One of the most glaring of these cultural challenges was how to accommodate the diverse religious beliefs represented among the *troupes indigènes*, ranging from Catholic and Protestant Christianity to Buddhism, to African animist beliefs, and to Islam. Men would want to practice these religions, to live and die according to their precepts. Thus, official French policy sought to provide *troupes indigènes* with the means to do so, erecting places of worship for them, observing their religious holidays and feasts, and burying the dead in accordance with their specific religious customs. Such efforts were often difficult to sustain in the chaos of war, but one issue in particular caused acute difficulties: how to cope with Muslims in the French Army. This involved, not only the religious sensibilities of hundreds of thousands of men, but long-standing French preconceptions and stereotypes about Islam and its followers. The government and the army made many efforts to accommodate the religious beliefs of North African Muslims—for example, burying dead soldiers according to Muslim practice and facilitating the observance of the fast of Ramadan—but authorities continued to worry that the religious identity of these men potentially compromised their loyalty and reliability. German and Ottoman efforts to appeal to the religious solidarity of North Africans heightened these fears, which combined with deeply entrenched prejudices and suspicions and led France to avoid the risk of putting its Muslim soldiers in direct combat with other Muslims. This last issue provided the most dramatic evidence of the continuing inability of French officials to solve what they regarded as the "problem" of Islam in the French Army.

Thus, as with many other issues surrounding the use of *troupes indigènes* in Europe during the war, an aspect of colonial subjects' culture and identity stood in the way of their full integration into the nation for which they might be making the ultimate sacrifice. Islam in particular was difficult for many French people to integrate both into the army and into an understanding of French national identity. General Mangin gave an indication of what that would mean for the postwar army when he summarized the soldierly qualities of various *races indigènes* in 1920. Even though he was more likely than most to see the benefits rather than the drawbacks of using *troupes indigènes* (in this report as in others, he was arguing for the expanded use of these soldiers to ensure French security both at home and abroad in the postwar period), and though he noted that the results of German propaganda on North African soldiers during the war had been "pitiful," he warned that the deployment of such fervent Muslims depended upon "certain preventative precautions" within the army and "a skillful counterpropaganda" in indigenous societies.[104] Both in and out of the army, then, the Islamic faith of North Africans remained an obstacle to their use as soldiers, an impediment to the French *mission civilisatrice,* a "problem" for French authorities to solve. Yet the French authorities also became aware of another, more intimate cultural challenge they faced as a result of the presence of *troupes indigènes* in France, and this problem potentially involved all of these men, not just Muslims. Reading soldiers' mail and observing their behavior, officials noted a troubling intimacy between many nonwhite colonial subjects and white Frenchwomen. As the next chapter shows, questions of race and questions of sex became intertwined and uncovered some of the deepest anxieties of imperialism.

# CHAPTER SIX

# Race, Sex, and Imperial Anxieties

On Sundays, we go strolling with [French]women, as we
would do in Indochina, with our own women at home.

—*Sergeant Hao, 1916*

If the attitude of our protégés is generally good, their private
conduct, such as we would wish it [to be] here in order to
maintain intact in Indochina the prestige of the European
woman, leaves more and more to be desired.

—*French postal censor, 1917*

The fact of the matter is that nationalism thinks in terms of
historical destinies, while racism dreams of eternal contamina-
tions, transmitted from the origins of time through an endless
sequence of loathsome copulations: outside history.

—*Benedict Anderson,* Imagined Communities

I wish to be acknowledged not as *black* but as *white*. Now . . .
who but a white woman can do this for me? By loving me
she proves that I am worthy of white love. I am loved like a
white man. I am a white man . . . I marry white culture, white
beauty, white whiteness.

—*Frantz Fanon,* Black Skin, White Masks

When in April 1916 Sergeant Hao, an Indochinese soldier serving in the
French Army on the Western Front, wrote a letter in which he described
his Sunday walks and the welcome and acceptance he and his compatriots

received from members of French society, particularly Frenchwomen, he touched upon one of the most striking phenomena that arose out of the presence of *troupes indigènes* in France during the Great War. Hao may have been surprised by the very ordinariness with which some French people treated interracial contacts, and even more intimate relationships, between nonwhite soldiers and white Frenchwomen, but these contacts were anything but ordinary. They ranged from simple strolls in the park, to sexual liaisons of a more or less short duration, to friendships, even to pregnancies and marriages. The women with whom these men became involved ranged from prostitutes, to nurses, to daughters of respectable bourgeois families. For many in France, particularly those in positions of authority, these relationships were deeply troubling, challenging as they did "the prestige of the European woman," by transgressing sexual mores and racial and colonial hierarchies. These "loathsome copulations" across the racial divide threatened to contaminate the French population and national identity—through both the simple fact of contact and the even more disconcerting possibility of mixed-race offspring—because nationalism and racism, far from being separate concerns, were fatefully intertwined. What if, as Frantz Fanon wrote, these relationships revealed a demand to be recognized not as colonial subjects but as French, not as inferiors but as equals, not as "*black* but as *white*"?

Official anxiety went beyond the fear of racial and national pollution. Authorities, in France and in the colonies, feared the effect that these relationships would have on the *indigènes*' respect for white women when the soldiers returned home. And it was not only the soldiers they were worried about, but the indigenous populations in general, because authorities feared that soldiers returning home would spread tales of easy conquests and Frenchwomen of dubious morals. In addition, postal censorship showed that the soldiers also sent home revealing letters and thousands of photographs of Frenchwomen. The French censors were particularly concerned about these photographs, which featured simple portraits of purported girlfriends or mistresses, or pictures of soldiers with their beloveds, or, worse yet, photos of nude women in suggestive poses. As these images flooded back to the colonies by the thousands, the authorities became increasingly worried about diminished respect for Frenchwomen and the society they lived in, and the corresponding destabilizing effect upon colonial rule.

One might argue that these men, by defending the French nation, had earned the right to interact with French people on a basis of some equality, but such an argument ran counter to distinct ideas about racial and colonial hierarchies, which called for the maintenance of a strict separation between the white colonizers and the nonwhite colonized. Making these men soldiers had already called into question this separation, making it more difficult to maintain, and relationships between white women and nonwhite men presented an even more profound and intimate (in the most literal sense of the term) challenge to the racial and colonial order. In short, these relationships between *troupes indigènes* and Frenchwomen represented grave transgressions of racial, sexual, and colonial boundaries and engendered anxiety among male French authorities.

Numerous scholars have elucidated the importance of intertwined ideas about race and gender in the construction and maintenance of European colonial rule, but what transpired during the war years differed in crucial respects from what usually took place in the colonies both before 1914 and after 1918.[1] Indeed, scholars have long recognized women's more general role defining, through reproduction, the boundaries of culture, ethnicity, and nationality within modern states.[2] And if in the colonies, as Ann Laura Stoler argues, "Creating and securing the European community's borders took on special significance when cultural, political, and sexual contagions were conjured everywhere—where European and native sensibilities and desires brushed against one another as they were borrowed and blurred," then how much more important would it be to create and secure borders in France itself?[3] Indeed, during the early part of the twentieth century, the state began to promote the settlement of European women in the colonies as vectors of civilization, domesticity, bourgeois morality, and racial purity, but what to do now that colonial men had arrived in Europe and were interacting with Frenchwomen who seemed stubbornly resistant to their roles as guardians of the culture and race?[4]

Perhaps most disconcerting, love and sex in France occurred between men from the colonies and white Frenchwomen, reversing the more frequent pairing of white men and indigenous women overseas. Thus, male authorities faced not only a colonial, political, and racial threat as authorities, but a sexual threat as men. They were menaced with the betrayal of formerly loyal colonial subjects and soldiers, on the one hand, and wives and daughters, on the other. This was an era in which modern European states and the male elites who governed them were increasingly concerned with power over people's bodies, what Michel Foucault calls "a certain mode of detailed political investment of the body," a "new micro-physics of power."[5]

As part of this process, states focused on sexuality in particular as a "dense transfer point for relations of power," a privileged site of state intervention, seeking to establish and wield new technologies of what Foucault calls "bio-power" over individuals and societies.[6] Stoler's work has shown how important the colonial context was for the emergence of these concerns, and how instrumental colonial states and their racialist categorization through sexual proscription and prescription were to the emergence of the European bourgeois order and European identity.[7] The concerns of the French state and military, and their attempts to investigate and regulate the sexual behavior of both colonial men and Frenchwomen, fall neatly into this story, but power and control proved more difficult to exercise in the metropole in a time of war than in the colonies. Officials often found themselves in a position of what one might call "bio-powerlessness," concerned with but largely unable to stop love and sex across racial lines, or to prevent the ominous effects they feared would result from such unions.

Wartime relationships across the racial divide provide an important window, then, not only into the experience and attitudes of *troupes indigènes* and French officials, but also into the role sex and race played more generally in the structure of white predominance and empire.[8] These men's status as soldiers fighting for France and their presence on French soil opened up many possibilities for the destabilization of hierarchies that were virtually immutable back in the colonies. The *troupes indigènes* observed a certain "desacralization" of one of the tenets of imperial rule—white superiority—both in seeing France as an often nearly prostrate victim of German aggression and in discovering that Frenchwomen in France were not as aloof and untouchable as their counterparts in the colonies. As officials watched the behavior of these soldiers, and of Frenchwomen and their families as they welcomed colonial subjects into their lives and homes, and particularly as censors read the correspondence of *troupes indigènes*, acute anxieties emerged. It seemed to them that these relationships were creating significant weaknesses and fissures that would undermine imperial rule.

## Crossing the Color Line

Colonial subjects serving in France wrote a great deal about their relationships with Frenchwomen across the "color line."[9] A censor's report for November 1917 noted that though Madagascans in France expressed opinions on a variety of issues, such as the quality of army food, leave policy, life in hospitals, and rumors of military operations, the "greatest part" of their correspondence dealt "with their adventures in the company of white women."[10]

Workers imported from the colonies, of whom there were over 200,000 by the end of the war, obviously had more opportunities to engage in these relationships, given their placement among the civilian population and their integration into an increasingly sexually diverse workplace.[11] Nonetheless, soldiers had ample opportunity as well, because the army employed many *troupes indigènes* behind the lines, performing labor such as construction, resupply, and guard duty. Even combat troops had contact with the civilian population. As one censor noted of soldiers from Indochina, "The soldiers themselves make conquests in the villages where they are encamped."[12]

All West African soldiers and some Indochinese spent the winter months away from the cold, wet north of France, and encamped near Bordeaux or the Mediterranean, they often had extensive interaction with nearby populations. Lucie Cousturier's experiences bringing Senegalese soldiers into her home in the south of France and teaching them French is probably the best-known of these interactions.[13] Stays in the hospital were also an occasion for soldiers to meet French women: nurses on their wards as well as other women in the surrounding communities. In short, it was difficult to prevent *troupes indigènes* from interacting with the French civilian population, or even from having relationships with women whose homes they had traveled thousands of miles to defend.

Many of these relationships were of a distinctly impermanent nature. Soldiers' letters make it clear that they paid for many of their "conquests." A Madagascan soldier wrote in September 1917, "Once one arrives and walks upon French soil, one is obliged to partake of or one is attracted by something: it is prostitution."[14] In the Mediterranean town of Fréjus, near a hospital and the largest winter camp for *troupes indigènes*, prostitution became a major health concern. In the summer of 1915, the Ministry of War instructed the commandant of the camp to prevent Senegalese troops from frequenting "houses of ill-repute," though "it would be prudent to tolerate certain establishments where prostitution, regulated and supervised, would be less dangerous for the health of the men than illicit prostitution."[15]

Yet despite this tolerance of (properly regulated) interaction between African men and French prostitutes, authorities recognized the danger of even commercial sex for the reputation of Frenchwomen overall. As one report noted of the letters of Madagascan soldiers, "It does not appear . . . that Madagascans make a distinction between women of the night and white women in general."[16] Madagascans were not alone in presenting prostitution to their correspondents as evidence of a general attraction Frenchwomen felt toward colonial subjects in uniform. In August 1918, an Indochinese sergeant noted this habit among his countrymen, warning a friend at home not to believe stories others told of their amorous conquests of Frenchwomen: "Do not believe that Frenchwomen have any passion for the Indochinese; just like the women of our country going for European men, they care only about money."[17]

Yet prostitution was not the only means through which *troupes indigènes* and Frenchwomen had contact, and the authorities had to admit as much. "Our Indochinese," one censor observed, "in fact, receive letters that indicate that their correspondents sometimes belong to the best society."[18] Moreover, each month brought reports of dozens of new engagements, marriages, and even births stemming from such liaisons. This presented a particular problem for the authorities, given their assumptions about the dangerous sexuality of colonial men. Europeans traditionally viewed nonwhites as especially sexually active, potent, and depraved, and censors clearly had such stereotypes in mind when they noted that the easy availability of prostitutes exacerbated the "natural lubricity" of the Indochinese.[19]

The first censor's report on "Madagascan soldiers in France," a document that its writer intended as a guide to the "general characteristics of the race," observed that a Madagascan man rarely attained an advanced age, because "[t]he tendency to promiscuity, which he often abuses, even from childhood, is for him a cause of degeneration and shortens his days." This promiscuity also had as a consequence widespread syphilis among the island's population, the report claimed.[20] Observers judged North Africans, too, according to the prevailing sexual stereotype. The practice of polygamy and the ease of divorce under Muslim law (involving a simple declaration by husband to wife before the man could take another wife) served for many as proof of North Africans' uncontrollable desires. Commenting on a legislative proposal that would require Muslim soldiers to renounce such customs in order to acquire French citizenship, the French resident-general of Tunisia wrote that such a sacrifice was out of the question for such men, given their limited ability to control their desire for more than one woman. The *indigène* who renounced such prerogatives as polygamy and easy divorce would be making "a sacrifice beyond his strength."[21]

Concerns over polygamy of a somewhat different sort plagued French authorities. With hundreds of thousands of oversexed nonwhite males in

France, Frenchwomen were in danger of being duped by soldiers with wives back in the colonies. Censors in Tunis noted that many Frenchwomen wrote letters to men they had met in France expressing their disappointment and anger at discovering that the soldiers had made promises of marriage despite having a family in Tunisia. Such duplicity was often explicitly calculated, as was evident from the words a Tunisian soldier in the artillery addressed to a friend back in the colony. Not only did he write that he was happy to be in France, "where pretty women are plentiful," but he advised his friend not to forget, in the event he also came to France, to say that he was a bachelor.[22]

Censors seemed to feel that Indochinese men presented a special problem in this regard. The serial adultery, dishonesty, and potential bigamy of the interpreter Pham Van Khuong was typical of the many men from this colony who found themselves in similar circumstances. He received several letters from his fiancée, Ninon, in Toulouse, who professed her love and her desire to go to Indochina with him after the war. However, Khuong was also receiving letters from another young Frenchwoman, who reproached him bitterly for having earlier promised marriage to her, only to admit later that he already had a wife back home.[23] Some of these men had worked themselves into the good graces of solidly respectable families, and French officials found this particularly worrisome. Another interpreter, Dinh Van Giah, expressed a desire to marry a nurse at the hospital where he worked, but he already had a wife and family in Tonkin, and his new French beloved was the daughter of an officer in the French Army.[24]

Also alarming to authorities were the motives of some of the *troupes indigènes*, quite apart from their sexual appetites. Some were quite open about the ultimate goal of marriage to a Frenchwoman: French citizenship and economic security. "I plan to obtain naturalization by marrying a Frenchwoman, which will permit me to set myself up in a job [here] later," Corporal Trong wrote home to his parents in August 1917.[25]

Other soldiers' aims were less ambitious, but no less threatening to the elevated status Frenchwomen were supposed to enjoy. Jacques Ngon, a nurse in Montpellier, described his girlfriend (whom he called *ma femme*, however, which could mean "my wife"), the daughter of an artillery captain, to his parents and sisters, but told them he had no intention of bringing her home to Saigon with him because he was using her to take care of him in case of illness during his stay in France. Ngon's colleague Theo said that he had taken up with a Frenchwoman, who did his washing, only for the duration of the war.[26] This was, of course, a dramatic inversion of the colonial order, in which indigenous women often served as concubines and performed domestic tasks, like washing, for white European men.[27] In November 1916, censors noted the engagement of a young Indochinese soldier serving at the front and a young woman who lived in the region where he was stationed. He was primarily interested in her because, as he put it to his parents, "She has a lot of money." With characteristic sarcasm and racial stereotyping, the censor remarked, "The contrary would have surprised us, because the Indochinese is nothing if not sentimental."[28]

Such opportunism at the expense of French womanhood was troublesome enough to French authorities, but some soldiers expressed even more threatening motives for their pursuit of white women. As the head of the office charged with reading the mail of Indochinese soldiers characterized it, France was now paying for the sins of its sons who had built the colonial empire and had often taken native women as concubines. For the *indigènes*, sex with white women in France was "like a revenge on the European, the Frenchman who down there causes old Indochina to blush and incites jealousy."[29] Some soldier's letters did indeed invoke revenge as a motive for many of the *indigènes'* "conquests." One wrote that he was proud to see that now there were *métis* (mixed-race) children produced by the union of Indochinese men and Frenchwomen, as well as those produced in the colony by Frenchmen and Indochinese women.[30]

But the *indigènes* did not merely seek revenge upon Frenchmen, but also Frenchwomen, specifically those who lived in the colonies. A report on Madagascan correspondence observed in December 1917 that to have sex with a white woman was "not only a pleasure not to be scorned, but also a form of vengeance." These intimate encounters were "a payback," making it "possible today to repay all the contempt in which European women, in Madagascar, hold the *indigène*." As one soldier wrote, women in the colonies "regard us rather like lepers; well, then, come on, don't deprive yourself, take as much as possible today."[31] Another Madagascan put it even more bluntly: "What to tell you of white women? Down there, we fear them. Here they come to us and solicit us by the attraction of their charm. . . . What delights in their smooches, . . . I am forgetting about Madagascar because of them."[32]

Clearly, too, Madagascans were not the only *indigènes* who thought this way. An Indochinese soldier wrote, "In our country, the women of this race are very difficult to approach, but us being here, two francs is enough for us to have fun with them."[33] The likely effect of such interracial relationships on the status of Frenchwomen in the colonies was apparent. If these women were supposed to be pillars of the community there, embodying French ideas about civilization and domesticity and defining the boundaries that separated colonizers from colonized, *indigènes* with such attitudes, many of whom would eventually return to their homes, presented a significant potential threat to the colonial order.

## Blurring the Color Line

Yet transgression was a two-way street, and authorities felt that native Frenchwomen and their families were often at least partially to blame for encouraging *indigènes* in their indiscretions. Ignorant of the imperative and impervious nature of the boundaries between colonizers and colonized, they blurred the color line by engaging in or abetting interracial relationships, thus threatening the social order in the metropole. This stemmed largely from what officials regarded as the ignorance of French civilians about the realities of colonial hierarchies and the special mentality of *indigènes*. Typical of this supposed lack of understanding was a letter from Mme Baudin to Larbi Arboui, an Algerian soldier convalescing in hospital. "The author of this letter is assuredly a courageous person, but ignorant of the mentality of our *indigènes*, she uses with her protégé a language he cannot possibly understand," the French *officier interprète* who intercepted the letter reported.[34]

But it was not merely the use of inappropriate language that posed a problem. From the letters of the soldiers, it was clear that many of them had found acceptance within respectable families, and as the censors in Tunis argued, French families failed to take into sufficient account the social rank of the *indigènes* whom they invited into their homes. One Tunisian, mobilized as a driver in the engineering corps at Montpellier, married the daughter of a lawyer in that city.[35] Jacques Ngon, the Indochinese nurse who had taken up with the daughter of a captain in the artillery, wrote that he ate lunch each day at the home of the father, who also provided the couple with an allowance of 60 francs per month.[36] Another army officer, a lieutenant, had agreed to the marriage of his daughter to an Indochinese interpreter, promised to help his future son-in-law obtain naturalization, and consented to the couple moving to Indochina after the war.[37] Indochinese soldier Dinh also benefited from parental benevolence, paying frequent visits to a twenty-two-year-old widow "in full view of her father and mother."[38] Lawyers, army officers, and other self-respecting parents, the thinking went, ought to have known better and to have shown greater discretion than to allow their daughters to consort with nonwhite truck drivers, nurses, or common soldiers who were racially and socially beneath them.

Even more subversive of racial and social hierarchies, given his motives, was the case of the recently naturalized Adjutant Victor Tru. He had become dissatisfied with girlfriends in Touraine and Champagne, who did not possess the kind of fortune he was seeking. Happily for him, a wealthy grocer in Saint-Dié had recently agreed to the engagement of his daughter to Tru. As of November 1917, Tru was working with a friend in Indochina, a functionary in the colonial administration who apparently had greater facility in written French, to craft a letter that would sufficiently reassure the now wavering father to allow the marriage to go forward.[39]

The case of Khamaci Mohamed, the Tunisian soldier who impressed a French family with his knowledge of French over dinner in their home, illustrated the dangers of inviting *indigènes* into the family, a postal censor noted. Taking him "for a Frenchman" and treating him "as a true child of the family," his hosts had disregarded racial and social conventions, and their excessive praise risked inflating the soldier's opinion of himself.[40] Military and colonial authorities feared this sort of acceptance, springing from what they regarded as the gullibility and naïveté of some French people, because such treatment would inevitably, they feared, raise the expectations of the *indigènes* and cause them to regard the more strictly segregated society of the colonies in an unfavorable comparative light. The effect of such egalitarian treatment was not limited to the soldiers who served in France either, because their letters home had the potential to amplify dissatisfaction with the colonial order throughout indigenous society.

In this respect, French families, and especially Frenchwomen, were damaging not only the colonial order but metropolitan society as well. When one officer claimed that Algerians were apprehensive about "contact with our women, who in their eyes are all prostitutes and whose conduct unfortunately, in many cases, only confirms them in their opinion," he was voicing not only his concern over the effect of Frenchwomen's behavior upon the mentality of colonial subjects but also his disappointment as a French male at the failure of these women to conform to sexual mores and social expectations.[41] This is unsurprising, given that this period saw an intense debate about traditional gender roles and the place of women in society, and heightened anxieties about the behavior of Frenchwomen.[42] Even more disturbing to officials and disruptive of the social order were the children of mixed race (*métis*) who began to appear with increasing frequency as the war wore on. The existence of métis, the product of unions between Frenchmen and nonwhite women, in the colonies was one thing, but Frenchwomen giving birth to such children in France was quite another. Authorities could only be stung by the wry comment of an Indochinese doctor to a friend who had also come to France: "Like many others, you can say that you have more than served France; you are defending her and you are repopulating her."[43]

The official attitude was clear and is best illustrated by a report referring to the new mothers as "contaminated unfortunates."[44] This term resonated with the discourse on *métissage* (miscegenation) as inevitably leading to the "degeneration of the race," but also indicated that such mixed-race unions and mixed-blood offspring were, as Ann Laura Stoler has put it, "sexual affronts." Behind ostensibly biological concerns about "contamination" lurked the larger and more unsettling questions about the permeability of political and cultural boundaries between European and "other," between colonizers and colonized. Crossing and blurring these lines destabilized the separation of people into categories upon which colonial domination depended, and confused questions of national identity in troubling ways.[45]

If the existence of métis was undesired and disturbing, at least that existence was not their fault, but the same could not be said of the women who had brought them into the world, whose behavior was distressing to male French officials irrespective of whether it produced children. One category of Frenchwomen who had a great deal of contact with *troupes indigènes*, which could easily deepen into intimacy, caused particular concern. Nurses at the various hospitals throughout France where wounded and sick men received treatment had perhaps the greatest opportunity to form relationships with soldiers, especially combat soldiers, because a prolonged period of recovery allowed sufficient time spent in one relatively confined place for men and women to get to know one another. These bonds often greatly comforted soldiers, as the experience of some West Africans demonstrated.[46]

The military, however, found soldiers' extended stays away from their units and in the company of nurses especially corrosive of morale. A July 1915 report on North African soldiers in the south of France asserted that many of them had lost their soldierly qualities as a result of hospitalization. This was in large part because "they have been treated in too benevolent a manner, especially by the female personnel." The men had come to expect such treatment, and their newly acquired arrogance became indiscipline when they did not receive the same kind of treatment from their officers outside the hospital. Worse still, the nurses' "benevolence" apparently extended beyond mere medical attention to

> sexual favors given to the soldiers by certain of their nurses and other of our female compatriots, favors that for reasons of national pride we would like to doubt, but that the letters enclosed with the present report and taken randomly from a batch of correspondence retained at the Aix Depot oblige us to observe. One finds in these letters proof that Frenchwomen have dared to deliver themselves up to these men and have not hesitated in their hysterical folly to commit the crime of turning these soldiers from their military duty, advising them to avoid leaving for the front.[47]

What else but hysteria, a constitutional weakness to which women were supposedly especially prone, could explain Frenchwomen's simultaneously betraying their race, Frenchmen, the war effort, and their nation? Nurses, as professionals, and like prostitutes, were predictable targets of official male anxiety, because they "fell outside the colonial space to which European women were assigned: custodians of family welfare and respectability and dedicated and willing subordinates to and supporters of men," Stoler observes. If "French family life and bourgeois respectability were conceived as the cultural bases for imperial patriotism and racial survival," these women were failing on many levels.[48]

These nurses' "hysterical folly" disrupted more than military order. Naïvely, some of these women had given to their North African patients photographs of themselves in their Red Cross uniforms. For anyone who knew the "boastfulness" of *indigènes* about anything to do with women, the author of the report argued, it was obvious that the soldiers would not fail to send these pictures back to friends in North Africa as evidence of their "innumerable mistresses." As the images and stories passed through many hands in indigenous society, they would excite "the amusement and derision of our *indigènes*." This would strike a blow to French prestige in France's Muslim colonies, especially given their "so particular conception of the woman—beast of burden, flesh for pleasure."[49] This belief in the male chauvinism of North Africans was widespread in official circles. In 1917, for instance, the Ministry of War discouraged Mme Régis, president of the Société "l'Algerienne," from visiting North African soldiers imprisoned in Switzerland, because "visits made by women to indigenous soldiers from North Africa are, in general, interpreted by these men in a sense little favorable to the visitors and always give only negative results."[50]

Official concerns repeatedly focused on the effect on the "special mentality" of *indigènes* of Frenchwomen's behavior. The author of the July 1915 report on North Africans' interactions with French nurses mentioned above admitted that the issue was not "of a purely military order" but asserted that it did relate to "the work of moral education of the Muslims of North Africa," the civilizing mission for which the army was partly responsible. Further upsetting the hierarchies that defined political and social relations between colonizers and colonized in France's overseas possessions, some nurses had written to their North African friends, not only expressing love, but also exalting the bravery of the *troupes indigènes* to such an extent that many of the soldiers would undoubtedly suppose "they have saved France."[51]

Another officer complained of the "new mentality of the Algerian *tirailleur* who has entered into intimate contact with the populations of France." Told that they had "saved" France, they repeated this contention often and with arrogance, but this officer had found a remedy in the forceful statement of French republican colonial ideology: "It has been profitable to explain to them with authority, and in front of hospital personnel [i.e., nurses] . . . that they were the saviors of their own African homes and that the tricolor flag is quite as much theirs as it is ours."[52]

Still, the idea that *troupes indigènes* were indispensable to the defense of the metropole went to the heart of one of the great paradoxes of the use of these troops: if France was such a powerful nation, if its moral and military superiority were such that it had every right to rule over distant lands and peoples in its colonial empire, why then did it need these peoples to save it from defeat at the hands of the Germans? This apparent need for help from the subject peoples, as well as the sight of large parts of France devastated by and prostrate before the invading German army, was subtly, but deeply, destabilizing to the colonial order. Military authorities were not happy to observe Frenchwomen adding to the problem by calling the *indigènes'* attention to it.

Authorities could intervene with the *indigènes* themselves, as when an Indochinese man was imprisoned for fifteen days for "daring to fall in love with a French girl."[53] But recommendations for preventing the problems stemming from these relationships often made it clear that the primary concern was to modify the behavior of the Frenchwomen in question. In 1915, a wealthy woman near Toulouse took a special interest in North African soldiers, sending food and money to the nearby hospital, hosting *tirailleurs* in her home, and listening with sympathy to their grievances. This led, an officer reported, to a "very unjustified arrogance and a discontentment" among the *indigènes* with their treatment at the hospital. Worse, this woman had persuaded two badly wounded men to stay with her after their convalescence, one of whom had had a good attitude while at the front, but had now acquired "a rebellious, arrogant, and very undisciplined spirit, hating his superiors and believing that he alone saved France." This situation, in addition to the presence of three North Africans (who had been discharged because of wounds) already living in Toulouse with their French wives, threatened to undermine the morale of other soldiers.[54]

The Ministry of War's response to this problem noted that though the soldiers had to be sent back to North Africa for processing before their formal discharge, they would be free to return to France after that. Still, the army could place the men under surveillance and deport them if they had a harmful effect upon the attitudes of their former comrades. But the measure likely to have the greatest effect was to have the intelligence service inform the woman discretely that the military authorities would not tolerate any incitement to indiscipline.[55]

Perhaps even more effective than a visit from intelligence officers would be to forbid all closed correspondence for the soldiers, requiring that they send and receive nothing but postcards. This would prevent writers from expressing the most intimate and subversive sentiments, "Or, then, must we irremediably doubt the modesty of our women?" Officials hoped they could count on the modesty of at least some Frenchwomen, and some clearly befriended their North African patients with the most innocent of motives, but it was still important to inform the nurses "of the danger of their enthusiasm, even the most modest, for our Muslim soldiers: to enlighten [the nurses] about [the soldiers'] military qualities, but also about their moral qualities, alas, deplorable."[56]

Still, it was not clear that it would be politically wise to interfere too overtly with the mail, even though wartime censorship was no secret, and in any case, soldiers and civilians often found ways around such measures. However, a more subtle campaign to educate Frenchwomen about the peculiar nature of *indigènes* and the sensitivity of relationships with them did appear appropriate. A December 1915 circular from the Service de santé militaire noted the problems with the "too maternal" behavior of the nurses, which presented "a real danger for our *indigènes*, as for our French families," and mandated that nurses were thenceforth to have periodic meetings with knowledgeable doctors and interpreters "to inform them of the very special mentality of our indigenous soldiers."[57]

Nonetheless, the problem did not go away. In May 1917, an *officier inter-prète* reported relationships between North Africans and their nurses at a military hospital in Guerche. Demonstrating the kind of "modesty" in his language that officials hoped nurses would display in their postcards to *indigènes*, this officer noted that the soldiers were "having conversations with the nurses," and that a letter intercepted from a Mme Laurent "leads one to believe that these conversations have been pushed a little too far."[58]

One solution to this problem, of course, was to staff the hospitals where *troupes indigènes* would be treated with male nurses. This was what one general decided after inspecting several of these facilities. Noting that the soldiers "acquire in France a morality, or rather an immorality, that does not honor us, and that they boast of in their correspondence with Algeria," he advocated forbidding closed letters and removing women from the hospitals. However, he admitted that the latter would be hard to do.[59] The authorities did in fact stipulate that only male nurses should treat wounded or sick West African soldiers, but that the army was unable to impose this strictly is shown by the relationships between these men and women in and around their hospitals.[60]

The authorities' uncomfortable suspicion that any interaction between West Africans and Frenchwomen was inappropriate, potentially subversive, and perhaps even sexual is apparent from their elliptical descriptions of these contacts. A report on correspondence from the large camp at Fréjus–Saint-Raphaël noted ambiguously that "our *indigènes* are cared for at the home of Madame Bourdieu," near their hospital, and that another local woman also had "many connections with the Senegalese world."[61] Despite official disapproval and discouragement, the effects of efforts to restrict these relationships were limited.

As these references made clear, the problem of interactions between *troupes indigènes* and French civilians stretched beyond nurses in hospitals to other women and even entire families in their homes. This expansion of contact was particularly alarming to officials, because it spread potential disorder both more broadly among more soldiers and more widely in French society and into the intimate spaces of French homes. These issues came to a head in the middle of 1915, when a proposal surfaced to allow North African soldiers, smarting under army policy that denied most of them leave to visit their families, to apply for a period of leave to visit French families willing to host the men in their homes. One Ministry of War official responded by pointing out that it was unlikely that a soldier's stay with "persons foreign to his race, his language, his mentality" would raise his morale, as a period of leave was designed to do. Such an experience would affect the *indigènes* negatively: "The debilitating influence exercised over our indigenous soldiers by the attentive care that the female personnel of our hospitals lavish upon them suggests that their admission to the homes of French families, [and] the care and well-being with which they will be surrounded [there], will lead to the same consequences." And French families would suffer as well: "Those of these families who are totally ignorant about the mentality and the ways of our Muslim soldiers will come to regret their generous offer."[62]

Another official also noted that allowing *indigènes* to associate with French families was unlikely to have better results than contact with Red Cross nurses, such as "often passionate correspondence." Families in the metropole would not be familiar with the *indigènes'* mentality, and these men would search out "indulgent" families and use the hospitality accorded them to move about freely in French cities, "to exploit the credulity and the generosity of the public." The soldiers would certainly have intimate encounters with Frenchwomen, and this unleashed primitive and degenerate sexuality would pose a danger to public health and hygiene, "considering that most of them are syphilitic."[63]

The exploitation of the French public's hospitality and gullibility was a recurring fear for French officials trying to police the behavior of thousands of colonial subjects let loose on the streets of the metropole. One *officier interprète* cautioned his superiors about the *indigènes'* native cunning: they sought out civilians, women in particular, who were "naïve," unlike the Europeans of Algeria, who would never fall for their wiles. At once persistent and hypocritical, these men would seek money or sexual favors, often skillfully using promises of marriage to obtain the latter, and the army could expect all manner of indiscipline from men whose military worth had thus been spoiled.[64]

Officers often seem to have had a difficult time deciding whose behavior they found more deplorable, that of their men or that of the naïve and fallen women who consorted with them. A nurse, who at one point drove all the way from Paris to the camp for North African soldiers at Aix in an automobile to see her paramour, persisted in sending him letters, which included some phrases she had learned to write in Arabic. Apparently, the officer who read them considered these unspecified phrases inappropriate, because he described her use of Arabic as "flouting decency." Her behavior had ruined the attitude of her correspondent, who had been punished for insubordination: he had been "a good soldier," but "today he appears [to have] irremediably lost [his] military spirit."[65] Still, this soldier was probably not as far gone as another whom an *officier interprète* met on the street in Marseilles. This Algerian had adopted "the attitude and dress of a pimp," with "long hair, curled [and] greased, a garish scarf, hat pushed back on his head with some sort of medal on the front," all this after spending seven days on leave with a Frenchwoman in the neighborhood.[66] The anxieties such behavior raised could provoke extreme reactions. In one case, an officer reported a North African soldier for having broken the rules by spending his leave periods after being treated for wounds at the apartment of a Parisian woman, even though the officer knew full well that the woman was the soldier's wife. Despite his legitimate marriage to a Frenchwoman, the officer felt that this and similar "deplorable practices" by other *indigènes* should be stopped.[67]

At the root of military authorities' worries was the conviction that Frenchwomen who became romantically involved with these soldiers did not adequately understand the "indigenous mentality." Censors noted that these women had formed "an erroneous ideal" of the soldiers and their way of life in the colonies. One letter that illustrated the phenomenon of women "steeped in Orientalism" particularly well, the censors in Tunis asserted, was that of Mme Marthe Crozat to the Tunisian soldier Salah Ben Amor. After having been posted back to his regiment at Bizerte, Ben Amor sent her a package containing a rug as a gift. Mme Crozat wrote in return: "In fact, looking at this rug, I cannot help but think of the luxury that is laid out in your beautiful homes, so firmly closed off, of your delicious harems, so well hidden away, where the women of Africa and of all the Orient are found, so perfectly happy because they have a comfort that many Frenchwomen envy, thanks to soft rugs of many colors."[68]

Another woman's correspondence a few months later also revealed the dangers of being "seduced by the mirage of the Orient." This woman had married a Tunisian with the intention of moving to North Africa with him, but he had been posted back to Bizerte, and she had lost contact with him. Her last letter to him had been returned marked "unknown," and she had learned that while their marriage was legal in France, at home in Tunisia, her husband had the right to take up to four wives and even to repudiate her if he so chose. She admitted to suffering terribly, but wrote that she "did not have the courage to leave him," even though with her property she could have made a better marriage. The censor noted the pathos of the situation; here was a woman "whom no moral consideration or material interest seemed to be able to restrain."[69] Even some *indigènes* expressed doubts about the good sense of some of the women who became involved in interracial relationships. One Madagascan counseled a friend who was talking of marriage to a Frenchwoman to let her know that he was poor, what life was like in Madagascar, and to be sure that she would not arrive in the colony, regret not having the status of other European women who lived there, and kill either herself or her new husband to escape her fate.[70]

## Images Across the Color Line

These kinds of situations exemplified for authorities the destabilizing effects that interracial relationships had upon metropolitan society, as Frenchwomen were apparently deluded and sometimes suffering for their transgression of racial and sexual boundaries. That they were deluded and suffered was bad enough, but it was all the more galling to male French officials that this was occurring at the hands of colonial subjects. Not only were these men allegedly dishonoring white Frenchwomen, but they also certainly spread tales of their conquests in their letters home and when they returned to the colonies, thus undermining French prestige and the assumptions of white superiority upon which it rested. But the *indigènes* did not just send and bring home tales of their success in love and sex, they often provided proof in the form of photographs, and these were not always merely pictures of nurses in their Red Cross uniforms.

In many ways, the censors were more concerned about the subversive effects of these images than they were about the written and verbal testimony of the soldiers. This was in part, no doubt, because, inasmuch as "traditional exoticism" had featured nude indigenous women for the fascinated gaze of European men, it represented another dramatic inversion of the colonial order.[71] In November 1916, the censors in Marseille reported that they had destroyed several postcards, bound for Indochina, which pictured "nude Frenchwomen in more or less academic poses, with some reflections of doubtful taste on the other side."[72] Since this was fairly early in the life of formal censorship, and the majority of Indochinese soldiers had yet to arrive in France, there were relatively few of these postcards, only thirteen in all. However, a few months later, the censors were alarmed to see the volume increase dramatically. By February of the next year, they were confiscating more and more numerous "photographs of nude women, the subjects of which only rarely decorate our museums of painting or sculpture," and, what was worse, the censors suspected that the traffic in these images had begun before the institution of regular censorship.[73] In March, they seized over 400 *nudités* (nude pictures) along with another 100 photographs accompanied by "libidinous or lewd comments." Shocked, the censor noted: "One of these is most obscene." This state of affairs was "absolutely disconcerting," all the more so because the Indochinese did not make any attempt to hide their "vices" from their families, sending lewd pictures and remarks to their mothers and fathers, wives, even their children. Often the soldiers accompanied the photos with the remark, "There are such marvels only in France," but censors observed that "this admiration of French beauty is not without irreverence." Remarkably, as disconcerted as they were about the *nudités,* the censors seem to have been even more worried about the photographs the Indochinese sent home of themselves in the company of white women. Such proof of interracial contact was damaging to "our prestige in the Far East," so the censors confiscated twenty-three of these images.[74]

That same month, Sergeant Thai Hu Tham wrote to his brother in Indochina warning him to be skeptical of the photos that soldiers sent home, because many had their pictures taken with prostitutes and then described them as their fiancées or wives. He assured his brother that the "women in the countryside" were not like these urban prostitutes, and such virtuous women were good conversationalists who sometimes let one hold their hand, "or kiss, but not. . . . " The censors observed, however, that such laudatory remarks were rare, and "the Indochinese repertoire has furnished some new terms for a comparative anatomy that is not at all flattering to Frenchwomen." The report noted that though many of the hundreds of pictures confiscated originated from Indochinese workers in France, many also came from soldiers, even those at the front in combat units. Six months later, a report noted that soldiers sent most of the *nudités,* "as usual."[75]

In December 1918, censors gave a final accounting of all the photos seized from mail to Indochina during the two years of their work. Almost 10,000 images were listed according to the following categories: nudes, undressed, bathers, kissing, mixed-race children, photographs of Frenchwomen, photographs of Franco-Indochinese couples.[76] These categories make it clear that French authorities considered any visual proof of interracial relationships—from suggestive or fully or partly nude pictures of Frenchwomen, to photos of mixed-race children, to photos of Frenchwomen in the company of *indigènes*—as potentially subversive. Moreover, it was not just Indochinese soldiers who sent such images home. Censors in Tunis reported that one North African sent home a photograph of a Muslim soldier with his arm around a very young French girl, along with a message in Arabic that read, "I ask you, my brother, to tell me if this young girl pleases you, in which case I will procure one for you [and] you can then do with her what you like." Others sent pictures of Frenchwomen with obscene captions, such as "One can have this young thing for a few francs."[77]

*Troupes indigènes* from all of the colonies engaged in this traffic in photos between the metropole and the colonies, rendering the problem very serious in the eyes of military officials. Consequently, on 5 June 1917, the Ministry of War issued a circular formally forbidding the photographs and ordering the seizure and destruction of all obscene pictures and postcards, though this had already been de facto policy for some time.[78] Yet the effect of this circular upon the behavior of the soldiers was at first limited. A report on Indochinese correspondence for the month in which the circular appeared observed that despite the new formal policy and severe punishments for transgressions, the number of *nudités* seized had only slightly decreased (from 480 during the previous month to 349).[79] By April, however, the strict policy seems to have begun working, because the number had decreased further (to 216).[80] Still, in later months, this number was sometimes higher, and there were other indications that the authorities were not entirely able to prevent transmission of such images. Some *indigènes* labored to find ways around the strictures, the most creative of which was probably that employed by Fang, a worker who wrote to a friend from the hospital that he could not get any more *nudités* as requested, because the sale of them was forbidden, but, "to simplify, I will draw some myself and send them to you."[81]

Moreover, the existence of the restrictive policy itself provided possible occasions for criticizing French assumptions of racial superiority. In August 1917, an Indochinese letter writer observed that officials had forbidden *nudités* because "the French fear ridicule."[82] It seemed, then, that French officials faced ridicule whether they allowed the traffic in these photos to continue (the *indigènes* laughing either at the nudity of their proud colonial masters or at the impotence of Frenchmen to prevent their women from behaving shamelessly, or both) or whether they forbade it (the French fearing their colonial subjects' laughter or Frenchmen, unable to exercise control over their women, resorting to cracking down on *indigènes* who looked at the photographs). If, as George Orwell contended, the white man's life in the colonies "was one long struggle not to be laughed at," then the traffic in these images and the resulting risk of ridicule presented a serious challenge to the white prestige upon which colonial rule rested.[83]

## Consequences

Photographs were striking visual proof of the willingness of Frenchwomen to have relationships with colonial men, and hence prized by *indigènes* eager to inform and titillate friends and family back home. However, they were not the only form of proof. Sergeant-Major Hô sent his brother in Indochina letters he had received from Frenchwomen, telling him to save them as "sacred things" that the sergeant could, upon his return, show to European *colons* who did not believe his stories and who might mock him for his pretensions to relations with white women. Censors were quite candid about the ultimate consequences for public order and French rule in the colonies: examples, like Sergeant Hô, of the "deplorable attitude" that many *troupes indigènes* had acquired during their stay in France would lead the population of Indochina to think that the French lived in a "shameful debauchery."[84]

The sexual (mis)conduct of *indigènes* in France, and its consequences, soon became the main preoccupation of the military officials charged with reading their mail. Censors worried, often explicitly, about the effect upon the "prestige" of white women in the colonies.[85] "Some of these letters are injurious to Frenchwomen," one report lamented.[86] And injuries to Frenchwomen and their prestige were equally injuries to France and to the white prestige that justified and supported European rule.

The authorities certainly did not want rumors spread in the colonies like the one Hussein el Gassem Blagui propagated in a letter to friends in Tunisia: "I would like to inform you that the minister has directed that as soon as the war is finished, each soldier must marry, whether he likes it or not, a young French girl; reservists will have the right to a virgin, and active soldiers to a young and beautiful woman. There we are, then, o my brother, stuck. No matter, thank God anyway!"[87] Nor was it gratifying to the officials who had brought these *indigènes* to France to see a Tunisian send home a picture of a young Frenchwoman and her younger sister, with an accompanying letter asserting that neither of these women wanted him to leave France. Of course, he wrote, he did not want to leave France either, because there were better women even than these around for the taking. Though another Tunisian complained of the cold of French winters, he was able to withstand them, he wrote, because Frenchwomen helped him keep warm, and he assured his correspondent that if he too came to France, he would be "very debauched."[88]

Officials hoped that *indigènes* would display enthusiasm for coming to

France and making war on Germany out of a sense of obligation to France for the benefits colonial rule had ostensibly brought to the colonies, or even a kind of patriotism. However, making love with Frenchwomen inspired some *troupes indigènes* to want to stay in France for very different reasons. A Madagascan slated to be sent home for health reasons (wounds or sickness), but who obtained leave to remain in France, wrote: "I invoked my great desire to continue to serve the fatherland, but in reality, I find Frenchwomen too pretty and nice and I would hate to leave them already." Another encouraged a friend in Madagascar not to be slow in volunteering for service in France because "the white women whom we believe haughty and disdainful at home are here before us just like little dogs, they lick the soles of our feet. . . . Some of them are as pretty as angels [there followed, the censor noted, 'obscene details,' which he did not specify] . . . each Madagascan has his own."[89] One exasperated officer asked how one could expect to maintain the loyalty of North Africans when they were "obsessed by the idée fixe of satisfying their violent passions and the image of defending the *patrie* is erased entirely from their minds."[90]

Eventually, officials began to suspect that their efforts to discourage and prevent liaisons between *indigènes* and Frenchwomen could not stop contact altogether, and despite what authorities often wanted to believe, many of these relationships were of a genuinely romantic and serious nature. By 1918, at least 250 Indochinese men had married Frenchwomen, and 231 such couples were living together in the metropole, with these and other relationships producing dozens of mixed-race children.[91] Other interracial couples no doubt escaped notice, and some Frenchwomen certainly emigrated to the colonies to be with their beloveds.

Such circumstances caused officials to reflect upon the consequences of these contacts and to consider their own role in policing them. In a March 1917 report, censors admitted that the problem of the liaisons between Indochinese men and Frenchwomen was not going to go away. When men returned home, whole families were left desolate in France, especially when the union had produced children, and the army received urgent requests for the return of the man to the metropole. "Should we," the report asked, "respect these consensual unions, especially when they are consecrated by a birth?" The obligation the state owed to the children seemed to indicate that the answer was yes. The situation of the young mothers was desperate. Should the authorities in certain cases condone the regularization of the union by marriage? Here the report seems to espouse a liberal view on the matter of integrating these (admittedly few) men into French society: "Assimilation increases day by day, to such an extent that this stage could be easily reached by a rather large number of *indigènes*, if their stay in France is prolonged for many more months."[92] In other words, perhaps these unions would perform the ideological work of French imperialism, civilizing colonial subjects.

Nevertheless, just as voices touted the benefits of *métissage* to bring the French and subject "races" closer together only occasionally during certain periods of French imperial history, there was never any doubt about the overall negative official attitude toward these wartime unions.[93] As the war continued and the stay of Indochinese men in France grew longer and longer, bringing evidence of more and more relationships and, especially, of the birth of métis children, alarmed censors admitted that there was little or nothing authorities could do to "prevent the liaisons and the consequences that result from them."[94]

In November 1917, a report summed up at length the predicament facing the authorities. The number and sincerity of "amorous letters" was beginning to give the censors pause. Whole families were evidently embracing Indochinese men who courted their daughters. The most intelligent letter writers were aware of official censorship of the mails and found alternative ways to correspond, while the less perceptive grew angry and bitter over the perceived failure of their beloveds to respond. "What can we do? . . . To protect the Frenchwoman is an urgent duty for us, but stopping a few letters is a palliative that loses all of its value when the writer remains in the country." Intrusive censorship might be too grave a restriction on individual liberty, as well as providing both French people and *indigènes* with a new complaint against the government. The Indochinese chafed at being treated "as little boys." Letters often indicated that these men found Frenchwomen in the metropole more approachable and likeable than those in the colonies. "While waiting for them to change their opinion of our female compatriots in the Far East, is it a good idea to spoil, to some degree, the opinion that they have of us all here?" As a more practical matter, too draconian a surveillance of this correspondence risked exposing the preventative efforts of the authorities to ridicule, because despite censorship, there were many "unfortunate Frenchwomen led astray in obviously grotesque liaisons," which were clearly a form of revenge for mixed unions between European men and indigenous women in the colonies. In the end, the report recommended discretely warning women and families of the risks they were running by welcoming colonial men into their homes, beds, and hearts.[95]

Ultimately, however, officials were concerned about the effects of these interracial relationships, not only upon French metropolitan society, but also upon the social and political order in the colonies. The problems overseas were potentially more destructive over the long term. Within weeks after the war ended in November 1918, the French Army began repatriating the *troupes indigènes* who had helped bring about the recent victory over Germany. By 1920, many of these men were home. Now the problem was no longer the stories and pictures that they sent home in envelopes, but those that they brought home in person, and there was no form of censorship that could effectively prevent these men from telling of their experiences. Moreover, these men had gained the kind of experience, skills, and, in some cases, education that would make them leaders in their societies in the postwar years. With their newfound perspective on the prestige of European women and white superiority, both of which helped underpin colonial rule, such men would in all probability be more difficult to rule. After the war, one official articulated this concern explicitly, worrying that some Indochinese men who had served in France would return to the colony with new ideas and be less "submissive" to "their traditional discipline."[96] The colonial administration in Indochina was a few steps ahead on this issue, having already instructed regional officials in June 1918 to interrogate and maintain close surveillance on returning soldiers.[97]

In the metropole, censors' reports noted the Faustian deal that France had made in calling upon its subject peoples for aid in defeating the Germans, and not only because colonial men discovered that they could approach white women and have relationships of some equality with them. Mail from *troupes indigènes* also revealed a fascination with the might of the German military machine that had caused such great devastation to the French nation, while these men did not fail to note that France had called upon the aid, not only of the colonies, but of Great Britain, Russia, and even the United States to defeat a powerful Germany that, in their eyes, stood virtually alone, with only Austria for an ally. When in 1918 *indigènes* called the French the "poor brothers" of the Entente and remarked upon the superior material wealth and energy of newly arrived Americans, French officials saw a vision of the postwar world order that they did not like.

A number of comments along these lines emanated from troops still in Europe during the years immediately after the war. The army stationed many *troupes indigènes* in the German Rhineland as occupation forces following the November 1918 armistice, including many Indochinese, whose activities and continuing sexual exploits, now carried on with German women, received a great deal of attention from censors charged with reading their mail. The troops commented often upon the technological prowess of the defeated enemy, one soldier writing in 1923, "From the point of view of scientific progress, this nation stands incontestably well above France. German civilization is thus without rival." Another soldier seemed to have had a hard time deciding whether he was more impressed by German women or by "the countryside and the cities, which are very pretty; the machines are even more magnificent." After seeing large parts of France battered and destroyed, it was not surprising that these men found Germany's villages and cities, physically untouched by war, impressive, but many followed their observations to a logical conclusion that was troubling for their colonial masters. One soldier compared the victors unfavorably the vanquished, writing, "I think that the Germans are more civilized and stronger than the French," while another quantified German superiority, asserting: "The Germans are ten times more skillful than the French." Yet more troubling was the often-repeated charge that the French emerged victorious from the war only because "Germany was merely alone against several very powerful nations." Another soldier resorted to hyperbole to drive home the point of German might: "If this nation is defeated, it is thanks to ten thousand nations allied to France."[98] French officials certainly did not like hearing their colonial subjects raising the specter of waning French power within Europe, a specter that could easily be exported overseas and into the empire.

Censors took equal note of comments revealing relationships with German women, which appeared to be numerous. Though these intimate encounters might be less of a concern than relations with Frenchwomen, any interracial relationships were disconcerting, because they violated the boundaries between European and colonial subject, white and nonwhite. Contacts across the color line, on both sides of the Rhine, then, threatened to sow disorder in the empire.

It would be difficult to determine whether French officials were correct about the effect of these relationships, because that would entail identifying colonial subjects who were involved with European women and then tracking their behavior as they spread out over the vast French colonial empire during the postwar period, a large, complicated, and perhaps impossible task. However, there are indications that military and colonial officials did observe the behavior of some of these men, and that, at the very least, authorities believed their wartime anxieties to be justified. To take one example, in

1921, an official in Tunisia claimed: "All the *tirailleurs* are coming back from France or the Army of the Rhine with ideas clearly turned around as far as French prestige, and European prestige in general, are concerned." Those who had served in France during the war "were welcomed too warmly into French families, where it was too often repeated to them that they were the saviors of the country." Unhappily, these men had now become aware of "their importance and their strength," and worse, "the license of certain milieux and the impropriety of too many women have succeeded in destroying the respect they had for us, and all of the countryside [*le bled*] now knows about the amusing adventures" these soldiers had in French society. As for soldiers coming back from Germany, they were no better.[99] Circumstances like these demonstrate how much "the First World War was experienced by colonial authorities as traumatic experiment," as Jean-Yves Le Naour puts it.[100]

In official French eyes, these attitudes did not bode well for the future of the French colonial empire. In this respect, though historians debate the significance of the experiences of *troupes indigènes* in raising political consciousness among colonized peoples and in stimulating nationalist and independence movements, the use of these troops and their experiences moving, and loving, back and forth across the color line did provoke significant fears that the colonial order would be seriously weakened because wartime experiences had fatally undermined the respect for racial boundaries that underpinned white prestige, upon which the colonial order ultimately depended.[101]

The high point of French imperialism in the postwar years, which saw the addition of former Ottoman territories in the Middle East to the French colonial empire, and the hyperbole of imperial propaganda that culminated in the celebratory Colonial Exposition of 1931 in Paris, then, perhaps masked a deeper fear that the Great War had produced circumstances that would doom European colonial empires. Indeed, as one historian has put it, the postwar years saw a "double movement of pride and worry, of pride in the work accomplished but also of fear for the fate that history might have in store for it."[102] In short, in a postwar context that saw a shift toward stricter notions of racial hierarchies in the justification of colonial rule, French officials worried that *indigènes'* less exalted view of white French people, whom they had visited, loved, and even seen naked, set the stage for challenges to that rule.[103]

At the beginning of the period of decolonization that would bring about an end to European colonial empires, the Tunisian writer Albert Memmi observed: "It is essential that this [colonial] order not be questioned by others, and especially not by the colonized."[104] French authorities recognized this as well, but the participation of *troupes indigènes* in the war effort in France after 1914 raised numerous discomfiting questions. Many of these arose out of contacts between colonial subjects in uniform and white Frenchwomen. These contacts, especially when intimate, violated the rigid separation between white and nonwhite that prevailed in the colonies. Such crossing over the color line threatened white prestige at a point French officials considered highly vulnerable and sensitive, a point loaded with sexual and racial significance. The behavior of French civilians, especially women, was a concern as well, because they too seemed to be questioning, or at least inspiring *indigènes* to question, the restrictions and boundaries of the colonial order. Citizens of the metropole blurred the color line by failing to observe strictures against interracial mixing that were much more vigorously, and much more easily, enforced in the colonies themselves. Métis offspring of interracial couples constituted the most spectacular and disturbing visual proof of grave moral, social, and racial transgressions. Visual proof also came in the form of pictures and postcards depicting the unrestrained sexuality of Frenchwomen and the access that *indigènes* had to that sexuality, either as partners or as voyeurs. This too caused French officials no end of trouble, because they feared the spread of these photographs into indigenous societies, and thus the amplification of a wartime metropolitan problem into a postwar, empirewide concern.

The fear that all of this activity provoked was of the undermining of white prestige, and thus of French power, in the colonies. Colonial subjects who had had sexual contact across the color line, or had seen evidence of such contact in photographs or heard about it from reliable sources, might very well not remain willingly subject to the colonial and racial order. Sex and love between colonial men and Frenchwomen was an intimate challenge to a racial order that was indispensable to the entire colonial system, for, as Memmi put it: "Racism appears then, not as an incidental detail, but as a consubstantial part of colonialism. . . . Not only does it establish a fundamental discrimination between colonizer and colonized, a *sine qua non* of colonial life, but it also lays the foundation for the immutability of that life."[105] Interracial relationships disproved both sides of the equation, demonstrating that discrimination did not have to be universal and showing that the relationship between colonizer and colonized was mutable and could change and take different, less restrictive forms.

Official reactions to these relationships demonstrated at least an instinctive awareness of just these sorts of dangers. Much like the existence of métis in the colony (almost always the offspring of a European man and indigenous woman), relationships between indigenous soldiers and white women provided "living proof of the impossibility of sustaining the very basis of colonial domination" because they violated the dualistic racial and cultural oppositions upon which colonialism depended.[106] This was "the fundamental contradiction of imperial domination: the tension between a form of authority simultaneously predicated on incorporation and distancing."[107] Colonial subjects, especially those in uniform fighting for France, were in theory part of the nation, but were also distanced from it by their racial identity. If that distance disappeared, then so would colonialism, the French empire, power, prestige, and much else that mattered very much to French officials. Their anxieties about these matters were all the more acute inasmuch as they recognized, to a certain extent, their powerlessness to stop much of this activity.[108] Colonial authorities had always been interested in extending bio-power into an area "where they had equivocal control—in the home."[109] Now, ironically, at home in the metropole, military and political officials found that their control was even more equivocal, because of the social and administrative disorder war brought with it; because of the greater liberality of the social order of the metropole when compared with the colonies; and because of the contradiction created by the leaders of the French state, asking men whom they did not regard as their equals to wear a uniform, to be a part of the nation, and perhaps to die to save France.[110]

This anxiety over the difficulties the use of *troupes indigènes* raised for the future of empire in France were not only apparent in reactions to interracial relationships, however, but also in one of the most difficult and contentious colonial political issues to emerge during the war. As the next chapter shows, nothing exposed the paradoxes of the use of indigenous soldiers and of the maintenance of an empire of colonial subjects as clearly as debates over offering citizenship to these men as a reward for their defense of what was supposed to be their "second fatherland."

# CHAPTER SEVEN

# *Between Subjects and Citizens*

❖

It is an obligation for France to seek to compensate the *in-digènes* who fight for her, or who, simply but loyally, have fulfilled their military duty. The highest, noblest recognition that France can perceive is to offer what she considers most precious, that is to say, French nationality.

—*Legislative proposal, Chamber of Deputies, 1 April 1915*

The vanquished are the [Indochinese] and we are the conquerors. Let us remain what we are! Let us remain the masters. We need soldiers, not electors.

—*Ulysse Leriche, 1895*

The colonial powers have always employed their overseas subjects [as soldiers] without linking in any way the rights that they grant to them and the duties they impose upon them.

—*Charles Mangin,* La force noire, *1910*

The legislative proposal that declared in 1915 that France had an "obligation" to its colonial subjects in uniform that could best be honored by offering them the "precious" gift of French nationality concisely articulated the liberal republican orthodoxy linking citizenship with service to the state in the military. As it applied specifically to colonial subjects, however, the issue was a contentious one and had been for years. In 1895, frustrated with those in the metropole who talked earnestly of assimilating or associating France's colonial subjects, of integrating them more closely into French political life, the colonist and journalist Ulysse Leriche called for his fellow French citizens to cast off their timidity and hypocrisy by embracing their role as "conquerors" and "masters," making use of Indochinese *indigènes* as soldiers without feeling compelled to offer them corresponding political rights as electors. Fifteen years later, Charles Mangin wrote similarly that France, like other European colonial powers, was under no obligation to reward the duty of military service imposed on colonial subjects with the expanded rights that French citizens enjoyed, along with their own duty to serve in the military.

Opponents of naturalizing *troupes indigènes* repeated these arguments after 1914, when the context of the debate had changed dramatically and France needed soldiers even more urgently. Leriche and Mangin had treated military service and political rights as separate issues, but the two were closely linked, as quickly became apparent when France began to recruit hundreds of thousands of colonial subjects to fight in Europe. Though these men were fighting and dying for their "adopted *patrie*," making the sacrifices that the state routinely demanded of its citizens, they remained colonial subjects, without the rights of French citizens. Powerful republican traditions and the need to attract more recruits prompted French officials to attempt to address this anomaly with measures such as the 1915 legislative proposal. However, such efforts proved controversial, and the debates they provoked among French officials and politicians highlighted the place of religion and culture in French conceptions of national identity, citizenship, and colonial ideology.

Revolutionary France was the birthplace of a new concept of national identity that closely linked the idea of citizenship with service to and defense of the state in the military. Thus, when, over a century later, France made extensive use of its colonial subjects on European battlefields to save itself from destruction at the hands of the Germans, it was entirely in keeping with traditional republican ideology that these men be offered the rights of French citizens. Opponents of this idea argued, however, that it was not necessary at all to reward these soldiers in such a manner, that military service was a just price for the colonized to pay in return for the benefits of French imperial rule, and that in fact such an idealistic approach to the question put the future of the French colonial empire gravely at risk. How France would maintain imperial control over naturalized and enfranchised colonial peoples was a crucial question, to be sure, but there was also another concern that took on special importance during the war. Many in France wondered if members of these "other" races, with cultural practices very different from those of the French, were worthy and capable of exercising the rights of French citizens.

The issue that most clearly revealed these anxieties was the naturalization of Muslim soldiers from North Africa, especially Algerians, and debate crystallized around these Muslims' traditional customs and the special legal status that preserved them, the *statut personnel*. Muslims in the colonies were in many ways subject to French law, but in matters not of direct or urgent concern to the colonial administration (property or personal disputes between Muslims, laws regarding the family, inheritance, and other issues), they were subject to Koranic law administered by local religious authorities. In this *statut personnel*, many French officials saw an insurmountable obstacle to the acquisition of French citizenship. On the other hand—and this was what made the issue so difficult to resolve—how could the men who ran the Third Republic in good conscience deny the benefits of citizenship to those who had sacrificed so much for the defense of the nation?

Scholars, and many French people themselves, consider understandings of nationhood in France to be "assimilationist," in contrast to more ethnically centered concepts of national belonging prevalent in many other countries. As such, France is supposed to be relatively open to the political and social integration of immigrants and other outsiders, no matter what their ethnic or cultural origins, who choose to embrace French law, traditions, and culture. In theory, political and cultural assimilation override ethnic and racial difference. Yet France's use of colonial subjects as soldiers in the Great War put its assimilationist impulses to the test and confronted the French with acute racial, ethnic, and cultural questions. Putting republican assimilationist theory into practice turned out to be very difficult indeed.

The most vexing of these questions for authorities were those involving customs and practices that authorities regarded as "uncivilized" and that they believed were linked with Islam. This was especially true of customs associated with the family and the rights of women, such as polygamy. That these fears were often more apparent than real did not lessen their importance in preventing the government from enacting any meaningful citizenship reform for Muslim colonial subjects. Such reform would have brought French policy into line with the republican ideology linking citizenship to military service, and with liberal traditions of assimilation that justified French colonialism by making indigenous peoples the targets of a "civilizing mission" designed to raise them up to the technological, intellectual, cultural, and eventually legal status of their colonial masters. However, despite the power of this ideology and these traditions, French officials were unable to integrate Islam into their conception of French national identity. In the final analysis, French assimilationist principles often gave way before what many regarded as insoluble racial, cultural, and religious differences. The limited access to naturalization in the colonies after the war brought into stark relief the ultimate weakness of the republican ideal of assimilation when it came to transforming colonial subjects into French citizens.

## Citizenship, Military Service, and Troupes indigènes

Revolutionary France was the birthplace of the modern idea of national citizenship as a legal state of belonging to a political entity that derived its power and legitimacy from its expression of the will of a sovereign people, not from God and the king. The Revolution of 1789 removed the mediated, indirect relations that characterized interactions between the individual and the state under the ancien régime and introduced the modern idea of citizenship as membership in the national community on an equal basis with other citizens, with shared privileges and obligations.[1] The Revolution gave legal and ideological shape to the distinction between citizens and foreigners, a distinction that would become sharper as the nineteenth century wore on and that would characterize thinking about nationality in the modern era. The French revolutionary government invented or at least institutionalized many of the trappings of modern citizenship, such as passports, a state bureaucracy devoted to defining and monitoring citizens, and strict legal requirements for the acquisition and proof of national belonging.[2]

Ideas about nationality took on a special character in France. As they have developed from their origins in the Revolution, French understandings of nationhood have stressed allegiance to the state and willing integration into national political and cultural life as signs of nationality, while many other modern nations have stressed ethnic identity, blood ties, language, and shared cultural history as important components of national identity. The French model is an expansive concept of the nation, in which "the status of citizen versus foreigner is defined less by birth or mother tongue than by political stance and cultural sympathies."[3]

Rogers Brubaker has illuminated this difference by contrasting the state-centered and assimilationist ideal in France with Germany's ethnocultural and "differentialist" model of national identity. His work reveals, not only the importance of the revolutionary heritage, but also the instrumental role that the Third Republic played in solidifying this heritage and enshrining the assimilationist ideal in the French consciousness and in law.[4] In 1882, Ernest Renan made the celebrated and oft-quoted pronouncement that the French nation was a "daily plebiscite," reflecting the conscious will of citizens to join freely together under a common government. It is the official republican adoption of this rhetoric since 1870 (excepting, of course, the attitude of the Vichy regime during World War II) that leads Maxim Silverman, in another important scholarly formulation of the nature of French national identity, to characterize the French model of the nation as "contractual," as opposed to competing "ethnic" models.[5]

These contrasting approaches are particularly evident in the historic embrace in France (and, for example, in the United States) of the *jus soli* legal conception of citizenship, which accepts as members of the national community those who are born within national borders or those who reside there and meet certain other legal requirements. In other words, if a child is born in a nation operating under this principle, then he or she is automatically a citizen, regardless of race, religion, ethnicity or other inherited characteristics. The individual becomes part of the national "daily plebiscite." An alternative definition of citizenship that prevails in many countries is known as *jus sanguinis*, which requires true members of the national community to have blood ties with the dominant ethnic group. Under this system, the nationality of a newborn child is entirely dependent upon the ethnic identity of the parents, and membership in the national community is thus restricted, even largely closed.

Yet the French universalist and assimilationist model, rooted in *jus soli* conceptions of citizenship, is neither unconditionally open to outsiders nor immune from seemingly particularist restrictions and exclusions. In the first place, the requirements of integration and assimilation can be absolute and unyielding. Those wishing to become French citizens must embrace French laws and customs, and this often requires sacrificing signs of ethnic and cultural difference. This has been especially true for Muslim North Africans. During the Great War, the most contentious debates revolved around how much of their distinctive cultural practices they could retain and still meet the requirements of French citizenship. In short, many officials doubted that Muslims could become truly French while retaining their religious identity. So France's "open" conception of nationality, while theoretically not limited by factors such as ethnicity, race, or religious belief, could be intolerant of diversity, of any deviation from prevailing notions of cultural identity. The use of *troupes indigènes*, however, posed particular difficulties, because these men were carrying out one of the most sacred duties of modern citizenship, taking up arms to defend the nation.

The French Revolution was not only the birthplace of the modern idea of citizenship, but also the origin of a view of citizenship tied explicitly to the performance of military service.[6] On 23 August 1793, the National Convention adopted the *levée en masse*, declaring that "the French people are in permanent requisition for army service," in order to defeat the invading armies of Europe's monarchies. Empowered by this decree, the state conscripted hundreds of thousands of young men, establishing the principle of the "nation in arms," which would over the next century transform European armies and the nature of modern war.[7] The *levée en masse* resulted from a transformation in the idea of citizenship that had been in the making since 1789. The measure rested upon the assumption that the state, now an expression and instrument of the popular will instead of the individual will of the monarch, could legitimately require all citizens to take up arms in defense of the nation. Now that all people had a stake in their government, they were obligated to protect its existence. In protecting the interests of the state, they were protecting their own interests. If not all French citizens perceived the logic and justice of this obligation, and some failed to volunteer for military service, the state would rightfully resort to conscription. In fact, official documents such as passports were originally most important for administering the new system of conscription.[8] Thus the first French republic established the enduring ideal of obligatory military service as "both the badge and moral consequence of citizenship," and the Third Republic embraced and extended this ideal of the citizen soldier.[9]

Thus, history and republican ideology prepared the ground for the linkage of military service and citizenship for colonial subjects in the French Army during the First World War. This link was particularly strong when it came to conscription, as the draft was one of the more specific and onerous demands that the state made of its citizens. How could France conscript colonial subjects without offering them naturalization? In a 1918 address to Parliament, the minister of the colonies offered the orthodox and idealistic republican answer that France could not deny *troupes indigènes* the opportunity to acquire French citizenship:

These populations must . . . understand that, by the very call that she addresses to them, France raises them up to her [level]. In the metropole, it is an honor as much as a duty to be a soldier, and our laws have always excluded indigenous citizens [i.e., colonial subjects] from the national army: to fight in the first ranks of the French Army is, for our African subjects, to stand forever on the side of civilization, threatened by our enemies. But, if she makes the *indigènes* a partner in her defense and demands of them their share of the sacrifices that she also imposes upon herself, France, in return, must take care to prove to them her spirit of justice and her recognition.[10]

Not everyone, however, agreed with this argument, many military and political officials preferring to avoid conscription, and thus the problem of compensation in the form of naturalization, altogether. In 1915, Senator Henry Bérenger explicitly rejected conscription as a means of recruitment, though he urged the French government to make greater use of *indigènes* in the army. He argued that obligatory military service was not a practice that the French could export to the colonies because

such as it functions today in French democracy, it is the complex work of time and liberty. It is the statute of a nation of citizens; it cannot be the regime of several races of subjects. Such sublime servitudes can be imposed by law only if they have first been consented to by the intellect and the heart. Conscription cannot be improvised any more than can the fatherland. We cannot require of our *indigènes* the same military obligations we require of ourselves while we have not conceded them the same civil rights.[11]

The Senator did not envision according *indigènes* these civil rights, and so he cautioned against conscripting men "who fight neither for their traditions nor for their homes."[12] Bérenger suggested that the government make use of volunteers, or mercenaries fighting for material benefits, and perhaps offer limited access to naturalization to those who volunteered for military service and met certain requirements. This vision was far from the maximal republican ideal linking obligatory service to the state in the military with the right to citizenship.

Claims that colonial subjects were not fighting to protect their own homes were objectively true, but in fact the republican ideology of assimilation allowed many to argue that *indigènes* were defending their own immediate interests by serving in the French Army. The 1918 address by the minister of the colonies was in this tradition. Colonial assimilationist ideology was similar and related to the assimilationism of French citizenship policy, but specific to the colonial context. As it related to military service, the doctrine dictated that France would raise the inhabitants of the colonies up to its own elevated level of civilization, and so it was proper that France conscript *indigènes* to fight alongside native Frenchmen to defend their common interests, in this case, to expel the Germans from French soil.

Men like Senator Bérenger favored the competing vision of the colonial relationship known as association, which advocated allowing colonial subjects to develop within their own cultures and social institutions while the French associated local indigenous elites with the colonizing project. Association seemed to abandon, at least in part, the republican ideal of "civilizing" and assimilating indigenous peoples, and to recognize an irreducible difference between the French and their colonial subjects. Subjects would remain associated with the colonial project, not assimilated into an expansive French national community. Bérenger's colleague in the Senate, Étienne Flandin, made this point explicit in a 1917 critique of the use of conscription in Algeria. He believed it a mistake to force ill-prepared *indigènes* to assimilate to French practices and ideals, in this case obligatory service in the French Army. A more prudent approach, he argued, would be to pursue a policy of association in military matters, which in this case amounted to a militia system based upon local tribal organization, to allow "the *indigène* to evolve not in our civilization, but in his own."[13]

The ideal of assimilation seemed to offer more hope for the eventual naturalization of colonial subjects, once they had achieved a certain level of cultural affinity and political maturity in the judgment of their colonial masters. Association, in contrast, did not seek such an allegedly utopian transformation of the mentality of *indigènes,* and seemed to maintain the political and cultural gulf that separated colonizers from colonized. Still, in practice, neither approach opened an easy path to French citizenship. Yet given the content of republican ideology and public discussion of military service for colonial subjects, *indigènes* themselves could be forgiven for being confused about the opportunities that existed if they joined the army. French officials routinely referred to France as the *indigènes'* "new" or "adopted" *patrie.* Invoking *la patrie,* or "the fatherland," implied an emotive, mystical bond between the nation and its "children." There was even more concrete discussion of compensation. In 1914, in an address to an important religious figure from Algeria who was touring France and visiting soldiers to improve their morale, the minister of war gave his assurance that Algerians were defending "not only their adopted *patrie,* but also the patrimony of liberty that they won nearly a century ago [i.e., in 1830, when France conquered

Algeria] and that will not cease henceforth to increase."[14] The implication was clear: Algerians contributing to the national defense were repaying the debt they owed for the benefits of French rule and paying installments on benefits that would accrue in the future.

Talk of future compensation emanated from many sources during the war. In the spring of 1915, a marabout from Guelma named Mbarek issued three proclamations to his fellow Algerians, urging them to be "grateful to our *patrie* France, which is our adoptive mother" and saying that the French government had two important qualities, "generosity and pity," and would compensate "its Muslim sons perfectly," especially those who had fought at the front and distinguished themselves with their bravery and loyalty.[15] Though such obsequious and self-serving displays of fidelity on the part of members of the indigenous elite, many of whom were anxious to curry favor with the French administration and thereby retain their positions of influence and power within the colonial order, did not often fool other *indigènes*, such talk of compensation probably both reflected and contributed to elevated expectations among those who served and their families.

The soldiers themselves sometimes embraced French republican ideals and expressed a desire to obtain citizenship. In late 1918, with the war ending in a French victory, a North African soldier wrote in a letter from the front: "These events fill us with joy and ensure that our lives are saved. . . . May France survive, she who represents the rights of man."[16] That some soldiers had internalized French rhetoric portraying France as a beacon of freedom and justice could only flatter the colonizers, but it also perhaps indicated the soldiers' expectation of a reward for loyal service.

Others were more direct. A report on morale among troops from North Africa written very early in the war noted that the men "count entirely on the fairness of France in no longer being treated as pariahs but as 'citizens' of their country after the war, having shed their blood without stinting."[17] Later, an Algerian told a French official that "it would be generous to grant us certain rights, which France without doubt will not refuse to the survivors of her Algerian children who will have died contributing to her triumph over Germany."[18] In January 1915, the Ministry of War observed that there were numerous demands emanating from Algeria for the naturalization of all soldiers then in the army.[19]

If North Africans' demands for citizenship were a particular concern for French officials, given the large numbers who served and the special legal status of Muslims, they were neither the only group nor even the only Muslims among the *troupes indigènes* whose desire to obtain political rights captured attention. In fact, the status of a relatively small group from West Africa, *originaires* from the Four Communes of Senegal, provided the most spectacular example of the possibilities for linking military service to citizenship. These men were the first to obtain concrete affirmation as citizen-soldiers, and their religious identity played a surprisingly small role in shaping official French attitudes toward their citizenship status, at least when compared with attitudes toward North African Muslims.

The *originaires'* success in obtaining recognition as citizen-soldiers was almost entirely due to the efforts of Blaise Diagne, who was the first black African to serve in the French Parliament, having been elected after an extraordinary campaign in February 1914. Diagne was highly assimilated: educated by French missionaries, he worked in the colonial administration, married a Frenchwoman in Paris in 1909, and, according to the eulogy of his fellow parliamentarian Fernand Buisson, "spoke our language with a skill that even many here envied." Diagne's election broke the power of more politically pliable mulattoes (*métis*) who had hitherto dominated local politics, who had not significantly challenged the French administration. The new deputy soon lived up to his election promise to represent better the interests of his black African constituents.[20] Though Diagne often saw himself as representing the interests of all West Africans, his immediate constituents were the natives, or *originaires*, of the Four Communes—Saint-Louis, Dakar, Gorée, and Rufisque—known as the *quatre communes de plein exercice* (i.e., with full rights), who were represented in French Parliament by virtue of their ancestors' loyalty to the Republic during the Revolution of 1848.[21] When the war began only six months after Diagne's election, he was presented with a unique opportunity to expand and solidify the status of *originaires* as full-fledged French citizens.

Diagne used the military service and conscription of his constituents to accomplish this goal. Immediately upon the outbreak of war, he fought for the right of his fellow *originaires* to serve in the French metropolitan army. The question of military service and conscription, Diagne knew, would pose the question of the status of *originaires* in a particularly acute manner, because full French citizens would be subject to metropolitan draft laws and would serve in units of the regular French Army alongside white Frenchmen, while colonial subjects would be conscripted into the *tirailleurs sénégalais* under the legislation that applied to the AOF. In the years prior to 1914, the colonial administration and the local métis elite had worked to erode the position of black Africans in the Four Communes, whose status as French citizens was ambiguous: they had voting rights, and were exempt from forced labor (corvée) and the repressive legal code applied to colonial subjects known as the *indigénat,* but the many *originaires* among them who were Muslims retained their special legal status, the *statut personnel* (personal status), instead of submitting to the French Code, a situation that ostensibly precluded full French citizenship.[22]

Though Charles Mangin and others had rejected any necessary link between military service and citizenship, Diagne knew better. The new Senegalese deputy also knew that politicians in Paris were more receptive than colonial authorities in West Africa to arguments rooted in republican idealism.[23] So Diagne began immediately in August 1914 to lobby the Ministry of War to include *originaires* in metropolitan units. Making no headway in these efforts, he brought the matter up in Parliament in April 1915, declaring in his first speech before that body, "If we can come here to legislate, we are French citizens; and if we are, we demand the right to serve as all French citizens do."[24] In legislation he later introduced on the subject, he called the *originaires'* exemption from the 1905 and 1913 French laws on conscription an "illegal privilege" and argued that his constituents saw "in this exceptional situation the spectacle of a veritable humiliation for the reputation of their patriotism and their French consciousness."[25] On 19 October 1915, Diagne finally succeeded in pushing through legislation that allowed *originaires* to serve in metropolitan units and subjected them to the same conscription laws as Frenchmen living in the metropole.[26]

Yet he had not achieved his main objective—an official and explicit recognition of *originaires* as French citizens—and over the next year, he sought to wring such an acknowledgment out of Parliament. In February 1916, Diagne submitted another legislative proposal, seeking to tighten up the provisions of the earlier legislation by explicitly stating that children of *originaires,* even if born outside the territories of the Four Communes, were also subject to metropolitan conscription laws. This seemingly innocuous proposal in fact had profound implications, because Diagne had chosen his words carefully. The new law would state that *originaires* and their descendants "are and remain French citizens subject to the military obligations contained in the law of 19 October 1915."[27] Incredibly, none of the other deputies seem to have grasped the import of this wording, and they passed without discussion the law as Diagne had written it on 13 July 1916.[28]

Diagne had discouraged his fellow *originaires* from enlisting until he had clarified their status, but his legislative victories in 1915 and 1916 opened the way for thousands more Africans to help defend France. Colonial administrators alleged that *originaires* were not at all eager to be subject to the draft: the lieutenant-governor of Senegal reported that *originaires* insulted and threatened Diagne when he appeared in Saint-Louis after the passage of the law of 19 October.[29] Yet many of his constituents appreciated his efforts on their behalf, largely because he explicitly paired the obligation of military service with *originaires'* privileges as French citizens. Years later, one veteran recalled that, "The métis and the *Tubabs* [Europeans] wanted to recruit us into the army as *tirailleurs*. And Blaise Diagne created the [conscription] law [so that we could] become citizens, [and] not be considered as *tirailleurs*. And the law was adopted and [later] all the 'black' Senegalese from the Four Communes became citizens."[30]

Despite difficulties with registering and incorporating *originaires*, conscription operations soon got under way and provided the French Army with nearly 6,000 men by April 1916.[31] In all, at least 7,200 *originaires* served in the French Army during the war, and over 5,000 served in Europe.[32] Though these numbers were of small military significance in the context of a French war effort that mobilized over eight million men, they had a profound effect upon *originaires* and their rights as French citizens. Moreover, Diagne soon transferred the same tactics he used in advocating the cause of his constituents in the Four Communes to recruitment policy throughout the AOF. When, in the desperate months of late 1917 and early 1918, the French government decided to call upon thousands more *tirailleurs* to defend the metropole, Diagne took the opportunity to tie recruitment and military service to a larger political "war to obtain rights" for all West Africans.[33] Before leaving France to lead the massive recruiting mission in French West Africa in 1918, he obtained several important concessions that emphasized the reciprocal duties of the colonizers and colonized. Among these measures, designed to ease resistance to recruitment and reward West Africans for their cooperation and aid in the war effort, was a decree allowing veterans who had won both the *croix de guerre* and the *médaille militaire* to obtain French citizenship (though Muslims had to renounce their special legal status, the *statut personnel*).[34] This hardly opened the door wide to mass naturalization, but it was still an important recognition of the links between military service and citizenship.

## Islam and French Citizenship

As the stipulation regarding the *statut personnel* in the 1918 recruitment legislation for the AOF indicated, the problem of reconciling the requirements of French citizenship with the legal customs of Muslim subjects often confounded French officials in discussions about the naturalizing of *troupes indigènes* during the war. Oddly enough, this issue did not loom large in considerations of the *originaires'* status, and this was probably due to the relatively small number of *originaires* and to Diagne's skill in exploiting both republican ideology and parliamentary procedure. Certainly, the laws of 1915 and 1916 provoked negative reactions once Parliament had passed them, primarily among French officials in the colonies.[35] Lamine Guèye, later deputy for Senegal during the Fourth Republic, discussed the Diagne Laws and the conflicts between Muslims' *statut personnel* and French law in his 1922 doctoral dissertation for the Faculty of Law at the University of Paris. He concluded that such problems were more apparent than real, because the French had never had any difficulty in the past either accommodating or suppressing certain elements of Koranic Law in order to bring the lives of the colonized into harmony with "modern civilization." The law was more important, he argued, for its political implications than its civil consequences, defining the electoral rights and military obligations of the *originaires*.[36]

French authorities were not as sanguine as Guèye about the relationship between French and Koranic law when it came to North Africans. Wartime discussions about the naturalization of Muslims from Tunisia, Morocco, and especially Algeria starkly illuminated the difficulties officials had in reconciling French citizenship with Islam. These problems stemmed from Muslims' *statut personnel.* This special "privilege" set Muslims apart from French citizens, who were subject to the Napoleonic Code in all matters. Moreover, French and Koranic law were in direct contradiction in some areas, notably in laws regarding the family. These contradictions raised grave concerns for many French officials when they contemplated the implications of naturalizing North African soldiers.

Algerians quickly became the focus of the debate over naturalization. Powerful colonial interests in all of the colonies, especially European settlers, opposed granting the rights of citizens to *indigènes*. Such objections sometimes carried more weight when they focused on black Africans or southeast Asians, whose racial identity dramatically separated them from

Frenchmen and North Africans, both "perfectible whites," in the words of Algeria's governor-general.[37] Within North Africa, the status of Tunisia and Morocco as protectorates complicated plans for naturalization considerably, requiring that the French respect the nominal sovereignty of the indigenous rulers. Converting those rulers' subjects into French citizens was hardly an effective way of doing so. Algeria, considered an integral part of France itself, was different. And though the numerous European settlers of Algeria adamantly opposed any political changes that would diminish their own power and prestige by enhancing the status of the much more numerous *indigènes*, legal anomalies arising out of Algeria's special position rendered the status of indigenous Algerians ambiguous and subject to debate. According to the *sénatus-consulte* of 14 July 1865, legislation of Napoleon III's Second Empire that regulated the status of Algeria's Muslims, indigenous Algerians were "French," though they were not fully citizens because of their *statut personnel*. Liberal politicians had for years sought ways to improve and define more clearly the status of Algerian Muslims, trying to find an arrangement more appropriate to residents of an integral part of France and more in line with republican ideals of equality. After 1914, the issue of naturalizing Algerians also had special prominence because more of them were serving in the French Army during the war than any other group among the *troupes indigènes*: about 175,000 Algerians served, comprising approximately one-third of all indigenous troops and almost two-thirds of those from all of North Africa.

If the *sénatus-consulte* of 1865 brought indigenous Algerians closer to French nationality, it also set the precedent of the separation of nationality from citizenship on the basis of religion, which would complicate the naturalization of soldiers during the Great War.[38] As early as 1836, the French legal system no longer considered indigenous Algerians to be foreigners, and in 1862, the Court of Algiers declared that "while not being a citizen, the *indigène* is French." The 1865 legislation, however, formalized the opposition between French citizenship and Islam, stating that "the Muslim *indigène* is French; nevertheless, he will continue to be governed by Muslim law."[39] In other words, Muslim Algerians could possess French nationality, because Algeria was more than a colony and part of the French nation, but could not be citizens, because they were not subject to French civil law. This ambiguous situation created a number of juridical difficulties, contradictions, and outright confusion, representing an anomaly at the heart of the republican edifice of law as it applied in Algeria. This compelled some jurists to quibble over even the language of potential reform, objecting to plans for the "natu-ralization" of *indigènes,* because they already possessed French nationality. Naturalization was for foreigners, they argued, and since Algeria was not a foreign country, *indigènes* were not foreigners, so it would be more accurate to speak of them as being "admitted into the title of a French citizen."[40]

Yet Algerians' religion did for all intents and purposes make them for-eigners. The idea that Islam was foreign to French national identity was in-scribed in the laws regulating Algerians' status. Though some liberal officials and legislators explored the possibility of granting *indigènes* the political rights of citizens while allowing them to retain the civil rights of Muslim law, the majority ultimately decided that, in the words of one administra-tor, "the full exercise of the rights of a French citizen is incompatible with the conservation of the *statut musulman* and its dispositions, [which are] contrary to our laws and our customs on marriage, divorce, and the civil rights of children." As Charles-Robert Ageron notes, this attitude and the resulting stipulations of the *sénatus-consulte* meant that "[n]either citizens nor subjects, Muslims thus enjoyed instead a mixed position between that of foreigners and that of a citizen."[41] In order to escape this ambiguous status, a Muslim would have to reject the *statut personnel* after he had turned twenty-one and apply to the colonial administration for citizenship.

Yet it was clear from the beginning that the vast majority of Muslims were unwilling to meet this requirement. Other factors besides religion were undoubtedly at work, because resentment of the French conquerors had an important political aspect as well, but fidelity to the tenets of Islam was crucial for many. For Muslims, to reject Koranic law was apostasy, "a kind of civil and moral death," which could lead to the legal dissolution of marriage and the confiscation of property. The apostate was excluded from the community of Muslims in this life and could only look forward to eternal damnation in the next.[42] Few Algerians were eager to make this sacrifice in order to obtain the rights of a French citizen: between 1865 and 1915, the government-general in Algeria received only 2,215 requests for naturalization.[43]

When the issue gained renewed prominence after 1915, Islam would re-main the major impediment to gaining French citizenship, in the eyes of both the Muslims themselves and French officials. Early in 1916, an *officier interprète* reported that some North African soldiers had heard stories cir-culating in the press about a project for the naturalization of *indigènes* and had expressed their unhappiness with the idea. The officer tried to explain to the men that proposal was intended only to confer upon them the advantages of French citizenship, but the men persisted in their belief that "our hidden motive was to suppress their *statut personnel* and to make them French only in order better to be able to subject them to obligatory military service, with the sole intention being to fill the gaps the war has created in the army."[44] Yet, if the soldiers were mistaken in thinking that the government was going to force Muslims to abandon their legal status in some sort of mass naturalization, they were justified in their suspicion that French authorities viewed French citizenship and the *statut personnel* as mutually exclusive. Ultimately, these views caused the most difficulty in drafting an effective plan to offer naturalization to Muslim North Africans.

Given these concerns, why then did the issue of granting French citizenship become so important to authorities? Paradoxically, it was their identity as Muslims that, in part, at first provoked efforts to reform naturalization procedures for soldiers. After the Ottoman empire joined in the war against France, the government in Paris sought ways to demonstrate to the *indigènes* that its commitment to furthering the interests of Muslims in the French colonies was more than just rhetorical. Such a demonstration was all the more important because Germany and Turkey encouraged the spread of anti-French propaganda among France's Muslim subjects both at the front and in North Africa. In February 1916, the French seized copies of brochures, written in Arabic, intended for distribution in North Africa. Among these tracts was one entitled *Mépris de la religion musulmane dans les rangs français* (Contempt for the Muslim Religion in the French Ranks), which, in addition to charging that the French Army did not provide dead Muslim soldiers with proper burials, claimed that the French had coerced North Africans to fight for their "second *patrie.*" The brochure's author admitted that it was possible that Arabs would serve willingly, "on the condition that France confer on them all the rights that Frenchmen enjoy, both advantages and obligations." But currently they were fighting "without any compensation." Muslim soldiers who served "this nation without honor," "ungrateful" for their sacrifice, "must disobey the laws that force them to go into combat as into the abattoir, to fight against the allies of their religion, of their land, and of the green standard of the Prophet."[45] The pamphlet asked whether "glorious France, humanitarian France," which demanded blood and sacrifice and reduced Muslims to the "the last degree of servitude," was in fact working, not only for the French, but also for Jews and other "thieves" to whom France had given rights of citizens.[46]

The author of *Mépris de la religion musulmane* skillfully exploited the evident gap between French demands for wartime aid from their subject populations and the republican ideal linking military service with the rights and duties of citizenship. It was precisely this gap, and the resulting vulnerability to anti-French propaganda, that efforts to naturalize Muslim soldiers sought to address. Many political authorities believed that charges of hypocrisy and bad faith threatened to undermine recruitment efforts, and as the war dragged on, and France's manpower crisis deepened, naturalization seemed to offer a way to make enlistment more attractive and conscription more palatable to North Africans. Yet despite the clear importance of military necessity in inspiring proposals to liberalize access to French citizenship, idealism also played a role. The various wartime legislative proposals emanated from the "liberal milieux" in French politics, and one should not discount the role of revolutionary "Jacobin idealism" in stimulating lawmakers to attempt to bring recruitment practices in line with republican ideology.[47]

This mix of pragmatic and idealistic motives was evident in the government's first consideration of naturalizing North African soldiers. In late 1914, the minister of war began a serious examination of the issue, noting that up to then, North Africans' "moral and civil education" had been insufficient for them to exercise the rights and fulfill the duties of citizens, but their service in France, and their courage, loyalty, and devotion to the French cause during the war rendered them "each day more worthy of acquiring the rights of French citizenship." Offering them the possibility of naturalization would also bring military and political benefits: it would, he hoped, stimulate voluntary enlistments, reducing the need to rely on conscription; and it "would further tighten the ties that unite our Algerian subjects with France," an objective ever more imperative given "the current situation in the Muslim world, agitated by the machinations of Turkey and Germany." The measure would also put an end to the complaints of the "Young Algerians," a loosely organized group of educated and assimilated *indigènes* who were clamoring for greater political rights, because naturalization through military service would permit them to acquire the same rights as Frenchmen by submitting to the same obligations.[48]

From the beginning officials conceived of naturalization and the Muslims' *statut personnel* as mutually exclusive legal states, and *indigènes* would have to choose between their religious practices and French citizenship. Given this, these officials were aware from the beginning that the ostensibly generous measures they were considering were in fact largely symbolic when offered to Muslims little disposed to sacrifice traditional customs protected by the *statut personnel*. The minister admitted that any measure would have very limited effects, because many of those in a position to obtain naturalization would prefer to retain their *statut personnel*.[49]

The representative of the Ministry of the Colonies on the Interministerial Commission on Muslim Affairs (CIAM), which also took up the issue of the naturalization of North Africans at about the same time, echoed this opinion, observing that many Muslims would reject naturalization, considering it "a sort of apostasy, because of the renunciation of the Koranic *statut personnel*." Colonel Jules Hamelin of the Ministry of War agreed that this was the case, but he thought the gesture was still worth making as a demonstration of French magnanimity. Another member of the commission agreed, citing an obligation that arose directly from the republican coupling of military service and civic rights. "Do we not," he asked, "owe them a debt of recognition, and would this not be a means of paying it?"[50]

Despite the existence of this debt, of propaganda that criticized the French for failing to pay it, and of indications that some soldiers expected France to honor their sacrifices with admission into *le droit de cité français* (the rights of French citizenship), military and political authorities continued to argue that such a gesture would be purely symbolic, because very few Muslims would renounce their *statut personnel* in return for French citizenship. One reason for this was the widespread characterization of the *troupes indigènes* as "mercenaries," who volunteered out of self-interest and were already adequately compensated with bonuses and elevated wages. As one general wrote of Algerian soldiers serving in his division, "The *indigènes* are mercenaries; they serve in our ranks because they find it worth their while."[51] Of Moroccan troops, another officer wrote, "Our Moroccans are warriors; they did not enlist out of a love of France, which is not their *patrie*, and the idea of *patrie* is not even very developed among them. They enlisted for certain benefits that were granted them: they are, then, mercenaries. Warriors and mercenaries, it is necessary to take them as they are."[52] This was the hard reality many believed underlay hopeful rhetoric about a "second *patrie*."

It was in this context that the CIAM worked on the issue and eventually reviewed various parliamentary proposals for the naturalization of *troupes indigènes*. The deliberations of this commission, in which the opinions of colonial administrators and members of the various governmental ministries were represented, offer some of the most revealing discussions of naturalization and its incompatibility with Islam. Hamelin and Georges Bèze, chief of the Algerian Service at the Ministry of the Interior, outlined a proposal early in 1915 to offer naturalization to all North African soldiers fighting in Europe, upon request and without age limits, after an investigation into the soldier's background and "morality" by the Ministry of War. One problem with this plan, as another member of the commission noted, was that Tunisia and Morocco were separate cases, which the government would have to handle differently from Algeria.[53] The French residents-general in Tunisia and Morocco were quick to make the same point. Alapetite wrote from Tunis that, as residents of a protectorate, Tunisians had no interest in citizenship, which would not confer upon them any electoral rights, as would be the case for Algerians. Even those currently eligible for naturalization rarely availed themselves of the opportunity, refusing to sacrifice their *statut personnel* and rejecting the status of French citizen as "a kind of apostasy." Moreover, the bey of Tunis, whose nominal sovereignty the French had to respect, would have to be involved in any such project.[54]

Lyautey was even more forceful about the problems of applying an identical approach in a protectorate such as Morocco and in Algeria, a formal possession of the French state administratively integrated into the metropole. Naturalizing Moroccans would be a direct challenge to the authority of the sultan of Morocco, because French citizenship would remove soldiers from his traditional authority. As one of Lyautey's subordinates put it, "it is the negation of the principle of the protectorate, that is to say the maintenance of the sovereignty of the sultan over his subjects."[55] The Moroccans themselves did not desire naturalization, Lyautey argued, and such a step would hurt recruitment, because they would think that the French were "making them 'roumis' despite themselves" (*roumi* was a term in use for hundreds of years among North Africans that referred generically to Europeans, deriving from their Christian allegiance to Rome). In a territory that France had ruled for only two years, it was unwise to destabilize the political situation, and, as in Tunisia, citizenship had no real meaning where there were no electoral institutions, "and where the indigènes are incapable of even understanding them." Most of all, Moroccans would not want to sacrifice their *statut personnel*, and, since they were recruited from "the coarsest elements of the population," Moroccan soldiers would not even understand what they were giving up when they obtained French citizenship. This would lead to major problems when they appeared before French courts, the judgments of which, necessary under French law, would be "contrary to their most serious interests and their most profound sentiments." Given that Muslims did not even want to become French citizens, it would be paradoxical to give the naturalized soldier no real advantages while putting him in a situation of inferiority in his own country. Naturalizing the Jews of Algeria in 1870 had already hurt the prestige of French citizenship in the eyes of Muslims, who would be further offended that the government had offered it to the *fétichistes* (a reference to Diagne's constituents in the Four Communes, who were in fact predominantly Muslim) of Senegal, because North Africans regarded black Africans "as an inferior race."[56] A few months later, Lyautey repeated his arguments against making naturalized soldiers "pariahs in Muslim society." He explicitly repudiated the idea that the greatest gift France could bestow was the honor of French citizenship, because Muslims did not share French esteem for that status. It was by material means—money, jobs, status, and protection—that France could best demonstrate its gratitude to Moroccan soldiers.[57]

Despite these objections to applying a uniform policy on naturalization to all of North Africa, the CIAM approved Hamelin and Bèze's proposal on 25 January. As the commission's president, Abel Ferry, argued, to restrict the proposal to Algeria would be too narrow and would not have the effect the government desired. Germany was busy promoting pan-Islamism throughout the region, and France had to take action to oppose this propaganda on all fronts. In recognition of the different political situations in the protectorates of Tunisia and Morocco, the ministers of war of the indigenous rulers, not the French minister of war, would carry out the investigations into the background of applicants for naturalization in those colonies. However, a French military officer held this position in both colonies, so it was hardly a dramatic concession to the indigenous authorities.[58]

Charles Lutaud, Algeria's governor-general, also objected to the CIAM's plans, offering instead his own proposal on naturalization, which would apply only to Algerian soldiers, but to all of them, not just those who served in Europe. They would make a simple declaration of intent to obtain French citizenship, and the colonial administration, not the minister of war, would conduct the investigation into their backgrounds. The wider application of the plan stemmed from its initial, prewar impulse: to compensate *indigènes* for newly introduced conscription measures. But this appearance of generosity was deceiving, because an investigation by colonial administrators promised to be more rigorous than one by the minister of war. Usually with good reason, colonists and the colonial administration generally feared the greater liberalism and idealism of metropolitan authorities, whom they accused of lacking a real understanding of the nature of colonial populations and how to control them. Noting the essential conservatism of Lutaud's plan, Abel Ferry observed that this aspect of the governor-general's plan seemed designed to give only "the appearance of satisfaction and to sabotage the reform."[59]

Algerian officials were indignant at this characterization, but the practices of the colonial administration in the years before the war gave credence to the charge. Between 1865 and 1899, the administration had rejected the requests for naturalization of 178 out of 1,309 applicants, or 13.59 percent. Between 1899 and 1909, the rate of rejection rose to 214 out of 551, or 38.83 percent. From 1910 to 1915, the rate fell somewhat: out of 355 applicants, 101 were refused, or 28.4 percent. Still, this last percentage was more than twice the rejection rate during the nineteenth century, indicative of a growing hostility in Algeria to the idea of *indigènes* gaining political rights.[60]

The idea that Islam and French citizenship were incompatible was implicit in all of these discussions. Ostensibly, naturalization did not require giving up one's faith, merely the special legal status of the *statut personnel*. Yet submitting to Koranic law was integral to the religious identity of many North African Muslims. Muslims were not the only ones, however, who regarded French citizenship and Islam as mutually exclusive; French officials too identified the *statut personnel* with a host of cultural practices that they considered synonymous with Islam. That religion was the primary problem that the French felt they had to solve in crafting a plan for the naturalization of North African soldiers is clear in all discussions of the issue. As Governor-General Lutaud succinctly put it, "A great fact dominates the entire question of naturalization of Muslim *indigènes:* it is the Islamic fact."[61] This "Islamic fact" ultimately revolved around one particular set of issues, Muslims' customs regarding marriage and the family. The heads of the colonial administrations in North Africa were perhaps the most vociferous and eloquent on this point, but Parisian legislators and bureaucrats had a similar outlook.

In Resident-general Alapetite's responses to the proposals of the CIAM, he pointedly called the attention of the commission to the cultural and religious obstacles to the naturalization of Muslims: "Naturalization would have, especially, the effect of conferring on their wives rights that [their naturalized husbands] do not want to recognize. They do not want to lose their rights, their property, in a word they do not want to renounce the Koran for the Civil Code; they do not know French and do not have their children learn it." It would be a mistake, he argued, to give *indigènes* the impression that "France wants to acquit itself [of the debt it owes] to those who risk their lives in her service by [giving them] a certificate of French citizenship, which costs her nothing and would tear them away, if it is taken seriously, from their religion, their family, and their customs." Since the "*statut personnel* is one and the same with religious law," the Muslim soldier's naturalization could only result from pressure, religious proselytism, or propaganda that played upon the soldier's ignorance of the consequences of his act, and he would be dismayed when he discovered that under French civil law he would not be able to repudiate his wife to marry another and that his daughters would have the same inheritance rights as his sons.[62]

Alapetite also provided specific examples of the unsuitability of Muslims for French citizenship. In April, he sent a long report to the minister of foreign affairs, describing naturalized Tunisians who had become "recidivists." In soldiers, who were the most likely to obtain naturalization, one could observe "a general regression . . . toward the original state," once these men left the military: "Hereditary and religious forces, and there is no reason to be surprised by this, immediately become predominant again." Alapetite's pairing of heredity and religion indicated the belief he shared with many other French people that the religious and racial identity of North African Muslims were inextricably intertwined. Any return to this identity was a regression from an acquired, assimilated "Frenchness." To cite one example, Salah Manoubi ben Manouba's naturalization did not seem to have changed him in any way, the resident-general noted. His mentality remained the same as that of other Muslims, and he took advantage of his status as a naturalized French citizen only when seeking favors from the colonial administration. He married following Muslim customs and lived like other Muslims. His wife spoke no French, never left the house, and dressed like other Muslim women.

The case of Balit Ouali ben Rabah was even more revealing. He was a Catholic, raised by missionaries, spoke and wrote French, took communion regularly, and wore European dress. He had lived alone for two years, saying he had divorced his wife. Yet as there was no official record of the action, one had to assume that he had done so according to traditional Muslim custom, with a simple declaration to her. On a more positive note, he was going to remarry a young Catholic in the Church, under French law, and any children would probably be raised as French. But despite these signs of assimilation, he wore a *chéchia* (traditional Muslim headgear) outside of work and frequented "Moorish cafés." Alapetite's point was clear: if such an apparently assimilated man—naturalized, Catholic, soon to be married in the Church, fluent in French, largely European in outward appearance (aside from his hat)—could not be counted upon to become truly French and to fulfill fully the duties of a French citizen, who could?[63] In short, "nationality does not change the Muslim," who found aspects of French law "repugnant," such as the legal rights of women in French society.[64]

## Algerians, Polygamy, and French Citizenship

The Tunisian resident-general's stress on family life, especially with regard to the rights French law accorded to women, was a recurring theme in discussions of naturalization. It was especially prominent in the case of Algeria, where most of the attention finally settled as 1915 wore on. In the spring of that year, Parliament took the initiative in offering proposals aimed at naturalizing *troupes indigènes*. Beginning on 1 April, legislators introduced five different proposals in six months, all designed to ease the administrative process by which soldiers could become French citizens. The first of these proposals applied to all soldiers from North Africa, while the second, introduced at the end of May, aimed at soldiers from all areas of the French empire. But the three proposals that followed by the end of September narrowed the focus to the naturalization of Algerians.[65]

As these proposed measures affected his administration most directly, Governor-General Lutaud voiced the most serious concerns about the dangers to French law and culture posed by Muslims' supposedly alien and incompatible practices, and he focused particularly on polygamy and other customs regarding women. Focusing on, or fantasizing about, the presumably deviant and uncontrolled sexuality of *indigènes* and the position of women in indigenous society to articulate the differences between French and Algerian culture had a long history—it had served officials of the early Third Republic in justifying their doubts about the fitness of *indigènes* for full political membership in the French nation.[66]

Lutaud's comments partook of this discourse, but he claimed to be speaking from concrete experience as a colonial administrator and catalogued quite specifically the practices of *indigènes* that made them poor candidates for naturalization. In one of his initial responses to the proposed reforms, the governor-general pointed out several problems with reconciling common (he alleged) Muslim familial customs with French law. How could an administration governed by the French Civil Code allow a man to retain his wife's property when he divorced her (especially a problem if he had to re-pudiate polygamous unions contracted before the naturalization); to arrange his daughter's marriage without her consent, even if she was not "nubile"; to exclude his daughters entirely from inheriting his property? Lutaud sug-gested that this was only the tip of the iceberg, and allowing Muslims to retain traditional family customs would introduce into French law many "oddities," and even worse. He argued that France could not declare com-patible with French law, *le droit de cité*, practices which were in such fla-grant contradiction with it, and that conserving such "outmoded and often inhumane" practices would be to fail in the civilizing mission the French had set for themselves in 1830 when they began the conquest of Algeria.[67]

By the end of 1915, Lutaud had had an opportunity to consider all of the various proposals for naturalization, and he submitted a 63-page report lay-ing out his arguments against them. He praised the *sénatus-consulte* of 1865, which did not allow naturalized Muslims to retain their *statut personnel*, for recognizing "the Islamic fact with its civil and religious consequences in-separably linked to each other, as one knows, by the Koran." Though the governor-general conceded that Algerians were "perfectible whites," just like Frenchmen, he maintained that "there exists between them such a differ-ence of culture that political equality is obviously not achievable for the mo-ment."[68] Assimilation, an integral part of the French *mission civilisatrice* and of the justification for republican colonialism, was a slow process, which would have to await the subsidence of a stubborn adherence to the tenets of Islam.

Lutaud described the contradictions between French law and Muslim cus-toms at great length, particularly with regard to polygamy, marriage rights, repudiation and divorce, and giving away in marriage very young women (a practice he now called "legalized rape"). He adamantly rejected any com-promise on the issue, such as a sort of "demi-naturalization" that would provide limited local electoral rights but allow the preservation of the *statut personnel*, which some officials had considered, because such a step "would risk crystallizing the *indigènes* in their laws and institutions, in a word in Muslim law, in Islam." What was needed, he argued, was "a wise assimila-tion, the gradual evolution of our subjects," so that France could open "the doors of *la cité française* progressively to the *indigènes*." Thus, any scheme for a hasty naturalization of Algerians was directly contrary to both French and indigenous interests.[69]

Lutaud had good reason to argue against "demi-naturalization," because officials and legislators had been considering such a compromise. Although work on the issue of naturalization had bogged down in the government and in Parliament by the end of 1915, this lull did not last long. On 20 April 1916, Deputy Henri Doizy introduced a new bill that offered Algerians "naturalization within the *statut personnel* and in a local capacity," an arrangement that increased *indigènes'* local political representation, but allowed Muslims to retain their religious customs and avoided clashes with the French Civil Code.[70]

This proposal also took direct aim at the colonial administration. Doizy quoted from a previous legislative proposal to support his assertion that the inertia and even ill will of colonial officials were blocking access to naturalization. The earlier proposal had asserted that, "One would like in the colonies"—"and," Doizy added, "this is particularly true in Algeria"—"the fewest possible French citizens. With subjects, the Administration can deal with them on its own terms; with citizens, that would become more delicate, and such an arbitrary regime could no longer blossom so freely. . . . A German would be naturalized more easily than would an Algerian." In view of the sacrifices of the *troupes indigènes*, "who at this very moment are giving a new and striking demonstration of devotion to the metropole," Doizy noted, it was appropriate and just to enhance the political rights of Algerians.[71]

Though not all members of the CIAM fully shared Lutaud's unbending hostility to the parliamentary projects for the naturalization of *indigènes*, neither did they all fully endorse the liberal approach of men like Doizy. Ultimately, members of the commission, like most other officials who wrestled with the issue, had trouble accepting any plan that would give full citizenship to Muslims without requiring the sacrifice of their *statut personnel*. Such difficulties prevented any real reforms from getting beyond the proposal stage, so in 1917, the Chamber of Deputies charged the socialist deputy and future minister of the colonies Marius Moutet with reconciling the various measures. In October, he presented his new plan to the CIAM, and the subsequent discussions of this body are quite revealing of attitudes about one of the issues that many French authorities felt most complicated the issue of naturalization: the practice of polygamy among Muslim men.

Some officials recognized that this did not necessarily present a serious problem. Commenting on a stipulation barring the naturalization of polygamists in one of the earlier proposals, Resident-general Alapetite wrote in May 1915 that such a restriction was unnecessary, because soldiers were almost always too young to be polygamists. The real problem, he argued, was that Muslims engaged in a sort of "progressive" polygamy, making use of the ease with which the *statut personnel* allowed them to renounce wives of whom they had tired and to take others. Citing what he seemed to regard as a congenital weakness in Muslim men, Alapetite asserted that *indigènes* would be unable to give up this convenient outlet for their overactive libidinous desires.[72] Doizy similarly dismissed the specific importance of polygamy as an impediment to naturalization, intimating that those who dwelled on the issue were merely looking for an excuse to bar the way to French citizenship for Muslims. In a sarcastic challenge to those who argued that assimilation was only an extremely long-term goal, he asked, "Does it follow that we must wait patiently, beatifically, for the centuries to do their work and for our *indigènes* to be resigned to abandoning their *statut*?"[73]

Yet it was clear that polygamy and other traditional family customs were a concern to many in the French government. Moutet's proposal explicitly barred polygamists from becoming French citizens, and this issue provoked a great deal of discussion in the CIAM. Some members of the commission foresaw problems with this stipulation. Edmond Doutté, professor at the madrasa of Tlemcen, pointed out that polygamists were often important figures in Algerian society, whom the French had an interest in conciliating. But another member noted that the issue went right to the heart of a delicate question: whether or not the Muslim *statut personnel* was compatible with French citizenship. There was general agreement that an Algerian living in France could not have multiple wives—preserving public order dictated that he submit to French law on the matter. Also, the law would not permit an Algerian to contract multiple marriages after his naturalization, no matter where he lived. The real issue was what to do about applicants for naturalization who already had more than one wife.

On this question there was much disagreement. Octave Depont, representing the Algerian colonial administration, cited a study that showed many Algerians continued to practice polygamy even after naturalization. Others pointed out the legal nightmares that would result from naturalizing polygamists. Even if an Algerian broke off his polygamous unions and kept only one wife upon his accession to citizenship, what rights would the former wives and their children retain? How could one have legitimate children with more than one wife? On the other hand, how could there be two sorts of French citizens, monogamous and polygamous? Depont then raised the objections that Lutaud had voiced earlier about many Muslim family customs, including polygamy, the right of *jabr* (by which, he alleged, fathers married off their pre-pubescent daughters without their consent and against their will), the "absolute and arbitrary" right to repudiate one's wife, the elimination of daughters from inheritance, and a host of other practices "as bizarre as [they are] inhumane." He painted a particularly lurid picture of the *jabr*, calling up the image of girls as young as eight or nine years old offered up to their husbands, then "damaged for life, when they do not die from the effects of these legal rapes." These, he said, were the kinds of practices that French law would consecrate as legal if the government allowed naturalized *indigènes* to retain their *statut personnel*. How could these men be allowed to vote—one of the critical rights and responsibilities of citizenship—in effect making laws that would govern French people but not themselves? This was a particular danger given the large margin by which *indigènes* outnumbered Europeans in Algeria.[74]

In the end, the CIAM altered the articles in Moutet's proposal that barred polygamists from citizenship, allowing men with multiple marriages contracted before the act of naturalization to keep them. This was no doubt dictated by the desire not to offend the kind of prominent and wealthy *indigènes* who could afford to have multiple wives, but the proposal still sought to limit the ramifications of this exceptional measure. Under no circumstances could an *indigène* contract polygamist unions after naturalization, and the effects of naturalization were restricted to the man: his wife or wives did not alter their status, and sons would make a declaration of intent during their twenty-second year to be considered a French citizen or to retain the *statut personnel*. In other words, the proposal still required a definitive rejection of a Muslim's *statut personnel* in order to obtain French citizenship. Some members of the commission still saw potential problems. For one, what of the inheritance rights of daughters? And the specter of polygamy was not so easily banished. What if a son was already a polygamist at the time his father became a French citizen? Would he be able to make a simple declaration of intent upon turning twenty-one? Despite such reservations, the commission and Moutet adopted the amended articles.[75]

In spite of the remarkable willingness to accept a certain limited amount of polygamy under French law, Moutet's proposal in the end emphatically rejected any measures that would preserve the *statut personnel* for those who became French citizens. The two legal states were still mutually exclusive. In many respects, though increased access to French citizenship was supposed to reward soldiers who had sacrificed so much for the defense of France, the direction of discussions on the issue of naturalizing Algerians ultimately tended toward tightening, not loosening, the restrictions of the 1865 *sénatus-consulte*. It was this fact that caused the humanitarian organization the Ligue des droits de l'homme (League of the Rights of Man) to charge that Moutet's proposal fell short of its goal.[76] As the prominent left-wing historian Alphonse Aulard put it in April 1917, the Ligue favored allowing "Algerians to retain their Muslim *statut* when becoming French citizens," along with granting them representation in the French Chamber of Deputies, and would eventually even cite American President Woodrow Wilson's appeal for national self-determination to argue for greater political rights for Muslims in Algeria.[77] On the other hand, the administration in Algeria remained adamantly opposed to Moutet's suggestions for reform, fearing the consequences of any increase in Muslims' electoral power.

When Georges Clemenceau became prime minister and minister of war in late 1917, his government gave special priority to the reform effort in Algeria, which he saw as an ideal means of achieving his overriding goal of increasing recruitment. As early as November 1915, Clemenceau, then chairman of the committee on foreign affairs in the Senate, had urged the government to make political reforms in Algeria in recognition of the loyalty and military service of the *indigènes*.[78] Now in power, the new premier recalled Lutaud, who was closely allied with the colonists and openly obstructing the reform efforts emanating from Paris, and installed Charles Jonnart as governor-general in January 1918. By the end of that month, Jonnart had drawn up the government's plans for reform in Algeria. This modified some of the provisions of Moutet's plan, eventually replacing it, but the war ended before the new plan could become law. And when it eventually did, in 1919, the results hardly constituted a dramatic liberalization of access to French citizenship in Algeria. In the end, attempts to facilitate the naturalization of Algerians foundered on the incompatibility French officials believed existed between Muslims' religious identity, symbolized by the *statut personnel* and practices such as polygamy, and French national identity, which required absolute conformity to French cultural and legal norms.

## Postwar Reform and Naturalization in the Colonies

By 1918, France had failed to close the gap that opened during the war between the inferior civil status of *troupes indigènes* fighting for France and traditional republican ideology that linked defense of the nation in the military with the rights and duties of full citizenship. This failure was particularly dramatic in the case of Algeria. Though the Jonnart Law, which passed in early 1919 and would define French policy toward *indigènes* for the next twenty-five years, was ostensibly motivated by a desire to remove or lower obstacles to the naturalization of Algerians, it actually made the requirements and procedures more rigorous. An applicant would have to satisfy several preliminary conditions: be aged twenty-five or older, be monogamous or single, have no convictions for serious crimes, and have two consecutive years of fixed residence. In addition, he would have to satisfy one of seven secondary requirements: be a veteran and in possession of a certificate of good conduct, know how to read and write French, be a settled and licensed farmer or businessman, hold or have held elective office, be a current or retired functionary in the colonial administration, have received a French decoration, or be the adult child of a naturalized father. The law represented the final rejection of the idea of naturalization with the retention of the Muslim *statut personnel,* and a repudiation of the colonial doctrine of assimilation as it applied to Algeria.[79]

In addition to the new requirements for French citizenship, the law enacted a "special naturalization," demi-naturalization in fact, that provided a limited expansion of electoral rights for over 400,000 Algerians (43 percent of the adult male population) while allowing them to retain their *statut personnel.* In his address introducing the law to the Chamber, Jonnart claimed that this was an "intermediary status," a "stage between the status of French citizen and that of a French subject." He implied that this was a temporary state of affairs until the Muslims evolved culturally and politically, but in reality it was more of a permanent condition for the vast majority of Algerians.[80] The *indigènes* had begun the war in an ambiguous state between subjects and citizens, and despite four years of efforts to clarify this status and reward them for their military service, most ended the war in similar ambiguity. In an irony that many contemporaries did not fail to appreciate, the requirements for full naturalization under the new law were actually more stringent in many respects (for example, in the minimum age for applicants) than was the *sénatus-consulte* of 1865.

The primary reason for this was Algerians' religious identity. French government officials and legislators could not reconcile the practice of Islam with the obligations and privileges of French citizenship. One clear indication of this was the requirement in the Jonnart Law that applicants for naturalization be monogamous. This served to "mark" Muslims as polygamists, something that the 1865 legislation had not done explicitly (though in practice the colonial administration had always refused the requests of polygamous applicants).[81] Polygamy was, in reality, in steep decline in Algeria.

A Senate report of March 1918 revealed that between 1891 and 1911 polygamous marriages had declined from 149,000 to 55,427.[82] This was part of an
even longer-term decrease in the frequency of polygamy: in 1886, 16 percent of married Algerian males had more than one wife; by 1948, this had
dropped to 3 percent, and the average age of these men was over sixty-five.[83]
Such men were unlikely to be interested in French citizenship after living
into old age without it, and even if the average age was somewhat lower in
the years immediately following the Great War (though there is no reason
to suppose that it was), polygamists were very unlikely to be recent veterans
of the French Army. Polygamy was more important as a symbol than as
an actual practice among Algerians. It came to represent for French officials all that was alien to and incompatible with French citizenship, particularly laws and customs relating to women and the family. This was hardly
surprising, given more general anxieties, both in the metropole and in the
colonies, about gender roles during the first part of the twentieth century.[84]
But the special mention of polygamy in the Jonnart Law also pointed to the
difficulty many in France had in integrating Islam as an acceptable component of French national identity. For polygamy stood, not just for alien ways
and customs, but for alien ways and customs that French officials believed
were peculiar to Muslims and an inextricable part of their religion.

The ultimate irony of the Jonnart Law was that it represented the failure of the French government to give *troupes indigènes* who were defending France precisely the access to French citizenship that officials had been
working for since the start of the war. Though public figures in the government, legislature, and press had debated various measures designed to liberalize and simplify the naturalization process in the years before 1914, the
new circumstances created by the war were clearly instrumental in stimulating the search for more dramatic ways to improve the lot of Muslims in
Algeria.[85]

That the service of Muslims in the army was the impetus for these efforts
is clear even from the comments of opponents of reform. During the discussion of Jonnart's measure in the Chamber of Deputies on 7 November 1918,
an Algerian deputy, Gaston Thomson, complained that reformers had allowed the sentimentality provoked by the presence of thousands of Algerian
*indigènes* in the army to play too large a role in shaping their ideas.[86] Yet opposition from colonists, the end of the war (which removed much of the ur-
gency for the reforms, because recruitment was no longer a burning issue),
and objections to sanctioning traditional Muslim customs under French law

ensured that the end result of all the efforts at reform would fall far short of the ideal imagined by those who felt republican ideology demanded both the obligation of military service and the privilege of citizenship. Inasmuch as the 1919 measures governing naturalization actually represented a regression from those contained in the *sénatus-consulte* of 1865, it is unsurprising that Doizy, author of one of the more ambitious reform proposals in 1916, summed up the Jonnart Law by saying, "I do not think that we have done anything important."[87]

Evidence of the failure of the reform efforts that culminated in the Jonnart Law of 1919 was clear in the postwar frequency of naturalizations. Between 1919 and 1923, the colonial administration received 317 requests for French citizenship under the terms of the new legislation, and denied 115.[88] As a consequence of the government-general's suspicion of and hostility to the naturalization of *indigènes*, the rejection rate of 36 percent was comparable to highest levels of the prewar years. Jonnart had intended his reforms, as he put it during his defense of the law in the Chamber, to make accession to citizenship a right for many Algerians, instead of a privilege or favor handed out by the administration to a select few.[89] Nevertheless, he doubted that Muslims would or could abandon their customs in order to qualify for French citizenship, and he was in any case gone by July 1919, replaced by Jean-Baptiste Abel. Moreover, Muslims were loath to sacrifice their *statut personnel* in return for naturalization, and so the law was flawed from the beginning. As one member of the Young Algerians put it, "Why, before according liberty to the Muslims and the improvement of their lot, require of them the cruel renunciation of their age-old traditions?"[90] In the end, the reform in the terms of accession to citizenship for Algerians, supposed to admit soldiers who had fought for France into the nation they had defended, remained a "dead letter."[91]

Algeria was not the only colony in which naturalization for veterans was an issue, and not the only colony in which very few subjects received the reward of citizenship in return for their military service. After Diagne had won official recognition of the *originaires* as citizens, he worked to increase the rights of West Africans outside the Four Communes as well. The 1918 legislation that governed the final, massive recruiting effort in the AOF contained several provisions that improved the lot of soldiers and their families, such as exemption from corvée, the *indigénat*, and the head tax. These represented intermediary steps on the road to assimilation, while stopping short of full recognition of West African soldiers' rights as citizens. Moreover, winners of both the *croix de guerre* and the *médaille militaire* were entitled to French citizenship, though, if Muslims, they had to renounce their *statut personnel.*

This promise was as empty as it was in Algeria, however, largely due to a colonial administration both doubtful of West Africans' ability to acquire the cultural attributes of Frenchness necessary for responsible citizenship and hostile to subjects' gaining more rights and power. Reflecting the "more conservative republicanism" and higher consciousness of immutable racial differences of the colonial administration in the postwar period, the governor-general of the AOF wrote in 1923, "We have an ever-greater interest in according naturalizations only to individuals whose absolute loyalty has been proven, and whose right to this exceptional favor has been well and truly earned." It was apparent that this was a small pool of potential citizens indeed, even among veterans: one observer reported that between 1914 and 1925, only eighty-eight Africans became French citizens, fourteen of whom were former soldiers.[92]

The situation in Indochina was no different, perhaps even worse. Years before the war, General Raoul de Boisdeffre had argued against conscripting Indochinese because of their inability to assimilate to French ways and thus to be worthy of the citizenship that usually accompanied compulsory military service: "If all *indigènes* do not have patriotic sentiment developed to the same degree, experience has proven that all, whatever their social standing, are assimilated only superficially. They acquire, in general, only the external appearances and especially the vices of European civilization."[93] Attitudes like Boisdeffre's no doubt explain the low number of naturalizations accorded in the prewar years: between 1882 and 1906, 161 *indigènes* were naturalized in Cochin China, 27 of them soldiers.[94] Nonetheless, during the war, some looked to naturalization to stimulate recruitment, such as the parliamentary deputies who proposed that the French Army solve its difficulties in recruiting suitable officer candidates among the Indochinese by offering the "the lure of naturalization" to encourage educated *indigènes* to volunteer.[95] Perhaps this was why an Indochinese journalist after the war claimed that many men had volunteered because the French government had promised citizenship in return.[96]

As was the case in other colonies, however, there was considerable resistance in Indochina to the idea of too generous an offer to too many *indigènes,* and it was not until 4 September 1919 that the government issued a new decree supposedly making it easier for soldiers who had served in France to obtain citizenship. Even then, the new decree did not significantly modify the essential structure of the 1913 measure that had governed naturalization in Indochina.[97] During the war, Governor-General Albert Sarraut had effectively opposed all proposals to naturalize soldiers en masse. He preferred a more cautious policy of association.[98] After the war, the colonial administration was no more accommodating of requests for naturalization than in other colonies. In 1921 and again in 1924, ministers of the colonies (first Albert Sarraut, in a curious reversal of position, then Édouard Daladier) wrote to the government-general to complain about the low number of requests granted. A report that accompanied one of these letters stated that of 71 requests for citizenship, 61 had been rejected; 19 requests had come from soldiers, and all of them had been denied.[99] The situation did not improve, despite the complaints from Paris: in 1929, of 165 requests, 65 were suspended for further consideration, while 42 were rejected outright. In all, between 1921 and 1930 about 270 *indigènes* (including men, women, and children) became French citizens in Indochina, bringing the estimated total in the whole of the colony to 600.[100] This hardly indicated a grateful France conferring upon the *tirailleurs indochinois* the benefits of French citizenship that they had earned on the battlefield.

Much the same was true in Madagascar. When organizing a recruiting mission there in the spring of 1918, the Ministry of War recommended applying the same measures to Madagascar that Parliament had applied to the AOF in the decree of 14 January, namely, that Madagascan soldiers who won both the *croix de guerre* and the *médaille militaire* would be entitled to French citizenship. This would require only a minor change in existing policy. Previously, applicants for naturalization in Madagascar had to prove they were able to read and write French and that they lived an assimilated, European lifestyle. Now the Ministry of War suggested that "the fact of having obtained the *médaille militaire* and the *croix de guerre* constitute, morally, qualifications [that are] at least equivalent."[101] As was the case with soldiers from the AOF, French officials knew that it was extremely unlikely that many would win both of these prestigious decorations. The measure served more as propaganda and an incentive, an indication of gratitude and of the ostensible willingness of the French, not only to open the ranks of the army to the *indigènes,* but also to offer them the possibility, however remote, of joining their colonial masters in the enjoyment of the rights of French citizenship. However, transportation difficulties, which prevented all but initial efforts to begin massive recruitment in 1918, and the end of the war intervened before any new French policy could have an effect.

After the war, there was some agitation outside of the military for facilitating naturalizations as a reward for Madagascans' military service, as a January 1921 meeting of the Ligue française pour l'accession aux droits de citoyens des indigènes de Madagascar (French League for the Attainment of the Rights of Citizens of the *indigènes* of Madagascar) indicates. From within the army, a *tirailleur* expressed the hope in 1919 that Great War veterans from Madagascar might form an association in order pressure the government to accord them French citizenship.[102]

Such hopes and raised expectations came up against the hard reality of a colonial administration more concerned with heading off any potential trouble from returning veterans, whose exposure to a relatively egalitarian social order in the army and in France stood in marked contrast to life back home in the strictly hierarchical colonial framework, than with rewarding *troupes indigènes* for their role in the recent victory. Officials denied or suspended requests from men who had volunteered for the duration of the war, either because they did not demonstrate sufficient knowledge of French or because of their lifestyles or social status. One former sergeant's request was denied because he had spent several days in prison while in the army. Authorities rejected the request of another soldier, even though he had submitted a letter of recommendation from the Ministry of War's director of colonial troops, General Famin, because they judged that his application was a means to avoid his labor obligations as a colonial subject. Even the most remote and casual of contacts with someone implicated in the anticolonial VVS conspiracy of 1915–16 was sufficient to doom a request. Moreover, having been a soldier did not seem to help an applicant; quite the opposite: eleven of the thirteen requests for naturalization that officials rejected in 1923 came from veterans of the war, some of them decorated. To add insult, and irony, to injury, the local branches of the League of the Rights of Man in Tananarive and Tamatave refused to accept non-naturalized Madagascans into their ranks. Madagascan noncommissioned officers in the French Army, usually the most assimilated among the island's indigenous population, had supposedly not yet reached the stage where they could handle or even understand "all the responsibility and all the duties that are attached to the rights and the prerogatives" of their military rank, which itself was already a "benevolent measure taken on their behalf."[103]

As this last comment makes clear, the widespread belief in the congenital inability of *indigènes* to assimilate fully and properly, stemming from their inherent inferiority to whites, was the real obstacle to naturalization both during and after the war. In this sense, French citizenship had a cultural and moral content, a content clear from the number of candidates for naturalization deemed unsuitable by reason of dubious "morality." The rigid understanding of this cultural "Frenchness" could conflict with the orthodox republican ideal of citizenship as a political construct theoretically open to all. French officials could and did point to many examples of this, but the issue of the *statut personnel* of Muslims, especially in Algeria, became the most important, and in a way symbolized the incompatibility of all colonial subjects and their customs with the requirements of French citizenship. This was the case even with the Senegalese *originaires*. In the prewar years, colonial officials cited the *statut personnel* of Muslims in the Four Communes as the reason that they would not recognize the *originaires* as full citizens, despite their special electoral rights.[104] It was only through shrewd manipulation of republican ideology, parliamentary skill, and the special circumstances created by the war that Blaise Diagne was able to obtain recognition of his constituents as French citizens, even as they retained their *statut personnel.*

Algerian *indigènes* had no such representation of their own in Paris, despite the presence of some well-disposed French liberals. Moreover, the Senegalese *originaires* were few in number, faced a relatively small settler population, and benefited from a long-standing tendency to view sub-Saharan Islam as less threatening than Arab and North African Islam.[105] The large number of Algerian *indigènes,* combined with a large European settler population fearful of the electoral consequences of naturalizing hundreds of thousands of unassimilated colonial subjects, also helped to prevent Algerians' accession to citizenship as long as they continued to observe their Muslim customs. In short, despite the attempts of French officials to bring policy toward naturalizing Algerian soldiers more into line with republican traditions that linked military service with citizenship, the religious identity of these men—the "Islamic fact," as Governor-General Lutaud put it—remained an insurmountable obstacle. Even the most assimilated among the *indigènes*, Lutaud argued in 1916, refused to sacrifice their religious identity in order to become truly French. Many whom the French had educated, and who had become lawyers, doctors, officers, or teachers, refused to sacrifice their *statut personnel* in order to obtain French citizenship. This refusal, he argued, stemmed from a mix of political and religious "fanaticism" that often resulted in subversion and even rebellion. He went on to say, in a blunt statement of the doctrine of association tinged with racist condescension, that he preferred the "simple fellahs" who did not display a false assimilation but still remained in their own culture and loyal to their colonial masters, learning to "become truly friendly with us, often even to love us."[106]

It was not just the conservative Lutaud who viewed Islam as an insurmountable obstacle to naturalization, the highest stage of assimilation. The agreement on this point of even liberal republicans ultimately doomed any measure granting of French citizenship with the retention of the *statut personnel*. Gustave Mercier, a prominent lawyer who in fact favored reform in French policy toward Algerians, wrote in 1918 that it was dangerous to "make them electors before making them civilized human beings."[107] The liberal, socialist-sympathizing journalist Jean Mélia refused to entertain the idea of two groups of French citizens governed by two different statutes. Similarly, the left-wing senator Raphaël Milliès-Lacroix, no friend to reactionary colonial interests, "quibbled constantly over the legal definition that it was proper to give to monogamy. The risk that the ballot of a monogamous Frenchman and that of a polygamous Frenchman might lie together in the ballot box filled him with dread."[108]

If the *statut personnel* stood for the *indigènes'* general lack of civilization, then specific cultural practices (regardless of the extent to which Muslims really engaged in them), especially polygamy, dramatically symbolized the supposedly irreconcilable differences between the observance of Islam and the demands of French citizenship. And these differences ran deeper than mere matters of outward religious observance or even faith itself. The label "Muslim," as Laure Blévis has put it, designated not only a religious confession, but "a state, a social condition . . . a fundamental otherness." The very use of the terms *musulman* and *indigène* by jurists and lawmakers concealed a rigid understanding of difference rooted in ethnicity and race.[109]

This state of affairs ran contrary, not only to the republican tradition linking defense of the state in the military with citizenship, but also to the ideal of French citizenship itself. Indeed, the fundamental basis of this ideal was the proposition that membership in the national community was not limited by skin color, race, religion, or historical background, but only by the willingness to adopt French language, culture, and political authority. Yet often when even the most assimilated of France's colonial subjects, many of whom had fought in the French Army during the Great War, applied for naturalization, colonial administrations rejected them for reasons such as "morality," lifestyle, or doubts about their mastery of the French language.

Often, these justifications hid more important doubts on the part of officials that people from "primitive" cultures could or would ever really assimilate fully to French ways. This situation encapsulated one of the great paradoxes of colonial policy under the Third Republic: if newly naturalized *indigènes* were to live among their compatriots in the colonies as examples, to "incarnate simultaneously French civilization (and its benefits) and possible emancipation," then their restricted numbers revealed just how narrow the path was to salvation, how essentially hollow and self-serving rhetoric about a republican "civilizing mission" could be.[110]

In many respects, the ideology of association, especially as expressed by men like Governor-General Lutaud, was an explicit denial of the possibilities of assimilation, a rejection of the republican ideal that justified France's possession of a colonial empire, and an excuse to maintain an essentially exploitative relationship with the colonies and their indigenous inhabitants.[111] One might argue that the resistance to naturalizing Muslims who retained their *statut personnel* was in keeping with the republican ideal of citizenship, because these *indigènes* were failing to accept French law and therefore undeserving of the benefits accorded to citizens. There was some truth in this, but it was more the idea that Muslims would remain Muslims, and not "civilized human beings," that prevented French authorities from facilitating their naturalization. In some respects this should not be surprising, because there is a religious component to French national identity—rooted in Catholic Christianity—that has coexisted with more secular republican notions.[112] Moreover, as Pierre Birnbaum has shown, this religious heritage, along with the Revolution's conception of the nation as an organic whole from which "autonomy and diversity are rejected; all manifestations of divergence are excluded as dysfunctional," has produced a sense of nationhood that is often hostile to cultural and political pluralism.[113]

Recent controversies over the integration of immigrants, most of whom are from the former colonies, have highlighted the often intolerant side of French ideas about citizenship and national identity, but this intolerance has a long history, which includes the experiences of the *troupes indigènes* who fought for France in the First World War. Indeed, understanding the colonial legacy is critical to understanding both the historical construction of French citizenship and its operation in contemporary France.[114] Many immigrants in France today are discovering what many of their ancestors found out in the years after 1914: demands for cultural conformity, even within a supposedly relatively open assimilationist system of national identity based upon *jus soli,* can be as imperious and difficult to satisfy as are the more straight-forwardly ethnic requirements of systems based upon *jus sanguinis.*[115]

The idea that Islam is incompatible with, even a threat to, French identity has consistently caused many of the difficulties. Right after the Second World War, France took steps to bring its colonial subjects closer into the nation by naming them citizens of an expansive "French Union," which sought to include the metropole and colonies in one closely knit entity, by means of the Loi Lamine Guèye of 1946 (the same Lamine Guèye, now a member of the French Chamber, had written his 1922 doctoral dissertation on the citizenship of the *originaires*). But a distinction remained between metropolitan and colonial citizens, so some French people were "more citizens than others," and in practice the *statut personnel* and Islam remained barriers to the exercise of full citizenship rights.[116]

Even after decolonization, the "problem" of integrating Islam into French national identity remained, due to the presence of millions of Muslim immigrants in France. In 1992, for instance, the Haut Conseil à l'intégration, a government agency charged with studying ways to encourage the integration of immigrants into French society, declared that the French "concept of the nation as a cultural community . . . does appear unusually open to outsiders, since it regards an act of voluntary commitment to a set of values as all that is necessary." However, this same pronouncement criticized the idea of "multiculturalism" in no uncertain terms and stressed the indispensability of full integration of prospective members of the national community into the dominant political and cultural ethos of France. Immigrants who wanted to become French citizens were to become truly French, legally and culturally, to leave behind past cultural particularities: "Notions of a 'multicultural society' and the 'right to be different' are unacceptably ambiguous . . . it would be wrong to let anyone think that different cultures can be allowed to become fully developed in France."[117] Muslim immigrants, especially North Africans, are often foremost in the minds of officials making such statements, just as they were in the minds of officials contemplating the naturalization of Muslim *indigènes* during the Great War.

New legislation in 1993 restricting the right of *jus soli* by making citizenship less easily accessible to children born of foreign parents in France is an even more dramatic example of the limits of the assimilationist ideal in contemporary France. Moreover, aspects of this legislation made it more difficult for Algerians, in particular, to take advantage of a liberal *jus soli* policy. Some aspects of this law were modified in 1998, but immigrants and their children still faced greater difficulties becoming French citizens than they had prior to 1993. Far from being a right-wing, xenophobic reaction against a rising tide of immigration, the new "constricted parameters of French [national] membership" had wide support across the political spectrum.[118] Indeed, people of diverse political convictions can share a conviction that Islam is a threat to French identity because some perceive Muslims as a threat to ethnic purity, while others regard Islam as a threat to the universal and secular values that make up the political content of what it means to be French.[119] To be sure, though, even complaints that Muslims fail to observe fundamental principles of human rights (in the past, by taking more than one wife; today, by wearing a headscarf in France's secular schools) often conceal more basic fears about the implications of inviting greater ethnic diversity into French society.[120]

Given the nature and ultimate outcome of debates over the naturalization of Muslims almost a century ago, today's consensus on the threat posed by Islam is unsurprising. It has a long history in France. A genuine commitment to the liberal ideals of universalism and egalitarianism led many in France to espouse an inclusive view of the nation that welcomed colonial subjects in uniform who wanted to become French, provided they demonstrated a willingness to accept republican political traditions and to integrate into French social and cultural life. Yet officials defined the process by which this transformation from foreigner to French would occur in such a way as to render the transformation complicated and difficult, if not impossible, to achieve. The experience of Algerian soldiers offers a particularly illustrative example, given the difficulties officials had in envisioning the transformation *troupes indigènes* from subjects to citizens, despite the strong links in French republican tradition between military service and citizenship. That efforts to offer naturalization to these men were so controversial, and in the end unsuccessful, demonstrates the very real limits of the assimilationist ideal in the face of ethnocultural and religious differences. Demands for cultural conformity were well within the republican tradition, but such demands often stemmed from grave doubts that Muslims could ever truly be French, precisely because they were Muslims.[121]

Of course, Islam was only the most salient of a host of factors that prevented *troupes indigènes* from all of the colonies from obtaining French citizenship, the greatest proof that they belonged to the nation which they were defending. The "Father of Victory" Georges Clemenceau once recalled visiting a group of "magnificent black soldiers" at the front and telling them "that they were in the process of liberating themselves by coming to fight with us, that we had become brothers, sons of the same civilization and the same idea."[122] These soldiers, if they were lucky enough to survive the war, might have wondered what became of this commonality of cause and purpose, this brotherhood of arms, during the years that followed, when French officials denied them legal acceptance into the brotherhood of the nation as full citizens.

Clemenceau had never been enthusiastic about restrictive French policies in the empire, but men like Albert Sarraut had more influence over colonial policy both during and after the war. In an influential book published in 1923, Sarraut, then minister of the colonies, admitted that perhaps naturalization should be easier for some *indigènes*, but he vehemently argued against "mass naturalization," because France's subject populations were simply incapable of exercising the rights of full citizenship. To grant them these rights "would be to decree the end of the civilization, the end of the benefits that it guarantees," to condemn the colonies to "anarchy" and to return "the masses under [our] guardianship to [their] former servitude."[123] Even the socialist deputy and charter member of the League of the Rights of Man Marius Moutet, who labored so hard to craft a reform in the naturalization process in Algeria, worked from an extremely narrow premise, writing in 1918, "If one wants to accomplish anything practical, one must certainly renounce the illusion of the mystical unity of human beings, who could receive the same laws and adapt themselves to them equally well."[124]

In the end, sentiments like these applied broadly to colonial subjects in general and submerged the kind of universalism and republican idealism that prompted the colonial newspaper *L'AOF* to call on the *tirailleurs séné-galais* to defend France "as in the days of Jemmapes or Valmy."[125] Invoking these revolutionary victories of 1792 was ironic, because they were fought by large armies of enthusiastic volunteers fired with revolutionary patriotism, defending their recently won rights. They validated the idea that citizen-soldiers defending those rights were the best means of beating back the invading armies of Europe's reactionary monarchies. Over a century later, the World War I battles of Verdun and the Somme merely confirmed the standing of the thousands of *troupes indigènes* who fought in them as inferior colonial subjects, instead of elevating their status to that of integral members of the French nation and fellow citizens with their French comrades-in-arms.

# Conclusion

❧

It should not be a question of assuming a permanent gulf,
never filled, between the white and the *indigène*; if, unlike
other nations, we do not accept as a dogma the eternal inferiority of certain races, we see, nevertheless, the delay in their
evolution and we devote ourselves to accelerating its stages.

—*Albert Sarraut, minister of the colonies, in a speech to the
Chamber of Deputies in 1921*

People are not, generally speaking, conscious hypocrites. No
one holds himself in contempt for thirty years. Anyone who
thinks that colonial imperialism was simply a case of capi-
talists snatching at profits from lucrative territories and of
defenceless populations has no idea what it was all about. In
the eyes of its agents, imperialism—like the humanitarianism that preceded it—was a worthy thing. Its chief advocates
evoked the great ideals of the period: the ideals of nationalism
and of humanitarianism. Unwitting of the problems and evils
they were engendering, they had clear consciences. This point
cannot be too strongly emphasised.

—*Henri Brunschwig*, French Colonialism, 1871–1914

France's use of *troupes indigènes* during the First World War highlights the
intertwined and often contradictory effects of French conceptions of republican principles, colonial ideology, and race. The need for more soldiers to
withstand the German invasion provided the immediate impetus to draw
upon the manpower resources of the empire, and the long war of attrition
gave momentum to further French demands for recruits. Yet the widespread
belief in France's civilizing mission in the colonies and the power of the ideal

of assimilation provided important justifications for demanding sacrifices from colonial subjects. These justifications were more than just cynical manipulation and empty rhetoric, and many of the men responsible for making policy with regard to *troupes indigènes* professed a genuine commitment to the republican ideal of equality. Officials like Albert Sarraut could believe, and expect others to believe, his claims that France was free of the "dogma" of racism and was carrying out a selfless humanitarian task in speeding the retarded "evolution" of the empire's colonized peoples. Such men spoke and acted with what the historian Henri Brunschwig has identified as "vital" to the imperialism of this period: a clear conscience.

This most certainly does not mean that these officials really were free of racial prejudice. Policies and attitudes toward *troupes indigènes* during the Great War prove definitively that this was not the case. But to achieve clear consciences, many officials clearly felt impelled at least to nod in the direction of color-blindness and equal treatment. They often moved in this direction only far enough to try to satisfy themselves, and efforts to live up fully to republican and humanitarian ideals fell short more often than not. In short, if military necessity led the French to consider using colonial subjects as soldiers, republican ideology and a view of race that placed minimal stress on the importance of essential, immutable differences often allowed them to do so without a sense of guilt or hypocrisy.

Some French officials no doubt viewed the use of *troupes indigènes* as a simple case of France making use of one of the tools at its disposal to defend itself. In this view, the French Army employed colonial subjects because it could, and the fact that these men were racially inferior made their use even easier. Others, however, made much of the reciprocal duties of the colonizers and colonized, grounding their justifications in appeals to equality among men and a universal humanity. Such pure exploitation and republican idealism could coexist even in the motivations of a single individual, and both impulses guided many military and political officials. This helps explain the often paradoxical policies toward *troupes indigènes,* and thus helps answer the questions that prompted this study. France acquired a reputation as a color-blind society because republican ideals pushed many French people to consider treating nonwhites as equal members of a universal humanity. Yet the pull of racism, the impulse to consider people who were not white Europeans as inherently inferior, caused many of these same French people to discriminate. As specific policies that governed the service of *troupes indigènes* in the French Army during the Great War demonstrate, despite a commitment to egalitarian republican principles and professions of racial tolerance, French authorities often failed to live up to these ideals in their treatment of colonial subjects. Racial and cultural prejudices prevented the integration of *troupes indigènes* into the nation for which they were fighting.

The importance of these conflicting impulses was apparent in French policy on a number of issues. Ideas about race had a profound influence on recruitment—affecting decisions about whom to recruit, where, and how intensively—both before and during the war. These same ideas affected the deployment of *troupes indigènes*. French officials viewed men from the colonies through a prism of racial stereotypes and ranked the different "races" of the French empire according to their martial ability. This resulted in distinctions between *races guerrières* and *races non-guerrières* both within and among different colonies, distinctions that often determined how the men would be deployed. Members of groups considered to be particularly warlike spent a disproportionate amount of time in combat, much of that time serving as attacking "shock troops." Men from supposedly less martial groups most often served as staging troops, performing labor, and officials' comments reveal the durability of the racial stereotypes associated with certain groups. The influence of racial prejudice is even clearer in army policy on promotion and officers, both white and indigenous. Conventional wisdom held that white officers were best equipped to lead racially inferior indigenous troops, playing a paternal role that emphasized the childlike nature of their men. Policy on indigenous officers highlighted even more starkly the conflict between republican principles of promotion based solely on merit, particularly important in the French Army, and the firm belief that the military hierarchy should reflect a racial hierarchy that placed whites firmly at the top and in control. In situations where race and rank conflicted, race prevailed.

Language policy in the army also reflected the conflicts between the republican imperative of "civilizing" colonial subjects and integrating them into the French nation, on the one hand, and racial prejudices that deemed nonwhites incapable of the "improvement" necessary to become members of the national community, on the other. The army often seemed to value interpreters more for their "moral" role in supporting and policing the *indigènes* than for their facilitation of communication. French officials failed to provide adequate language instruction to soldiers, and the instruction they did provide was clearly predicated upon the alleged intellectual simplicity of nonwhites. Language policy toward West Africans dramatically underscored this assumption, and the French that the army taught these *tirailleurs* only reinforced their status as outsiders. The French language was supposed to be one of the most powerful agents of "civilization" and integration, but officials failed to use this tool adequately.

Policies on religion in the army, on sex and love across the color line, and on the naturalization of *indigenes* who served during the war also reveal the conflict between the supposition that military service would tighten the bonds that linked the metropole to the colonies and racial and cultural prejudices that separated the colonizers from the colonized. Long-standing stereotypes about Islam and fears about the loyalty of North African Muslims, who might balk at fighting against an alliance that included the Ottoman empire and its sultan, stood between France and its Muslim soldiers. Suspicion and hostility prevented a true merging of interests, and underlined the status of colonial subjects as outsiders.

Suspicion and hostility also marked French officials' reactions to the even more intimate challenge that interracial relationships posed to French national identity. Fraternization, love, and sex between nonwhite colonial subjects in uniform and white Frenchwomen living in the metropole confronted authorities with disturbing questions about the consequences of bringing *troupes indigènes* to fight in Europe. Official reactions to these relationships, anxieties about their effects upon the *indigènes'* mentalities and the stability of colonial rule, and dismay at limits on the ability to prevent and control the behavior of both colonial subjects and Frenchwomen all underlined the conflict between inclusionary impulses driven by republican ideology and exclusionary urges stemming from racial prejudice.

This same conflict characterized debates over offering French citizenship to *troupes indigènes*. Republican tradition and history created a close link between service to the state in the military and the rights and duties of citizens, but efforts to offer naturalization to soldiers, thus bringing their service into line with republican principles, foundered upon allegedly insurmountable racial and cultural differences. Islam, and customs French officials held to be synonymous with Islam, symbolized the difficulties many French officials had in incorporating Muslims and other colonial subjects into their conception of French national identity.

These policies all underlined the significant limits that race and culture placed upon the republican ideals of universalism and egalitarianism. That there were conflicts between race and ideology at all, however, indicates the power of the latter. The issue of citizenship is a good example. If pure exploitation lay behind the use of *troupes indigènes,* why consider offering them naturalization at all? In part, the motive was to provide more incentives to potential recruits in the colonies, but discussions often focused on offering compensation to men already in the army. Thus, the impetus to liberalize naturalization policies also came from attempts to reconcile the service of *troupes indigènes* with republican principles linking military service with citizenship. These efforts ultimately failed, but they highlighted the importance of republican ideology and the role it played in shaping policy toward *troupes indigènes.* As Alice Conklin has put it: "It is very easy to condemn colonialism's most visible excesses. It is considerably harder to lay bare the myriad more subtle ways in which colonialism worked its way into the life of the nation over the course of the last century—ways which linger (and malinger) still."[1] The key to understanding France's use of *troupes indigènes* during the First World War is to understand how mixed motives—the sense of entitlement to exploit an imperial resource, enhanced by a sense of racial superiority, and the impulsion to leaven this exploitation with attempts to observe republican orthodoxy—produced specific policies. Then one can see more clearly both how racism and colonial ideology worked their way into the life of the French nation during the Great War and how the life of the nation, in the form of political impulses molded by republican principles, worked its way into French colonialism and the lives of colonial subjects.

## The "Black Shame"

An episode that highlighted these issues, and one of the most famous episodes of the war involving *troupes indigènes,* actually occurred after the armistice of 11 November 1918 that brought an end to the fighting on the Western Front. The occupation of German territory by colonial subjects in French uniform, and the resulting international controversy, contributed mightily to convincing many French people that their commitment to republican ideals was sincere and uncorrupted by racial prejudice, that France did not make distinctions between its native white soldiers and its *troupes indigènes,* even if other nations did. Many *troupes indigènes* remained in Europe after the armistice, either because of the terms of their enlistment (in many cases, the duration of the war plus six months), or due to a lack of transport capacity to ship them home. Moreover, the army was not eager to let these men go. The end of active fighting reduced the need for soldiers but did not eliminate it. The armistice was not necessarily a permanent peace, and France had to remain on a war footing, ready to resume hostilities if Germany proved reluctant to come to final terms set by the victors. Moreover, French troops occupied areas in western Germany, most notably, the Rhineland. French forces in this area numbered approximately 200,000 men at their peak in the winter of 1919, falling to about 85,000 a year later. *Troupes indigènes* eventually made up about half of this occupation force.[2]

The presence of non-Europeans among the occupiers became an international scandal. The fiercest controversy surrounded France's "black" soldiers. In reality, these consisted of two regiments of West Africans and one regiment of Madagascans, but most of the *troupes indigènes* in the Rhineland were North Africans. Nevertheless, German propaganda eventually referred to all French indigenous soldiers as "black," or at least "colored," and objected to their presence among the occupiers, denouncing *die schwarze Schande* (the black shame) in the Rhineland, and publicists in Great Britain and America took up the outcry against "the black horror on the Rhine." German officials did everything they could to capitalize upon the racial fears and prejudices present in the societies of other nations around the world once the occupation began and "colored" troops moved in. This reflected not only racial prejudice in Germany but also the desire of many Germans to portray themselves as the victims of an unreasonable and vindictive French government and thereby to win concessions at the negotiating table over peace terms and reparations. But Germany had also sought to exploit the issue of race and France's use of *troupes indigènes* as a means of winning sympathy for its cause and driving a wedge between the Entente powers during the war. In June 1915, the German government had published a white paper alleging atrocities committed by French and British colonial soldiers. These men, the Germans claimed, had imported their savage methods of warfare into the heart of civilized Europe, taking the heads, fingers, and ears of their opponents as trophies, killing unarmed and wounded men, gouging out their opponents' eyes, raping white women, and generally terrorizing all Europeans with whom they came into contact. With unintentional irony, given that during the First World War, the European powers introduced many unprecedentedly brutal and cruel weapons and forms of warfare, the German government protested before the nations of the world against the use of "troops whose brutality and cruelty are a disgrace to the conduct of war in the twentieth century."[3]

In January 1917, a group of French legislators, among them Blaise Diagne, formally protested against a similar diplomatic note that the German government had addressed to the world's neutral nations. The German note had declared, "The use of colored troops in Europe and the extension of the war to the African colonies, which has taken place contrary to treaties and which diminishes the prestige of the white race in this part of the world, are no less irreconcilable with the principles of international law and civilization." The French lawmakers protested in the name of the *troupes indigènes* who fought so valiantly for France, charging the Germans with hypocrisy, because their actions in occupied France and Belgium were the true affronts to civilization.[4]

In one sense, this was merely a part of the larger struggle between France and Germany to claim the mantle of "civilization" in a struggle both sides defined explicitly as a battle of "civilization against barbarism."[5] Both sides sought to ennoble their causes and win the sympathy, and even the help, of neutral nations like the United States. Of course, British and French propaganda accusing German troops of atrocities in occupied Belgium and France was another part of this contest.[6] Race was a particularly effective theme upon which to play, not least because of the well-known prejudices of white Americans against blacks in their own country, prejudices personified by President Woodrow Wilson, himself a racist segregationist.[7] Yet these wartime events also revealed sharp divergences in racial attitudes between France and the other belligerent nations. The so-called black shame of the occupation of the Rhineland was merely the most dramatic episode in the long history of international tensions over race and France's use of *troupes indigènes.*[8]

The intensity of the German reaction to the presence of non-Europeans among the occupiers tended to increase immediately prior to international conferences on reparations, indicating once again that they were as intent upon exploiting the racial prejudices of other nations as they were on venting their own prejudices.[9] Germans protested against the "black shame" and spread lurid tales of rape and violence through the world press, with the help of foreign figures such as the English humanitarian activist E. D. Morel (who before the war had led the international campaign against human rights abuses in the Belgian Congo, but whose sympathy for Africans apparently waned when they did not stay put in Africa).[10] Soon, prominent figures such as H. G. Wells, Philip Snowden, and Bernard Shaw had entered the debate, condemning France for introducing uncivilized men into the heart of Europe.[11] By 1923, the Rhenish Women's League had printed four editions of a long pamphlet describing alleged atrocities committed by French indigenous troops in their homeland, listing everything from rape and murder, to attempted rape, molestation of boys, and the "unnatural usage" of men. Nothing, it seemed, was beyond the lustful and demonic appetites of these "savage" foreigners. One alleged complaint told of a man and his horse being followed home by a Moroccan soldier, "who at first attempted to misuse the horse . . . but as this was not possible, he turned on the man himself, crying "Horse too high, Horse too high."[12]

By compiling such lengthy lists of allegations, in all their lurid details, often including names, places, and dates, opponents of French policy added an air of verisimilitude to their charges and hoped to outrage readers. Of course, one cannot rule out a kind of voyeurism and perhaps even an attempt to titillate. The Rhenish Women's League pamphlet contains over 100 descriptions of incidents, including all but the most pornographic details. The authors do not seem to have omitted any outrage that might occur to the imagination: gang rape, sodomy, violations of boys, "unnatural lust" (a euphemism for homosexuality and pedophilia), rape in the presence of women's husbands, children, parents, or sweethearts. Typical of the descriptions is that of the rape of a 71-year-old woman, allegedly attacked on the road by "a coloured French soldier. He seized her from behind on the right arm and dragged her forcibly into the bushes . . . then pulled his bayonet . . . and forced her to her knees and violated her in a most obnoxious and brutal manner."[13]

The propagandists intended the incidents to reflect the essentially savage nature of non-European troops, and to imply that the French were equally uncivilized for stooping to employ such primitives in their army. Allegations sometimes graphically illustrated this point, as when the Rhenish Women's League charged that during the rape of a young girl by two black soldiers, "a white French soldier in the company of the blacks . . . just stood and looked on without interfering in the least."[14] Yet virtually none of the accusations were true, and Germans who lived in the Rhineland often found the behavior of indigenous troops preferable to that of haughty and vengeful Frenchmen. In fact, most of the complaints originated outside the Rhineland and were clearly part of an orchestrated propaganda campaign.[15]

In 1922, French authorities published *La campagne allemande contre les troupes noires: Rapport du capitaine Bouriand sur ses missions en pays rhénans*, the report of an officer who had toured the Rhineland investigating German claims and the behavior of France's occupying forces. This report focused on West African and Madagascan troops, taking aim at allegations of a "black" shame by asserting that French authorities had received only one complaint about the behavior of a West African soldier, who was acquitted for lack of evidence, and sixteen charges against Madagascans, only six of which were proved and resulted in convictions. The report then went on to reproduce numerous letters and testimonials by inhabitants of the Rhineland who praised the conduct of the Africans.[16] Moreover, the undeniable existence of consensual relationships and marriages, sometimes resulting in children, revealed the positive attitude of at least some Germans to the presence of *troupes indigènes*. French military censors' reports on mail emanating from troops stationed in the Rhineland indicate fraternization between French colonial men and German women, and the existence of mixed-race offspring from these unions haunted those in Germany who considered it a mark of "shame" for decades after French troops had withdrawn from the region.[17]

France might have expected some kind of backlash from its Rhineland policy, and British and American officials had warned their French counterparts very early on that using non-Europeans would meet with international disapproval and controversy. Why, then, use *troupes indigènes* in the occupation? Contemporary propaganda was nearly unanimous in attributing the French decision to a desire to humiliate the Germans, and American and British authorities largely shared this view.[18] Some historians take a similar view, crediting French officials with a wish to demonstrate to the Germans the full extent of their defeat at the hands of France and its mighty colonial empire.[19] Others maintain that there was no premeditated plan to use black troops, asserting that after demobilization, France had barely enough troops to go around and thus had to use those available, or that Mangin's 10th Army was designated to hold half the French zone of occupation and so his Senegalese units simply followed their commander to his new posting.[20] Some scholars, citing widespread racism, hostility, and fears of sexual pollution and miscegenation by West African troops in France, argue that a desire to separate these troops from the French population impelled authorities to send them to Germany.[21]

There was, of course, widespread racism in French society and among military and political officials, as French policy during the war itself demonstrates, and fears of primitive sexuality and racial mixing were very real. There is little evidence, however, that the French military authorities viewed their decision to include *troupes indigènes* among the occupying forces in the Rhineland as a policy of expulsion. Manpower shortages certainly played a role. The government felt constrained by the political imperative of demobilizing as many Frenchmen as possible as quickly as possible. After over four long years of war, no *poilu* wanted to be marching off to the Rhine for garrison duty after the shooting had stopped. Keeping under arms *indigènes* already thousands of miles away from home and unable to vote, or to mount protests in France along with their relatives, was a safe political course. Officials could be explicit on this point. In July 1919, the High Command expressed enthusiasm about using Madagascans in the Rhineland because "there are only advantages in increasing the use of colonial elements there in order to diminish the burdens on French recruitment."[22] The presence of Mangin's 10th Army among the occupiers was important in ensuring *troupes indigènes* ended up in the Rhineland. Mangin saw the deployment as a critical component of his campaign to expand the importance of indigenous colonial forces in the postwar French defense structure.

Blaise Diagne, however, was most instrumental in ensuring that West Africans were among the occupation troops.[23] It was the presence of these men, even as a minority of the *indigènes* in the Rhineland, that propelled the controversy and defined it as a "black" shame even after the *tirailleurs sénégalais* had departed. There were good reasons why they should not be stationed in the Rhineland: the winter weather would be terrible for their health, the German and international reaction would be predictably hostile (though its ultimate extent and intensity seems to have taken the French by surprise), and many of these men wanted to go home at least as badly as did their white French comrades now that the war had ended and there seemed to be no urgent need for their extraordinary presence in Europe. However, longer-term political and colonial considerations were decisive. In part, occupying the Rhineland was a reward for services rendered to France over the course of four years of war.[24] Just after the armistice went into effect, the Ministry of War argued that excluding *troupes noires* from the occupation forces would be unjust, because "these troops and their officers . . . have rendered, in the course of the campaign, services recognized by all, and have suffered glorious losses under fire," and they "would have difficulty understanding why they were excluded from participation in the occupation of enemy territories."[25]

But sending these men to Germany was much more than a gesture designed to make the troops happy. Officials intended the experience to serve the political goals of French imperial rule. Even as he sought to defend and expand the rights of indigenous peoples, Diagne, an ardent assimilationist and defender of French colonial interests, had long argued that service in the French Army would hasten their "social education from the point of view that is best suited to the goal of colonization."²⁶ When the war ended, he stressed "the greatest interest, from the political and social point of view, of putting the largest number of men possible through the School of the Army, so that they are returned to their colony of origin more educated and more penetrated by French influence."²⁷ Having *troupes indigènes* occupy the Rhineland would serve a similar purpose.

Many officials were worried about the effect on the *indigènes* of seeing France prostrate before German aggression and obliged to call, not only on them, but also on the British and the Americans to defend French soil. Sending *troupes indigènes* to the Rhineland was a way to emphasize the French victory in the eyes of the *indigènes*. Diagne made this goal explicit early in his efforts to have *tirailleurs sénégalais* included in the occupation forces, arguing that beyond the notion of rewarding these soldiers, as the Ministry of War had advocated, "it is necessary, from the point of view of our indigenous policy, to mark in a tangible way our victory in the eyes of our African populations, by having the *tirailleurs* contribute to the occupation of a portion of enemy territory."²⁸

Although not everyone concurred with this reasoning—in December 1918, Marshal Pétain wrote to oppose the deployment of West Africans in the Rhineland, primarily because they would be useless in the cold weather there—Clemenceau and other Ministry of War officials ultimately agreed with Diagne, especially as the West Africans would not be sent to Germany until the spring.²⁹ As one official put it, articulating Diagne's and Clemenceau's colonial policy, it was "of major interest, from the point of view of our indigenous policy, to give the Senegalese a concrete idea of French Victory and Power. This result will be achieved only if they are stationed in German territory. It is there, on the spot, that the *tirailleurs sénégalais,* in their simplistic mentality, will acquire the intimate conviction that France has conquered the enormous military power of Germany. They will take this sentiment back to the various regions of our West Africa; the turbulent populations impressed by the power of France will no longer be tempted to cause disturbances."³⁰

That these goals differed from Mangin's was apparent when Diagne complained to Clemenceau about the general's plan to use the *tirailleurs sénégalais* in the Rhineland even during the winter. This plan, Diagne charged, had a purely military aim, "the permanent use of the Senegalese in their totality," while he and the prime minister aimed at "a goal above all political in its colonial repercussion." Mangin's proposals were also dangerous to the health of West African soldiers, who would suffer from the winter cold in Germany.[31] In the end, two regiments of *tirailleurs sénégalais* took up their posts in the Rhineland in the spring of 1919.

Stung by the international criticism, France withdrew these West African troops in June 1920. By then, however, those propagandizing against the "black shame" on the Rhine, both inside and outside Germany, had come to consider Madagascans and even North Africans to be just as black and shameful as the *tirailleurs sénégalais*, and the uproar continued.

Nonetheless, many *troupes indigènes* remained in Germany, and the issue gained renewed prominence in 1923 when the French included some among the forces that invaded the Ruhr to enforce the payment of reparations. Ultimately, despite the sound and fury of propaganda, and German hopes to the contrary, the controversy over race in the occupation of the Rhineland had very little concrete effect upon postwar international diplomacy.[32]

The episode did, however, reverberate through German culture and national consciousness, enhancing Germans' sense of victimhood and playing a role in exacerbating racial tensions through the Nazi period.[33] Most important, though, the "black shame" highlighted the ways in which French racial attitudes and colonial policies differed from those of other nations. Rather than see the use of nonwhite soldiers in Europe as an immoral and dangerous attack upon white prestige, French officials viewed *troupes indigènes* as embodying the republican assimilationist tradition of national belonging. Their use was a symbol of France's unwavering commitment to republican ideals of egalitarianism and universal humanity, and the objections of other nations to this use only served as evidence that France's commitment was unique.

Of course, this attitude allowed French officials to ignore their own racial prejudices, evident in other policies toward *troupes indigènes*. Moreover, practical considerations, such as manpower needs and a desire to lessen the burden of military service upon the domestic French population, played an important role in the decision to send *indigènes* into Germany as occupiers. The political imperative to demonstrate the power of France that motivated Diagne and Clemenceau also stemmed in part from practical concerns over the mentality of *indigènes* who would soon return to the colonies. As much as this policy sought to include colonial subjects as partners in the victory over Germany, to bring them closer into the fold of the French nation, just as military service in general was the "school of the nation," the use of *troupes indigènes* in the Rhineland and elsewhere was complicated throughout the war by real manifestations of racial prejudice. As this study has shown, policies on recruitment, deployment, promotion, language, religion, sexual activity, and citizenship often distanced *troupes indigènes* from the nation rather than integrating them, and policies governing the occupation of the defeated enemy's territory were no different.

Despite all of this, the extensive use of these soldiers, and their deployment in the Rhineland, demonstrated how much further than other nations France was willing to go at least to give the appearance of integrating nonwhites and colonial subjects into the national community. Many of the issues that troubled French officials did so only because they felt obligated to consider, for instance, promoting colonial subjects up the military hierarchy, or offering them citizenship in return for their sacrifices on behalf of the nation. The idea of "rewarding" these men by allowing them to participate in postwar manifestations of the French victory such as the occupation of the Rhineland stemmed, at least in part, from the same impulses. To fail even to consider such measures, in short, would have given some French authorities stabs of conscience. The pull of republican principles was strong and difficult to ignore. In the end, the pull of racism proved similarly powerful, of course, and this placed significant limits on the fulfillment of the very lofty ideals of civilization that France and its colonial subjects had defended against German aggression.

## Colonial Ideology and Troupes indigènes

The impulse to downplay racial differences and hold up integration as the model relationship France should have with its colonial subjects exerted a strong influence over even those officials who advocated association—with its stress on enduring differences between the French colonizers and indigenous peoples, who would learn to work in partnership with the colonizers rather than becoming one with them—as a more appropriate colonial ideology than assimilation—which envisioned, essentially, transforming colonized indigenous peoples into French people. Albert Sarraut, former governor-general of Indochina and minister of the colonies for over four years following the war, was a leading spokesman for association, and his 1921 statement that France did not subscribe to the idea "the eternal inferiority of certain races" shows his adherence to prevailing ideas about race.[34] Indeed, for Sarraut and others, there was a great deal of slippage between association and assimilation, because republican orthodoxy limited the ability of associationists to deny completely that the gaps between different peoples could be filled by political and cultural assimilation.

Two years after his 1921 speech, Sarraut repeated and expanded these comments in his widely influential 1923 book *La mise en valeur des colonies françaises,* which explicitly tied French racial ideas to the use of *troupes indigènes* in Europe. He condemned those in other nations who upheld "the indelible inequality of the superior race and the inferior races . . . which explains the too complaisant echoes that one could find, in certain European countries, in defiance of the truth as in defiance of the heroic memories of yesterday, of the passionate attacks of the German press on our admirable black troops stationed on the Rhine."[35] He went on to give a broad justification of France's use of *troupes indigènes,* in a statement that is worth quoting at length, highlighting as it does intertwined ideas about military service, republican principles, race, and colonial policy:

> France, by calling these indigenous auxiliaries to the honor of defending her flag has only done so within the very logic of her colonial doctrine. She has not, according to the Carthaginian method, enlisted mercenaries. She has mobilized "her children of the colonies." It is that she does not accept, as a dogma, the "eternal" inferiority of certain races. She sees the delay in their evolution, and devotes herself to correcting its effects and tries hard to accelerate its stages. Kindness, indeed, sublime virtue, is at the base of her civilizing work, but also the great thought of justice that permeates the tradition of the nation of the Declaration of the Rights of Man. The dignity and the capacity of the human being is not measured for her by the nuance, more or less marked, of his color, but certainly by the value of the individual conscience and the coefficient of personal virtues that he shows. And as soon as he shows himself capable, by the indisputable proof of his moral and intellectual elevation, of rising to a higher destiny, no text nor any dogma will deny him on French territory the right to claim the benefit of this attainment [i.e., equality and citizenship].[36]

So allegiance to republican principles compelled even associationists like Sarraut to reject, at least rhetorically, rigid racism and to envision a close union of French and colonial subjects, not divided by racial difference, but joined by culture and a shared adherence to the universal principles outlined in the Declaration of the Rights of Man of 1789. To be sure, Sarraut was a leading advocate of *mise en valeur,* or rational economic development, in the colonies, which certainly seemed at times to be a purely cynical attempt to exploit the empire economically, in other words, to make it pay. Sarraut, at least in part, "considered colonial activity at its origin but an egotistical act of force, the justification of which was to be found in its utility, in the development and distribution of new wealth."[37] Moreover, Sarraut's later writings and his reactions to increasing immigration from the colonies during the interwar period show a greater willingness to emphasize biology and heredity in explaining racial difference, and to incorporate these views into restrictive policies.[38]

Still, in the immediate aftermath of a victory over Germany won by colonizers and colonized fighting side by side, Sarraut and many other officials believed that uniquely French ideas about race, culture, and human rights made France's colonial policy exceptional, and exceptionally generous. In this view, serving France in the military was a privilege for colonial subjects, a privilege that could open the door to other benefits of a closer association with the metropole, even citizenship. Yet, even as French officials congratulated themselves on their humanitarian approach to colonialism, this belief blinded them to their own very real racial and cultural prejudices, and served as a virtually insurmountable barrier to the acceptance of colonial subjects as true members of the national community. As naturalization policy during the war demonstrated, racial and cultural prejudices prevented real reform in French policy in this area, despite the close linkage of military service and citizenship in traditional republican ideology. Indeed, even as he asserted that individual worth, not color, defined the ability of colonial subjects to accede to the full benefits and rights of being French, Sarraut condemned those who were so carried away by ideological commitment and a concern to reward *indigènes* for their military service during the war that they had the temerity to suggest "the error and the peril" of mass naturalization.[39] The preparation of colonial subjects for French citizenship would require a long process of tutelage. Perhaps many generations would have to pass before they were ready.

This was certainly convenient. It allowed French officials to proceed with a clear conscience, to declare themselves unconstrained by the racism that compromised the colonial rule of other less enlightened powers (such as those that had objected so strenuously to the presence of *troupes indigènes* in the occupied Rhineland) and unmoved by their purely exploitative motives. And these officials would not have to confront the consequences of a truly liberal colonialism (if there could even be such a thing), which would have involved real concessions to indigenous peoples. In short, French colonialism would live up to the republican ideals of egalitarianism and universalism, just not today. Bringing policy into line with these ideals, the argument went, would be a long-drawn-out process.

Both during the war and afterwards, French officials were careful to stress that France's enlightened colonial policies lay behind its use of *troupes indigènes*, not, as Sarraut put it, the cynical "Carthaginian method" of hiring mercenaries. The clearest statements of this point of view often emerged when the French attempted to justify the presence of these soldiers in Europe to other nations. In the summer of 1918, Lieutenant-Colonel Édouard Jean Réquin, a member of the French military delegation to Washington, D.C., submitted a memo on the "Use of Colored Troops in the French Army" to American officials, who had it translated and distributed it to the press. Concentrating primarily on West Africans, Réquin described the situation in the French Army as one of idyllic racial harmony, in which whites and blacks served side by side and were cared for in the same hospitals and by the same personnel. "Thus," he wrote, "we have delivered these blacks from African barbarism, we have brought them civilization and justice. They come in their turn to defend in our country this justice and this civilization against Prussian barbarism."

This last statement reflected a theme French officials never tired of emphasizing: the irony and symbolism of "uncivilized" Africans defending civilized humanity (unhesitatingly equated with France) against the true barbarians, the Germans. Widening his focus to encompass *troupes indigènes* from all the French colonies, Réquin cited the unwavering service of thousands of Moroccans, so recently brought under French imperial control in the years immediately before the war, as particularly dramatic proof of the loyalty France inspired in its colonial subjects. All of France's colonies were doing their part, providing "volunteers" (this assertion of course obscured the importance of conscription and coercion in the colonies): "Arabs, Kabyles, Moroccans, Tunisians by hundreds of thousands, Senegalese, [other West Africans], Madagascans and Somalis, and even Indochinese have come to fight on French soil for the defense of liberty, all the benefits of which they have learned, under our tutelage, to appreciate." The presence of so many *troupes indigènes* fighting in France was not only due to the genius of specific colonial administrators and their efficient methods, it

shows equally what a prodigious faculty of assimilation the French possess, if one considers that in North Africa the Islamic faction is in essence resistant to all foreign intervention. The voluntary participation of colored men in the defense of French soil definitively consecrates the guiding principles of our colonial expansion. It is, outside of any question of national interest, and solely from the point of view of humanity and morality, the finest justification of the role of France outside of France.[40]

Alongside this idealized picture of the place of *troupes indigènes* in France's civilizing mission, and claims that skin color did not matter in France, one must place the attitudes of French officials and the policies they produced. During the war and the deployment of *troupes indigènes* Réquin was lauding as shining examples of French benevolence and egalitarianism, French policies on the promotion of indigenous officers and on naturalization demonstrated the limits of the integration of colonial subjects into the French nation, while methods of recruitment and deployment, and approaches to linguistic and religious diversity in the ranks, and reactions to love and sexual activity across the color line were heavily influenced by prevailing notions of the racial and cultural inferiority of nonwhites.

Despite idealistic public rhetoric, many contemporaries were well aware that such a contradictory situation existed. To take a particularly revealing example from debates over the vexed questions surrounding the status of *officiers indigènes,* a group of officers studying the question in Indochina after the war admitted that restrictive policies toward the promotion of *indigènes* might seem ungrateful, considering the sacrifices that hundreds of thousands of colonial subjects had made to help defend the metropole. Still, these officers argued that despite the contributions of *troupes indigènes* to the war effort, the army had to maintain clear distinctions between French soldiers and their indigenous counterparts "in a way that safeguards, in our colonies, the ascendancy and the prestige of the French soldier over the indigenous soldier." Though "this way of looking at it, after the appeal made by France to the contingents of our colonies to defend her independence, might shock our egalitarian ideals," caution was still necessary: "Whatever the loyalty of the indigenous soldier, he is not yet sufficiently adapted to our conceptions of patriotism, abnegation and sense of duty. In other words, he has not yet internalized the French mentality."[41] So in the end, though the dictates of republican ideology and the civilizing mission of France in its colonies left some room for *indigènes* to acquire a "French mentality," racial differences constituted a barrier that would in theory take many years to break down. In practice, it often seemed that this theory merely masked a deeper conviction that this barrier would never disappear.

## Race in France

How, then, can one make sense of the paradoxical blend of tolerance and intolerance on display in French use of *troupes indigènes?* Republican ideals required a commitment to equality, but some other nations, like the United States, also professed such a commitment and still seemed to hold different, more rigid ideas about racial inequality. For many white Americans, the inherent inferiority of nonwhites legitimized their exclusion from the democratic principles that applied to members of the superior race. Great Britain did not share the same kind of revolutionary and republican traditions with France, but professed some of the same democratic and egalitarian values, and certainly adhered to its own version of an imperial "civilizing mission." Yet authorities in these other nations considered the use of nonwhites as soldiers in Europe to be a largely unjustifiable risk, even when, as in the case of African Americans, these nonwhites were citizens and not colonial subjects. And, to put it simply, the unequal treatment of nonwhites by these nations did not seem to give officials quite the same bad conscience that such treatment gave many of their French counterparts.

Race prejudice pushed French officials to pursue exclusionary practices in many areas, and to deny *troupes indigènes* full integration into the French nation, but republican principles prompted at least some nods in policy toward egalitarianism. To resolve apparent contradictions in colonial policy, French officials integrated their use of *troupes indigènes* into a certain vision of republican ideology reflected in a universalizing French *mission civilisatrice*. This mission in turn rested upon a uniquely French interpretation of racial difference, an interpretation that often downplayed strictly biological and scientific notions that stressed inherited and immutable characteristics in favor of an emphasis on cultural, and thus somewhat mutable, ideas of difference.

Scientific ideas about race, which gained growing acceptance in many countries during the nineteenth century, did have an influence on French racial thinking. Concepts associated with evolution combined with physical anthropological views of racial difference to reinforce a racial hierarchy, with white Europeans firmly at the top. Yet cultural and environmental factors never receded, at least in France, to the extent that one can speak of a "triumph of scientific racism" in the late nineteenth and early twentieth centuries.[42] The two strands of French racial thinking—cultural and biological—coexisted throughout the period, and the greater prominence of the former in comparison with thinking in other nations set France apart. Though after the First World War hard, scientific perspectives on racial difference gained greater currency in the French medical and scientific community, strict biological racism never fully defined the field. Up to the 1920s, the ideas of famous French theorists of scientific racism, such as Arthur de Gobineau and Georges Vacher de Lapouge, were much more influential outside France than inside it. French eugenicists remained marginal until the interwar period and the Vichy years provided an opportunity for them to influence state policy more directly with their ideas about biology and race.[43]

Similarly, in the colonial context, it was during the 1920s that French policy began to display a heightened consciousness of race and of the irreducible difference between white Europeans and, especially, black Africans.[44] Even so, one can find during the same period a resurgence of cultural understandings of difference in the work of French ethnographers working in West Africa, what one historian terms a continuing "strain of relativism" in French racial attitudes.[45] In fact, these attitudes demonstrated a marked continuity throughout this period, with both scientific and cultural assumptions clearly in evidence.

Though these competing strands of thought manifested themselves in debates over colonial policies of "assimilation" and "association," the power of cultural understandings of race also blurred the distinction between these competing ideologies. The conventional historical narrative points to the growing importance of "scientific" notions of race in the years before 1914 as contributing to the shift from assimilation to association.[46] Theories of inherent biological difference helped to discredit the idea of assimilating allegedly inferior "natives" to superior white culture, and many French observers thus deemed association a more realistic approach in the face of biological realities largely impervious to change. Yet even historians who tie increasing racism to the rise to prominence of associationist colonial ideology concede that assimilationist ideas never really died out completely, and the two approaches tended to overlap even after association became official policy after 1918.[47] Moreover, as Albert Sarraut's statements above make clear, even the most ardent associationist felt compelled to reject the notion of "the eternal inferiority of certain races," stressing the importance, not of "color," but of "individual conscience" and "personal virtues." If he had subscribed to rigid scientific notions of racial difference, Sarraut would not have made such a claim and then gone on to define France's mission in the colonies as accelerating the evolution of the inhabitants. France could not hasten their biological evolution, but it could contribute to their cultural development, their "intellectual and moral elevation." Their culture was the predominant factor defining them as racially inferior, not their biology.

To be sure, biology was not totally absent from considerations of race in France, but cultural and historical factors frequently tempered, or at least complicated, strict biological determinism. Charles Mangin provides one of the clearest examples of this. In *La force noire*, Mangin argued passionately that black Africans were "born soldiers," hardened by the primitive conditions of life in West Africa and uncorrupted by modern European ways of life and work.[48] Their legendary endurance, he claimed, also stemmed from the "much less developed" nervous systems of black Africans. This characteristic rendered *tirailleurs* more stable under fire, especially heavy artillery fire, than white soldiers. The "extreme nervousness of civilized peoples" was one of the main dangers of their participation in modern warfare, and the use of West African soldiers would address this problem.[49] Throughout its history, Mangin claimed, Africa had been "a vast battlefield," and this warlike past had prepared Africans for service in the French Army. In Mangin's view, living conditions, the biology of the nervous system, and history all combined to define the difference between white Europeans and black Africans. Clearly, understandings of the history of racial thought and racism that draw distinct lines between early modern notions about culture and the development of modern scientific notions rooted in biological understandings of difference fail to capture the complexity of such thinking.

Some scholars seeking to explain French conceptions of race today have noted the predominance of culture over biology, especially when compared to racial ideas in other nations. David Beriss has argued that the dominant tendency in France is to discriminate and exclude foreigners on the basis of culture, though cultures "constrain people in ways that resemble race."[50] Similarly, Gérard Noiriel has pointed to the power of republican ideology in explaining "why France is one of the countries in which racial prejudice has been the least pronounced." The undeniable manifestations of discrimination evident in French society, "the essential divide between 'us' and 'them'," stem more from legal and cultural distinctions between French and foreigner than between white and nonwhite.[51]

This cultural understanding of French identity often results in a sort of cultural chauvinism that is similar to racial discrimination, but different from the racism predicated on "biological" difference prevalent, for instance, in American society. Though Beriss and others are quick to admit the important role that "harder" notions of race play in current debates over national identity and immigration, notably in the recent prominence and electoral success of the xenophobic and overtly racist Front National, "softer," more ambiguous cultural understandings of difference are predominant.

The power of this cultural understanding of difference has led the French demographer Emmanuel Todd to assert the continuing power of assimilationist attitudes in informing contemporary reactions to immigrants. As a result, he downplays the existence of racism in France, attributing the success of the Front National and other manifestations of xenophobia to "a perversion of French egalitarian and universalist principles," rather than to "a manifestation of racism in the narrow sense of the word." For him, the French attitude stands in stark contrast to British and American "differentialism" and biological racism.[52] Todd's ideas are based to a large extent on an overly optimistic vision of race relations in France and a stereotypical view of the American and British racial contexts, but he is correct in discerning a difference, rooted in culture, in the ways that many French people view race.[53]

Part of the problem, to be sure, is the difficulty of defining race and racism in general, let alone in the specific national context of one nation. George Fredrickson's recent attempt to define racism illustrates the difficulty of dispensing with notions of biology in defining racism. He argues that the permanence of ethnic difference is an essential component of racism, and if "conversion or assimilation is a real possibility, we have religious or cultural intolerance but not racism." The second essential component is social and political power exercised in the name of race, "and the resulting patterns of domination and exclusion."[54]

Yet, though French notions of race explicitly hold out the possibility of assimilation, they are still clearly notions of race, attached as much to perceived racial identities as to culture. And it is hard to label the resulting policies of discrimination as anything but racism. Neil MacMaster has offered a more flexible and serviceable definition, which manages to encompass the myriad, complex, and contradictory ways in which people understand racial difference, including in cultural terms. He notes that the label of racism, as it has operated in modern European history, is appropriate to "belief systems which categorized individuals in a deterministic way, whether expressed through biology or culture." Yet he too adds that this categorization insisted that the racialized individuals "were incapable of moving from one social position to another."[55]

Again, such a restriction conceals the extent to which some people who think in terms that are self-evidently racist are willing to entertain the notion that racial identities are not in fact fixed and permanent. Of course, as this study has shown, people who claim to believe in assimilation often fail to live up to that belief in practice, but it is not simply dishonesty that drives them to do so. What is in fact behind these contradictory attitudes is a conception of race that does not depend entirely on the scientific and biological conceptions that racial theorists carefully worked out over the course of the nineteenth and twentieth centuries. If we accept that many people "think of race as a fuzzy jumble of behavior, culture, and biology," and that this jumble takes particular forms and shapes according to the national, historical, and cultural environment in which it develops, then we can begin to understand how important it is to think in terms of "racisms" rather than racism.[56]

MacMaster's work is important for reminding us that the use of the plural form can help us recognize the different ways in which race and racial discrimination operate in different historical contexts, but it is also important to keep in mind that spatial borders can be as important as temporal ones in separating different understandings of what race is and what it means. In this light, we have to take seriously the idea that French thinking about race developed in a historical context specific to that nation, and that understanding how race operates in France involves paying close attention to the ways prevailing French attitudes differ from those of people in other nations. This is most assuredly not to argue that race and racism was and is not important in France, or that France is somehow "less racist" than other nations in which more restrictive notions of biology have played a more salient role in defining race. It is, however, critical not to assume that a phenomenon as complicated, malleable, and protean as racism takes the same form everywhere and all the time.

The contemporary stress in France on culture as opposed to biology, then, is much easier to understand and explain if we problematize the notion of a triumph of biological racism in the late nineteenth century, identifying instead a greater continuity in French racial attitudes. Though "scientific" racism was an important aspect of racist thought in France during the late nineteenth and early twentieth centuries, many in France continued to consider cultural and environmental factors of great importance in explaining racial difference. Pierre-André Taguieff has identified these two discourses on race as "hetero-racialization" and "auto-racialization," the former type being universalizing and assimilationist, while the latter is particularist and more exclusionary.[57] Michel Wieviorka has further explored these discourses, arguing that they constitute two "logics" of racism that often coexist in racist attitudes and practices.[58] This coexistence was evident in the approach of French military and political officials to racial difference during the First World War. Both biology and culture were important in informing French racial attitudes throughout this period, but the importance of cultural understandings of difference combined with republican ideology and the sense of a civilizing mission to allow French officials to claim that race did not limit membership in the national community. In practice, of course, the real racial prejudices that these claims often obscured complicated and undermined this ideal. French policies toward *troupes indigènes* reflected the tension between prejudice and the desire to deny that prejudice and minimize the importance of racial difference.

This tendency toward the elision or minimization of the discrimination and racism that marked the use of colonial subjects in the French Army during the Great War continued well beyond 1918. In the immediate aftermath of the war, when many French people found a new source of national pride in the colonies because of the aid they had offered to the distressed metropole, the indigenous soldier came to symbolize the close and mutually beneficial relationship between France and its overseas possessions. These African and Asian men seemed to confirm the integrative power of republican ideals, "above all question of origin or race," as the black deputies Diagne and Candace had put it during the war.[59] The loyal service of the *troupes indigènes* had supposedly testified to the truth of the claim that France reckoned its true strength in terms, not of its 40 million metropolitan inhabitants, but of the 100 million souls scattered across its worldwide empire. In the public memory, the *tirailleur* occupied a place of honor next to the *poilu* as a symbol of France's suffering and glory in the great national trial of the First World War.[60] Even as the war became more distant, and as different groups within France instrumentalized the image of the indigenous soldier for their own purposes, he has often been a symbol of nostalgia, fraternity, and integration.[61] Such memories continue to obscure the importance of racism in wartime policies on indigenous troops, but remain well within the republican ideal that sought to minimize or ignore the importance of race during the war itself.

Making sense of French policies toward troupes indigenes requires taking into account conflicting impulses: republican egalitarianism and cultural understandings of race that left room for "improvement," assimilation, and integration; and real racial prejudices stemming from a vision of difference that was more permanent and at least partly rooted in biology, and that resulted in discrimination. Without such a nuanced view of French racial thinking, it is also impossible to make sense of the experience of the *troupes indigènes* themselves in France. These experiences were often as paradoxical and contradictory as French policy. In September 1917, Madagascan Corporal Ramananjanahary wrote in a letter, "I believe that Malagasy kings would not be as well treated as we are here in France."[62] Yet only a few months earlier, Tunisian Sergeant bel Gassem Soultan had written, "We are in France made perfectly aware that we are FOREIGNERS, and we fight every day; we die like dogs."[63] The difference between these two statements was not due to different treatment of Madagascans and Tunisians, because men from all the colonies expressed similarly conflicting sentiments. What these statements reflect is the curious blend of tolerance and intolerance, the tension between republicanism and racism, that marked France's approach to colonial subjects in its army.

*Ranks in the French Army, with Approximate U.S. Army Equivalents*

PETITS GRADÉS

| | |
|---|---|
| *soldat de 1er classe* | specialist |
| *caporal (infanterie)* | specialist |
| *brigadier (cavalerie)* | specialist |
| *caporal-chef (infanterie)* | private 1st class |
| *brigadier-chef (cavalerie)* | private 1st class |

SOUS-OFFICIERS

| | |
|---|---|
| *sergent (infanterie)* | corporal |
| *maréchal des logis (cavalerie)* | corporal |
| *sergent-chef (infanterie)* | sergeant |
| *maréchal des logis-chef (cavalerie)* | sergeant |
| *sergent-major* | staff sergeant; there are no first or master sergeants, or sergeants 1st class |
| *adjudant* | 1st sergeant; there are no sergeant majors |
| *adjudant-chef* (1912) | warrant officer W1 |
| *major* (rank created in 1975) | chief warrant officer W2, W3, W4 |

OFFICIERS SUBALTERNES

| | |
|---|---|
| *aspirant* | none |
| *sous-lieutenant* | 2nd lieutenant |
| *lieutenant* | 1st lieutenant |
| *capitaine* | captain |

OFFICIERS SUPÉRIEURS

| | |
|---|---|
| *commandant chef de bataillon (infanterie) ou d'escadron (cavalerie)* | major |
| *lieutenant-colonel* | lieutenant-colonel |
| *colonel* | colonel |

OFFICIERS GÉNÉRAUX

| | |
|---|---|
| *général de brigade* | brigadier general |
| *général de division* | major general |
| *général de corps d'armée* | lieutenant general |
| *général d'armée* | general |
| *maréchal de France* | general of the Army |

## Acronyms

| | |
|---|---|
| AEF | Afrique équatoriale française (French Equatorial Africa) |
| AMAE | Archives du Ministère des affaires étrangères (Paris) |
| AN | Archives nationales |
| AOF | Afrique occidentale française (French West Africa) |
| AP | [CAOM] Affaires politiques |
| BTI | *bataillon de tirailleurs indochinois* |
| BTM | *bataillon de tirailleurs malgaches* |
| BTS | *bataillon de tirailleurs sénégalais* |
| CA | *corps d'armée* |
| CAC | *corps d'armée colonial* |
| CAOM | Centre des archives d'Outre-mer (Aix-en-Provence) |
| CIAM | Commission interministérielle des affaires musulmanes (Interministerial Commission on Muslim Affairs) |
| CITI | Commission interministérielle des troupes indigènes (Interministerial Commission on Indigenous Troops) |
| COA | *commis et ouvriers d'administration* (administrative clerks and workers) |
| DI | *division d'infanterie* |
| DIC | *division d'infanterie coloniale* |
| DM | *division marocain* |
| DSM | Direction des services militaires |
| DTC | Direction des troupes coloniales |
| EMA | État-major de l'armée |
| GCC | *général commandant en chef* |
| GGA | *gouverneur général de l'Algérie* |
| GQG | Grand quartier général |
| MAE | *ministre des affaires étrangères* |
| MC | *ministre des colonies* |
| MCC | *maréchal commandant en chef* |
| MG | *ministre de la guerre* |
| MI | *ministre de l'intérieur* |

PC           *président du Conseil* (prime minister)
RGM          *résident général du Maroc*
RGT          *résident général de la Tunisie*
SA           [EMA] Section d'Afrique
SHAT         Service historique de l'armée de terre
SLOTFOM      Service de liaison avec les originaires des territoires français d'Outre-mer

## Introduction

*Epigraphs:* Senator Henry Bérenger, SHAT 7N2121: "Rapport sur le recrutement d'une armée indigène, présenté à la commission sénatoriale de l'armée par M. Henry Bérenger, sénateur" (26 November 1915). Blaise Diagne and Gratien Candace, AN C7537: dossier 1468, "Blaise Diagne et Gratien Candace, proposition de loi no. 1795, autorisant les indigènes et sujets français de l'Algérie, du Maroc, et des colonies françaises à contracter des engagements volontaires, en temps de paix comme en temps de guerre, dans les corps français de l'armée métropolitaine et coloniale et dans l'armée de mer" (15 February 1916).

1. About 20,000 additional nonwhite troops came to Europe from the so-called *vieilles colonies* (old colonies) of Réunion, Guyane, Martinique, Guadeloupe, and French possessions in India. From French islands in the Pacific came a battalion of mixed white and indigenous troops, and 2,000 or so Africans from the Côte française des Somalis (Djibouti) also formed a combat battalion. However, these smaller contributions provoked fewer comments and problems than did the larger contingents from other areas. Moreover, as French citizens, *créoles* from the *vieilles colonies* served in integrated metropolitan army units, making them more difficult to trace in the archives and reducing their relevance to the present study. Men from North and West Africa, Madagascar, and Indochina served in larger numbers and confronted French authorities with the kinds of questions about race and national identity that are most revealing for present purposes.

2. Quoted in Tyler Stovall, *Paris Noir: African Americans in the City of Light* (New York: Houghton Mifflin, 1996), 18.

3. Arthur E. Barbeau and Florette Henri, *The Unknown Soldiers: African-American Troops in World War I* (Philadelphia: Temple University Press, 1974; rpt., New York: Da Capo Press, 1996), 112–13, argues that racial prejudice and a low opinion of the value of African American troops to the U.S. war effort motivated Pershing's actions, while Robert B. Bruce, *A Fraternity of Arms: America and France in the Great War* (Lawrence: University Press of Kansas, 2003), 161–62, disputes the notion that Pershing was particularly racist and argues that a desire to satisfy French demands with good-quality troops underlay the decision.

4. For an account of the U.S. 93rd Division in France during World War I, see Barbeau and Henri, *Unknown Soldiers*, 111–36.

5. SHAT 6N97: Col. J. A. Linard, Mission militaire française près de l'armée américaine, "Au sujet des troupes noires américaines" (7 August 1918).

6. SHAT 6N97: Diagne to MG, "AS d'une circulaire relative aux troupes de couleur" (16 November 1918).

7. Barbeau and Henri, *Unknown Soldiers,* 114.

8. Quoted in Marc Michel, *L'appel à l'Afrique: Contributions et réactions à l'effort de guerre en AOF, 1914–1919* (Paris: Publications de la Sorbonne, 1982), 391. For Du Bois's promotion of France as a color-blind society, see Jennifer D. Keene, "French and American Racial Stereotypes During the First World War," in William L. Chew, ed., *National Stereotypes in Perspective: Americans in France, Frenchmen in America* (Atlanta: Rodopi, 2001), 261–62.

9. Barbeau and Henri, *Unknown Soldiers,* 113.

10. Barbeau and Henri describe American military officials as dismayed to see that "the integration of black troops with the white French troops was all too complete, without social or other discrimination," and saw "sinister implications for the future" (ibid., 114). André Kaspi writes similarly that white Americans were "at first astonished, then offended" by French treatment of African American soldiers. See his *Le temps des américains* (Paris: Publications de la Sorbonne, 1976), 303–4. See also Yves Pourcher, *Les jours de guerre: La vie des Français au jour le jour entre 1914 et 1918* (Paris : Plon, 1994), 199–201.

11. Jean-Charles Jauffret, "La Grande Guerre et l'Afrique française du Nord," in Claude Carlier and Guy Pedroncini, eds., *Les troupes coloniales dans la Grande Guerre* (Paris: Economica, 1997), 106. See also Charles John Balesi, *From Adversaries to Comrades-in-Arms: West Africans and the French Military, 1885–1918* (Waltham, Mass.: Crossroads Press, 1979), 112–13; and Michel, *Appel,* 396.

12. Stovall, *Paris Noir,* 17.

13. Hoover Institution Archives, Réquin Papers, "La collaboration Franco-Américaine, 1917–1918": Lt. Col. Édouard Jean Réquin, "Emploi des troupes de couleur dans l'armée française" (15 July 1918).

14. Stovall, *Paris Noir,* 19–23; quotation from 23. See also Tyler Stovall, "The Color Line Behind the Lines: Racial Violence in France During the Great War," *American Historical Review* 103, 3 (June 1998): 737–69; and "Colour-blind France? Colonial Workers During the First World War," *Race and Class* 35, 2 (1993): 35–55.

15. Keene, "French and American Racial Stereotypes." See also her *Doughboys: The Great War, and the Remaking of America* (Baltimore: Johns Hopkins University Press, 2001), 126–30. For an early and very influential scholarly challenge to the myth of a color-blind France, see William B. Cohen, *The French Encounter with Africans: White Responses to Blacks, 1530–1880* (Bloomington: Indiana University Press, 1980). For an analysis of the different ways in which "color-blindness" manifests itself in policies on race in France and the United States, see Robert C. Lieberman, "A Tale of Two Countries: The Politics of Color Blindness in France and the United States," *French Politics, Culture & Society* 19, 3 (Fall 2001): 32–59.

16. Herrick to secretary of state, 16 August 1923, U.S. National Archives and Records Administration, Record Group 59, 851.00/432. Thanks to Hubert Dubrulle for bringing this material to my attention.

17. SHAT 6N96: Maj. Arnaud, "Note au sujet de l'organisation d'unités offensives mixtes sénégalaises" (12 February 1917).

18. SHAT 16N197: unattributed, "Note sur l'utilisation des Sénégalais" (n.d.). This appears to be the same report Marc Michel cites (*Appel,* 323) as being written on 5 Janu-

ary 1918 by Col. Eugène Petitdemange, who was in charge of training West Africans at the large camp for *troupes indigènes* at Fréjus–Saint-Raphaël in southern France.

19. *The Times History of the War*, vol. 1 (London: The Times, 1914), 155.

20. On the Indian Army in World War I, see Byron Farwell, *The Armies of the Raj: From the Mutiny to Independence, 1858–1947* (New York: Norton, 1989), 248–66.

21. David Killingray, "The Idea of a British Imperial African Army," *Journal of African History* 19 (1979): 421–36.

22. For evidence that the British feared that fighting whites would make their colonial subjects more difficult to rule, see Farwell, *Armies of the Raj*, 253.

23. Byron Farwell, *The Great War in Africa* (New York: Norton, 1986). On the role of military and police forces in various areas of the empires of European colonial powers, see David Killingray and David Omissi, eds., *Guardians of Empire: The Armed Forces of the Colonial Powers, c. 1700–1964* (Manchester, England: Manchester University Press, 1999).

24. See Myron Echenberg, *Colonial Conscripts: The* Tirailleurs Sénégalais *in French West Africa, 1857–1960* (Portsmouth, N.H.: Heinemann, 1991), 5.

25. For a discussion of the often problematic application of revolutionary principles to marginalized groups during the Revolution itself, see Shanti Marie Singham, "Betwixt Cattle and Men: Jews, Blacks, and Women, and the Declaration of the Rights of Man," in Dale Van Kley, ed., *The French Idea of Freedom: The Old Regime and the Declaration of Rights of 1789* (Stanford, Calif.: Stanford University Press, 1994), 114–53; and Alyssa Goldstein Sepinwall, "Eliminating Race, Eliminating Difference: Blacks, Jews, and the Abbé Grégoire," in Sue Peabody and Tyler Stovall, eds., *The Color of Liberty: Histories of Race in France* (Durham, N.C.: Duke University Press, 2003), 28–41.

26. Alice Conklin, "Colonialism and Human Rights, a Contradiction in Terms? The Case of France and West Africa, 1895–1914," *American Historical Review* 103, 2 (April 1998): 419–42. See also id., *A Mission to Civilize: The Republican Idea of Empire in France and West Africa, 1895–1930* (Stanford, Calif.: Stanford University Press, 1997).

27. On assimilation, see Raymond F. Betts, *Assimilation and Association in French Colonial Theory, 1890–1914* (New York: Columbia University Press, 1961); and Martin D. Lewis, "One Hundred Million Frenchmen: The Assimilationist Theory in French Colonial Policy," *Comparative Studies in Society and History* 4, 2 (1962): 129–53.

28. Herman Lebovics, *True France: The Wars over Cultural Identity, 1900–1945* (Ithaca, N.Y.: Cornell University Press, 1992).

29. Betts, *Assimilation and Association*, 165ff.

30. Conklin, "Colonialism and Human Rights."

31. The term "school of the nation" was a common way of referring to the army's assimilating function within the nation under the Third Republic. For a typical example of the application of this function this way to the colonies, see Antoine-Vincent Passols, *L'Algérie et l'assimilation des indigènes musulmans: Étude sur l'utilisation des ressources militaires de l'Algérie* (Paris: Charles Lavauzelle, 1903).

32. Eugen Weber, *Peasants into Frenchmen: The Modernization of Rural France, 1871–1914* (Stanford, Calif.: Stanford University Press, 1976).

33. AN C7537: dossier 1468, "Blaise Diagne et Gratien Candace, proposition de loi no. 1795 . . . " (15 February 1916).

34. SHAT 7N2121: Bérenger, "Rapport sur le recrutement . . . " (26 November 1915).

35. After 1918, conservative outlooks on race, empire, and republicanism among the French officer corps and colonial administration became more pronounced. On the former, see André Lambelet, "Back to the Future: Politics, Propaganda and the Centennial of the Conquest of Algeria," in *French History and Civilization: Papers from the George Rudé Seminar,* vol. 1 (Melbourne, Australia: George Rudé Society, 2005): 62–72; on the latter, see Conklin, *Mission.*

36. See Douglas Porch, *The March to the Marne: The French Army, 1871–1914* (Cambridge: Cambridge University Press, 1981); David B. Ralston, *The Army of the Republic: The Place of the Military in the Political Evolution of France, 1871–1914* (Cambridge, Mass.: MIT Press, 1967); Alistair Horne, *The French Army and Politics, 1871–1970* (New York: Peter Bedrick Books, 1984); and John Kim Munholland, "The Emergence of the Colonial Military in France, 1880–1905" (Ph.D. diss., Princeton University, 1964).

## One • *Reservoirs of Men*

*Epigraphs:* Adolphe Messimy's comment appeared in an interview in the Parisian daily *Le Matin* on 3 September 1909; it is quoted in Marc Michel, *L'appel à l'Afrique: Contributions et réactions à l'effort de guerre en AOF, 1914–1919* (Paris: Publications de la Sorbonne, 1982), 7. Henri Simon made the statement quoted when introducing legislation governing the new recruiting efforts of 1918 in West Africa; it is cited in *Journal officiel,* 17 January 1918, 677. The mother's lament to a French officer in Senegal is quoted in Joe Lunn, *Memoirs of the Maelstrom: A Senegalese Oral History of the First World War* (Portsmouth, N.H.: Heinemann, 1999), 41.

1. Jean-Charles Jauffret, *Parlement, gouvernement, commandement: L'armée de métier sous la Troisième République, 1871–1914* (Vincennes: Service historique de l'armée de terre, 1987), 2: 1103.

2. Charles John Balesi, *From Adversaries to Comrades-in-Arms: West Africans and the French Military, 1885–1918* (Waltham, Mass.: Crossroads Press, 1979), 3–6; Jacques Razafindranaly, *Les soldats de la grande île: D'une guerre à l'autre, 1895–1918* (Paris: L'Harmattan, 2000), 48–50, 86–89; Jauffret, *Parlement, gouvernement, commandement,* 2: 1063–81, 1108–9; Maurice Reeves and Eric Deroo, *Les Linh Tâp: Histoire des militaires indochinois au service de la France (1859–1960)* (Paris: Charles Lavauzelle, 1999), 8–49; Mark McLeod, *The Vietnamese Response to French Intervention, 1862–1874* (New York: Praeger, 1991), 114–20; Henri Eckert, "Les militaires indochinois au service de la France (1859–1939)" (doctoral thesis, Université de Paris IV, 1998), 1: 13–14.

3. The term "Armée d'Afrique" had no official existence, but colloquially referred to troops stationed in North Africa. In 1873, the military designated the territory of Algeria as the nineteenth military district of France, and the troops there formed the 19th Army Corps. This military administrative integration corresponded with the political integration of the colony as three *départements* (Oran, Alger, Constantine), with parliamentary representation in Paris, while internal affairs in Algeria were technically the responsibility of the minister of the interior, not the minister of the colonies. By 1914, the military, if not political, integration of the area had extended to Tunisia and Morocco (they remained protectorates), and troops there were also part of the 19th Army Corps.

4. Anthony Clayton, *France, Soldiers, and Africa* (London: Brassey's Defence Publishers, 1988), 244–46.

5. Jauffret, *Parlement, gouvernement, commandement,* 2: 1041–46; Clayton, *France, Soldiers, and Africa,* 246; Augustin Bernard, *L'Afrique du Nord pendant la guerre* (Paris: Presses universitaires de France, 1926), 5.

6. Jauffret, *Parlement, gouvernement, commandement,* 2: 1066.

7. Philip D. Curtin, *Disease and Empire: The Health of European Troops in the Conquest of Africa* (Cambridge: Cambridge University Press, 1998), 74–112, 175–94; William B. Cohen, "Malaria and French Imperialism," *Journal of African History* 24 (1983): 23–36.

8. Balesi, *From Adversaries to Comrades-in-Arms,* 4; Myron Echenberg, *Colonial Conscripts: The* Tirailleurs Sénégalais *in French West Africa, 1857–1960* (Portsmouth, N.H.: Heinemann, 1991), 8–13.

9. On Galliéni's policies, see Marc Michel, *Galliéni* (Paris: Fayard, 1989); John Kim Munholland, "The Emergence of the Colonial Military in France, 1880–1905" (Ph.D. diss., Princeton University, 1964), 77–120; and Douglas Porch, "Bugeaud, Galliéni, Lyautey: The Development of French Colonial Warfare," in Peter Paret, ed., *Makers of Modern Strategy from Machiavelli to the Nuclear Age* (Princeton, N.J.: Princeton University Press, 1986), 376–407.

10. Jauffret, *Parlement, gouvernement, commandement,* 2: 1113–14; Munholland, "Emergence of the Colonial Military in France," 249–58; Chantal Valensky, *Le soldat occulté: Les Malgaches de l'armée française, 1884–1920* (Paris: L'Harmattan, 1995), 162–63.

11. Bernard, *Afrique du Nord pendant la guerre,* 6.

12. Jauffret, *Parlement, gouvernement, commandement,* 2: 1051.

13. This was the case in Cochin China and Tonkin, two of the most important provinces of the Indochinese Federation. Eckert, "Militaires indochinois au service de la France (1859–1939)," 1: 198–220; Jauffret, *Parlement, gouvernement, commandement,* 2: 1064–94.

14. For the political context of events during these years, see Eugen Weber, *The Nationalist Revival in France, 1905–1914* (Berkeley: University of California Press, 1968) and J. F. V. Keiger, *France and the Origins of the First World War* (New York: St. Martin's Press, 1983). Efforts to meet the demographic and military challenges posed by Germany culminated in the passage of a law in 1913 increasing the length of universal obligatory military service to three years. See Gerd Krumeich, *Armaments and Politics in France on the Eve of the First World War: The Introduction of Three-Year Conscription,* trans. Stephen Conn (Leamington Spa, England: Berg, 1984).

15. On Mangin and his ideas, see Balesi, *From Adversaries to Comrades-in-Arms,* esp. 57–78; Echenberg, *Colonial Conscripts,* 28–32; and Michel, *Appel,* 2–12.

16. Michel, *Appel,* 7. Charles Mangin, "Troupes noires," *Revue de Paris* 16 (1 and 15 July 1909): 61–80, 383–98.

17. Charles Mangin, *La force noire* (Paris: Hachette, 1910), 247–48, 252–54. See also Mangin's lecture, "Caractères physiques et moraux du soldat nègre," presented to the Société d'anthropologie and published, along with comments from the audience, as

"L'utilisation des troupes noires," *Bulletins et mémoires de la Société d'anthropologie de Paris* 2 (2 March 1911): 80–100. The same lecture appeared as "De l'emploi des troupes noires," *Revue anthropologique* 21 (April 1911): 9–28.

18. Mangin, *Force noire*, 283. He devotes the first 100 pages of the work to discussing the military implications of France's declining birthrate. On the declining birthrate and the anxieties it produced in French society, see Joseph J. Spengler, *France Faces Depopulation* (1938; rpt., New York: Greenwood Press, 1968); John C. Hunter, "The Problem of the French Birth Rate on the Eve of World War I," *French Historical Studies* 11 (1962): 490–503; Richard Tomlinson, "The Disappearance of France, 1896–1940: French Politics and the Birth Rate," *Historical Journal* 28 (1985): 405–15; Karen Offen, "Depopulation, Nationalism, and Feminism in Fin-de-Siècle France," *American Historical Review* 89, 3 (June 1984): 648–76; Joshua H. Cole, *The Power of Large Numbers: Population, Politics, and Gender in Nineteenth-Century France* (Ithaca, N.Y.: Cornell University Press, 2000), 180–211.

19. Balesi, *From Adversaries to Comrades-in-Arms*, 65–66; Echenberg, *Colonial Conscripts*, 29.

20. SHAT 7N81: Mangin to Ponty, mission summary, 2 November 1910. Cited also in Michel, *Appel*, 24, which provides the most thorough account of the 1910 "Mission Mangin" (pp. 21–29).

21. Michel, *Appel*, 33–34.

22. Gilbert Meynier, *L'Algérie révélée: La guerre de 1914–1918 et le premier quart du XXe siècle* (Geneva: Droz, 1981), 89.

23. Belkacem Recham, *Les musulmans algériens dans l'armée française (1919–1945)* (Paris: L'Harmattan, 1996), 17; Meynier, *Algérie révélée*, 90–95.

24. Meynier, *Algérie révélée*, 96–97.

25. Jauffret, *Parlement, gouvernement, commandement*, 2: 1033.

26. Recham, M*usulmans algériens dans l'armée française*, 21; Meynier, *Algérie révélée*, 100–102.

27. Bernard, *Afrique du Nord pendant la guerre*, 4.

28. Jauffret, *Parlement, gouvernement, commandement*, 2: 1067–71; Eckert, "Les militaires indochinois au service de la France (1859–1939)," 1: 199–201.

29. Meynier, *Algérie révélée*, 102–3.

30. There were 48,700 *troupes indigènes* in the Colonial Army, and 39,408 in the Armée d'Afrique, for a total of 88,108. Jean-Charles Jauffret, "Les armes de 'la plus grande France,'" in Guy Pedroncini, ed., *Histoire militaire de la France*, vol. 3: *De 1871 à 1940* (Paris: Presses universitaires de France, 1992), 61.

31. Precise accurate figures for losses in World War I are difficult to come by, and many sources vary widely in their calculations. A source used commonly by historians, Louis Marin, "Rapport sur le bilan des pertes en morts et en blessés des nations belligérentes," *Journal officiel*, Documents parlementaires, annexe no. 633, 1920, reflects only the best statistics available at that early date. See also *Données statistiques relatives à la Guerre, 1914–1918* (Paris: Imprimerie nationale, 1922). Alistair Horne, writing of the varying estimates of casualties at Verdun, rightly notes that "the accounting in human lives was never very meticulous in that war" (*The Price of Glory: Verdun 1916* [New

York: Penguin Books, 1962], 327). Nevertheless, 1.3 million combat deaths is the most common estimate, though others range as high as 1.5 million, and it is likely that about three times that number were wounded.

32. Exact figures are extremely difficult to determine, and these represent the best estimates drawn from numerous archival and published sources. Scholars have established fairly precise figures for West Africa (Michel, *Appel*), Indochina (Mireille Favre–Le Van Ho, "Un milieu porteur de modernisation: Travailleurs et tirailleurs vietnamiens en France pendant la Première Guerre mondiale" [doctoral thesis, École nationale des chartes, 1986]), and Algeria (Meynier, *Algérie révélée*), while the estimated numbers of Madagascans and Tunisians recruited during the war vary, sometimes considerably, from source to source. The number of men already under arms in August 1914, the number who remained in the colony, and the number who served in the army but not in the infantry (as nurses or specialized laborers, for example) further clouds the picture. Still, the table represents a reasonable rough estimate of the number of men recruited in each colony after the war began. For the French Army's own early estimates, see SHAT 7N440: "Note au sujet de la situation actuelle des effectifs en indigènes coloniaux" (11 September 1918).

33. Echenberg, *Colonial Conscripts*, 32–38. For French images of West African soldiers, see also Michel, *Appel*, 356–57, 393–96.

34. William B. Cohen, *The French Encounter with Africans: White Responses to Blacks, 1530–1880* (Bloomington: Indiana University Press, 1980); William H. Schneider, *An Empire for the Masses: The French Popular Image of Africa, 1870–1900* (Westport, Conn.: Greenwood Press, 1982); Brett A. Berliner, *Ambivalent Desire: The Exotic Black Other in Jazz-Age France* (Amherst: University of Massachusetts Press, 2002).

35. SHAT 16N198: GQG, *Notice sur les Sénégalais et leur emploi au combat* (19 October 1918).

36. Lunn, *Memoirs*, 145. Lunn examines French officers' ideas about ethnicity in West Africa in his "'Les Races Guerrières': Racial Preconceptions in the French Military About West African Soldiers During the First World War," *Journal of Contemporary History* 34, 4 (1999): 517–36.

37. Michel, *Appel*, 50.

38. SHAT 7N2121: Mangin to Minister of War Alexandre Millerand, "Note sur la création d'une armée coloniale indigène pour le printemps 1916" (2 August 1915).

39. SHAT 16N195: Gen. Pierre Famin, DTC, "Note au sujet de la création d'une nouvelle armée coloniale indigène pour le printemps 1916 proposée par le général Mangin" (18 August 1915).

40. AN C7537: dossier 1461, "Proposition de loi no. 1246 sur le recrutement de l'armée indigène, par Pierre Masse, Pierre Ajam, Maurice Bernard" (16 September 1915).

41. Ibid. Emphasis in original.

42. Michel, *Appel*, 79–80.

43. There were 7,000 volunteers out of 52,000 or 53,000 recruits. Clozel quoted in Michel, *Appel*, 84.

44. Lunn, *Memoirs*, 42.

45. Ibid., 38, 51n15.

46. Ibid., 40–41.

47. Allen Douglas, *War, Memory, and the Politics of Humor: The* Canard Enchainé *and World War I* (Berkeley: University of California Press, 2002), 169–70.

48. Quoted in Michel, *Appel*, 82.

49. Lunn, *Memoirs*, 38.

50. SHAT 7N2121: Bérenger, "Rapport . . . (cited n. 34 above).

51. Michel, *Appel*, 50–57, 85–88; Lunn, *Memoirs*, 44, 51n15; Balesi, *From Adversaries to Comrades-in-Arms*, 90. On the more serious revolts, see Michel, *Appel*, 100–116; Alice Conklin, *A Mission to Civilize: The Republican Idea of Empire in France and West Africa, 1895–1930* (Stanford, Calif.: Stanford University Press, 1997), 148–49; Luc Garcia, "Les mouvements de résistance au Dahomey, 1914–1917," *Cahiers d'études africaines* 10, 1 (1971): 144–78; Hélène d'Almeida-Topor, "Les populations dahoméens et le recrutement militaire pendant la Première Guerre mondiale," *Revue française d'histoire d'Outre-mer* 60, 2 (1973): 196–241.

52. Conklin, *Mission*, 150.

53. Michel, *Appel*, 132–33; Balesi, *From Adversaries to Comrades-in-Arms*, 88–92.

54. Patricia Lorcin, *Imperial Identities: Stereotyping, Prejudice and Race in Colonial Algeria* (London: I. B. Taurus, 1995). See also her "Imperialism, Colonial Identity, and Race in Algeria, 1830–1870: The Role of the French Medical Corps," *Isis* 90, 4 (December 1999): 653–79.

55. Lorcin, *Imperial Identities*, 17–34.

56. Ibid., 155. In fact, these inhabitants of the Aurès were Chaouia, but many French observers in the nineteenth century used the term Kabyle to denote all Algerian mountain Berbers.

57. Clayton, *France, Soldiers, and Africa*, 262.

58. For a detailed description of these differing perceptions of the warlike qualities of North Africans, see Chapter 2.

59. Jauffret, *Parlement, gouvernement, commandement*, 2: 993–95; id., "Les armes de 'la plus grande France,'" 43.

60. Meynier, *Algérie révélée*, 393–95; SHAT 16N195: Gen. Moinier (commander of French forces in North Africa), to MG, "Situation des dépôts de tirailleurs" (23 June 1915); 17N491: SA, "Bulletin de renseignements sur les questions musulmanes" (26 April 1916).

61. SHAT 7N2081: SA, "Bulletin politique, mois d'août 1914."

62. SHAT 16N194: Minister of War Alexandre Millerand to Joffre, "Corps des spahis auxiliaires algériens" (17 March 1915); SHAT 7N2103, passim; Meynier, *Algérie révélée*, 260. On Captain Khaled, see Ahmed Koulakssis and Gilbert Meynier, *L'Emir Khaled, premier za'îm? Identité algérienne et colonialisme français* (Paris: L'Harmattan, 1987).

63. Meynier, *Algérie révélée*, 267ff.

64. Ibid., 394–95.

65. SHAT 7N2081: SA, "Bulletin politique, mois de décembre 1914."

66. Ibid., "Bulletin politique, mois d'octobre 1914."

67. SHAT 7N443: Lutaud to PC, MG, and MI, telegrams of 5, 6, and 9 October 1914.

68. SHAT 7N2081: SA, "Bulletin politique, mois d'octobre 1914."

69. Meynier, *Algérie révélée*, 269.

70. AMAE G1670: CIAM, session 4 (12 January 1915).

71. Ibid.: SA, "Note au sujet du développement des contingents indigènes" (23 December 1915).

72. SHAT 17N491: SA, "Bulletin de renseignements sur les questions musulmanes" (26 April 1916).

73. SHAT 7N446: Gen. Langle de Cary, "Inspection des troupes et armées de l'Afrique du Nord," 15 June 1916. See also his preliminary reports of 17 and 30 May in the "Dossier Afrique du Nord, prélèvements (Mission de Cary), 1916."

74. Meynier, *Algérie révélée*, 399.

75. SHAT 7N2081: SA, "Bulletin de renseignements sur les questions musulmanes" (12 November 1916).

76. SHAT 7N2081 and 17N491: "Bulletins de renseignements sur les questions musulmanes" (November 1916–February 1917); Meynier, *Algérie révélée*, 591–98.

77. SHAT 7N1001: "Rapport sur les opérations de la commissions militaires de contrôle postal de Tunis, pendant le mois de décembre 1916."

78. SHAT 7N2107: Commission militaire de contrôle postal, Tunis, "Rapport sur les opérations de la commission pendant le mois de mars 1917."

79. CAOM DSM6: EMA, Bureau de l'organisation et de la mobilisation de l'armée, "Note sur la classe 1917" (9 December 1916).

80. Meynier, *Algérie révélée*, 405, 570–71.

81. SHAT 16N199: "Ressources fournis par le recrutement de l'Afrique du Nord" (April 1919).

82. SHAT 7N443: "Dépôts d'indigènes à Arles et à Aix" (n.d.); 16N194: Gen. Drude, cdr., 45th Algerian Division, to cdr., 33rd CA [Pétain], 14 November 1914.

83. SHAT 16N194: Drude to Pétain, 14 November 1914; SA to Joffre, "Entretien des effectifs des battalions de tirailleurs indigènes" (6 December 1914); SHAT 16N194: "Dossier relatif à la répression d'un acte d'indiscipline devant l'ennemi au 8e tirailleurs"; Gilbert Meynier, "Pour l'exemple: Un sur dix! Les décimations en 1914," *Politique aujourd'hui* 1–2 (January–February 1976): 55–70.

84. CAOM DSM6: Resident-général Gabriel Alapetite, "Note déstinée à accompagner la remise au ministre des colonies des documents relatifs au recrutement militaire indigène tunisien" (22 April 1917); SHAT 16N199: "Ressources fournis par le recrutement de l'Afrique du Nord" (April 1919).

85. SHAT 7N446: Gen. Langle de Cary, "Inspection des troupes et armées de l'Afrique du Nord" (15 June 1916). See also his preliminary reports of 17 and 30 May in the "Dossier Afrique du Nord, prélèvements (Mission de Cary), 1916."

86. SHAT 16N194: Resident-général Alapetite to Minister of War Millerand, 29 December 1914.

87. Ibid.: Millerand to Alapetite, 9 January 1914; MG to cdr., 15th Region, Marseille, "Repatriation des militaires indigènes pour l'encadrement des dépôts d'Afrique" (2 February 1915); MAE to Alapetite, telegram, 6 February 1915; Alapetite to MAE, 9 February 1915; SA to cdr., 15th Region, Marseille, "Envoi en Tunisie des militaires indigènes tunisiens destinés à l'encadrement des dépôts d'Afrique" (14 March 1915).

88. Ibid.: MAE to Alapetite, telegram. 6 February 1915. On leave policy, see also Meynier, *Algérie révélée*, 420ff.

89. CAOM DSM6: RGT, "Note déstinée à accompagner la remise au ministre des colonies des documents relatifs au recrutement militaire indigène tunisien" (22 April 1917).

90. SHAT 7N1001: "Rapport sur les opérations de la commission militaires de contrôle postal de Tunis pendant le mois de mars 1917."

91. Ibid.: "Rapport sur les opérations de la commission militaires de contrôle postal de Tunis pendant le mois d'avril 1917."

92. SHAT 17N491: SA, "Bulletin de renseignements sur les questions musulmanes" (11 July 1917); CAOM DSM6: MAE to MG, 4 July 1917.

93. CAOM DSM6: MC to Alapetite, "Recrutement militaire" (14 April 1917).

94. William Thomas Dean III, "The Colonial Armies of the French Third Republic: Overseas Formation and Continental Deployment, 1871–1920" (Ph.D. diss., University of Chicago, 1999; 3 vols.), 3: 441.

95. Clayton, *France, Soldiers, and Africa*, 263; Mohamed Bekraoui, "Les soldats marocains dans la bataille de Verdun," *Guerres mondiales et conflits contemporaines* 182 (April 1986): 40–41.

96. SHAT 16N195: Lyautey to MG, "Emploi des tirailleurs marocains en France" (11 June 1915).

97. SHAT 7N445: SA to Lyautey, "Au sujet des tirailleurs marocains" (27 September 1915); 16N195: MG to Joffre, 19 September 1915.

98. SHAT 7N2103: "Rapport de l'officier interprète Reymond sur l'état d'esprit des militaires indigènes de l'Afrique du Nord" (14 July 1915).

99. SHAT 16N195: Lyautey to MG, "Au sujet des tirailleurs marocains" (4 September 1915).

100. CAOM DSM6: MC to Lyautey, "Recrutement militaire" (14 April 1917).

101. SHAT 17N491: SA, bulletins, "Renseignements sur les questions musulmanes" (February 1917–January 1918).

102. CAOM DSM6: Lyautey to MAE, 26 March 1917; "Note sur le Maroc" (15 June 1917).

103. Clayton, *France, Soldiers, and Africa*, 364–65.

104. SHAT 8H106: *Manuel à l'usage des gradés européens servant dans les régiments de tirailleurs malgaches* (Tananarive: État-major, 1904), 22.

105. Valensky, *Soldat occulté*, esp. 32–35, 116–37.

106. See Michel Foucault, *Discipline and Punish: The Birth of the Prison* (New York: Vintage Books, 1979), and *The History of Sexuality, Volume I: An Introduction* (New York: Vintage Books, 1990).

107. See Laura Ann Stoler, *Carnal Knowledge and Imperial Power: Race and the Intimate in Colonial Rule* (Berkeley: University of California Press, 2002), and *Race and the Education of Desire: Foucault's History of Sexuality and the Colonial Order of Things* (Durham, N.C.: Duke University Press, 1995).

108. SHAT 8H106: *Manuel à l'usage des gradés européens*, 21.

109. Razafindranaly, *Soldats de la grande île*, 87, 89.

110. SHAT 8H106: *Manuel à l'usage des gradés européens*, 2.

111. Razafindranaly, *Soldats de la grande île*, 205–6; Valensky, *Soldat occulté*, 130, 244.

112. Valensky, *Soldat occulté*, 244.

113. Quotation from Razafindranaly, *Soldats de la grande île*, 267; Valensky, *Soldat occulté*, 163.

114. Maurice Gontard, *Madagascar pendant la Première Guerre mondiale* (Tananarive: Éditions universitaires, 1969), 11–18

115. Razafindranaly, *Soldats de la grande île*, 283.

116. Ibid., 282–88.

117. SHAT 7N2121: Mangin to Minister of War Alexandre Millerand, "Note sur la création . . . " (2 August 1915).

118. SHAT 16N195: Famin, DTC, "Note . . . " (cited n. 39 above).

119. AMAE G1666: SA, "Note au sujet du développement des contingents indigènes" (23 December 1915).

120. SHAT 7N2121: Bérenger, "Rapport . . . (cited n. 34 above).

121. Gontard, *Madagascar pendant la Première Guerre mondiale*, 39.

122. *Journal officiel*, 18 December 1915, 9291.

123. Razafindranaly, *Soldats de la grande île*, 291.

124. Ibid., 291; Valensky, *Soldat occulté*, 292–302.

125. The initials stood for the Malagasy words *vy* (iron), *vato* (stone), and *sakelika* (ramification), implying that the movement was strong, hard, and durable like iron and stone, and would spread out into Madagascan society as it grew more powerful. Dedicated to expulsion of the French, and to indigenous control of the island, the members of this group had become increasingly restive over the course of 1915. See Gontard, *Madagascar pendant la Première Guerre mondiale*, 45–64.

126. Hubert Garbit, *L'effort de Madagascar pendant la guerre* (Paris: A. Challamel, 1919), 37–38.

127. Gontard, *Madagascar pendant la Première Guerre mondiale*, 66–68; Valensky, *Soldat occulté*, 299.

128. Garbit, *L'effort de Madagascar*, 38; SHAT 16N198: Col. Garbit, "Rapport au sujet des possibilities de recrutement à Madagascar, pour le service en Europe, dans la période de transition qui suivra la guerre," 19 February 1919.

129. SHAT 7N997: Contrôle postal malgache, "Rapport du mois de Septembre 1917."

130. Valensky, *Soldat occulté*, 300.

131. Ibid., 306–9; Gontard, *Madagascar pendant la Première Guerre mondiale*, 68.

132. SHAT 7N2121: SA, "Renseignements concernant le recrutement indigène à Madagascar en 1917 (tirailleurs, COA, infirmiers, travailleurs)" (n.d.). On the economic crisis and political changes in the colony in 1917, see Gontard, *Madagascar pendant la Première Guerre mondiale*, 79–103.

133. Gontard, *Madagascar pendant la Première Guerre mondiale*, 89.

134. SHAT 7N2121: SA, "Renseignements concernant le recrutement indigène à Madagascar en 1917" (n.d.); Valensky, *Soldat occulté*, 301.

135. Jauffret, *Parlement, gouvernement, commandement*, 2: 1094–96.

136. Ibid., 1096.

137. Eckert, "Militaires indochinois au service de la France (1859–1939)," 1: 217–19.

138. Quoted in Jauffret, *Parlement, gouvernement, commandement*, 2: 1101.

139. Favre–Le Van Ho, "Milieu porteur de modernisation," 1: 8–35.

140. Ibid., 1: 46–51.

141. SHAT 7N2121: Mangin to Millerand, "Note . . . " (cited n. 117 above).

142. Ibid.: Gen. Théophile Pennequin to Minister of War Millerand, 5 October 1915.

143. AN C7537: dossier 1461, "Proposition de loi no. 1246 . . . " (16 September 1916); SHAT 7N2121: Bérenger, "Rapport . . . (cited n. 34 above).

144. SHAT 16N195: Famin, DTC, "Note . . . " (cited n. 39 above).

145. AN C7494: Commission de l'armée, procès-verbaux, 1915, 21 September 1915.

146. SHAT 16N195: Joffre to MG, 20 October 1915.

147. *Journal officiel*, 18 December 1915, 9291.

148. AMAE G1666: SA, "Note au sujet du développement des contingents indigènes" (23 December 1915); CAOM SLOTFOM I, 4: "Les Indochinois en France" (undated report, probably written sometime in 1921); Favre–Le Van Ho, "Milieu porteur de modernisation," 1: 114–22, 182–83.

149. Favre–Le Van Ho, "Milieu porteur de modernisation," 1: 131.

150. Ibid., 150.

151. Ibid., 241–51.

152. Quotation from *Histoire militaire de l'Indochine française*, vol. 1 (Hanoi-Haiphong: Imprimerie d'Extrême-Orient, 1931), 245. Published by military officials in the colonial administration on the occasion of the International Colonial Exposition in Paris that year, the work displays the optimism and triumphalism that marked the event as a whole.

153. Quoted in Favre–Le Van Ho, "Milieu porteur de modernisation," 1: 208.

154. Ibid., 184–87; on resistance in Cambodia and Cochin China, see 201–30.

155. SHAT 7N2121: "Renseignements concernant le recrutement dans l'Indo-chine en 1917" (n.d.).

156. Shelby Cullom Davis, *Reservoirs of Men: A History of the Black Troops of French West Africa* (Geneva: Chambéry, 1934), 150.

157. Clemenceau told the Chamber of Deputies on 20 November 1917, "Nous nous présentons devant vous dans l'insigne pensée d'une guerre intégrale." Gregor Dallas, *At the Heart of a Tiger: Clemenceau and His World, 1841–1929* (New York: Carroll & Graf, 1993), 501.

158. AN C7499: Commission de l'armée, procès-verbaux, October 1917–February 1918, 12 December 1917. Also quoted in Michel, *Appel*, 226.

159. SHAT 6N97: Mangin, "Mesures à prendre immédiatement au sujet du recrutement indigène coloniale" (8 December 1917).

160. Ibid.: Clemenceau to MC, "Recrutement indigène" (17 December 1917).

161. Bernard, *Afrique du Nord pendant la guerre*, 6; SHAT 16N199: "Ressources fournis par le recrutement de l'Afrique du Nord" (April 1919).

162. SHAT 7N1001: Commission de contrôle postal, Tunis, "Rapport Mensuel, Mois d'avril 1918."

163. Meynier, *Algérie révélée*, 401–2.

164. CAOM DSM6: "Observations de M. Reymond officier interprète principal sur le rapport de M. Flandin, sénateur, relatif à la conscription des indigènes de l'Algérie" (28 November 1917).

165. SHAT 7N2081: SA, "Observations sur le rapport de M. E. Flandin, sénateur, en date du 26 novembre 1917, sur la circonscription [*sic*] indigène en Algérie" (27 November 1917); SA, "Résultats des conférences des 4 &5 décembre 1917, entre M. Flandin, sénateur, rapporteur de la commission de l'armée, et la SA de l'état-major de l'armée" (6 December 1917); CAOM DSM6: "Note du gouverneur général de l'Algérie" (26 November 1917); Meynier, *Algérie révélée*, 402–3.

166. Meynier, *Algérie révélée*, 403–4.

167. SHAT 7N447: Jonnart to Clemenceau, "Incorporation de la classe indigène 1918" (19 June 1918).

168. Ibid.: Gen. Rabier, inspecteur général de l'instruction de l'infanterie à l'intérieur, "Note pour l'EMA" (13 June 1918); 7N1992: Rabier to SA, 27 June 1918; and SA to Gen. Nivelle, "Class indigène 1918" (12 July 1918).

169. SHAT 7N1992: Gen. Nivelle to SA, 22 July 1918.

170. On Diagne's campaign to subject residents of the Four Communes to obligatory military service and thereby confirm their claim to French citizenship, see Chapter 7.

171. As Charles Balesi points out (*From Adversaries to Comrades-in-Arms*, 93), a principled defense of his prerogatives as governor-general and oposition to recruitment in the colony precipitated Vollenhoven's resignation, not racial prejudice and a refusal to share power with a black African, as some writers have charged.

172. *Journal officiel*, 17 January 1918, 677–81. The decree reinstituted conscription, but offered the same bonuses, pay, and family allowances accorded to volunteers; exempted soldiers and their families from the *indigénat*, head tax, and corvée; established a medical and agricultural school at Dakar, as well as a number of sanitoria to care for returning wounded; reserved positions in the colonial administration for veterans; and allowed soldiers who had won both the *croix de guerre* and the *médaille militaire* to obtain French citizenship (though Muslims had to renounce their special legal status, the *statut personnel*).

173. SHAT 7N2120: SA, "Note sur le recrutement des Sénégalais en Afrique occidentale française" (21 February 1918).

174. CAOM AP661: dossier O2, "Troupes indigènes, tirailleurs, recrutement en AOF 1918," press clipping from Jean Peyraud, "M. Diagne reçoit une mission délicate," an article supressed by the censors.

175. SHAT 6N97: Angoulvant to MC, telegram, 28 June 1918.

176. Shelby Cullom Davis attributes the large number of recruits both to the attraction of the incentives outlined in the decrees of 17 January and to "the popularity of Diagne, who touched the black's psychology" (Davis, *Reservoirs of Men*, 155). Marc Michel concurs, though he gives equal weight to the legislative incentives, efficient administration in the colony, cooperation among indigenous elites, and skillful and systematic preparation (Michel, *Appel*, 239–60; see also his "La génêse du recrutement de 1918 en Afrique noire francaise," *Revue française d'histoire d'Outre-mer* 58, 213 [1971]:

433–50). G. Wesley Johnson is less sure of Diagne's ability to rally genuine support, though he does not offer an alternative reason for Diagne's success (G. Wesley Johnson, *The Emergence of Black Politics in Senegal: The Struggle for Power in the Four Communes, 1900–1920* [Stanford, Calif.: Stanford University Press, 1971], 194–95). Charles Balesi argues that rather than material incentives, "it was Diagne's presence which had won the impossible wager" (Balesi, *From Adversaries to Comrades-in-Arms*, 95), and Joe Lunn's interviews with Senegalese veterans support this conclusion (Lunn, *Memoirs*, 78–81).

    177. SHAT 6N97: Diagne to MC, telegram, 15 February 1918.

    178. Ibid.: Diagne to MC, telegram, 17 March 1918.

    179. Lunn, *Memoirs*, 78.

    180. SHAT 6N97: Angoulvant to MC, telegram, 7 August 1918. This figure embraced recruits from the AOF as well as Afrique équatoriale française (AEF).

    181. Michel, *Appel*, 243.

    182. SHAT 7N447: Angoulvant to MC, telegram of 22 June 1918.

    183. SHAT 7N2121: Bérenger, "Rapport . . . (cited n. 34 above); AN C7537: dossier 1468, "Blaise Diagne et Gratien Candace, proposition de loi no. 1795 . . . " (15 February 1916).

## Two • *Race and the Deployment of Troupes indigènes*

*Epigraphs:* Reymond, CAOM DSM6: "Observations de M. Reymond officier interprète principal sur le rapport de M. Flandin sénateur relatif à la conscription des indigènes de l'Algérie" (28 November 1917). Vrenière, SHAT 16N195: "Rapport du Colonel Vrenière au sujet de rgt marocain" (15 September 1915).

    1. CAOM DSM5: "Note de M. l'officier interprète de 1ère classe Reymond" (17 July 1917).

    2. See Chapter 3 for a detailed discussion of the role of officers in indigenous units.

    3. James F. McMillan, *Housewife or Harlot: The Place of Women in French Society, 1870–1940* (New York: St. Martin's Press, 1981); Joan Wallach Scott, *Only Paradoxes to Offer: French Feminists and the Rights of Man* (Cambridge, Mass.: Harvard University Press, 1996); Mary Louise Roberts, *Disruptive Acts: The New Woman in Fin-de-siècle France* (Chicago: University of Chicago Press, 2002).

    4. Robert Nye, *Masculinity and Male Codes of Honor in France* (New York: Oxford University Press, 1993); Edward Berenson, *The Trial of Madame Caillaux* (Berkeley: University of California Press, 1992); William M. Reddy, *The Invisible Code: Honor and Sentiment in Postrevolutionary France 1814–1848* (Berkeley: University of California Press, 1997).

    5. SHAT 7N2107: MG, note to Gen. Moinier, 10 May 1915.

    6. Jean-Charles Jauffret, *Parlement, gouvernement, commandement: L'armée de métier sous la Troisième République, 1871–1914* (Vincennes: Service historique de l'armée de terre, 1987), 2: 1083.

    7. On language policy, see Chapter 4.

    8. SHAT 7N444: Ménestrel, "Inspection des troupes d'Afrique" (20 June 1915); EMA, Bureau de l'organisation et de la mobilisation de l'armée, "Note au sujet des question

soulevées dans le rapport établi par le général Ménestrel, à la suite de son inspection de l'Afrique du Nord" (n.d.).

9. Ibid.: GQG to EMA, 1st Bureau, 22 August 1914.

10. Unlike the better-prepared Germans, the French Army "had only six of the despised St. Étienne machine guns per regiment" and these were poorly integrated into tactical battle plans, according to Alistair Horne, *The Price of Glory: Verdun 1916* (New York: Penguin Books, 1962), 15.

11. SHAT 16N196: "Rapport du lt-col Maurice, cdt le Rgt marocain, sur la situation de l'encadrement français (troupe) du rgt" (1 June 1916).

12. SHAT 16N195: DTC to GCC-GQG, "Bataillons sénégalais" (18 April 1918).

13. SHAT 16N196: GQG, État-major, 3rd Bureau, "Note pour le 1er Bureau" (18 December 1916).

14. SHAT 16N197: GCC to armies, 6 July 1917.

15. SHAT 16N195: "Rapport du général Niessel, cdt. le 37e DI (II Armée, 30e Corps) sur le recrutement des cadres des régiments indigènes" (4 March 1916).

16. SHAT 16N197: "Rapport du lt-col de Saint Maurice cdt le 2e Régiment de marche de tirailleurs sur l'encadrement en tirailleurs français des régiments de tirailleurs algériens" (2 June 1917).

17. AMAE G1671*bis*: CIAM, session 47 (18 October 1917).

18. SHAT 16N197: GCC to armies, 6 July 1917.

19. An officer seeking to persuade his superiors to increase the number of Europeans in West African units gave the proportion in January 1918 as about 15 percent (SHAT 16N197: "Note sur l'utilisation des Sénégalais"), but Joe Lunn, *Memoirs of the Maelstrom: A Senegalese Oral History of the First World War* (Portsmouth, N.H.: Heinemann, 1999), 145n18, cites 22 to 24 percent by 1918.

20. SHAT 7N2121: DTC, "État numérique faisant ressortir la situation des militaires indigènes au dépôt commun des formations indigènes d'infanterie et d'artillerie coloniale, à la date du 1er Janvier 1919."

21. SHAT 16N198: Garbit, "Rapport au sujet des possibilités de recrutement à Madagascar" (19 February 1919). The existence of institutions like the École de médecine in the Madagascan capital of Tananarive certainly accounted for the presence of doctors. In Indochina, a 1907 decree established a Corps des médecins auxiliaires indigènes, who would be trained at the École de médecine in Hanoi, but the corps was suppressed in 1909. Consequently, upon the outbreak of war in 1914, there was only one indigenous doctor in the French Army in Indochina. See Maurice Reeves and Eric Deroo, *Les Linh Tâp: Histoire des militaires indochinois au service de la France (1859–1960)* (Paris: Charles Lavauzelle, 1999), 45.

22. SHAT 16N198: Lt. Col. Le Duc, "Historique du 1er régiment de chasseurs malgaches," 9 March 1919.

23. See SHAT 7N997: Commission militaire de contrôle postal de Marseille, "Les soldats malgaches en France: Rapport mensuel, juillet–août 1917" summarizes the prevailing stereotypes of Madagascans.

24. See Eckert, "Les militaires indochinois au service de la France (1859–1939)," 2: 539–52; Mireille Favre–Le Van Ho, "Un milieu porteur de modernisation: Travailleurs

et tirailleurs vietnamiens en France pendant la Première Guerre mondiale" (doctoral thesis, École nationale des chartes, 1986), 2: 330–32; CAOM SLOTFOM III, 139–40: "Rapports de M. Przyluski"; CAOM SLOTFOM I, 4: "Les Indochinois en France" (n.d.).

25. CAOM SLOTFOM III, 139–49: "Rapport trimestrielle de M. Przyluski" (n.d.).

26. Ibid., "Rapport de M. Przyluski, controleur des contingents indochinois, sur les conducteurs annamites à la réserve Stenbock," 18 March 1918. The commandant of the training center at Stenbock made a similar observation, noting that Indochinese drivers took better care of their trucks than did their French counterparts. See Favre–Le Van Ho, "Milieu porteur de modernisation," 2: 331.

27. CAOM SLOTFOM I, 4: "Les Indochinois en France" (n.d.).

28. SHAT 7N81: Mangin, "Note relative à l'emploi des races indigènes dans les divers armes et sur les différents théâtres d'opération" (12 March 1920).

29. SHAT 16N199: Mangin to Pétain, MCC des armées du nord et du nord-est, "Objet: Demande de spécialistes indigènes" (17 June 1919).

30. Officers used the adjective "white" to distinguish units composed of native Frenchmen from indigenous units.

31. In the French Army, four sections (corresponding to a platoon in the American military) formed a company; four companies, a battalion; three battalions, a regiment; two regiments, a brigade; two brigades, a division. (The army did not always formally designate brigades, forming divisions directly out of autonomous regiments.) These were general rules, and battalions sometimes had more than four companies, regiments more than three battalions. The exigencies of wartime often produced such irregular formations, and they were fairly common among *troupes indigènes*.

32. Emmanuel Bouhier, "Les troupes coloniales d'Indochine en 1914–1918," in Claude Carlier and Guy Pedroncini, eds., *Les troupes coloniales dans la Grande Guerre* (Paris: Economica, 1997), 79–80.

33. See Jacques Razafindranaly, *Les soldats de la grande île: D'une guerre à l'autre, 1895–1918* (Paris: L'Harmattan, 2000), 303–42.

34. Clayton, *France, Soldiers, and Africa*, 263.

35. Ibid., 248.

36. Meynier, *Algérie révélée*, 419.

37. Marc Michel, *L'appel à l'Afrique: Contributions et réactions à l'effort de guerre en AOF, 1914–1919* (Paris: Publications de la Sorbonne, 1982), 294–95.

38. SHAT 16N195: "Note au sujet de l'emploi des bataillons sénégalais" (January 1916).

39. Ibid., from a marginal note signed by Joffre.

40. Ibid.: GQG, "Projet d'utilisation des troupes sénégalaises" (14 January 1916).

41. Michel, *Appel*, 301–2; Lunn, *Memoirs*, 122, 149n13.

42. See SHAT 6N96: DTC, "Programme d'utilisation des troupes indigènes au printemps" (8 February 1917).

43. *Panachage* is best rendered in English as "variegation," which conveys the sense of placing different units together in a sort of mosaic. In fact, both the English and French terms most often refer to combining colors in such a manner, and this is exactly

what officers like Major Arnaud had in mind, with varying combinations of "black" and "white" units. "Mixed" formations were generally larger units that contained both French and African units on a more or less permanent basis, which commanders might then variegate before attacks. The army also sometimes referred to such a process of combination as "amalgamation," though Arnaud preferred *panachage*. See Lunn, *Memoirs*, 121–27.

44. SHAT 6N96: Maj. Arnaud, "Note au sujet de l'organisation d'unités offensives mixtes sénégalaises" (12 February 1917).

45. SHAT 16N198: GQG, *Notice sur les Sénégalais et leur emploi au combat* (19 October 1918), 27.

46. SHAT 16N197: GQG, "Note sur l'emploi des bataillons sénégalais dans les divisions métropolitaines" (3 May 1917).

47. Michel, *Appel*, 315.

48. SHAT 16N197: Blondlat to 8th Army commander, "Au sujet des btns sénégalais" (24 June 1917).

49. Ibid.: GQG, "Note sur les emplois des battalions sénégalais" (26 August 1917).

50. Ibid.: "Note sur l'utilisation des Sénégalais" (January 1918). See also Michel, *Appel*, 323.

51. Michel, *Appel*, 323.

52. SHAT 7N441: "Projet d'organisation d'une armée coloniale dans la 15ème région pendant l'hiver 1918–1919" (n.d., but related documents approving and elaborating upon the plan date from July through October 1918). See also 7N1991: dossier 1: "Organisation des divisions mixtes."

53. SHAT 7N443: DTC to MC, "AS des 2 bataillons malgaches destinés à aller au Cameroun" (10 November 1914).

54. SHAT 7N2120: SA, "Note à la DTC, Tirailleurs malgaches" (14 October 1915). The *non approuvé* scrawled across the top of this document and the eventual use of Madagascan troops in Tunisia for a brief time indicate that higher authorities eventually overruled these objections.

55. See, e.g., SHAT 7N2121: Gen. Losserre to Gen. Archinard, 8 November 1915.

56. Gen. Noguès, "Notice sur les tirailleurs indochinois," *Revue des troupes coloniales* 157 (1922), quoted in Henri Eckert, "Les militaires indochinois au service de la France (1859–1939)" (doctoral thesis, Université de Paris IV, 1998), 90.

57. Albert de Pouvourville, "Des jaunes? Un peu, beaucoup, pas du tout," *La dépêche colonial et maritime*, 28 December 1915.

58. SHAT 16N195: Joffre to MG, "Troupes indigènes" (24 January 1916).

59. SHAT 7N2121: Henry Bérenger, "Rapport sur le recrutement d'une armée indigène" (26 November 1915).

60. Razafindranaly, *Soldats de la grande île*, 302–3; Rives and Deroo, *Lính Tâp*, 58.

61. SHAT 7N144: DTC, "Instruction relative à l'emploi de la main-d'œuvre annamite" (20 February 1916).

62. CAOM SLOTFOM III, 139–40: "Rapport de M. Przyluski, controlleur des contingents indochinois sur les tirailleurs indochinois en service à Châlons-sur-Marne" (9 May 1918); Rives and Deroo, *Lính Tâp*, 58.

63. SHAT 16N198: Le Duc, "Historique . . . " (cited n. 22 above)..

64. SHAT 7N2121: Losserre to Archinard, 8 November 1915.

65. Rives and Deroo, *Lính Tâp*, 56.

66. CAOM SLOTFOM I, 8: Contrôle postal indochinois, "Rapport du mois d'octobre 1917."

67. CAOM SLOTFOM III, 139–40: "Rapport de M. Przyluski controleur des contingents indochinois sur les tirailleurs des 7ème et 21ème bataillon en Alsace" (16 January 1919).

68. J. Merimée, *De l'accession des Indochinois à la qualité de citoyen français* (Toulouse: Andrau & La Porte, 1931), 52. Also quoted in Denise Bouche, *Histoire de la colonisation française*, vol. 2: *Flux et reflux (1815–1962)* (Paris: Fayard, 1991), 289.

69. SHAT 16N198: Le Duc, "Historique . . . " (cited n. 22 above).

70. Ibid. See also Razafindranaly, *Soldats de la grande île*, 303–42, for a complete account of the actions of the 12th BTM.

71. SHAT 16N198: Le Duc, "Historique . . . " (cited n. 22 above)).

72. Ibid.: Daugan to MCC, 11 March 1919.

73. Ibid.: Garbit, "Rapport des possibilités de recrutement à Madagascar" (19 February 1919).

74. Valensky, *Soldat occulté*, 367–69.

75. AMAE G1664: Consul general [and *secrétaire interprète*] Piat to Foreign Minister Théophile Delcassé, 29 October 1914.

76. SHAT 16N196: GQG, État-major, 3rd Bureau, "Note . . . " (cited n. 13 above).

77. SHAT 16N194: MG to GCC, "Emplois aux armées des formations marocaines" (20 August 1914); Lyautey, telegram to MG, 17 August 1917. Lyautey and the minister of war were concerned about a cavalry regiment that had yet to embark.

78. Ibid.: Maunoury to GCC (n.d., but probably October 1914); see also SHAT 16N198: "Historique très succinct des opérations de la brigade de chasseurs indigènes (troupes marocains), du 15 août au 20 octobre 1914," the detailed (and not very succinct) account of these actions that prompted Maunoury's report.

79. SHAT 16N194: SA , "Note au sujet de l'emploi des chasseurs indigènes provenant du Maroc" (12 August 1914).

80. Clayton, *France, Soldiers, and Africa*, 263.

81. SHAT 16N195: Lyautey to MG, "Au sujet des tirailleurs marocains" (4 September 1915).

82. SHAT 16N196: Lt. Col. Dupertuis, "Au sujet du repatriement de spahis marocains" (29 August 1916).

83. SHAT 16N194: SA, "Note au sujet de l'emploi des chasseurs indigènes provenant du Maroc" (12 August 1914).

84. SHAT 7N2103: "Rapport de l'officier interprète Reymond sur l'état d'esprit des militaires indigènes de l'Afrique du Nord dans les dépôts de passage d'Aix, Tarascon & Beaucaire et sur les mesures les plus susceptibles de l'améliorer" (14 July 1915).

85. SHAT 16N195: "Rapport du colonel Vrenière au sujet de rgt marocain" (15 September 1915).

86. Ibid.: Lt. Col. Auroux to Vrenière, "Au sujet d'une proposition de relève des bataillons" (14 September 1915).

87. CAOM DSM6: "Rapport de M. Delphin: Recrutement des indigènes en Algérie" (17 December 1915).

88. Ibid.: "Études algériens, l'administration des indigènes: La conscription" (n.d.).

89. See Lorcin, *Imperial Identities*, 17–34.

90. SHAT 7N2081: SA, "Bulletin politique" (October 1914).

91. CAOM DSM6: "Observations de M. Reymond sur le rapport de M. Flandin relatif à la conscription des indigènes de l'Algérie" (28 November 1917).

92. SHAT 16N196: GQG, État-major, 3rd Bureau, "Note . . . " (cited n. 13 above).

93. See Gilbert Meynier, *L'Algérie révélée: La guerre de 1914–1918 et le premier quart du XXe siècle* (Geneva: Droz, 1981), 404–5; Charles-Robert Ageron, *Les Algériens musulmans et la France, 1871–1919* (Paris: Presses universitaires de France, 1968), 2: 1165–66; Augustin Bernard, *L'Afrique du Nord pendant la guerre* (Paris: Presses universitaires de France, 1926), 8; Sarraut, 44; SHAT 7N440: "Note au sujet de la situation actuelle des effectifs en indigènes coloniaux" (11 September 1918).

94. SHAT 16N194: Minister of War Millerand to Joffre, "Militaires tunisiens" (9 January 1915).

95. Ibid.: Gen. Drude, cdr., 45th Algerian Division, to cdr., 33rd Army Corps [Pétain], 14 November 1914.

96. AMAE G1664: Minister of War Millerand to MAE, "Au sujet du rapport de M. Piat" (3 January 1915).

97. SHAT 16N194: SA to GQG, "État d'esprit des militaires indigènes du dépôt d'Arles" (1 November 1914).

98. Michel, *Appel*, 289–90.

99. Ibid., 290–291; and Charles John Balesi, *From Adversaries to Comrades-in-Arms: West Africans and the French Military, 1885–1918* (Waltham, Mass.: Crossroads Press, 1979), 97–98.

100. Léon Bocquet and Ernest Hosten, *Un fragment de l'épopée sénégalais: Les tirailleurs noirs sur l'Yser* (Paris: Librairie national d'art et d'histoire, 1918), 11, 6–7.

101. Michel, *Appel*, 291–92.

102. SHAT 7N2121: "Renseignements fournis par le capitaine DeLettre, du 2ème bataillon de tirailleurs sénégalais d'Algérie" (n.d.).

103. Ibid.: Maj. Pelletier, 19 January 1915.

104. SHAT 16N194: Mangin to cdr., 3rd CA, 29 September 1914.

105. Charles Mangin, *Comment finit la Guerre* (Paris: Plon, 1920), 7, quoted in Leonard V. Smith, *Between Mutiny and Obedience: The Case of the French Fifth Infantry Division During World War I* (Princeton, N.J.: Princeton University Press, 1994), 102.

106. Bakary Diallo, *Force-bonté* (Paris: F. Reider, 1926), 113.

107. SHAT 7N2121: 10th Colonial Division, "Objet: Utilisation des Sénégalais" (19 October 1916). See also Diallo's description in *Force-bonté*, 123; Michel, *Appel*, 344–50; and the German white paper "Völkerrechtswidrige Verwendung farbiger Truppen auf dem europäischen Kriegsschauplatz durch England und Frankreich" (30 July 1915), in AMAE G1668.

108. SHAT 16N196: Gen. Antoine Dessort, crd., 16th DIC, to Berdoulat, 12 September 1916.

109. SHAT 16N196: "Rapport du Chef de bataillon Trouilh, cdt le 5e BTS, sur l'emploi des Sénégalais" (13 August 1916).

110. SHAT 16N196: 1st CAC, État-major, 3rd Bureau, "Rapport sur l'utilisation et le rendement des Sénégalais dans la guerre européen" (18 September 1916).

111. Lunn, "'Races Guerrières,'" esp. 531–35; id. *Memoirs*, 140–47.

112. Lunn, "'Races Guerrières.'"

113. SHAT 7N2121: 10th Colonial Division, "Objet . . . " (cited n. 107 above).)

114. SHAT 16N198: GQG, *Notice sur les Sénégalais* . . . (cited n. 45 above).

115. SHAT 16N194: Médecin divisionnaire Spillman, Moroccan Division, Service de santé militaire, reports, 16 and 17 November 1914.

116. On cold weather and respiratory illnesses among West Africans, see Pierre Jandeau, *Contribution à l'étude de pneumonie chez le tirailleur sénégalais* (Bordeaux: Imprimerie de l'Université, 1916); Henry Templier, *Observations étiologiques, cliniques, pronostiques et thérapeutiques sur la pneumonie des noirs de l'Afrique occidentale française au camp du Courneau* (Bordeaux: Imprimerie de l'Université, 1917); Lucien Viéron, *Quelques réflexions sur la pneumonie des troupes noires et son traitement* (Bordeaux: Imprimerie de l'Université, 1917); Richard Fogarty and Michael A. Osborne, "Constructions and Functions of Race in French Military Medicine, 1830–1920," in Sue Peabody and Tyler Stovall, *The Color of Liberty: Histories of Race in France* (Durham, N.C.: Duke University Press, 2003), 206–36.

117. SHAT 16N197: MG, Bureau de l'organisation et de la mobilisation de l'armée, "Au sujet de l'hivernage des coloniaux" (10 August 1917).

118. Ibid.: DTC to Général inspecteur des contingents indigènes des troupes coloniales, "Organisation des unités indigènes pendant l'hiver 1918–1919" (10 October 1918); CAOM SLOTFOM I,4: "Les Indochinois en France" (n.d.); Eckert, "Les militaires indochinois au service de la France (1859–1939)," 2: 476–501.

119. SHAT 7N443: DTC to MC, "AS des 2 bataillons malgaches destinés à aller au Cameroun" (10 November 1914).

120. The French heavy artillery grew from 428,000 men and 10,650 officers in the summer of 1914 to 1,090,000 men and 26,000 officers by the end of the war. See Razafindranaly, *Soldats de la grande île*, 342–46, and on Garbit's role, 347–52; see also Valensky, *Soldat occulté*, 343–44.

121. SHAT 16N198: Garbit, "Rapport au sujet des possibilités de recrutement à Madagascar" (19 February 1919).

122. SHAT 16N588: DTC to GCC, "Direction d'artillerie" (20 October 1917).

123. Ibid.: MG, Direction d'artillerie, to GCC and directeurs des dépôts d'artillerie malgaches, 24 October 1917.

124. SHAT 6N97: DTC to MC, "Recrutement à Madagascar" (24 March 1918).

125. Ibid.: Capitaine Estreme, 3rd Group cdr., 106th RAL, 27 April 1918.

126. SHAT 16N588: "Rapport du général Paloque, sur la valeur des contingents malgaches, versés dans les batteries lourdes" (26 July 1918).

127. On this question, and the ways in which soldiers try to answer it, see Samuel Hynes, *The Soldiers' Tale: Bearing Witness to Modern War* (New York: Penguin Books, 1997).

128. Michel, *Appel*, and Meynier, *Algérie révélée*, both include some interviews with veterans, but Lunn, *Memoirs* (esp. 127–37), makes the most extensive use of such evidence to describe the combat experience of West Africans.

129. On sex and love across the color line, see Chapter 6.

130. SHAT 7N995: Commission de contrôle postal de Marseille, "Annamites en France, note" (2 January 1917).

131. On French soldiers' lives at the front during World War I, see Pierre Miquel, *Les poilus* (Paris: Plon, 2000); Smith, *Between Munity and Obedience;* and Horne, *Price of Glory.*

132. SHAT 7N995: Commission de contrôle postal de Marseille, "Annamites en France, note" (2 January 1917).

133. AN 94AP135: "Note relative au recrutement de la main-d'œuvre coloniale nord- africain et chinoise" (16 August 1916). On the "Kabyle myth," see Lorcin, *Imperial Identities.*

134. SHAT 7N81: Mangin, "Note . . . " (cited n. 28 above). For an examination of this durability of racial stereotypes throughout the war, even when tested by intimate personal experience in the ranks, in the writings of one French officer who served with West Africans, see Nicole Zehfus, "From Stereotype to Individual: World War I Experiences with *Tirailleurs sénégalais," French Colonial History* 6 (2005): 137–57.

## Three • *Hierarchies of Rank, Hierarchies of Race*

*Epigraphs:* Dessort, SHAT 16N196: Gen. Antoine Dessort, cdr., 16th DIC, to cdr., 1st CAC, 12 September 1916 (report on West African troops). Algerian *officier indigène,* AMAE G1664: letter to Deputy Albin Rozet, 3 January 1915.

1. Lt. El Hadj Abdallah [pseudonym under which Boukabouya published the first edition of his pamphlet], *L'Islam dans l'armée française* (Constantinople, 1915), 4.

2. Ibid., 5.

3. Ibid., 13.

4. SHAT 16N196: Gen. Berdoulat, cdr., 1st CAC, "Rapport sur l'utilisation et le rendement des Sénégalais dans la guerre européen" (18 September 1916); emphasis in original.

5. SHAT 16N194: Mangin, cdr., 5th DI, to cdr. 3rd CA.

6. Ibid.: SA, "Note au sujet de l'emploi des chasseurs indigènes provenant du Maroc" (12 August 1914). For more on language policy in the army, see Chapter 5.

7. Ibid.: GCC to MG to Bordeaux, telephone message no. 3725, 15 November 1914.

8. Besides the Zouaves, other obvious white candidates for service in indigenous units were members of the Foreign Legion, but as Gen. Degoutte of the Moroccan Division pointed out, they were not legally able to serve in French regiments. See SHAT 16N196: Degoutte, cdr., DM, to cdr., 4th Army, "Spécialistes nécessaire pour les régiments indigènes" (30 April 1917).

9. SHAT 16N196: Gen. Degoutte, cdr., DM to cdr., 10th CA, "Objet: a/s de l'encadrement des régiments indigènes" (19 February 1917).

10. SHAT 7N443: Gen. Moinier, GCC des armées de terre et de mer de l'Afrique du Nord, to EMA, 2 September 1914.

11. SHAT 7N444: Gen. Ménestrel, inspecteur général des régions, to SA, 23 January 1915; Ménestrel remarked that this *sentiment de la tribu* was less pronounced among Algerians, but they still preferred to serve under officers whom they knew. The difference between Tunisians and Algerians was merely one of degree.

12. Abdallah [Boukabouya], *L'Islam dans l'armée française* (1915), 11.

13. Édouard Montet, *L'Islam et la France* (Paris: Levé, n.d. [1915–16]), 7.

14. SHAT 6N97: "Rapport de Monseigneur LeMaître" (15 June 1918).

15. SHAT 16N198: GQG, *Notice sur les Sénégalais et leur emploi au combat* (29 October 1918), 5–6.

16. Hubert Lyautey, "Du role social de l'officier," *Revue des Deux Mondes* 104 (15 March 1891): 443–59.

17. Gabriel Hanotaux, ed., *Histoire des colonies françaises*, vol. 6 (Paris, 1933), 1, quoted in Robert Aldrich, *Greater France: A History of French Overseas Expansion* (New York: St. Martin's Press, 1996), 4.

18. Hubert Lyautey, "Du rôle colonial de l'armée," *Revue des Deux Mondes* 157 (15 January 1900): 308–28.

19. SHAT 16N195: "Rapport du général Niessel cdt. la 37e DI sur le recrutement des cadres des régiments indigènes" (4 March 1916).

20. SHAT 16N194: cdr., 35th CA, to cdr., 6th Army, "Renforcement en caporaux des cadres des régiments de tirailleurs" (30 April 1915); GQG, "Note pour les armées" (5 May 1915), indicates that the number of corporals was indeed increased.

21. Ibid.: Gen. Deshayes de Bonneval, cdr., 37th DI, to cdr., 35th CA, "A/S des déserteurs indigènes" (23 April 1915).

22. SHAT 16N198: GQG, *Notice sur les Sénégalais . . . (cited n. 15 above)*, 20–21.

23. SHAT 16N196: GQG, Bureau de personnel (infanterie), 18 May 1917; id., "Note pour les armées," 29 May 1917, extended the provision, originally applied to Moroccan, Algerian, and Tunisian troops, to West Africans, Indochinese, Madagascans, and Somalis.

24. SHAT 16N197: Gen. Louis Franchet d'Esperey, cdr., Northern Army Group to GCC, 14 October 1917.

25. Yves de Boisboissel, *Peaux noires, cœurs blancs*, 2nd ed. (1931; Paris: Peyronnet, 1954), 42.

26. SHAT 16N198: GQG, *Notice sur les Sénégalais . . . (cited n. 15 above)*, 23.

27. Ibid., 24–25.

28. Ibid.: Garbit, "Rapport au sujet des possibilités de recrutement à Madagascar" (19 February 1919); emphasis in original.

29. Ibid.: Gen. Daugan, cdr., DM, to MCC, 11 March 1919.

30. SHAT 16N195: DTC, "Note pour l'état-major de l'armée" (11 April 1916).

31. SHAT 16N194: Lyautey to MG, 17 and 18 August 1914.

32. Ibid.: "Rapport du général cdt. la 38e Division sur l'état physique et moral des régiments de tirailleurs de 38e division" (26 December 1914).

33. SHAT 7N2121: DTC to regional cdrs., 11 October 1914.

34. Alistair Horne, *The Price of Glory: Verdun 1916* (New York: Penguin Books, 1962), 63.

35. SHAT 16N194: Mangin, cdr., 5th DI, to cdr., 3th CA, 29 September 1914.

36. SHAT 16N195: Mangin, "Note sur la création . . . " (2 April 1915).

37. SHAT 7N2121: Lt. Col. Nogues, cdr., 6th colonial mixte, letter from Gallipoli to Gen. Archinard, 17 May 1915.

38. SHAT 7N2103: "Rapport de l'officier interprète Reynaud sur l'état d'esprit des militaires indigène de l'Afrique du Nord" (14 July 1915).

39. SHAT 16N196: Lt. Col. Martelly, "Rapport succinct sur les services rendus par les Sénégalais dans les affaires auxquelles ils ont participé et les conclusions qui en résultent" (14 August 1916).

40. SHAT 6N96: Maj. Arnaud, cdr., 64th BTS, "Note au sujet de l'organisation d'unités offensives mixtes sénégalaises" (12 February 1917); emphasis in original.

41. SHAT 7N444: Ménestrel to SA, 1 February 1915.

42. SHAT 16N196: "Rapport du Chef de bataillon Trouilh, cdt. le 5ᵉ BTS, sur l'emploi des Sénégalais" (13 August 1916). Also quoted in Marc Michel, *L'appel à l'Afrique: Contributions et réactions à l'effort de guerre en AOF, 1914–1919* (Paris: Publications de la Sorbonne, 1982), 304.

43. SHAT 16N197: Gen. Maistre, cdr., 6th Army, to GCC, 6 November 1917.

44. SHAT 6N97: Diagne to MG, 31 August 1918. In November, the Ministry of War claimed that an inquiry into the incident was under way, though it is unclear if and how the problem was resolved. It is not clear where exactly the confrontation took place in order for the officer to throw the soldier from a height of almost twenty-three feet; Diagne merely speaks of a *chemin*, though perhaps he meant a bridge.

45. SHAT 7N445: Gen. Urbal to EMA, 3rd Bureau, "Rapport sur les conditions d'installation en France des indigènes Algériens de la class 1917" (12 February 1917).

46. Abdallah [Boukabouya], *L'Islam dans l'armée française* (1915), 17.

47. Lieutenant indigène Boukabouya Rabah (Hadj Abdallah), *L'Islam dans l'armée française*, pt. 2 (Lausanne: Librairie nouvelle, 1917), 39–51.

48. Ibid., 30.

49. SHAT 16N195: "Note pour le général cdt. le 36e CA Hely d'Oissel" (17 June 1915).

50. SHAT 16N194: Col. Cherrier, cdr., 3rd Moroccan Brigade, to cdr., 37th Division, 10 December 1914.

51. SHAT 7N997: Commission militaire de contrôle postal de Marseille, December 1917–January 1918.

52. SHAT 16N194: Gen. Ebener, cdr., 35th CA, to cdr., 6th Army, 24 April 1915.

53. SHAT 7N2104: Cpl. Zitouni Salah, spahis auxiliaires, interrogation after repatriation from Germany, Algiers, 3 December 1917.

54. SHAT 7N446: Maginot, "Note pour Monsieur le général Foch" (n.d.); and CAOM DSM5: [ Lt. Col. Métois], note, "Mesures à prendre à l'égard des tirailleurs de l'Afrique du Nord" (May 1917).

55. SHAT 6N97: MG, "Analyse: Incidents survenus à Espira de l'Agly du 3 au 10 décembre 1917" (9 January 1918). For more information on these and other similar outbreaks of indiscipline among créoles and originaires, see SHAT 7N440 and Marc Michel, *Appel*, 385–86.

56. SHAT 16N196: Col. Nogues, Fréjus–Saint-Raphaël, "Compte rendu: Rixe entre Somalis et Malgaches" (26 March 1917).

57. See the reports gathered by Gen. Berdoulat in SHAT 16N196.

58. SHAT 6N96: Maj. Arnaud, "Note au sujet de l'organisation d'unités offensives mixtes sénégalaises" (12 February 1917).

59. AMAE G1664: "Rapport du M. Piat" (30 October 1914).

60. SHAT 16N196: "Rapport du chef de bataillon Fortin au sujet l'utilisation des troupes sénégalais" (13 August 1916).

61. SHAT 6N97: PC/MG to MC (n.d., but between 5 and 19 February 1918).

62. SHAT 7N1001: "Rapport sur les opérations de la commission militaires de contrôle postal de Tunis, pendant le mois d'octobre 1917."

63. SHAT 7N997: Commission militaires de contrôle postal de Marseille, "Rapport mensuel: Les soldats malgaches en France" (July–August 1917).

64. Mokrani Boumezraq el-Ouennoughi and Katrandji Abderrahmane, *L'Islam dans l'armée française: Réplique à des mensonges* (n.p.: n.d. [probably 1916]), 15.

65. Ibid., 31.

66. The term *gradé* usually referred to a noncommissioned officer (in the French Army of the time, a man holding the rank of sergeant or *adjudant*), but many French military personnel of the time applied the term loosely to both NCOs and corporals.

67. Boukabouya, *Islam* (1917), 37–38.

68. Ibid., 74–75.

69. Gilbert Meynier, *Algérie révélée: La guerre de 1914–1918 et le premier quart du XXe siècle* (Geneva: Droz, 1981), 419. The Frenchman who was promoted over Boukabouya was a European from Algeria, which may help explain some of the virulent hatred for settlers evident in the pages of Boukabouya's pamphlets. There are also indications that the man was an *adjudant*, not a lieutenant, and thus Boukabouya's subordinate in rank, which would have made the slight all the more insulting.

70. SHAT 16N196: "Rapport du chef de bataillon Ehrhard au sujet des tirailleurs sénégalais" (13 August 1916).

71. Ibid.: "Rapport du chef de bataillon Trouilh sur l'emploi des Sénégalais" (13 August 1916).

72. SHAT 16N198: GHQ, *Notice sur les Sénégalais . . .* (cited n. 15 above), 22–25.

73. Ibid.: Lt. Col. Le Duc, "Historique de 1er régiment de chasseurs malgaches, citations à l'ordre de l'armée du 12e bataillon de chasseurs malgache" (9 March 1919).

74. SHAT 7N2121: Gen. Losserre to Gen. Archinard, 8 November 1915. Gen. Théophile Pennequin had developed an ambitious plan to train Indochinese officers in 1912, only to see his ideas rejected by colonists and colonial administrators opposed to such an elevation of status for *indigènes*. See Favre–Le Van Ho, "Milieu porteur de modernisation," 1: 8–33.

75. AN C7537: dossier 1461, "Proposition de loi no. 1246 sur le recrutement de l'armée indigène, par Pierre Massé, Pierre Ajam, Maurice Bernard" (16 September 1915).

76. SHAT 6N97: DTC, "Analyse" (16 May 1918).

77. SHAT 16N198: GQG, *Notice sur les Sénégalais . . .* (cited n. 15 above), 18–19.

78. SHAT 6N97: "Proposition de nomination au grade de sous-lieutenant indigène d'un aspirant d'infanterie coloniale" (23 April 1918); "Propositions de nomination au

grade de *sous-lieutenant* à titre temporaire de sous-officiers sénégalais" (23 April 1918). In 1920, another son of the *fama* of Sansanding also became an officer in the French Army. Of the several *gradés* listed in these nominations, only two appear to have become officers, according to Charles Balesi's listing of "Native Black Officers, 1862–1921" in *From Adversaries to Comrades-in-Arms*, 129.

79. SHAT 7N2103: Lutaud to MG, 6 February 1915.

80.Ibid.: SA, "Note au sujet du télégramme du gouverneur général de l'Algérie" (8 February 1915).

81. Ibid.: Lutaud to MG, "Au sujet de Si Brahim El Hadj Mohammed" (28 December 1915).

82. AMAE G1671: CIAM, session 19 (20 January 1916).

83. CAOM DSM6: "Note du gouverneur général de l'Algérie" (n.d.).

84. SHAT 7N445: SA to Moinier, "Pelotons spéciaux" (14 July 1916).

85. AMAE G1671*bis*: CIAM, session 47 (18 October 1917).

86. SHAT 7N2081: "Résultats des conférences entre M. Flandin et la SA" (6 December 1917).

87. For information on the issue of replacement and the special schools for future officers and *gradés*, see SHAT 7N446, dossier "Remplacement des indigènes," and Meynier, *Algérie révélée*, 541–45.

88. SHAT 6N97: "Répartition des contingents noirs dans les unités de nouvelle formation" (11 March 1918).

89. SHAT 7N441: DTC, "Circulaire résumant les principales dispositions arrêtées pendant la guerre au sujet des tirailleurs . . . " (26 April 1917).

90. SHAT 7N1992: Direction d'artillerie, "Circulaire au sujet d'utilisation des Malgaches dans l'artillerie" (24 February 1918).

91. SHAT 17N491: SA, "Bulletin de renseignements sur les questions musulmanes" (13 January 1918).

92. SHAT 16N1507: "Comptes rendus des chefs d'unités relatifs au moral des troupes 7e BTI" (7 July 1918).

93. SHAT 7N81: Mangin, "Note relative à l'encadrement des troupes indigènes" (21 April 1920).

94. Joe Lunn, *Memoirs of the Maelstrom: A Senegalese Oral History of the First World War* (Portsmouth, N.H.: Heinemann, 1999), 110–11.

95. AN C7537: dossier 1461, "Proposition de loi No. 1246 sur le recrutement de l'armée indigène, par Pierre Massé, Pierre Ajam, Maurice Bernard" (16 September 1915).

96. SHAT 6N97: DTC to regional cdrs., 16 July 1918.

97. AMAE G1670: CIAM, session 4, 12 January 1915.

98. Policy on this matter was in fact quite complicated, with differences among soldiers from different areas of the empire, and underwent several changes during the conflict. Tunisians and Algerians did in fact receive some family allocations, but the Algerian administration had to work hard to persuade the government in Paris that most Algerian families were poor and needed assistance. See Meynier, *Algérie Révélée*, 548–49, which underlines the racist motivations behind these policies.

99. AMAE G1664: letter to Albin Rozet, a deputy in the Chamber from Haute-Marne who championed the interests and political rights of indigenous Algerians (always with a view toward their assimilation) until his death in a car accident on 15 September 1915. See Jean Jolly, ed., *Dictionnaire des parlementaires français: Notices biographiques sur les ministres, députés et sénateurs de 1889–1940*, vol. 8 (Paris: Presses universitaires de France, 1977), 2929–30.

100. SHAT 7N144: SA, "Objet: Hospitalisation" (22 March 1916).

101. SHAT 7N444: SA to Moinier, "Organisation des spahis auxiliaires algériens" (15 September 1914).

102. SHAT 7N144: Ménestrel to SA, 23 January 1915.

103. AMAE G1664: letter to Albin Rozet.

104. Rives and Deroo, *Linh Tâp*, 14–15.

105. AMAE G1665: Alapetite to MAE, "Naturalisation des indigènes musulmans" (16 May 1915).

106. SHAT 7N2081: SA, "Observations sur le rapport de M. E. Flandin" (27 November 1917); "Résultats des conférences entre M. Flandin et la SA" (6 December 1917).

107. CAOM DSM5: "Note de M. l'officier interprète de 1ere Classe Reymond" (17 July 1917).

108. CAOM DSM6: "Observations de M. Reymond officier interprète principal sur le rapport de M. Flandin sénateur relatif à la conscription des indigènes de l'Algérie" (28 November 1917).

109. SHAT 16N196: "Rapport du lt-col Pasquier sur l'utilisation des Sénégalais dans les combats de Juillet 1916" (12 September 1916).

110. CAOM DSM6: "Observations de M. Reymond officier interprète principal sur le rapport de M. Flandin" (28 November 1917).

111. SHAT 16N196: Lt. Col. Martelly, "Rapport succinct sur les services rendus par les Sénégalais dans les affaires auxquelles ils ont participé et les conclusions qui en résultent" (14 August 1916).

112. AMAE G1669: SA, "Note au sujet de la proposition de MM. Diagne, Candace . . . en ce qui concerne les indigènes algériens et marocains" (10 October 1917).

113. For the role of education in France's civilizing mission in West Africa, see Alice Conklin, *A Mission to Civilize: The Republican Idea of Empire in France and West Africa, 1895–1930* (Stanford, Calif.: Stanford University Press, 1997), 75–86, 130–41; Gail Paradise Kelly, *French Colonial Education: Essays on Vietnam and West Africa* (New York: AMS Press, 2000); and Bob H. White, "Talk About School: Education and the Colonial Project in French and British Africa (1860–1960)," *Comparative Education* 32, 1 (1996): 9–25.

114. AMAE G1671: CIAM, session 19 (20 January 1916).

115. On language policy in the army, see Chapter 5.

116. AMAE G1671: CIAM, session 19.

117. Ibid.

118. Captain Khaled was the most prominent figure to hold this rank.

119. For Hamelin's comments, see AMAE G1671: CIAM, session 19. For documents relative to the legislation, the passage of which dragged on until after the war, see docu-

ments in AMAE G1667; SHAT 7N443 and 7N2081; AN C7537, V., "Armée coloniale: Service des indigènes."

120. AMAE G1671: CIAM, session 19.

121. AMAE G1671*bis*: CIAM, session 47 (18 October 1917).

122. Under both systems, even naturalized soldiers served *au titre indigène*, and could only serve *au titre français* by virtue of a special decree, which was, needless to say, rarely issued.

123. Charles-Robert Ageron, *Les Algériens musulmans et la France, 1871–1919* (Paris: Presses universitaires de France, 1968), 2: 1211–12.

124. Recham, M*usulmans algériens dans l'armée française*, 71.

125. Ibid., 71–72.

126. Meynier, *Algérie révélée*, 419.

127. John Kim Munholland, "The Emergence of the Colonial Military in France, 1880–1905" (Ph.D. diss., Princeton University, 1964), 107; Jean-Charles Jauffret, "L'officier français (1871–1919)," in Claude Croubois, ed., *L'officier français des origines à nos jours* (Saint-Jean-d'Angély: Éditions Bordessoules, 1987), 296.

128. Gontard, *Madagascar pendant la Première Guerre mondiale*, 11.

129. Balesi, *From Adversaries to Comrades-in-Arms*, 129.

130. Michel, *Appel*, 325.

131. SHAT 7N2306: CITI, "Rapport d'ensemble de la Commission des troupes indigènes" (8 June 1920); 7N2351: CITI, 2nd subcommission, "Note sur la constitution d'un corps d'officiers indigènes" (n.d.). On Mangin's postwar plans for a large force of *troupes indigènes* (200,000 in the Colonial Army and another 100,000 in the Armée d'Afrique), see SHAT 7N81: Mangin, "Note relative à l'encadrement des troupes indigènes" (21 April 1920).

132. SHAT 7N2351: CITI, 2nd subcommission, "Note sur la constitution d'un corps d'officiers indigènes" (n.d.).

133. Ibid.: Direction de l'artillerie, "Droit au commandement entre militaires français et indigènes" (7 December 1921).

134. Ibid.: "Rapport du lieutenant-colonel Lame, commandant le Centre de transition des troupes indigènes coloniales, relatif au droit au commandement et aux marques extérieurs de respect des indigènes coloniaux" (24 November 1925); emphasis in original. For more on the work of the CITI and postwar debates over indigenous officers, see Henri Eckert, "Les militaires indochinois au service de la France (1859–1939)" (doctoral thesis, Université de Paris IV, 1998), 2: 828–40; and Marc Michel, "Colonisation et défense nationale: Le général Mangin et la force noire," *Guerres mondiales et conflits contemporains* 145 (January 1987), 39ff.

135. SHAT 7N2351: SA, "Réponse de section d'Afrique et d'Orient aux objections contenues dans le rapport ci-contre" (EMA report on Mangin's proposals; n.d. [14 October 1922]).

*Four • Race and Language in the French Army*

*Epigraphs:* Frantz Fanon, *Black Skin, White Masks*, trans. Charles Lam Markmann (New York: Grove Press, 1967), 18. French Foreign Ministry, AMAE G1666: "Hôpital au

Jardin colonial" (1916). West African soldier quoted in Marc Michel, *L'appel à l'Afrique: Contributions et réactions à l'effort de guerre en AOF, 1914–1919* (Paris: Publications de la Sorbonne, 1982), 391. Banania advertising slogan in the pidgin French of West African soldiers; difficult to translate, it is probably best rendered as "Is good!"

1. Stéphane Audoin-Rouzeau and Annette Becker, *La Grande Guerre, 1914–1918* (Paris: Gallimard, 1998), 61. For more on Banania and images of the *tirailleurs*, see Anne Donadey, "'Y'a bon Banania': Ethics and Cultural Criticism in the Colonial Context," *French Cultural Studies* 11 (February 2000): 9–29; Jean Garrigues, *Banania: Histoire d'une passion française* (Paris: Du May, 1991); John Mendenhall, *French Trademarks: The Art Deco Era* (San Francisco: Chronicle Books, 1991); Anne-Claude Lelieur and Bernard Mirabel, *Negripub: L'image des noirs dans la publicité depuis un siècle* (Paris: Société des amis de la Bibliothèque Forney, 1987).

2. Benedict Anderson, *Imagined Communities: Reflections on the Origin and Spread of Nationalism*, rev. ed. (New York: Verso, 1991), 133.

3. Ibid., 134.

4. Fanon, *Black Skin*, 17–18.

5. Dennis Ager, *Language, Community and the State* (Exeter, England: Intellect Books, 1997), 72

6. Dennis Ager, *Identity, Insecurity and Image: France and Language* (Philadelphia: Multilingual Matters, 1999), 6.

7. Eugen Weber, *Peasants into Frenchmen: The Modernization of Rural France, 1870–1914* (Stanford, Calif.: Stanford University Press, 1976), 67–70.

8. David A. Bell, *The Cult of the Nation in France: Inventing Nationalism, 1680–1800* (Cambridge, Mass.: Harvard University Press, 2001), 175–77. For the wider context of the role of language in constructing national identity during the French Revolution, see ibid., 169–97; and Sophia Rosenfeld, *A Revolution in Language: The Problem of Signs in Late Eighteenth-Century France* (Stanford, Calif.: Stanford University Press, 2001), esp. 123–80.

9. Weber, *Peasants*, 495.

10. Quoted ibid., 489–90. Bell, *Cult of the Nation*, 198–217 passim, also notes the importance of the Third Republic in continuing the Revolution's civilizing work through language instruction, both within France and in the colonies.

11. Quoted in Tzvetan Todorov, *On Human Diversity: Nationalism, Racism, and Exoticism in French Thought* (Cambridge, Mass.: Harvard University Press, 1993), 145–46.

12. Quoted in Raoul Girardet, *Le nationalisme français: Anthologie, 1871–1914* (Paris: Seuil, 1983), 94.

13. Alice Conklin, *A Mission to Civilize: The Republican Idea of Empire in France and West Africa, 1895–1930* (Stanford, Calif.: Stanford University Press, 1997), 84, 132.

14. The Mission laïque, founded in 1901 by Pierre Deschamps, director of education in Madagascar, and its specially trained "secular missionaries" explicitly tied the French language to the lofty principles of republican France and sought to spread the benefits of French civilization through language and education.

15. CAOM DSM5: Mission laïque française, Secretary-general Besnard to Clemenceau, 7 January 1918.

16. SHAT 7N81: Mangin, "Note relative à l'emploi des races indigènes dans les divers armes et services et sur les différents théatres d'opération" (12 March 1920).

17. SHAT 16N198: Gen. Daugan to MCC, 11 March 1919.

18. CAOM SLOTFOM I, 9: "Rapport de M. Peche: Infirmiers indochinois, Amélie-les-Bains" (24 August 1917).

19. SHAT 16N588: "Rapport du général Palque, adjoint R.G.A. au général I.G.A., sur la valeur des contingents malgaches, versés dans les batteries lourdes" (26 July 1918).

20. SHAT 16N194: SA, "Note au sujet de l'emploi des chasseurs indigènes provenant du Maroc" (12 August 1914).

21. SHAT 16N1507: "Comptes rendus des chefs d'unités relatifs au moral des troupes 1er rgt. de tirailleurs marocains, 153e division" (29 November 1918).

22. SHAT 16N197: "Rapport du lt-col de Saint Maurice commandant le 2e régiment de marche de tirailleurs sur l'encadrement en tirailleurs français de régiments de tirailleurs algériens" (2 June 1917).

23. SHAT 16N196: Gen. Berdoulat, 1st CAC, État-major, 3rd Bureau, "Rapport sur l'utilisation et le rendement des Sénégalais dans la guerre européen" (18 September 1916). See also ibid.: MG, État-major, Bureau de l'organisation et de la mobilisation de l'armée to GCC des troupes françaises de l'Afrique du Nord, "Ravataillement personnel des unités de tirailleurs indigènes des armées" (27 February 1917).

24. The dozens of different dialects spoken among the West African troops further complicated the situation. Though Bambara and Wolof were the major languages of the region, French authorities estimated the number of dialects at between 29 and 80 (there was no consensus, and everyone seemed to have his own figure). As officers familiar with West African troops were quick to point out, there was no way to find anyone who knew or could master all of these languages.

25. SHAT 16N 194: "Rapport du général commandant la 38e Division sur l'état physique et moral des régiments de tirailleurs de la 38e division" (25 December 1914).

26. SHAT 16N195: Gen. Pierre Famin, "Note au sujet de la opération d'une nouvelle armée coloniale indigène pour le printemps 1916 par le Général Mangin" (18 August 1915).

27. SHAT 7N440: DTC to GCC, "Formules de correspondance pour les tirailleurs sénégalais" (15 October 1918).

28. SLOTFOM I, 8; SHAT 7N1001.

29. CAOM DSM5: "Note de M. l'officier interprète de 1ere classe Reymond" (17 July 1917).

30. SHAT 7N2107: MC, "Rapport du cdt. Marcel controleur des contingents indigènes nord-africains sur sa visite aux régiments indigènes de la division marocaine" (19 March 1918).

31. SHAT 7N441: DTC, "Circulaire résumant les principales dispositions arrêtées pendant la guerre au sujet des tirailleurs, infirmiers et commis et ouvriers d'administration indigènes des troupes coloniales en service en Europe, Algérie ou Tunisie" (26 April 1917).

32. SHAT 7N2107: MC, "Rapport du commandant Marcel" (19 March 1918).

33. CAOM DSM5: IVe Région, État-major, Service d'assistance et de surveillance des

militaires indigènes de l'Afrique du Nord, "Rapport hebdomadaire du 29 avril au 5 mai" (29 April–5 May 1917).

34. To boost the morale and see to the needs of wounded North African soldiers, Consul general [and *secrétaire interprète*] Piat visited hospitals in southern France as early as mid October 1914. AMAE G1664: Piat to Foreign Minister Théophile Delcassé, 30 October 1914.

35. On Islam, the Ottoman empire, and France's North African soldiers, see Chapter 6.

36. SHAT 7N144: SA, "Instructions confidentielles, à communiquer aux interprètes militaires détachés ou en mission près les dépôts de militaires indigènes musulmans, ou les formations sanitaires désignées pour le traitement de ces militaires" (23 November 1914).

37. Ibid.

38. CAOM DSM5: SA to regional cdrs., "Surveillance de la correspondance des militaires indigènes de l'Afrique du Nord" (2 September 1915).

39. SHAT 16N194: SA to GCC, "État d'esprit des militaires indigènes du dépôt d'Arles" (11 January 1915).

40. Ibid.: MG to GCC, "Intervention des Puissances alliées en Turquie" (12 March 1915).

41. SHAT 7N2103: SA to GGA, "Intervention française en Orient" (11 March 1915).

42. SHAT 16N196: SA, "Note pour les officiers interprètes chargés du Service d'assistance et de surveillance des militaires indigènes" (14 July 1916). SA to GQG, 1 December 1916, contains the text of a letter from the sharif of Mecca to the president of France thanking him for France's sympathy. Interpreters were instructed to publicize the existence of this letter and its contents.

43. SHAT 7N2104: SA, "Note pour les officiers interprètes chargés du Service d'assistance aux militaires indigènes musulmans" (11 May 1917). Interpreters were instructed to emphasize that all British soldiers were forbidden by their commanders to enter mosques and Muslim holy places, that Muslim soldiers were placed at the doors of these places, and that General Sir Frederick Maude, the British military commander in Mesopotamia, had personally instructed his subordinates to allow free exercise to Muslim religious observance.

44. CAOM DSM5: SA to cdrs. of the 15th, 16th, 17th, and 18th Regions, "Assistance des jeunes recrues indigènes de la classe 1917" (3 February 1917).

45. AMAE G1670: CIAM, session 3 (31 December 1914).

46. Eileen Crofton, *The Women of Royaumont: A Scottish Women's Hospital on the Western Front* (East Lothian, Scotland: Tuckwell Press, 1996), 109. The hospital at Royaumont Abbey (about thirty miles north of Paris) was staffed entirely by women volunteers from Scotland throughout the war.

47. SHAT 16N194: SA to GCC, "Role des officiers interprètes détachés auprès des formations sanitaires" (n.d.; probably mid February 1915).

48. AMAE G1664: Lyautey to MAE, 21 October 1914; Resident-general Gabriel Alapetite to MAE, 14 October 1914. The Germans had the same problem when their interpreters wrote letters for French Muslim prisoners of war. A November 1917 censor's

report noted that the language in letters from POWs in Germany was not typical of that used by North Africans and the texts contained many "solecisms," so they must have been written by German interpreters, "not very up to date with the customs" of North Africans." SHAT 7N1001: "Rapport sur les opérations de la commission de contrôle postal de Tunis, pendant le mois de novembre 1917."

49. SHAT 7N2103: Sergent interprète auxiliaire Soulah Mohammed, "Nos troupes d'Afrique et l'Allemagne" (n.d.).

50. SHAT 7N144: GQG, "Interprètes français attachés to EM des bataillons indigènes" (8 July 1918).

51. CAOM DSM5: "Rapport hebdomadaire de l'officier interprète Mercier" (21 May 1917).

52. Ibid.: SA to regional cdrs., "Assistance religieuse aux militaires musulmans" (22 May 1915).

53. SHAT 16N194: SA to cdr., 15th Region, "Rapatriement des militaires indigènes pour l'encadrement des dépôts d'Afrique" (2 February 1915).

54. SHAT 7N144: Sous-secrétariat d'état du Service de santé militaire, "AS de l'état d'esprit des militaires indigènes musulmans" (7 December 1915).

55. SHAT 16N 196: 1st CAC, 16th DIC, 31st Colonial Brigade, État-major, "Rapport sur l'emploi des tirailleurs sénégalais, Colonel Venel" (16 August 1916).

56. CAOM DSM5: "Note du ministre des colonies" to chef d'état-major [Foch] and MG, 24 July 1917.

57. SHAT 16N198: GQG, *Notice sur les Sénégalais et leur emploi au combat* (19 October 1918), 17–18.

58. CAOM DSM5: SA, "Note sur l'Organisation et le fonctionnement du Service d'assistance et de surveillance des militaires indigènes et des bureaux régionaux des affaires indigènes" (22 May 1917).

59. AMAE G1671: CIAM, session 29 (6 July 1916).

60. AN C7537: dossier 1460, "Projet de loi no. 1052 concernant l'incorporation dans les conditions prévues par la loi du 21 mars 1905, modifié le 7 août 1913, des indigènes originaires des 4 communes de pleine exercise de Sénégal. Présenté au nom de M. le président de la République Raymond Poincaré par Alexandre Millerand (MG) et Gaston Doumergue (MC)" (24 June 1915).

61. CAOM DSM6: "Note du governeur général d'Algérie" (26 November 1917).

62. AMAE G1671: CIAM, session 19 (20 January 1916).

63. AMAE G1669: SA, "Note au sujet de la proposition de loi de MM. [Blaise] Diagne [et Gratien] Candace, députés, no. 1795, en ce qui concerne les indigènes algériens et marocains" (10 October 1917).

64. AMAE G1671: CIAM, session 30 (24 August 1916).

65. CAOM SLOTFOM I, 8: Contrôle postal malgache, September 1918.

66. CAOM SLOTFOM I, 4: "Les Indochinois en France" (n.d. [1921]).

67. AMAE G1666: "Hôpital au Jardin colonial." This description was destined to form the basis of an article in a Tunisian newspaper.

68. AMAE G1669: MAE to MG, ministre d'instruction publique, GGA, RGT, and RGM, "AS de la création de cours de français dans les hôpitaux spécialement affectés aux

soldats nord-africains" (27 March 1918); ministre de l'instruction publique to MAE, 5 April 1918.

69. Ibid.: "Rapport de M. Jouanneau, instituteur to l'École des garçons, Commune de Mesnil le Roi: Enseignement donné aux blessés indigènes pendant l'hiver 1917" (4 March 1918); and Département de Seine et Oise, École publique de Moisselles, L. Houan, "Cours d'adultes" (7 February 1918).

70. CAOM SLOTFOM I, 4: "Rapport Salles, 1916."

71. CAOM SLOTFOM I, 8: Contrôle postal annamite, March 1917.

72. SHAT 7N997: Contrôle postal indochinois, September 1917.

73. CAOM SLOTFOM III, 139–40: "Rapport de M. Przyluski controleur des contingents indochinois sur les COA indochinois au magasin central des troupes coloniales, à Paris" (23 August 1917); CAOM SLOTFOM I, 9: "Rapport de M. Peche: Infirmiers indochinois, Amélie-les-Bains" (24 August 1917). Many soldiers wrote letters, or had letters written for them, in French, even though their correspondents were unlikely to be any more fluent than they were in that language. The idea undoubtedly was to have the local colonial administrator, school teacher, or priest or missionary translate the letter.

74. SHAT 7N997: Contrôle postal malgache, "Rapport du mois de septembre 1917."

75. Fanon, *Black Skin*, 23, 36.

76. SHAT 7N997: Contrôle postal malgache, "Rapport du mois de septembre 1917."

77. SHAT 7N 2107: Commission militaire de Contrôle postal, Tunis, "Rapport sur les opérations de la commission pendant le mois de février 1917."

78. CAOM SLOTFOM I, 8: Contrôle postal indochinois, August 1918.

79. Conklin, *Mission*, 138. See also Gail Paradise Kelly, *French Colonial Education: Essays on Vietnam and West Africa* (New York: AMS Press, 2000); Bob H. White, "Talk about School: Education and the Colonial Project in French and British Africa (1860–1960)," *Comparative Education* 32, 1 (1996); and Denise Bouche, "L'enseignement dans les territoires français de l'Afrique occidentale de 1817 à 1920: Mission civilisatrice ou formation d'une élite?" (2 vols.; doctoral thesis, l'Université de Paris I, 1974).

80. In fact, a syncretic form of pidgin French, Spanish, and Italian mixed with Arabic and Berber, known as *sabir*, had evolved in North Africa.

81. Michel, *Appel*, 20. In *La force noire* (Paris: Hachette, 1910), 299, Charles Mangin warned of the decreasing utility of Bambara as recruitment widened.

82. *Le français tel que le parlent nos tirailleurs sénégalais* (Paris: L. Fournier, 1916). Both Joe Lunn (*Memoirs of the Maelstrom: A Senegalese Oral History of the First World War* (Portsmouth, N.H.: Heinemann, 1999), 180n22) and Marc Michel (*Appel*, 372–73) refer briefly to this pamphlet in their works on West African soldiers. On the relationship between the pidgin French of *Le français tel que le parlent nos tirailleurs sénégalais* and the French of uneducated West Africans today, see Gabriel Manessy, *Le français en Afrique noire: Mythe, stratégie, pratiques* (Paris: L'Harmattan, 1994), 111–19.

83. *Le français tel que le parlent nos tirailleurs sénégalais*, 5.

84. Ibid., 6.

85. Ibid.

86. This and all subsequent examples of the simplified rules of grammar are outlined in ibid., 7–16.

87. SHAT 6N97: Mangin, "Répartition des contingents noirs dans les unités de nouvelle formation" (11 March 1918).

88. Ironically, one of the best known assertions in Antoine de Rivarol's celebrated and often quoted 1783 essay *De l'universalité de la langue française* is: "What distinguishes our language from [other] ancient and modern languages is the order and the construction of the sentence. French names first the subject of the discourse, then the verb which [designates] the action, and finally the object of this action: that is the natural logic of all men; that is what constitutes common sense." Antoine de Rivarol, *De l'universalité de la langue française* (Paris: Obsidiane, 1991), 38–39; also quoted in Ager, *Identity*, 194. Thus, the same logic and simplicity that made French the greatest human language made West African languages primitive and unsophisticated.

89. Explanations accompanying the translations defined vocabulary alterations, such as substituting *faire manière* for *s'efforcer*, and *mirer* for *voir. Le français tel que le parlent nos tirailleurs sénégalais*, 19.

90. Ibid., 33. Marc Michel also notes the ironic nature of this passage in *Appel*, 372–73.

91. A reproduction of this cartoon appears in Paul Ducatel, *Histoire de la IIIe République: Vue à travers l'imagerie populaire et la press satirique*, vol. 4: *La Grande Guerre (1911–1923)* (Paris: Jean Grassin, 1978), 148.

92. Michel, *Appel*, 373.

93. Lucie Cousturier, *Des inconnus chez moi* (Paris: Éditions de la Sirène, 1920).

94. SHAT 6N97: Mangin, "Répartition des contingents noirs dans les unités de nouvelle formation" (11 March 1918).

95. Ibid.: Mordacq to DTC, 23 March 1918.

96. Ibid.: Mangin to Mordacq, 21 April 1918.

97. Ibid.: Gen. Mazillier, cdr., 1st CAC, to PC/MG, 27 April 1918.

98. Maurice Delafosse, *Vocabulaires comparatifs de plus de 60 langues ou dialectes parlés à la Côte d'Ivoire et dans les régions limitrophes* (Paris: Leroux, 1904), 264; quoted in Manessy, *Le français en Afrique noire*, 117.

99. SHAT 16N196: "Rapport du lt.-col. Debrieuvre, commandant le 58e colonial sur l'utilisation des Sénégalais au cours des récentes opérations" (12 September 1916).

100. SHAT 16N198: GQG, *Notice sur les Sénégalais*... (cited n. 57 above), 18.

101. AMAE G1669: Sous-secrétariat d'état du Service de santé militaire à Marseilles, "AS cours de français aux militaires indigènes de l'Afrique du Nord" (12 April 1918).

102. Allen Douglas, *War, Memory, and the Politics of Humor: The* Canard Enchaîné *and World War I* (Berkeley: University of California Press, 2002), 178–79.

103. SHAT 2107: Mission laïque française, "Enseignement du français aux travailleurs coloniaux" (n.d.).

104. Fanon, *Black Skin*, 20.

105. Cousturier, *Des inconnus*, 105. See also Michel, *Appel*, 373, and Balesi, *From Adversaries to Comrades-in-Arms*, 118–20.

106. Michel, *Appel*, 374.

107. Cousturier, *Des inconnus*, passim.

108. Lunn, *Memoirs*, 162.

109. Michel, *Appel*, 373. For the additional training of NCOs and specialists, see also Lunn, *Memoirs*, 106, and SHAT 16N198: GQG, *Notice sur les Sénégalais* . . . (cited n. 57 above).

110. Michel, *Appel*, 391.

111. Fanon, *Black Skin*, 17.

112. Conklin, *Mission*, 137. Both Kelly, *French Colonial Education*, and White, "Talk about School," place greater stress on French educators' desire to transform Africans, but the goal was still to do so in order to render them more useful as adjuncts and supports of the colonial edifice.

113. Ager, *Identity*, 79.

## Five • Islam in the French Army

*Epigraphs:* Djilani ben Smail, letter in SHAT 7N2107: Commission militaire de con-trôle postal, Tunis, "Rapport sur les opérations de la commission pendant le mois de Décembre 1917." Charles Lutaud on the dangers of a proposal for naturalizing Algerian soldiers that would have encouraged the spread of the Arabic language by making the ability to read and write it a qualification for citizenship, in AMAE G1665: Lutaud to MAE, 14 July 1915.

1. Few North Africans were Christians. North African Jews either did not serve in the French Army or (if Algerian) served in the Zouaves.

2. Stéphane Audoin-Rouzeau and Annette Becker, *14–18, retrouver la guerre* (Paris: Gallimard, 2000), 134ff. Annette Becker, *War and Faith: The Religious Imagination in France, 1914–1930* (Oxford: Berg, 1998) is primarily concerned with the importance of Christianity in shaping the experience of the war and of its commemoration and mem-ory in France: . For other treatments of religion in France during World War I, see Annette Becker, "The Churches and the War," in Jean-Jacques Becker, *The Great War and the French People*, trans. Arnold Pomerans (Leamington Spa, England: Berg, 1985), 178–91; Jacques Fontana, *Les Catholiques français pendant la Grande Guerre* (Paris: Cerf, 1990); Gérard Cholvy and Yves-Marie Hilaire, *Histoire religieuse de la France contempo-raine*, vol. 2: *1880–1930* (Paris: Privat, 1986); and Jean-Marie Mayeur, "La vie religieuse en France pendant la Première Guerre mondiale," in Jean Delumeau, ed., *Histoire vécu du peuple chrétien* (Paris: Privat, 1979).

3. For brief treatments of the importance of faith to some of the soldiers them-selves, see Gilbert Meynier, *L'Algérie révélée: La guerre de 1914–1918 et le premier quart du XXe siècle* (Geneva: Droz, 1981), 455–56; and Joe Lunn, *Memoirs of the Maelstrom: A Senegalese Oral History of the First World War* (Portsmouth, N.H.: Heinemann, 1999), 133–34.

4. The literature on immigration is extensive; see esp. Gérard Noiriel, *The French Melting Pot: Immigration, Citizenship, and National Identity* (Minneapolis: University of Minnesota Press, 1996); Alec G. Hargreaves, *Immigration, "Race" and Ethnicity in Contemporary France* (London: Routledge, 1995); Maxim Silverman, *Deconstructing the Nation: Immigration, Racism and Citizenship in Modern France* (London: Routledge, 1992); Neil MacMaster, *Colonial Migrants and Racism: Algerians in France, 1900–1962*

(London: Macmillan, 1997); Patrick Weil, *La France et ses étrangers: L'aventure d'une politique de l'immigration, 1938–1991* (Paris: Calmann-Lévy, 1991); Tahar Ben Jelloun, *French Hospitality: Racism and North African Immigrants* (New York: Columbia University Press, 1999); and Paul A. Silverstein, *Algeria in France: Transpolitics, Race, and Nation* (Bloomington: Indiana University Press, 2004).

5. On Islam in contemporary France, see Claude Liauzu, *L'Islam de l'Occident: La question de l'Islam dans la conscience occidentale* (Paris: Arcantère Éditions, 1989); Rémy Leveau and Gilles Kepel, eds., *Les musulmans dans la société française* (Paris: Presses de la Fondation nationale des sciences politiques, 1988); Rémy Levau and Shireen T. Hunter, "Islam in France," in Shireen T. Hunter, ed., *Islam, Europe's Second Religion* (Westport, Conn.: Praeger, 2002), 3–28; and Alain Boyer, *L'islam en France* (Paris: Presses universitaires de France, 1998); and Jocelyne Cesari, "The Muslim Presence in France and the United States: Its Consequences for Secularism," *French Politics, Culture & Society* 25, 2 (Summer 2007): 34–45.

6. Much of the current discourse frames Islam as a "problem" to be examined and perhaps solved, one indication being the numerous titles that invoke "la question de l'Islam." Another is the apparent necessity for a recent book that asks *Peut-on vivre avec l'islam? Le choc de la religion musulmane et des sociétés laïques et chrétiennes* (Paris: Favre, 1999), by Jacques Neirynck and Tariq Ramadan. Since the rise to prominence of international terrorism after 2001, this discourse has only intensified.

7. CAOM DSM5: Sous-secrétariat d'état du Service de santé militaire, EMA, and DTC, "Instruction générale sur l'hospitalisation et les décisions consécutives au traitement des militaires et ouvriers indigènes" (25 November 1916).

8. SHAT 6N97: Gen. Henri Mordacq, chef du cabinet militaire in Clemenceau's Ministry of War, undated *avis* in response to an 18 April 1918 request from Monseigneur LeMaître, a Catholic missionary, for the nomination of a (Catholic) chaplain to serve *troupes noires* in France.

9. SHAT 7N997: Contrôle postal de Marseille, Rapport mensuel, "Les soldats malgaches en France" (July–August 1917).

10. SHAT 7N995: Commission de contrôle postal de Marseille, "Annamites en France" (2 January 1917).

11. SHAT 7N997: Contrôle postal indochinois, September 1917.

12. CAOM SLOTFOM I, 9: "M. Peche: Rapport trimestrielle" (20 July 1918).

13. SHAT 7N144: Service de santé militaire, "Inhumation des travailleurs annamites et transmission des avis de décès concernant ces indigènes" (15 June 1916). Procedures for soldiers were identical. See also CAOM DSM5: Sous-secrétariat d'état du Service de santé militaire et al., *Instruction générale sur l'hospitalisation. . .* (cited n. 7 above).

14. CAOM SLOTFOM I, 9: M. [Gaston] Dupuy, "Hospitalisations, décès, inhumations des Indochinois à Marseille" (n.d.; probably 1917).

15. CAOM SLOTFOM I, 8: Contrôle postal indochinois, April 1917.

16. SHAT 6N97: Armée de l'Afrique du Nord, État-major, 3rd Bureau, "Note sur les modifications à apporter au régime des Sénégalais" (December 1916). The prestige of the Middle East (broadly defined as the area stretching from Morocco to Afghanistan) in the eyes of Muslims from outside the Middle East is a long-standing phenomenon, often

combined with a reverence or nostalgia for Islam's medieval "Golden Age," as Stephen Humphreys observes in *Between Memory and Desire: The Middle East in a Troubled Age* (Berkeley: University of California Press, 1999), xiv–xv.

17. SHAT 6N97: "Rapport de Monseigneur LeMaître" (15 June 1918).

18. Ibid.: Mordacq, *avis* in response to LeMaître's letter of 18 April 1918 (cited in n. 8 above); Cabinet du ministre, "Note au sujet de la proposition faite par Monsieur Le-Maître de créer un corps d'interprètes dans les bataillons indigènes" (n.d.). This last document summarized the opinions of Mangin and others. Indeed, why Clemenceau would have appointed LeMaître in the first place, given the prime minister's well-known anticlericalism, is somewhat puzzling, as is his continuing tolerance of the priest's mission even in the face of nearly unanimous opposition from army officers. Mordacq was instrumental in the initial appointment of LeMaître, but he did not show himself to be at all favorable to the priest's suggestions. In the end, Diagne's appointment as head of the Commissariat des troupes noires made LeMaître's mission redundant, and Clemenceau terminated it in November. On LeMaître, see also Marc Michel, *L'Appel à l'Afrique: Contributions et réactions à l'effort de guerre en AOF, 1914–1919* (Paris: Publications de la Sorbonne, 1982), 354–55, 382–83. For the role of missionaries in the empire and in influencing the development of republican colonial ideology, see J. P. Daughton, *An Empire Divided: Religion, Republicanism, and the Making of French Colonialism, 1880–1914* (New York: Oxford University Press, 2006).

19. See Christopher Harrison, *France and Islam in West Africa, 1860–1960* (Cambridge: Cambridge University Press, 1988), and David Robinson, *Paths of Accommodation: Muslim Societies and French Colonial Authorities in Senegal and Mauritania, 1880–1920* (Athens, Ohio: Ohio University Press, 2000).

20. SHAT 6N97: "Note sur les modifications . . . " (December 1916).

21. On the development by colonial "scholar-administrators" of this distinction between the benign "Islam *noir*" in West Africa and "fanatical" North African Islam, see Harrison, *France and Islam*, 93ff.

22. SHAT 16N194: SA to GCC, 25 November 1914; GCC to SA, 27 November 1914.

23. SHAT 7N2107: "Situation islamique au Sénégal et dans les pays maures" (n.d.; probably early 1915).

24. CAOM AP907: governor-general of the AOF to MC, 23 November 1914. Both AP907 and AP907*bis* contain many similar declarations from the AOF.

25. On the general quiescence of Muslims in West Africa during the war, see Harrison, *France and Islam*, 118–36; and Michel, *Appel*, 58–60, 83–84.

26. SHAT 16N198: GQG, *Notice sur les Sénégalais et leur emploi au combat* (19 October 1918), 15–16, 19.

27. Michel, *Appel*, 380–82.

28. SHAT 7N441: Diagne to DTC, "Objet: Au sujet d'une armée noire à constituer pour l'après guerre" (6 December 1918).

29. SHAT 7N81: Mangin, "Note relative à l'emploi des races indigènes dans les divers armes et services et sur les différents théâtres d'opération" (12 March 1920).

30. Edward Said's *Orientalism* (New York: Vintage Books, 1993) is the most important and pioneering work on the subject, particularly as it developed among French and

British writers in the nineteenth century. Henry Laurens's *Les origines intellectuelles de l'expédition d'Egypte: L'orientalisme islamisant en France (1698–1798)* (Istanbul: Éditions Isis, 1987) and Ann Thomson's *Barbary and Enlightenment: European Attitudes Toward the Maghreb in the 18th Century* (Leiden: Brill, 1987) trace the change in attitudes over the course of the previous century. For a critique of Said's and others' work on Orientalism, see Bernard Lewis (who himself has been accused of Orientalism), *Islam and the West* (New York: Oxford University Press, 1993), 99–118.

31. For a wide-ranging exploration of the relationship between France and the Islamic world, from the eighth century to the twenty-first, see William E. Watson, *Tricolor and Crescent: France and the Islamic World* (Westport, Conn.: Praeger, 2003). See also the essays in the special issue, "France and Islam," of *French Historical Studies* 30, 3 (Summer 2007).

32. François-René de Chateaubriand's *Itinéraire de Paris à Jérusalem* appeared in 1811, after his 1806–7 trip. Quoted in Bernard Lewis, *A Middle East Mosaic: Fragments of Life, Letters and History* (New York: Random House, 2000), 11–12.

33. Quoted in Lewis, *Middle East Mosaic*, 15. See also Alexis de Tocqueville, *Writings on Empire and Slavery*, ed. and trans. Jennifer Pitts (Baltimore: Johns Hopkins University Press, 2001).

34. AMAE G1671: CIAM, session 19 (20 January 1916).

35. Ibid. On the CIAM, as well as more generally on French policy on Islam in the twentieth century from a political point of view, see Pascal Le Pautremat, *La politique musulmane de la France au XXe siècle: De l'Hexagone aux terres d'Islam. Espoirs, réussites, échecs* (Paris: Maisonneuve & Larose, 2003).

36. AMAE G1671: CIAM, session 28 (10 June 1916).

37. AMAE G1671*bis*: CIAM, session 47 (18 October 1917).

38. SHAT 16N1555: SA to GQG, "Correspondance des militaires indigènes," "Chanson sur la guerre, expédié par un fils à son père" (21 November 1916).

39. SHAT 2103: "Rapport de l'officier interprète Reymond sur l'état d'esprit des militaires indigènes de l'Afrique du Nord dans les dépôts de passage d'Aix, Arles, Tarascon, & Beaucaire" (14 July 1915).

40. SHAT 7N2107: Commission de contrôle postal, Tunis, "Rapport sur les opérations de la commission pendant le mois de février 1917."

41. Ibid.: Commission de contrôle postal, Tunis, "Rapport sur les opérations de la commission pendant le mois de mai 1918."

42. SHAT 7N997: Contrôle postal malgache, "Rapport du mois de novembre 1917."

43. SHAT 16N198: GQG, *Notice sur les Sénégalais*... (cited n. 26 above), 23.

44. SHAT 16N1555: "Chanson . . . " (cited n. 38 above).

45. SHAT 7N2107: Commission de contrôle postal, Tunis, "Rapport sur les opérations de la commission pendant le mois d'avril 1917"; SHAT 16N194: SA to GQG, "État d'esprit des militaires indigènes tunisiens" (11 February 1915).

46. SHAT 7N1001: "Rapport sur les opérations de la commission militaire de contrôle postal de Tunis, pendant le mois d'août 1917."

47. SHAT 16N1555: "Chanson . . . " (cited n. 38 above).

48. SHAT 7N2107: Commission de contrôle postal, Tunis, "Rapport sur les opérations de la commission pendant le mois de mars 1917."

49. SHAT 16N1555: "Chanson . . . " (cited n. 38 above)

50. Lt. El Hadj Abdallah [Boukabouya], *L'Islam dans l'armée française* (Istanbul, 1915), 26–28.

51. SHAT 2103: Tabti Mostapha Ould Kaddour, "'Nos troupes d'Afrique et l'Allemagne': Impressions et chant de guerre. Recueillis, traduits et annotés par Soulah Mohammed, sergent interprète auxiliaire" (n.d.).

52. AMAE G1667: Senator Étienne Flandin, president of the Comité parlementaire d'action à l'étranger, to PC/MAE Aristide Briand, 29 September 1916. See SHAT 7N2104 for a French translation of the pamphlet "Contempt for the Muslim Religion in the French Ranks."

53. AMAE G1664: Lyautey to MAE, 21 October 1914.

54. SHAT 16N194: Minister of War Alexandre Millerand to regional cdrs. 1–21, "Règles à suivre pour l'inhumation des militaires musulmans" (16 October 1914).

55. Ibid.: MG, Direction du Service de santé militaire, "Règles à suivre pour l'inhumation des militaires musulmans" (3 December 1914).

56. Édouard Montet, *L'Islam et la France* (Paris: Levé, n.d. [1915–16]), 11–12.

57. CAOM DSM5: Officier interprète Mercier to cdr., 15th Region, "Rapport hebdomadaire no. 339" (21 May 1917).

58. SHAT 16N195: SA to GCC, "Au sujet de Ramadan" (28 June 1915).

59. SHAT 16N196: DTC, Service de l'organisation des travailleurs coloniaux en France, Ouvriers musulmans, "Au sujet de Ramadan" (19 June 1916). Though the statement here refers to workers, the DTC was equally responsible for soldiers, and the attitude expressed applied to Muslims in general.

60. SHAT 16N1555: Gen. de Salins, cdr., 38th DI, to cdr. 18th CA, 16 June 1918.

61. SHAT 16N195: SA to GQG, 22 July 1915; GGA to MG, 22 July 1915; French translations of fatwas of Sheikh ul Islam of Tunis and Missoum Abderrahman ben Cheikh el Missoum.

62. SHAT 16N196: SA to GQG, "AS du Ramadan" (2 July 1916).

63. SHAT 7N2103: Lutaud to MG, 6 November 1914.

64. AMAE G1670: CIAM, session 3 (31 December 1914).

65. Ibid.: CIAM, session 5 (13 January 1915).

66. Ibid.: CIAM, session 7 (2 April 1915).

67. CAOM DSM5: SA to regional cdrs., "Assistance religieuse au militaires musulmans" (22 May 1915); AMAE G1665: SA to MAE, "Traitement des soldats musulmans" (13 June 1915).

68. AMAE G1667: Flandin to Briand, 29 September 1916 (cited n. 52 above).

69. Ibid.: SA to MAE, "Imams aux armées" (24 December 1916); G1670: CIAM, session 6 (25 January 1915).

70. AMAE G1667: Lyautey to SA, 11 November 1916.

71. Ibid.: SA to MAE, "Imams aux armées" (24 December 1916).

72. SHAT 7N2104: Lutaud to PC/MAE Aristide Briand, "AS d'une brochure allemande intitulée: L'Islam dans l'armée française, guerre 1914–1915" (7 March 1916); CAOM DSM5: Sous-secrétariat d'état du Service de santé militaire et al., "Instruction générale sur l'hospitalisation . . . " (cited n. 7 above).

73. Mokrani Boumezraq el-Ouennoughi and Katrandji Abderrahmane, *L'Islam dans l'armée française: Réplique à des mensonges* (n.p.: n.d. [probably 1916]), 37–39.

74. Boukabouya, *Islam* (1917), 45–47.

75. Boukabouya, *Islam* (1915), 31–37; quotation from 31.

76. Boukabouya, *Islam* (1917), 60–71.

77. SHAT 7N2103: see numerous documents in the dossier entitled, "Prisonniers de guerre indigènes en Allemagne, 1914–1915."

78. Ibid.: SA, "Rapport fait au ministre: Au sujet des mesures propres à combattre l'action de la Turquie sur les populations musulmanes de l'Afrique du Nord" (21 November 1914).

79. AMAE G1664: Consul general [and *secrétaire interprète*] Piat to MAE Delcassé, 30 October 1914.

80. Ibid.: Officier interprète Galtier, "Note sur la situation morale des troupes indigènes de l'Afrique du Nord (Arles et Aix)" (n.d.).

81. Ibid.: Piat to Delcassé, 30 October 1914 (cited n. 79 above). This bizarre claim was actually not that unusual. German and Ottoman propaganda sometimes claimed that the Kaiser was a Muslim, had made a pilgrimage to the Holy Land, and descended from the family of Mohammed's sister.

82. SHAT 7N2081: SA, "Bulletin politique" (November 1914).

83. SHAT 7N2103: SA to MAE, "Action allemande sur les militaires indigènes" (5 December 1914); accompanied by French translation of an Arabic proclamation to French troops.

84. SHAT 16N194: Alapetite to MG Millerand, 29 December 1914.

85. SHAT 7N2104: Lutaud to PC/MAE Briand, "AS d'une brochure allemande . . . " (cited n. 72 above). Emphasis in original.

86. SHAT 7N2103: Tabti Mostapha Ould Kaddour, "Nos troupes d'Afrique et l'Allemagne" (n.d.).

87. Ibid.: Consul general Piat, note, "AS du Chérif si Ibrahim des Rahmanya" (n.d.).

88. Ibid.: MG to Lyautey, 23 December 1914.

89. Ibid.: Lutaud to MG, 5 May 1915.

90. SHAT 7N2081: SA, "Bulletin politique" (November 1914).

91. AMAE G1670: CIAM, session 3 (31 December 1914).

92. SHAT 7N2081: SA, "Bulletin de renseignements politiques" (24 February–18th March 1915).

93. SHAT 7N2103: SA to MAE, "Politique musulmane" (3 March 1915).

94. SHAT 7N444: Ménestrel, "Inspection des troupes d'Afrique" (20 June 1915). Ménestrel submitted this report nearly two months after the land phase of the Dardanelles campaign had begun in April, but he seems to have based his comments upon earlier inspections he undertook in January and February.

95. SHAT 7N2103: Lutaud to MG, 5 May 1915. Though the landing of troops at the Dardanelles had begun ten days before Lutaud sent this letter, the text indicates that he had written it much earlier. In any case, the question of deploying North Africans in Turkey would remain open as the operation bogged down and the Entente's forces needed reinforcements.

96. SHAT 7N444: MG, EMA, Bureau de l'organisation et de la mobilisation de l'armée, "Rapport fait au Ministre . . . au sujet de l'utilisation des indigènes de l'Afrique du Nord, sur le théâtre d'opérations d'Orient" (27 September 1916).

97. SHAT 7N445: MG, EMA, Bureau de l'organisation et de la mobilisation de l'armée, "Note pour les Sous-secrétariats d'état de l'artillerie et munitions, du ravataillement, et de l'intendance, et pour la direction du génie, utilisation des indigènes de l'Afrique du Nord sur le théatre d'opérations d'Orient" (2 October 1916).

98. SHAT 16N194: MG to GCC, "Intervention des Puissances alliées en Turquie" (12 March 1915).

99. Ibid.: SA to GCC, "Envoi au corps expéditionnaire d'Orient d'un bataillon de tirailleurs algériens" (29 April 1915); Joffre to SA, "Envoi en Orient d'un bataillon de tirailleurs" (3 May 1915).

100. SHAT 7N2104: "Rapport de l'officier interprète Auger" (30 October 1917).

101. AMAE G1667: Lt. Doynel de Saint-Quentin, Mission militaire française en Égypte, note no. 63: "Les prisonniers musulmans français à Zössen et à Constantinople (d'après le tirailleur marocain Aiyesch Ben Mohamed et le journal de campagne du Lieutenant Allemand Grobba)" (13 August 1916). See also Le Pautremat, *La politique musulmane de la France*, 158–61.

102. Ibid. Lt. Doynel Saint-Quentin to MAE, 18 July 1916; Mission militaire française en Égypte, note no. 60 (19 July 1916).

103. SHAT 7N2103: "Rapport de l'officier interprète Reymond sur l'état d'esprit des militaires de l'Afrique du Nord . . . " (14 July 1915).

104. SHAT 7N81: Mangin, "Note relative à l'emploi des races indigènes dans les divers armes et services et sur les différents théâtres d'opération" (12 March 1920).

## Six • *Race, Sex, and Imperial Anxieties*

*Epigraphs:* Hao, SHAT 7N995: Commission de contrôle postal de Marseille, "Annamites en France" (2 January 1917). Postal censor, CAOM SLOTFOM III, 143: M. Lacombe, Contrôle postal annamite (12 February 1917). Benedict Anderson, *Imagined Communities: Reflections on the Origin and Spread of Nationalism*, rev. ed. (New York: Verso, 1991), 149. Frantz Fanon, *Black Skin, White Masks*, trans. Charles Lam Markmann (New York: Grove Press, 1967), 63.

1. See Ann Laura Stoler and Frederick Cooper, "Between Metropole and Colony: Rethinking a Research Agenda," in id., eds., *Tensions of Empire: Colonial Cultures in a Bourgeois World* (Berkeley: University of California Press, 1997); Margaret Strobel, "Gender, Sex, and Empire," in Michael Adas, ed., *Islamic and European Expansion: The Forging of a Global Order* (Philadelphia: Temple University Press, 1993), 345–75; Nupur Chaudhuri and Margaret Strobel, eds., *Western Women and Imperialism: Complicity and Resistance* (Bloomington: Indiana University Press, 1992); Robert J .C. Young, *Colonial Desire: Hybridity in Theory, Culture and Race* (New York: Routledge, 1995); Julia Clancy-Smith and Frances Gouda, eds., *Domesticating the Empire: Race, Gender, and Family Life in French and Dutch Colonialism* (Charlottesville: University Press of Virginia, 1998); Martin Thomas, *The French Empire Between the Wars: Imperialism, Politics*

*and Society* (Manchester, England: Manchester University Press, 2005), 151–84; Floya Anthias and Nira Yuval-Davis, eds., *Racialized Boundaries: Race, Nation, Gender, Colour and Class and the Anti-Racist Struggle* (New York: Routledge, 1992); Ronald Hyam, *Empire and Sexuality: The British Experience* (Manchester, England: Manchester University Press, 1990); Kenneth Ballhatchet, *Race, Sex and Class under the Raj: Imperial Attitudes and Policies and Their Critics, 1793–1905* (London: Weidenfeld & Nicolson, 1980).

2. Nira Yuval-Davis and Floya Anthias, eds., *Woman—Nation—State* (New York: St. Martin's Press, 1989).

3. Ann Laura Stoler, *Carnal Knowledge and Imperial Power: Race and the Intimate in Colonial Rule* (Berkeley: University of California Press, 2002), 6. For the role racial prejudice played in debates over immigration and repopulation in the metropole after the Great War, see Elisa Camiscioli, "Producing Citizens, Reproducing the 'French Race': Immigration, Demography, and Pronatalism in Early Twentieth-Century France," *Gender & History* 13, 3 (November 2001): 593–621.

4. On European women's changing roles in the colonies, see Tyler Stovall, "Love, Labor, and Race: Colonial Men and White Women in France During the Great War," in id. and Georges Van Den Abbeele, eds., *French Civilization and Its Discontents: Nationalism, Colonialism, Race* (Lanham, Md.: Lexington, 2003), 299, 301–2; Stoler, *Carnal Knowledge;* and Alice Conklin, "Redefining 'Frenchness': Citizenship, Race Regeneration, and Imperial Motherhood in France and West Africa, 1914–1940," in Clancy-Smith and Gouda, *Domesticating the Empire,* 65–83.

5. Michel Foucault, *Discipline and Punish: The Birth of the Prison* (New York: Vintage Books, 1979), 139.

6. Michel Foucault, *The History of Sexuality, Volume I: An Introduction* (New York: Vintage Books, 1990), 103, 143.

7. Ann Laura Stoler, *Race and the Education of Desire: Foucault's History of Sexuality and the Colonial Order of Things* (Durham, N.C.: Duke University Press, 1995). See also id., *Carnal Knowledge,* 140–61.

8. The main concern here is with men, both *troupes indigènes* and French officials, though these relationships also provide at least an indirect view of the experiences of the Frenchwomen who were the objects of, on the one hand, desire and love, and on the other, concern and dismay.

9. The term "the color line" was made famous in the context of American race relations in an 1881 essay with that title by Frederick Douglass, then given renewed prominence by W. E. B. Du Bois's later use of the term. The image of a "color line" is useful in thinking about the rigid racial boundaries imposed by French colonialism, and Tyler Stovall has made effective use of it in his "Love, Labor, and Race" (cited n. 4 above) and "The Color Line Behind the Lines: Racial Violence in France During the Great War," *American Historical Review* 103, 3 (June 1998): 737–69. So too has Brett A. Berliner in *Ambivalent Desire: The Exotic Black Other in Jazz-Age France* (Amherst: University of Massachusetts Press, 2002), 37–70.

10. SHAT 7N997: Contrôle postal malgache, "Rapport du mois de Novembre 1917." On wartime postal censorship in France, see Maurice Rajsfus, *La censure militaire et policière (1914–1918)* (Paris: Le Cherche Midi, 1999); and Georges Liens, "La Commission de censure

et la Commission de contrôle postal à Marseille pendant la Première Guerre mondiale," *Revue d'histoire moderne et contemporaine* (October–December 1971).

11. On colonial workers in France during the war, see Bertrand Nogaro and Lucien Weil, *La main-d'œuvre étrangère et colonial pendant la guerre* (Paris: Presses universitaires de France, 1926); John Horne, "Immigrant Workers in France During World War I," *French Historical Studies* 15, 1 (Spring 1985): 57–88; and Tyler Stovall, "Colour-blind France? Colonial Workers during the First World War," *Race and Class* 35, 2 (October–December 1993): 35–55. On women in the World War I labor force, see James F. Mc-Millan, *Housewife or Harlot: The Place of Women in French Society, 1870–1940* (New York: St. Martin's Press, 1981), 131–62; Margaret H. Darrow, *French Women and the First World War: War Stories of the Home Front* (Oxford: Berg, 2000), 169–228.

12. SHAT 7N997: Contrôle postal des indochinois, September 1917.

13. Lucie Cousturier, *Des inconnus chez moi* (Paris: Éditions de la Sirène, 1920).

14. SHAT 7N997: Contrôle postal malgache, "Rapport du mois de Septembre 1917."

15. SHAT 9N691 (suppl.): Direction des troupes coloniales to cdr., Fréjus–Saint-Raphaël, "AS dépôt de convalescents sénégalais à Menton" (14 July 1915).

16. SHAT 7N997: Contrôle postal malgache, "Rapport du mois de Septembre 1917."

17. CAOM SLOTFOM I, 8: Contrôle postal indochinois, August 1918.

18. SHAT 7N997: Contrôle postal indochinois, September 1917.

19. Ibid. On perceptions of black Africans' sexual potency and depravity, which led to anti-miscegenation legislation as early as the eighteenth century, see William B. Cohen, *The French Encounter with Africans: White Responses to Blacks, 1530–1880* (Bloomington: Indiana University Press, 1980). Similar perceptions prevailed about other nonwhites in the colonial empire; see Stovall, "Love, Labor, and Race," 300, 310.

20. SHAT 7N997: Commission militaire de contrôle postal de Marseille, "Rapport mensuel: Les soldats malgaches en France" (July–August 1917),

21. AMAE G1665: Resident-general Gabriel Alapetite to MAE, "Naturalisation des indigènes musulmans" (16 May 1915).

22. SHAT 7N2107: Commission militaire de contrôle postal, Tunis: "Rapport sur les opérations de la commission pendant le mois de Décembre 1916." For more examples of duplicitous romantic behavior by Indochinese men, see Kimloan Hill, "A Westward Journey, an Enlightened Path: Vietnamese Linh Tho, 1915–30" (Ph.D diss., University of Oregon, 2001), 165–66.

23. SHAT 7N997: Contrôle postal indochinois, August 1917.

24. CAOM SLOTFOM I, 8: Contrôle postal indochinois, April 1917.

25. SHAT 7N997: Contrôle postal indochinois, August 1917.

26. Ibid.

27. Ann Laura Stoler, "Making Empire Respectable: The Politics of Race and Sexual Morality in Twentieth-Century Colonial Cultures," *American Ethnologist* 16, 4 (November 1989): 636–39.

28. CAOM SLOTFOM I, 8: Commission de contrôle de Marseille, "Note sur la correspondance annamite lue du 20 Octobre au 20 Novembre 1916."

29. CAOM SLOTFOM III, 143: M. Lacombe, Contrôle postale annamite, 12 February 1917.

30. CAOM SLOTFOM I, 8: Contrôle postal indochinois, "Rapport du mois d'Octobre 1917."

31. Ibid. I, 8: Contrôle postal malgache, December 1917.

32. SHAT 7N997: Contrôle postal malgache, "Rapport du mois de Septembre 1917."

33. Mireille Favre–Le Van Ho, "Un milieu porteur de modernisation: Travailleurs et tirailleurs vietnamiens en France pendant la Première Guerre mondiale," 2 vols. (doctoral thesis, École nationale des chartes, 1986), 2: 539.

34. CAOM DSM5: Officier interprète Dijan, "Rapport hebdomadaire du 29 avril au 5 mai, 9 mai 1917."

35. SHAT 7N2107: Commission militaire de contrôle postal, Tunis, "Rapport sur les opérations de la commission pendant le mois de Janvier 1917."

36. SHAT 7N997: Contrôle postal indochinois, August 1917.

37. Favre–Le Van Ho, "Milieu porteur de modernisation," 2: 541.

38. SHAT 7N997: Contrôle postal indochinois, August 1917.

39. Ibid.: Contrôle postal indochinois, November 1917.

40. SHAT 2107: Commission militaire de contrôle postal, Tunis, "Rapport sur les opérations de la commission pendant le mois de Février 1917."

41. CAOM DSM6: "Observations de M. Reymond officier interprète principal sur le rapport de M. Flandin sénateur relatif à la conscription des indigènes de l'Algérie" (28 November 1917).

42. See Mary Louise Roberts, *Civilization Without Sexes: Reconstructing Gender in Postwar France, 1917–1927* (Chicago: University of Chicago Press, 1994). James McMillan, "The Great War and Gender Relations: The Case of French Women and the First World War Revisited," in Gail Braybon, ed., *Evidence, History and the Great War: Historians and the Impact of 1914–1918* (New York: Berghahn, 2003), 135–53, disputes Roberts's claim that the Great War constituted a "crisis" in gender relations, instead seeing developments during the war years as part of a longer-running debate about the role of women in French society.

43. Favre–Le Van Ho, "Milieu porteur de modernisation," 2: 539–40. That repopulating France in this way was certainly not what even pronatalists had in mind became clear during debates over immigration after the war. See Camiscioli, "Producing Citizens, Reproducing the 'French Race.'"

44. CAOM SLOTFOM I,8: Contrôle postal indochinois, "Rapport du mois d'Octobre 1917."

45. Stoler, *Carnal Knowledge*, 79–111. See also Owen White, *Children of the Empire: Miscegenation and Colonial Society in French West Africa, 1895–1960* (Oxford: Clarendon Press, 1999); Emmanuelle Saada, "Race and Sociological Reason in the Republic: Inquiries on the *Métis* in the French Empire (1908–37)," *International Sociology* 17, 3 (September 2002): 361–91; Alice Bullard, *Exile to Paradise: Savagery and Civilization in Paris and the South Pacific, 1790–1900* (Stanford, Calif.: Stanford University Press, 2000), 210–33; Françoise Vergès, *Monsters and Revolutionaries: Colonial Family Romance and Métissage* (Durham, N.C.: Duke University Press, 1999); Ruth Harris, "The 'Child of the Barbarian': Rape, Race, and Nationalism in France During the First World War," *Past and Present* 141 (November 1993): 170–206. On attitudes toward *métissage* during

the interwar period, see Owen White, "Miscegenation and the Popular Imagination," in Tony Chafer and Amanda Sackur, eds., *Promoting the Colonial Idea: Propaganda and Visions of Empire in France* (Basingstoke, England: Palgrave, 2002), 133–42; Berliner, *Ambivalent Desire*, 37–70; Thomas, *French Empire Between the Wars*, 166–168; and Elizabeth Ezra, *The Colonial Unconscious: Race and Culture in Interwar France* (Ithaca, N.Y.: Cornell University Press, 2000), 36–46, 53–57. On similar attitudes in Britain in the years immediately after 1918, see Lucy Bland, "White Women and Men of Colour: Miscegenation Fears in Britain after the Great War," *Gender & History* 17, 1 (April 2005): 29–61.

46. See Joe Lunn, *Memoirs of the Maelstrom: A Senegalese Oral History of the First World War* (Portsmouth, N.H.: Heinemann, 1999), 172.

47. SHAT 7N2103: "Rapport de l'officier interprète Reymond sur l'état d'esprit des militaires indigènes de l'Afrique du Nord" (14 July 1915).

48. Stoler, *Carnal Knowledge*, 61. For generalized suspicions about nurses and their sexuality, see Darrow, *French Women*, 142–51; for more general suspicions of working women, see McMillan, *Housewife or Harlot*; Roberts, *Civilization Without Sexes*, 188–96; Stovall, "Love, Labor, and Race," 300–301.

49. SHAT 7N2103: "Rapport de. . . Reymond" (cited n. 47 above).

50. SHAT 7N2107: Section d'Afrique to Inspection générale des prisonniers de guerre, 23 October 1917. On the consensus in France that Frenchwomen in relationships with non-European men suffered from diminished status because attitudes toward women outside Europe were so debased, see Elisa Camiscioli, "Intermarriage, Independent Nationality, and the Individual Rights of French Women: The Law of 10 August 1927," *French Politics, Culture & Society* 17, 3–4 (Summer–Fall 1999): 63–65.

51. SHAT 7N2103: "Rapport de. . . Reymond" (cited n. 47 above).

52. SHAT 7N2112: Officier interprète Galtier, "Rapport hebdomadaire no. 41" (11 September 1915).

53. Hill, "Westward Journey," 166.

54. SHAT 7N2112: Officier interprète Brudo to cdr., 17th Region, 14 December 1915.

55. Ibid. : MG to cdr., 17th Region, 28 December 1915.

56. SHAT 7N2103: "Rapport de. . . Reymond" (cited n. 47 above).

57. CAOM DSM5: Sous-secrétariat d'état du Service de santé militaire, "AS de l'état d'esprit des militaires indigènes musulmans" (7 December 1915).

58. Ibid. : Officier interprète Benhazera, "Rapport hebdomadaire no. 42" (26 May 1917).

59. SHAT 7N2107: Inspection générale des régions, Gen. Menestrel, no. 126, "Extrait du rapport sur l'inspection des 14e et 15e régions, infanterie" (2 September 1915).

60. SHAT 7N144: Service de santé militaire circular, "Hospitalisation des militaires indigènes sénégalais" (27 March 1916); Lunn, *Memoirs*, 172.

61. CAOM DSM5: Interprète stagiaire Denant, Fréjus–Saint-Raphaël, "Contrôle de correspondance, 25 janvier 1918."

62. SHAT 7N2311: MG, 1 June 1915.

63. Ibid.: SA, "Note pour monsieur le ministre au sujet de l'hébergement dans les familles françaises des militaires indigènes" (8 June 1915).

64. SHAT 7N2112: Galtier, "Rapport . . . no. 41" (cited n. 52 above).

65. Ibid.: Officier interprète Galtier, "Rapport hebdomadaire no. 60" (22 January 1916).

66. Ibid.: Officier interprète Galtier, "Rapport hebdomadaire no. 32 (10 July 1915).

67. Ibid.: Gen. Pontavice to military governor of Paris, 14 June 1915.

68. SHAT 7N1001: Commission de contrôle postal, Tunis, "Rapport sur les opérations de la commission pendant le mois de Décembre 1916."

69. SHAT 7N2107: Commission de contrôle postal, Tunis, "Rapport sur les opérations de la commission pendant le mois de Février 1917."

70. SHAT 7N997: Contrôle postal malgache, "Rapport du mois de septembre 1917."

71. Jean-Yves Le Naour, *Misères et tourments de la chair durant la Grande Guerre: Les mœurs sexuelles des Français, 1914–1918* (Paris: Aubier, 2002), 261; Stovall, "Love, Labor, and Race," 312.

72. CAOM SLOTFOM I, 8: Commission de contrôle de Marseille, "Rapport morale et politique: Note sur la correspondance annamite lue du 20 Octobre au 20 Novembre" (25 November 1916).

73. CAOM SLOTFOM III, 143: M. Lacombe, Contrôle postal annamite, 12 February 1917.

74. CAOM SLOTFOM I, 8: "Rapport de Monsieur Lacombe chargé du contrôle postal annamite au Dépôt de Marseille" (8 March 1917).

75. Ibid.: Contrôle postal annamite, March 1917; Contrôle postal indochinois, September 1918.

76. Ibid.: Contrôle postal indochinois, December 1918

77. SHAT 7N1001: "Rapport sur les opérations de la commission militaires de contrôle postal de Tunis, pendant le mois de juin 1917; Rapport . . . octobre 1917."

78. CAOM SLOTFOM III, 143: Direction des troupes coloniales, circular, 5 June 1917.

79. CAOM SLOTFOM I, 8: Contrôle postal indochinois, June 1917.

80. Ibid., April 1917.

81. Ibid., June 1917.

82. SHAT 7N997: Contrôle postal indochinois, August 1917.

83. George Orwell, "Shooting an Elephant," in Sonia Orwell and Ian Angus, eds., *The Collected Essays, Journalism and Letters of George Orwell*, vol. 1: *An Age Like This, 1920–1940* (New York: Harcourt, Brace, & World, 1968), 239.

84. CAOM SLOTFOM III, 143: M. Lacombe, Contrôle postal annamite, 12 February 1917.

85. SHAT 7N997: Contrôle postal indochinois, September 1917.

86. SHAT 7N2107: Commission militaire de contrôle postal, Tunis, "Rapport sur les opérations de la commission pendant le mois de Février 1917."

87. AMAE G1670: CIAM, session 8 (27 May 1915).

88. SHAT 7N2107: Commission militaire de contrôle postal, Tunis, "Rapport . . . " (cited n. 86 above).

89. SHAT 7N997: Contrôle postal malgache, "Rapport du mois de septembre 1917."

90. SHAT 7N2112: Galtier, "Rapport . . . no. 41" (cited n. 52 above).

91. Hill, "Westward Journey," 168.

92. CAOM SLOTFOM I, 8: Contrôle postal indochinois, March 1918.

93. On the positive value sometimes attributed to miscegenation in the French colonial context, see Owen, *Children of the French Empire;* Saliha Belmessous, "Assimilation and Racialism in Seventeenth- and Eighteenth-Century French Colonial Policy," *American Historical Review* 110, 2 (April 2005): 322–49; Seymour Drescher, *From Slavery to Freedom: Comparative Studies in the Rise and Fall of Atlantic Slavery* (New York: New York University Press, 1999), 295–99. Even the famous racialist Arthur de Gobineau believed that racial mixing could provide benefits; see Young, *Colonial Desire*, 102ff., and Cohen, *French Encounter*, 181, 218.

94. CAOM SLOTFOM I, 8: Contrôle postal indochinois, January 1918. The report for the following month repeated the same observation in slightly different language.

95. SHAT 7N997: Contrôle postal indochinois, November 1917.

96. CAOM SLOTFOM I, 4: "Les indochinois en France" (n.d. [1921]).

97. CAOM, Papiers d'agents, 9PA13: circular, 2 June 1918.

98. See SHAT 7N2308: dossier containing extracts from Indochinese mail from the Army of the Rhine.

99. SHAT 7N2305: Unattributed, "Note sur l'état d'esprit des tirailleurs tunisiens libérés" (n.d.; probably written by a French colonial or military official in Tunisia in the summer of 1922).

100. Le Naour, *Misères et tourments*, 275.

101. For works that emphasize the contribution of veterans and their wartime experiences in weakening French colonial control, see Favre–Le Van Ho, "Milieu porteur de modernisation"; Hill, "Westward Journey"; and Meynier, *Algérie révélée*. For similar arguments about the role of colonial veterans of World War I in the British Empire, see Glenford Howe, *Race, War and Nationalism: A Social History of West Indians in the First World War* (Kingston, Jamaica: Ian Randle, 2002); and Richard Smith, *Jamaican Volunteers in the First World War: Race, Masculinity and the Development of National Consciousness* (Manchester, England: Manchester University Press, 2004). On the other hand, Gregory Mann, *Native Sons: West African Veterans and France in the Twentieth Century* (Durham, N.C.: Duke University Press, 2006), shows that former *tirailleurs sénégalais* occupied an ambiguous, to say the least, position in the evolution of nationalism and independence in Mali.

102. Raoul Girardet, *L'idée coloniale en France, 1871–1962* (Paris: La Table Rond, 1972), 136. On the expansion of the French empire as a result of the war, see Christopher M. Andrew and A. S. Kanya-Forstner, *The Climax of French Imperial Expansion, 1914–1924* (Stanford, Calif.: Stanford University Press, 1981). Denise Bouche, *Histoire de la colonisation française*, vol. 2: *Flux et reflux (1815–1962)* (Paris: Fayard, 1991), points out the way in which the 1931 Colonial Exposition in Paris masked systemic weaknesses in the empire, while Lebovics, *True France*, 51–52, points to broader anxieties masked by the Exposition.

103. Alice Conklin, *A Mission to Civilize: The Republican Idea of Empire in France and West Africa, 1895–1930* (Stanford, Calif.: Stanford University Press, 1997), discusses this shift to more rigid notions of race in the colonial context in postwar French West

Africa. See also William H. Schneider, *Quality and Quantity: The Quest for Biological Regeneration in Twentieth-Century France* (Cambridge: Cambridge University Press, 1990).

104. Albert Memmi, *The Colonizer and the Colonized*, rev. ed. (Boston: Beacon, 1991), 76. (Originally published in French in 1957.)

105. Ibid., 74.

106. White, *Children of the French Empire*, 182.

107. Stoler, *Carnal Knowledge*, 83. See also Ann Laura Stoler and Frederick Cooper, "Introduction," in Cooper and Stoler, eds., *Tensions of Empire*, 1–56.

108. Le Naour, *Misères et tourments*, 270, notes that official attempts to prevent contacts by a policy of segregation did not work. Stovall, "Love, Labor, and Race," though in some respects more confident in the success of official intervention (298), also points out that officials succeeded "not so much in preventing or even limiting individual interracial contacts, but rather in establishing the very idea of a color line in France, particularly one governing relations between members of the opposite sex" (313).

109. Stoler, *Carnal Knowledge*, 153.

110. Stovall, "Love, Labor, and Race," 310–11, notes that "opportunities for interracial contact were largely a creation of the French government," which only intensified officials' concern.

## Seven • *Between Subjects and Citizens*

*Epigraphs:* Legislative proposal, CAOM AP534: "Proposition de loi, no. 280, à faciliter l'accession des militaires et des militaires anciens algériens, tunisiens, et marocains au statut de citoyen français, Chambre des députés, Albin Rozet, Georges Leygues, Louis Doizy, Lucien Millevoye, 1 avril 1915." Ulysse Leriche quoted in Jean-Charles Jauffret, *Parlement, gouvernement, commandement: L'armée de métier sous la Troisième République, 1871–1914* (Vincennes: Service historique de l'armée de terre, 1987), 2: 1094. Charles Mangin, *La force noire* (Paris: Hachette, 1910), 94–95.

1. Renée Waldinger, Philip Dawson, and Isser Woloch, eds., *The French Revolution and the Meaning of Citizenship* (Westport, Conn.: Greenwood Press, 1993).

2. John Torpey, *The Invention of the Passport: Surveillance, Citizenship and the State* (Cambridge: Cambridge University Press, 2000), 21–56.

3. David A. Bell, *The Cult of the Nation in France: Inventing Nationalism, 1680–1800* (Cambridge, Mass.: Harvard University Press, 2001), 204. See also Robert C. Lieberman, "A Tale of Two Countries: The Politics of Color Blindness in France and the United States," *French Politics, Culture & Society* 19, 3 (Fall 2001): 35.

4. Rogers Brubaker, *Citizenship and Nationhood in France and Germany* (Cambridge, Mass.: Harvard University Press, 1992). On the construction of republican citizenship in the early years of the Third Republic, see also James R. Lehning, *To Be a Citizen: The Political Culture of the Early French Third Republic* (Ithaca, N.Y.: Cornell University Press, 2001); and Bertrand Taithe, *Citizenship and Wars: France in Turmoil, 1870–1871* (New York: Routledge, 2001).

5. Maxim Silverman, *Deconstructing the Nation: Immigration, Racism and Citizenship in Modern France* (London: Routledge, 1992), 19.

6. Alan Forrest, "Citizenship and Military Service," in Waldinger et al., eds., *French Revolution*, 153–65.

7. Richard D. Challener, *The French Theory of the Nation in Arms, 1866–1939* (New York: Columbia University Press, 1955); Daniel Moran and Arthur Waldron, eds., *The People in Arms: Military Myth and National Mobilization Since the French Revolution* (Cambridge: Cambridge University Press, 2003). For a discussion of the *levée en masse* as the origin of mass armies, total war, and twentieth-century "industrialized killing," see Omer Bartov, "The European Imagination in the Age of Total War," in his *Murder in Our Midst: The Holocaust, Industrial Killing, and Representation* (New York: Oxford University Press, 1996), 33–50.

8. Isser Woloch, *The New Regime: Transformations of the French Civic Order, 1780–1820s* (New York: Norton, 1994), 130, cited in Torpey, *Invention of the Passport*, 21.

9. Challener, *French Theory*, 4. On the extension of the principle of the "nation in arms" under the Third Republic by means of universal obligatory military service, see ibid., 10–90; Douglas Porch, *The March to the Marne: The French Army, 1871–1914* (Cambridge: Cambridge University Press, 1981), 23–44 and 191–212; and David B. Ralston, *The Army of the Republic: The Place of the Military in the Political Evolution of France, 1871–1914* (Cambridge, Mass.: MIT Press, 1967).

10. *Journal officiel*, 17 January 1918, 677.

11. SHAT 7N2121: Bérenger, "Rapport sur le recrutement d'une armée indigène" (26 November 1915).

12. Ibid.

13. CAOM DSM6: "Rapport fait à la Commission de l'armée sur la question de la conscription indigène en Algérie par M. E. Flandin" (16 November 1917).

14. SHAT 7N2103: SA, "Note sur le Chérif Si Brahim" (15 November 1915).

15. SHAT 16N195: Marabout Mbarek of Guelma, three proclamations, May 1915.

16. SHAT 7N2107: Commission militaire de contrôle postal, Tunis, "Rapport sur les opérations de la commission du 15 octobre au 15 novembre 1918."

17. AMAE G1664: Consul general [and *secrétaire interprète*] Piat, report, 27 December 1914.

18. Ibid.: Consul general [and *secrétaire interprète*] Piat, report, 30 October 1914.

19. SHAT 7N2081: SA, "Bulletin politique" (1–15 January 1915).

20. Buisson's statement appears in Jean Jolly, ed., *Dictionnaire des parlementaires français: Notices biographiques sur les ministres, députés et sénateurs de 1889–1940*, vol. 8 (Paris: Presses universitaires de France, 1977), 1448. On Diagne's life and political career, see G. Wesley Johnson, *The Emergence of Black Politics in Senegal: The Struggle for Power in the Four Communes, 1900–1920* (Stanford, Calif.: Stanford University Press, 1971), and Amody Aly Dieng, *Blaise Diagne: Député noir de l'Afrique* (Paris: Éditions Choka, 1990).

21. Charles John Balesi, *From Adversaries to Comrades-in-Arms: West Africans and the French Military, 1885–1918* (Waltham, Mass.: Crossroads Press, 1979), 5; Denise Bouche, *Histoire de la colonisation française*, vol. 2: *Flux et reflux (1815–1962)* (Paris: Fayard, 1991), 142. The French legislature confirmed the *originaires'* special status during the opening years of the Third Republic.

22. On the prewar legal status of *originaires*, see Johnson, *Emergence of Black Politics in Senegal*, 3–89 passim; Alice Conklin, *A Mission to Civilize: The Republican Idea of Empire in France and West Africa, 1895–1930* (Stanford, Calif.: Stanford University Press, 1997), 151–54; and Lamine Guèye, *De la situation politique des Sénégalais originaires des communes de plein exercise* (Paris: Éditions de "La Vie Universitaire," 1922).

23. Conklin, *Mission*, 155.

24. Quoted in Johnson, *Emergence of Black Politics in Senegal*, 186. For details on Diagne's early efforts to win *originaires* the right to serve in the metropolitan army, see Balesi, *From Adversaries to Comrades-in-Arms*, 80–85; and Marc Michel, "Citoyenneté et service militaire dans les quatre communes du Sénégal au cours de la Première Guerre mondiale," in *Perspectives nouvelles sur le passé de l'Afrique noire et de Madagascar* (Paris: Publications de la Sorbonne, 1974), 299–314.

25. AN C7537: dossier 1459, Chambre des députés, "Proposition de loi no. 941 par Diagne et al. tendant à soumettre aux obligations militaires prévues par les lois de 1905 et de 1913 les Sénégalais des communes de plein exercise de la colonie, 20 mai 1915."

26. For details on the law and the parliamentary debates that led to its passage, see Marc Michel, *L'appel à l'Afrique: Contributions et réactions à l'effort de guerre en AOF, 1914–1919* (Paris: Publications de la Sorbonne, 1982), 62–63; and Johnson, *Emergence of Black Politics in Senegal*, 185–87.

27. AN C7537: dossier 1467, Chambre des députés, "Proposition de loi no. 1794 par Diagne et al. étendant aux déscendants des originaires des communes de plein exercise du Sénégal les dispositions de la loi militaire du 19 octobre 1915" (15 February 1916).

28. Johnson, *Emergence of Black Politics in Senegal*, 191.

29. Balesi, *From Adversaries to Comrades-in-Arms*, 86.

30. Joe Lunn, *Memoirs of the Maelstrom: A Senegalese Oral History of the First World War* (Portsmouth, N.H.: Heinemann, 1999), 68–69.

31. Michel, *Appel*, 91.

32. Figures on the numbers of *originaires* incorporated and sent to France are difficult to determine with any great precision. For varying estimates, see SHAT 7N2121: Bonnier to Clemenceau, "Contribution des originaires à la défense nationale" (24 May 1919); Diagne to Clemenceau, October 1919; Lunn, *Memoirs*, 87n57; Michel, *Appel*, 404.

33. Lunn, *Memoirs*, 73.

34. *Journal officiel*, 17 January 1918, 677–81.

35. See Johnson, *Emergence of Black Politics in Senegal*, 189–91.

36. Guèye, *De la situation politique des Sénégalais*.

37. See AMAE G1671: CIAM, session 19 (20 January 1916).

38. Laure Blévis, "Les avatars de la citoyenneté en Algérie coloniale ou les paradoxes d'une catégorisation," *Droit et société* 48 (2001): 557–80; "La citoyenneté française au miroir ce la colonisation: Étude des demandes de naturalisation des 'sujets français' en Algérie coloniale," *Genèses* 53 (December 2003): 25–47.

39. Charles-Robert Ageron, *Les Algériens musulmans et la France, 1871–1919* (Paris: Presses universitaires de France, 1968), 1: 343.

40. Blévis, "Avatars de la citoyenneté," 567. For an examination of anomalies that continued to plaugue citizenship policy toward Algerians after the Great War, see Blévis,

"L'usage du droit dans le rapport colonial: L'exemple de l'inscription des Algériens sur les listes électorales de métropole, 1919–1939," *Bulletin de l'Institut d'histoire du temps présent* 80 (December 2002).

41. Ageron, *Algériens*, 1: 344.

42. Ibid. See also Blévis, "Citoyenneté française au miroir de la colonisation," 45.

43. Ageron, *Algériens*, 2: 1118, 1120.

44. AMAE G1666: MG to MAE and MI, "Extrait du rapport de l'officier interprète Pons de la XIe Région" (13 February 1916).

45. SHAT 7N2104: *Mépris de la religion musulmane dans les rangs français* (1915).

46. Ibid. In 1870, a decree sponsored by the Algerian Jewish jurist and politician Adolphe Crémieux granted French citizenship to all Algerian Jews. See Ageron, *Algériens*, 1: 13–17, and Daniel Amson, *Adolphe Crémieux: L'oublié de la gloire* (Paris: Seuil, 1988).

47. See Gilbert Meynier, *L'Algérie révélée: La guerre de 1914–1918 et le premier quart du XXe siècle* (Geneva: Droz, 1981), 552–63.

48. AMAE G1664: Projet de lettre of Minister of War Alexandre Millerand, undated, but probably written sometime in December 1914.

49. Ibid.

50. AMAE G1670: CIAM, session 3 (31 December 1914).

51. SHAT 16N194: Gen. Deshayes de Bonneval, cdr., 37th DI, to cdr., 35th CA, 23 April 1915.

52. SHAT 16N 195: "Rapport du colonel Vrenière, cdt. la 96e Brigade au sujet du régiment marocain" (15 September 1916).

53. AMAE G1670: CIAM, session 5, 13 January 1915.

54. Ibid.: CIAM, session 6 (25 January 1915).

55. AMAE G1665: Lyautey to MAE, 15 June 1915.

56. AMAE G1670: CIAM, session 7 (2 April 1915), telegrams of 2 and 21 February from Lyautey to the minister of foreign affairs.

57. AMAE G1665: Lyautey to MAE, 15 June 1915.

58. AMAE G1670: CIAM, session 6, 25 January 1915.

59. Ibid.

60. Ageron, *Algériens*, 2: 1118, 1120. See also AMAE G1671: CIAM, session 33 (26 October 1916).

61. AMAE G1671: CIAM, session 19 (20 January 1916), communication from Governor-general Lutaud.

62. AMAE G1670: CIAM, session 9 (8 July 1915), telegram from Alapetite to MAE, 1 July 1915.

63. AMAE G1665: Alapetite to MAE, 6 April 1915.

64. Ibid.: Alapetite to MAE, "Naturalisation des indigènes musulmans" (16 May 1915).

65. For details on these five proposals, see Ageron, *Algériens*, 2: 1191–92.

66. Lehning, *To Be a Citizen*, 128–54.

67. AMAE G1665: Lutaud to MAE, 15 July 1915.

68. AMAE G1671: CIAM, session 19 (20 January 1916). Lutaud's description of Algerians as "white" did not make the usual distinction between "white" Kabyles and Arabs,

but his comment was no doubt inspired by the discourse that made such distinctions. See Patricia Lorcin, *Imperial Identities: Stereotyping, Prejudice and Race in Colonial Algeria* (London: I. B. Taurus, 1995); Jean-François Guilhaume, *Les mythes fondateurs de l'Algérie française* (Paris: L'Harmattan, 1992), 83ff.; and Taoufik Djebali, "Ethnicity and Power in North Africa: Tunisia, Algeria, and Morocco," in Paul Spickard, ed., *Race and Nation: Ethnic Systems in the Modern World* (New York: Routledge, 2005), 135–54.

69. AMAE G1671: CIAM, session 19 (20 January 1916).

70. For details, see Ageron, *Algériens*, 2: 1197–98.

71. AMAE G1671: CIAM, session 28 (10 June 1916). The text of Doizy's *proposition* is annexed to the *procès-verbal*; he was quoting from a bill introduced on 23 September 1915 by Maurice Violette, vice president of the Chamber of Deputies.

72. AMAE G1665: Alapetite to MAE, "Naturalisation des indigènes musulmans" (16 May 1915).

73. AMAE G1671: CIAM, session 28 (10 June 1916).

74. AMAE G1671*bis*: CIAM, session 51 (13 November 1917).

75. Ibid.: CIAM, sessions 53 (29 November 1917) and 59 (1 February 1918).

76. See Ageron, *Algériens*, 2: 1201–3; and Meynier, *Algérie révélée*, 555.

77. Ageron, *Algériens*, 2: 1199; Vincent Confer, *France and Algeria: The Problem of Civil and Political Reform, 1870–1920* (Syracuse, N.Y.: Syracuse University Press, 1966), 100.

78. Confer, *France and Algeria*, 99.

79. Ageron, *Algériens*, 2: 1221–23.

80. Confer, *France and Algeria*, 111.

81. Jeanne Bowlan, "Polygamists Need Not Apply: Becoming a French Citizen in Colonial Algeria, 1918–1938," *Proceedings of the Western Society for French History* 24 (1997): 113; Blévis, "Citoyenneté française au miroir de la colonisation," 37–39.

82. Bowlan, "Polygamists," 111.

83. John Ruedy, *Modern Algeria: The Origins and Development of a Nation* (Bloomington: Indiana University Press, 1992), 128.

84. Bowlan, "Polygamists," 115. On anxieties over practices considered demeaning to Frenchwomen who married men from outside Europe, such as polygamy, and the consequences for laws on citizenship, see Elisa Camiscioli, "Intermarriage, Independent Nationality, and the Individual Rights of French Women: The Law of 10 August 1927," *French Politics, Culture & Society* 17, 3–4 (Summer–Fall 1999): 52–74. See also James F. McMillan, *Housewife or Harlot: The Place of Women in French Society, 1870–1940* (New York: St. Martin's Press, 1981); id., "The Great War and Gender Relations: The Case of French Women and the First World War Revisited," in Gail Braybon, ed., *Evidence, History and the Great War: Historians and the Impact of 1914–1918* (New York: Berghahn, 2003), 135–53, and Mary Louise Roberts, *Civilization Without Sexes: Reconstructing Gender in Postwar France, 1917–1927* (Chicago: University of Chicago Press, 1994). On the role of gender, and gender anxieties, in debates over citizenship in another colonial context, see Elizabeth Thompson, *Colonial Citizens: Republican Rights, Paternal Privilege, and Gender in French Syria and Lebanon* (New York: Columbia University Press, 2000).

85. Confer, *France and Algeria*, 100; Blévis, "Avatars de la citoyenneté," 561. For the wider prewar context of reforms and policy toward *indigènes* in Algeria, see Confer, *France and Algeria*, 14–95; Blévis, "Avatars de la citoyenneté," and "Citoyenneté française au miroir de la colonisation"; Ruedy, *Modern Algeria*, 80–113; and Ageron, *Algériens*.

86. Confer, *France and Algeria*, 110.

87. Meynier, *Algérie révélée*, 557.

88. Ageron, *Algériens*, 2: 1223. The administration also accepted fifty-four requests made under the old *sénatus-consulte* of 1865, because, through a legislative quirk, both laws remained in place simultaneously.

89. Confer, *France and Algeria*, 111.

90. Ageron, *Algériens*, 2: 1222.

91. Confer, *France and Algeria*, 114.

92. Conklin, *Mission*, 166–67. Naturalizations of West Africans became even more infrequent in the following decades; see Catherine Coquery-Vidrovitch, "Nationalité et citoyenneté en Afrique occidentale français: Originaires et citoyens dans le Sénégal colonial," *Journal of African History* 42, 2 (2001): 285–305. On the postwar drift toward stricter notions of racial difference and more conservative policies toward colonial subjects, see also William H. Schneider, *Quality and Quantity: The Quest for Biological Regeneration in Twentieth-Century France* (Cambridge: Cambridge University Press, 1990), 116 ff.; Raoul Girardet, *L'idée coloniale en France, 1871–1962* (Paris: La Table Rond, 1972), 136ff.; Clifford Rosenberg, "Albert Sarraut and Republican Racial Thought," *French Politics, Culture & Society* 20, 3 (Fall 2002): 97–114.

93. Quoted in Jauffret, *Parlement, gouvernement, commandement*, 2: 1083.

94. Eckert, "Militaires indochinois au service de la France (1859–1939)," 2: 434–35.

95. AN C7537: "Proposition de loi no. 1246 sur le recrutement de l'armée indigène, par Pierre Masse, Pierre Ajam, Maurice Bernard, 16 septembre 1916."

96. Kimloan Hill, "A Westward Journey, an Enlightened Path: Vietnamese Linh Tho, 1915–30" (Ph.D diss., University of Oregon, 2001), 188.

97. J. Merimée, *De l'accession des Indochinois à la qualité de citoyen français* (Toulouse: Andrau & La Porte, 1931), 107, 225–29.

98. Favre–Le Van Ho, "Milieu porteur de modernisation," 1: 46. On Sarraut's attitudes, see also Rosenberg, "Albert Sarraut and Republican Racial Thought."

99. Eckert, "Militaires indochinois au service de la France (1859–1939)," 2: 441. The report is undated, so it is not clear whether it accompanied the 1921 or the 1924 letter.

100. Merimée, *De l'accession des Indochinois à la qualité de citoyen français*, 155–56.

101. SHAT 6N97: "Note au sujet de l'envoi d'une mission de recrutement à Madagascar" (21 March 1918).

102. Chantal Valensky, *Le soldat occulté: Les Malgaches de l'armée française, 1884–1920* (Paris: L'Harmattan, 1995), 362–63.

103. Ibid., 366–67. The number of Madagascans naturalized remained low, which was typical of the general situation throughout the French colonial empire during the 1920s. One expert was "astonished" to find that only thirty-six *indigènes* from the colonies outside North Africa were naturalized in 1925—eight from Madagascar, twenty

from Indochina, seven from West Africa, and one from New Caledonia. See Henry Solus, *Traité de la condition des indigènes en droit privé* (Paris: Sirey, 1927), 117–18.

104. See Conklin, *Mission*, 102–5.

105. Christopher Harrison, *France and Islam in West Africa, 1860–1960* (Cambridge: Cambridge University Press, 1988). See also Sylvia A. Diouf, "Invisible Muslims: The Sahelians in France," in Yvonne Yazbeck Haddad and Jane I. Smith, eds., *Muslim Minorities in the West: Visible and Invisible* (Walnut Creek, Calif.: Altamira Press, 2002),

106. SHAT 7N2104: GGA Lutaud to PC/MAE Aristide Briand, "A.s. d'une brochure allemande intitulée: L'Islam dans l'armée française, 'Guerre 1914–1915,'" (7 March 1916).

107. Gustave Mercier, "Les indigènes nord-africains et la guerre," *Revue de Paris* 25, 4 (1 July 1918): 203–22, cited in Confer, *France and Algeria*, 98.

108. Meynier, *Algérie révélée*, 559. On Mélia's ideas, see also his *L'Algérie et la guerre (1914–1918)* (Paris: Plon-Nourrit, 1918).

109. Blévis, "Avatars de la citoyenneté," 577–99. See also Patrick Weil, *Qu'est-ce qu'un Français? Histoire de la nationalité française depuis la Revolution* (Paris: Grasset, 2002), 234–38.

110. Quotation from Blévis, "Citoyenneté française au miroir de la colonisation," 40. See also Lehning, *To Be a Citizen*, 154.

111. John Laffey has shown how the doctrine of association could be transformed and used to support racist policies in prewar Indochina, see "Racism in Tonkin before 1914: The *Colons*' View of the Vietnamese," *French Colonial Studies* 1 (1977): 65–81.

112. See Bell, *Cult of the Nation*; James B. Collins, *From Tribes to Nation: The Making of France, 500–1799* (Toronto: Wadsworth, 2002); Norman Ravitch, "Your People, My People; Your God, My God: French and American Troubles over Citizenship," *French Review* 70, 4 (March 1997): 515–27.

113. Pierre Birnbaum, *The Idea of France* (New York: Hill & Wang, 2001), 65.

114. Nicolas Bancel, Pascal Blanchard, and Françoise Vergès, *La Republique coloniale: Essai sur une utopie* (Paris: Albin Michel, 2003), 122.

115. Patrick Weil suggests that scholars have made too much of distinctions between *jus soli* and *jus sanguinis,* and that either open or discriminatory practices can be inscribed in systems based upon "soil" or "blood" depending upon the prevaling political climate. See his *Qu'est-ce qu'un Français?* and also "Nationalities and Citizenships: The Lessons of the French Experience for Germany and Europe," in David Cesarini and Mary Fulbrook, eds., *Citizenship, Nationality and Migration in Europe* (London: Routledge, 1996), 74–87. On ambiguities within German conceptions of citizenship as it applied to race and gender in a colonial context, see Lora Wildenthal, "Race, Gender, and Citizenship in the German Colonial Empire," in Cooper and Stoler, eds., *Tensions of Empire*, 263–83.

116. Bancel, Blanchard, and Vergès, *La Republique coloniale*, 123. For the example of West Africa, see Ruth Dickens, "Citoyens de statut français, citoyens de statut africain: Multiple Faces of Citizenship in the French Union, 1946–1956," *Proceedings of the Western Society for French History* 24 (1997): 516–24.

117. Quoted in Alec Hargreaves, "Multiculturalism," in Christopher Flood and Laurence Bell, eds., *Political Ideologies in Contemporary France* (London: Pinter, 1997), 184.

On the stress in France on full cultural and political integration as a prerequisite for citizenship, see Adrian Favell, *Philosophies of Integration: Immigration and the Idea of Citizenship in France and Britain*, 2nd ed. (Basingstoke, England: Palgrave, 2001); and David Blatt, "Immigrant Politics in a Republican Nation," in Alec G. Hargreaves and Mark McKinney, eds., *Post-Colonial Cultures in France* (London: Routledge, 1997), 40–55.

118. Miriam Feldblum, *The Politics of Nationality Reform and Immigration in Contemporary France* (Albany: State University of New York Press, 1999), 151. On contemporary immigration and citizenship in France, see Favell, *Philosophies of Integration*; Tahar Ben Jelloun, *French Hospitality: Racism and North African Immigrants* (New York: Columbia University Press, 1999); Gérard Noiriel, *The French Melting Pot: Immigration, Citizenship, and National Identity* (Minneapolis: University of Minnesota Press, 1996); Maxim Silverman, *Deconstructing the Nation*; id., *Facing Postmodernity: Contemporary French Thought on Culture and Society* (London: Routledge, 1999); and id., "Rights and Difference: Questions of Citizenship in France," in Alec G. Hargreaves and Jeremy Leaman, eds., *Racism, Ethnicity and Politics in Contemporary Europe* (Aldershot, England: Edward Elgar, 1995), 253–63.

119. Dennis Ager, *Identity, Insecurity, and Image: France and Language* (Philadelphia: Multilingual Matters, 1999), 85. On the difficulty, if not impossibility, of integrating Islam into a broader European sense of identity, see Talal Asad, "Muslims and European Identity: Can Europe Represent Islam?" in Anthony Pagden, *The Idea of Europe: From Antiquity to the European Union* (Cambridge: Cambridge University Press, 2002), 209–27.

120. Controversy surrounding the wearing of headscarves in France's rigorously secular schools by young Muslim women has provoked a tremendous amount of commentary and articles too numerous to list. For the history of the controversy in the 1990s, see Miriam Feldblum, *Reconstructing Citizenship: The Politics of Nationality Reform and Immigration in Contemporary France* (Albany: State University of New York Press, 1999), 129–45. On more recent events, see Patrick Weil, "Lifting the Veil," *French Politics, Culture & Society* 22, 3 (Fall 2004): 142–49; and Joan W. Scott, "Symptomatic Politics: The Banning of Islamic Head Scarves in French Public Schools," *French Politics, Culture & Society* 24, 4 (Winter 2005): 106–27.

121. Muslims' ability to conform continues to dominate controversies about the integration of immigrants today in France and elsewhere. See Christopher T. Husbands, "'They must obey our laws and customs!': Political Debate About Muslim Assimilability in Great Britain, France, and The Netherlands," in Hargreaves and Leaman, eds., *Racism, Ethnicity and Politics in Contemporary Europe*, 115–30. See also Catherine Wihtol de Wenden, "North African Immigration and the French Political Imaginary," in Maxim Silverman, ed., *Race, Discourse and Power in France* (Aldershot, England: Avebury, 1991), 99–110. On the links between attitudes toward Muslims and Islam formed during the colonial period to contemporary debates over immigration and national identity, see Hafid Gafaiti, "Nationalism, Colonialism, and Ethnic Discourse in the Construction of French National Identity," and Driss Maghraoui, "French Identity, Islam, and North Africans: Colonial Legacies, Postcolonial Realities," in Tyler Stovall and Georges Van Den Abbeele, eds., *French Civilization and Its Discontents: Nationalism, Colonialism, Race* (Lanham, Md.: Lexington Books, 2003), 189–212 and 213–34.

122. Quoted in Charles-Robert Ageron, "Clemenceau et la question coloniale," in André Wormser, ed., *Clemenceau et la justice* (Paris: Publications de la Sorbonne, 1983), 81.

123. Albert Sarraut, *La mise en valeur des colonies françaises* (Paris: Payot, 1923), 102–3.

124. Quoted in Merimée, *De l'accession des Indochinois à la qualité de citoyen français*, 74.

125. Quoted in Jacques Thobie et al., *Histoire de la France coloniale, 1914–1990* (Paris: Armand Colin, 1990), 79.

## Conclusion

*Epigraphs:* Albert Sarraut quoted in SHAT 7N2351: "Rapport de la Commission (I) présidée par le général Sicre, cdt. la division de l'Annam-Tonkin et chargé par le général cdt. supérieur des troupes, d'étudier la question posé par le ministre des colonies au sujet des prérogatives respectives des militaires français et indigènes" (5 October 1923). Henri Brunschwig, *French Colonialism, 1871–1914: Myths and Realities*, trans. William Granville Brown (New York: Praeger, 1964), 167.

1. Alice L. Conklin, review of Emmanuelle Sibeud, *Une science impériale pour l'Afrique? La construction des savoirs africanistes en France, 1878–1930* (Paris: Éditions de l'École des hautes études en sciences sociales, 2002), in *H-France Review* 3, 31 (April 2003), www.h-france.net/vol3reviews/conklin.html (accessed September 28, 2007).

2. Keith Nelson, "The 'Black Horror on the Rhine': Race as a Factor in Post-World War I Diplomacy," *Journal of Modern History* 42, 4 (December 1970): 610–11.

3. AMAE G1668: "Völkerrechtswidrige Verwendung farbiger Truppen auf dem europäischen Kriegsschauplatz durch England und Frankreich" (30 July 1915). Though ostensibly a protest against both British and French practices, the document lists only three atrocities by Indian troops, out of sixteen specific examples (twelve were attributed to French North African and West African troops, and in one instance the culprits' were described only as "black colonial soldiers" and "enemy colonial cavalry").

4. AN C 7537: dossier 1470, "Proposition de resolution no. 2881, relative à l'utilisation des troupes de couleur en Europe, présenté par René Boisneuf, Gratien Candace, Blaise Diagne, et al." (16 January 1917).

5. Jean-Yves le Naour, *La honte noire: L'Allemagne et les troupes coloniales françaises, 1914–1945* (Paris: Hachette, 2003).

6. John Horne and Alan Kramer, *German Atrocities, 1914: A History of Denial* (New Haven, Conn.: Yale University Press, 2001).

7. On Wilson's racism, see Wyn C. Wade, *The Fiery Cross: The Ku Klux Klan in America* (New York: Simon & Schuster, 1987), 115–51; Nancy J. Weiss, "Wilson Draws the Color Line," in Arthur Mann, ed., *The Progressive Era* (Hinsdale, Ill.: Dryden, 1975); and Kathleen Wolgemuth, "Woodrow Wilson and Federal Segregation," *Journal of Negro History* 44 (1959): 158–73.

8. On the long-standing German objections to France's use of *troupes indigènes* on racial grounds, see Le Naour, *Honte noire*, 15–36. For a different view, see Jean-Luc Susini, in his "La perception des 'troupes noires' par les allemands," in Claude Carlier

and Guy Pedroncini, eds., *Les troupes coloniales dans la Grande Guerre* (Paris: Economica, 1997), 53–67.

9. Nelson, "'Black Horror on the Rhine,'" 614.

10. See Morel's pamphlet, *The Horror on the Rhine*, which originally appeared in August 1920 and had gone through eight editions by 1921 (8th ed., London, 1921); and Robert C. Reinders, "Radicalism on the Left: E. D. Morel and the 'Black Horror on the Rhine,'" *International Review of Social History* 13 (1968): 1–28. On Morel and the Belgian Congo, see Adam Hochschild, *King Leopold's Ghost: A Story of Terror, Greed, and Heroism in Colonial Africa* (Boston: Houghton Mifflin, 1998).

11. John C. Cairns, "A Nation of Shopkeepers in Search of a Suitable France: 1919–1940," *American Historical Review* 79, 2 (June 1974): 718. For a complete account of the internationalization of the controversy, see Le Naour, *Honte noire*, 147–68.

12. *Coloured French Troops on the Rhine*, 4th rev. ed. (Rhenish Women's League, 1923), 44.

13. Ibid., 36–37. See also Sally Marks, "Black Watch on the Rhine: A Study in Propaganda, Prejudice and Prurience," *European Studies Review* 13, 3 (1983): 297–334.

14. *Coloured French Troops on the Rhine*, 12.

15. Marks, "Black Watch on the Rhine," 299–301.

16. *La campagne allemande contre les troupes noires: Rapport du capitaine Bouriand sur ses missions en pays rhénans* (Paris: Gauthier-Villars, 1922) originated with the Commissariat général des troupes noires, a government office headed by Blaise Diagne. The Ministry of Foreign Affairs bought 6,000 copies to distribute outside France. See CAOM AP534: dossier 12, "Envoi de brochures relative aux troupes noires, réponse à la campagne allemande" (1922).

17. See SHAT 7N2308; Le Naour, *Honte noire;* Annabelle Melzer, "Spectacles and Sexualities: The 'Mise-en-Scène' of the 'Tirailleur Sénégalais' on the Western Front, 1914–1920," in Billie Melman, ed., *Borderlines: Genders and Identities in War and Peace, 1870–1930* (London: Routledge, 1998), 213–44; Clarence Lusane, *Hitler's Black Victims: The Historical Experiences of Afro-Germans, European Blacks, Africans, and African Americans in the Nazi Era* (New York: Routledge, 2003), 69–91; Elisabeth Schäfer-Wünsche, "On Becoming German: Politics of Membership in Germany," in Paul Spickard, ed., *Race and Nation: Ethnic Systems in the Modern World* (New York: Routledge, 2005), 195–211.

18. Nelson, "'Black Horror on the Rhine,'" passim; Cairns, "Nation of Shopkeepers," 718–19.

19. "'Black Horror on the Rhine,'" 611–13; Le Naour, *Honte noire*, 245.

20. Marks, "Black Watch on the Rhine," 297–98; Balesi, *From Adversaries to Comrades-in-Arms*, 123.

21. Melzer, "Spectacles and Sexualities," 228–29; Nelson, "'Black Horror on the Rhine,'" 611–13.

22. SHAT 16N199: GQG to DTC, "Objet: Malgaches servant dans les formations stationnées dans les territoires d'occupation" (17 July 1919).

23. Marc Michel, *L'appel à l'Afrique: Contributions et réactions à l'effort de guerre en AOF, 1914–1919* (Paris: Publications de la Sorbonne, 1982), 417.

24. Nelson, "'Black Horror on the Rhine,'" 611–13.

25. SHAT 6N97: DTC, "Note pour l'EMA, 3e Bureau" (27 November 1918).

26. AN C7537: dossier 1468, "Blaise Diagne et Gratien Candace, proposition de loi no. 1795 . . . " (15 February 1915).

27. SHAT 6N97: Diagne to PC/MG, 29 January 1919.

28. SHAT 16N198: Diagne to PC/MG, 29 November 1918.

29. Ibid.: Pétain to MG, 15 December 1918.

30. Ibid.: DTC (Mordacq) to Pétain, "AS emploi des Sénégalais dans les territoires ennemis occupés" (31 December 1918).

31. SHAT 6N96: Diagne to Clemenceau, 5 February 1919.

32. Nelson, "'Black Horror on the Rhine,'" 626–27.

33. Le Naour, *Honte noire;* Lusane, *Hitler's Black Victims;* Schäfer-Wünsche, "On Becoming German."

34. Sarraut, in a speech to the Chamber of Deputies in 1921; quoted in SHAT 7N2351: "Rapport de la Commission . . . " (5 October 1923).

35. Albert Sarraut, *La mise en valeur des colonies françaises* (Paris: Payot, 1923), 100.

36. Ibid., 100.

37. Raymond F. Betts, *Assimilation and Association in French Colonial Theory, 1890–1914* (New York: Columbia University Press, 1961), 105. For the long history of the duplicity of French advocates of imperialism, who disguised the gross exploitation inherent in French imperialism with the lofty rhetoric of republican universalism, see Gilles Manceron, *Marianne et les colonies: Une introduction à l'histoire colonial de la France* (Paris: La Découverte, 2003).

38. Clifford Rosenberg, "Albert Sarraut and Republican Racial Thought," *French Politics, Culture & Society* 20, 3 (Fall 2002): 97–114.

39. Sarraut, *Mise en valeur,* 101. Sarraut was in fact fairly consistent throughout his career in trying to walk a fine line between an openness in line with orthodox republican assimilationism and the need to take into account the special and very different circumstances among "uncivilized" colonial subjects. In 1931, he wrote that France could not "show two faces," one of "liberty" in France and one of "tyranny" in the empire, but neither could France simply transfer its political structure (i.e., democracy) to such primitive cultures [*Grandeur et servitude coloniales* (Paris: Éditions du Sagittaire, 1931), 102–3]. See also Carole Reynaud Paligot, *La république raciale: Paradigme racial et idéologie républicaine (1860–1930)* (Paris: Presses universitaires de France, 2006), 272–75.

40. Hoover Institution Archives, Réquin Papers, "La collaboration Franco-Américaine, 1917–1918": Lt. Col. Édouard Jean Réquin, "Emploi des troupes de couleur dans l'armée française" (15 July 1918). Réquin had served in North Africa before the war, and would command the 4th French Army upon the outbreak of World War II. Requin's language in this passage is remarkably similar to the sociologist Roland Barthes's famous meditation on the symbolism of a photograph of a young black African in uniform saluting: "I see very well what it signifies to me: that France is a great empire, that all her sons, without any color discrimination, faithfully serve under her flag, and that there is no better answer to the detractors of an alleged colonialism than the zeal shown by this Negro in serving his so-called oppressors." Roland Barthes, *Mythologies* (New York: Hill & Wang, 1987), 125–26.

41. SHAT 7N2351: "Rapport de la Commission . . . " (5 October 1923).

42. William B. Cohen, *The French Encounter with Africans: White Responses to Blacks, 1530–1880* (Bloomington: Indiana University Press, 1980), 210–63, is the most influential exponent of the idea of such a triumph. William H. Schneider, *An Empire for the Masses: The French Popular Image of Africa, 1870–1900* (Westport, Conn.: Greenwood Press, 1982), also identifies a rising predominance of scientific racism, though his later work, *Quality and Quantity: The Quest for Biological Regeneration in Twentieth-Century France* (Cambridge: Cambridge University Press, 1990), reveals the marginal nature of much of this kind of thinking in France until the 1930s and 1940s.

43. And the end of Vichy marked the end of this brief period of ascendancy. See Schneider, *Quality and Quantity* and "Towards the Improvement of the Human Race: The History of Eugenics in France," *Journal of Modern History* 54 (1982): 268–91. See also Pierre-André Taguieff, "Eugénisme ou décadence? L'exception française," *Ethnologie française* 24 (1994): 81–103.

44. Alice Conklin, *A Mission to Civilize: The Republican Idea of Empire in France and West Africa, 1895–1930* (Stanford, Calif.: Stanford University Press, 1997), esp. 164–73.

45. Stephen R. Wooten, "Colonial Administration and the Ethnography of the Family in the French Soudan," *Cahiers d'études africaines* 131: 33–3 (1993), 419–46; quotation on page 426.

46. Betts, *Assimilation and Association.*

47. Ibid., 165ff.

48. Mangin, *Force noire,* 247–48, 252–54. See also Mangin's lecture, "Caractères physiques et moraux du soldat nègre," presented to the Société d'anthropologie and published, along with comments from the audience, as "L'utilisation des troupes noires," *Bulletins et mémoires de la Société d'anthropologie de Paris* 2 (2 March 1911): 80–100. The same lecture appeared as "De l'emploi des troupes noires" in *La Revue anthropologique* 21 (April 1911): 9–28, an indication that his ideas gained fairly wide exposure even in scholarly circles.

49. Mangin, "Utilisation," 90–91; see also id., *Force noire,* 252.

50. David Beriss, "Culture-as-Race or Culture-as-Culture: Caribbean Ethnicity and the Ambiguity of Cultural Identity in French Society," *French Politics, Culture & Society* 18, 3 (Fall 2000), 40. See also his *Black Skins, French Voices: Caribbean Ethnicity and Activism in Urban France* (Boulder, Colo.: Westview Press, 2004), 36–42; and Herrick Chapman and Laura L. Frader, "Introduction: Race in France," in id., eds., *Race in France: Interdisciplinary Perspectives on the Politics of Difference* (New York: Berghahn, 2004), 6.

51. Noiriel, *French Melting Pot,* 260–61. Among other scholars who have pointed to the importance of culture in constructing understandings of racial difference, in France and elsewhere, see esp. Ann Laura Stoler and Frederick Cooper, "Between Metropole and Colony: Rethinking a Research Agenda," in Frederick Cooper and Ann Laura Stoler, eds., *Tensions of Empire: Colonial Cultures in a Bourgeois World* (Berkeley: University of California Press, 1997), 1–56; Ann Laura Stoler, *Carnal Knowledge and Imperial Power: Race and the Intimate in Colonial Rule* (Berkeley: University of California Press, 2002); Emmanuelle Saada, "Race and Sociological Reason in the Republic: Inquiries on the *Métis* in the French Empire (1908–1937)," *International Sociology* 17, 3 (September

2002): 361–91; Étienne Ballibar and Immanuel Wallerstein, *Race, Nation, Class: Ambiguous Identities* (New York: Verso, 1991); and Paul Gilroy, *'There Ain't No Black in the Union Jack': The Cultural Politics of Race and Nation* (London: Hutchinson, 1987).

52. Emmanuel Todd, "Le paradoxe français," *L'histoire* 193 (1995)" 36. See also his *Le destin des immigrés: Assimilation et ségrégation dans les démocraties occidentales* (Paris: Seuil, 1994).

53. For a discussion of the problems with viewing American and British racial attitudes as simply and straightforwardly formed by scientific, biological notions of race, see Elazar Barkan, *The Retreat of Scientific Racism: Changing Concepts of Race in Britain and the United States Between the World Wars* (Cambridge: Cambridge University Press, 1992).

54. George M. Fredrickson, *Racism : A Short History* (Princeton, N.J.: Princeton University Press, 2002), 170

55. Neil MacMaster, *Racism in Europe, 1870–2000* (New York: Palgrave, 2001), 27.

56. Alan Goodman, "Two Questions About Race," in *Is Race "Real"?* (A web forum organized by the Social Science Research Council, http://raceandgenomics.ssrc.org/ Goodman [accessed October 2, 2007]) points out the confused mixture of behavior, culture, and biology in most people's thinking about race, though he does note that most racial thinking at least privileges biology over culture, "a bit of culture, and a lot of nature." MacMaster's *Racism in Europe* argues forcefully against a monolithic view of racist ideologies, insisting on the term "racisms" to capture the varying nature of racist thought and action over time.

57. Pierre-André Taguieff, *La force du préjugé: Essais sur le racisme et ses doubles* (Paris: La Découverte, 1988).

58. Michel Wieviorka, "Introduction," in id., ed., *Racisme et modernité* (Paris: La Découverte, 1993), 7–20.

59. AN C7537: dossier 1468, "Blaise Diagne et Gratien Candace, proposition de loi no. 1795 . . . " (15 February 1916).

60. Raoul Girardet, *L'idée coloniale en France de 1871 à 1962* (Paris: La Table Ronde, 1972), 119.

61. Serge Barcellini, "Les monuments en hommage aux combattants de la 'Grande France' (Armée d'Afrique et Armée coloniale)," in Carlier and Pedroncini, eds., *Troupes coloniales dans la Grande Guerre*, 113–53. For the ambiguous ways in which different constituencies can interpret such monuments and commemoration, see Gregory Mann, "Locating Colonial Histories: Between France and West Africa," *American Historical Review* 110, 2 (April 2005): 409–34. On the place of West Africans in French public memory after the Great War, see Jean de la Guérivière, *Les fous d'Afrique: Histoire d'une passion française* (Paris: Seuil, 2001), 51–68. For the effects of colonial participation in the war on postwar perceptions of French power and role in the world, see Jacques Frémeaux, *Les colonies dans la Grande Guerre: Combats et épreuves des peuples d'Outre-mer* (Paris: 14–18 Éditions, 2006), 324–44.

62. SHAT 7N997: Contrôle postal malgache, "Rapport du mois de septembre 1917."

63. SHAT 7N1001: "Rapport sur les opérations de la commission militaire de contrôle postal de Tunis, pendant le mois d'avril 1917."

*Archival Sources*

The French military archives at the Service historique de l'armée de terre (cited as SHAT), housed just outside Paris in the Château de Vincennes, provide the bulk of documentary material for any study of the French military. The holdings relating to the period of the Third Republic (1870–1940)—Series N, Troisième République—and to the Great War are particularly extensive, though documents relating to *troupes indigènes* are scattered throughout a number of different collections and among the administrative records of a number of different departments of the Ministry of War and of the army itself. Some collections, however, primarily address the use of *troupes indigènes*. Series 7N, carton 81 (7N81): État-major de l'armée (EMA), 1er Bureau (Organisation et mobilisation de l'armée), Organisation, Troupes coloniales, 1873–1912, contains materials relating, most notably, to Charles Mangin and West African troops through 1920. More materials on *troupes coloniales* (soldiers from areas of the French colonial empire outside of North Africa) are in 6N96–97: Fonds Clemenceau, Troupes coloniales et indigènes, 1916–1918; 7N2306: EMA, 1er Bureau, TOE (Théatres d'opérations extérieures); 7N2351: EMA, 1er Bureau, Troupes coloniales, 1920–1939; and 16N1507: Grand quartier général (GQG), 2ème Bureau: Comptes rendus des chefs d'unités au moral des troupes, 1917–1918: Troupes coloniales. Materials primarily on North African troops are in collections of the Section d'Afrique of the EMA, including 7N2081: EMA, Section d'Afrique (SA); 7N2103–2104: EMA, SA: Politique musulmane, 1914–1917; 7N2107: EMA, SA; and 7N2120–2121: EMA, SA. Also relevant to North Africans troops are records of the French military mission to Egypt in 17N491: Campagne contre Allemagne, 1914–1918, Mission militaire française en Égypte.

A particularly important source for uncovering attitudes and concerns about *troupes indigènes* are the records of the army's postal censors, the *contrôle postal*. These are concentrated in 7N949: EMA, 2e Bureau, Section de contrôle, 1914–1921; 7N993, 995, 997, and 1001: EMA, 2e Bureau, Commissions de contrôle postal, 1915–1918; and 16N1555: GQG, 2ème Bureau: Documentation diverse provenant du contrôle postal. Some censors' reports appear scattered throughout other series and cartons as well. This scattered distribution of records is typical, in fact, of materials that address all issues relating to the use of troops from the colonies. Thus, important documents appear in 3N2: Comité de guerre, séances; as well as in the Fonds Clemenceau—6N114: Fonds Clemenceau, Renseignements Allemagne, 1914–1921; 6N152: Fonds Clemenceau, Renseignements France, 1916–1921; and 6N157: Fonds Clemenceau, Renseignements Grande Bretagne, 1920–1922. Records produced by the EMA relating to military operations and general policies toward soldiers are also relevant: 7N144: EMA, 1er Bureau, Effectifs (Circulaires, principes); 7N440–447: EMA, 2ème Section, Effectifs, 1905–1919; and 7N1990–1992: EMA, 3e Bureau (Opérations militaires et instructions générales de l'armée), 1914–1919. The same is true for records emanating from the High Command directly responsible for military operations at the front: 16N194–199: GQG, 1er Bureau; 16N1588: GQG, 1er Bureau; and 16N919–924: GQG, 2ème Bureau. A final, and indispensable, source for French military policy toward Madagascan soldiers is in series 8H, Madagascar—8H106: Madagascar, JMO, Documentation générale.

The richest collection of documents on the French colonial empire is housed at the Centre des archives d'Outre-mer (CAOM), in Aix-en-Provence in the south of France. Both administrative and military records here are helpful in elucidating policies toward colonial subjects in general and *troupes indigènes* in particular. The documents emanating from the Service de liaison avec les originaires des territoires français d'Outre-mer (SLOTFOM), a department within the Ministry of the Colonies set up in 1916 and charged with surveillance of colonial subjects in metropolitain France, are particularly relevant: SLOTFOM I, cartons 4, 8, and 9; SLOTFOM III, cartons 139–40 and 143; and SLOTFOM XI, carton 2. The series Affaires politiques (AP) contains information on recruitment and other policies toward *troupes indigènes,* especially cartons 533–34, 661, 907, 907*bis*, and 913. The papers of Albert Sarraut, governor-general of Indochina during much of the war, provide some information on Indochinese soldiers: Papiers d'agents (PA): 9PA13 (Papiers Sarraut). Finally, the Direction des services militaires (DSM), cartons 5 and 6, provide insight into military policies as they affected the colonies and colonial administrations.

The archives of the French Foreign Ministry (Archives du Ministère des affaires étrangères, AMAE), in Paris, are particularly valuable for the information they contain on matters relating to North Africa and Islam. In series G, "Guerre 1914–1918," record groups G1664–69 focus on North African troops (Affaires musulmanes: Soldats musulmans dans l'armée française, 1914–1918), while G1670–71*bis* comprises records from meetings of the Commission interministérielle des affaires musulmanes (CIAM), a group made up of representatives from various government ministries who examined and debated policies on France's relations with the Muslim world and its own Muslim colonial subjects (Panislamisme, Procès-verbaux de la Commission interministérielle des affaires musulmanes, CIAM, 1914–1918).

The national archives of France (Archives nationales, AN) in Paris are important for revealing some aspects of the political issues at stake in the use of troops from the colonies during the war. Series C, Assemblée nationale, Chambre des députés contains information on legislative initiatives relative to *troupes indigènes,* particularly C7537: V. Armée coloniale: Service des indigènes (dossiers 1459–76). On parliamentary oversight of the army on issues of recuitment and staffing of indigenous units, see C7494–7501: Commission de l'armée, procès-verbaux, 1915–1919, and C7691: EMA, dossier 5341, Troupes coloniales, circulaires. The papers of Albert Thomas, a cabinet official responsible for matters relating to armaments and war industries, illuminate comparative perspectives on colonial subjects of different ethnicities and from different parts of the French colonial empire: series AP, Archives privées—94AP134–35: Papiers Albert Thomas.

In the United States, the Hoover Institution Archives in Stanford, California, contain a collection of the papers of Lt. Col. Édouard Réquin, who served on the French military delegation in Washington, D.C. Part of his activites focused on explaining the French use of *troupes indigènes* to Americans skeptical of the wisdom of such a policy: Réquin Papers, "La collaboration Franco-Américaine, 1917–1918." The Hoover Institution also contains a large collection of wartime posters from France, many of which feature *troupes indigènes*, revealing prevailing racial stereotypes in France: Hoover Institution Archives Poster Collection, series FR. The Library of Congress in Washington, D.C., also holds a number of similiarly useful French wartime posters in its poster collection (POS-Fr.).

## Selected Published Sources

In addition to extensive archival work, this study builds upon the works of other historians who have examined France's use of *troupes indigènes*. Where this study differs from those earlier works is in its focus on troops from across the French empire, and its primary concern with questions of race and racism. One of the earliest general works that focuses on a particular colony or area of the empire alone is Shelby Cullom Davis, *Reservoirs of Men: A History of the Black Troops of French West Africa* (Geneva: Chambéry, 1934). Davis's focus on troops from West Africa is representative, in that troops from this region attracted the most attention and notoriety both during and after the war. Works that followed include Charles John Balesi, *From Adversaries to Comrades-in-Arms: West Africans and the French Military, 1885–1918* (Waltham, Mass.: Crossroads Press, 1979); Myron Echenberg, *Colonial Conscripts: The* Tirailleurs Sénégalais *in French West Africa, 1857–1960* (Portsmouth, N.H.: Heinemann, 1991); and Joe Lunn, *Memoirs of the Maelstrom: A Senegalese Oral History of the First World War* (Portsmouth, N.H.: Heinemann, 1999). This last is particularly notable because of the number of veterans the author interviewed who could tell their stories in their own words (see also Lunn's "'Les Races Guerrières': Racial Preconceptions in the French Military About West African Soldiers During the First World War," *Journal of Contemporary History* 34, 4 [1999]: 517–36). Another source for the perspective of a West African in his own words is Bakary Diallo, *Force-bonté* (Paris: F. Reider, 1926; reprint, Abidjan: Nouv. éd. africaines; Paris: Agence de coopération culturelle et technique, 1985); and the perspective of an officer who served with West Africans is explored in Nicole Zehfus, "From Stereotype to Individual: World War I Experiences with *Tirailleurs sénégalais*," *French Colonial History* 6 (2005): 137–57. The most important and thorough work on West Africans in the Great War remains, however, Marc Michel's seminal *L'appel à l'Afrique: Contributions et réactions à l'effort de guerre en AOF, 1914–1919* (Paris: Publications de la Sorbonne, 1982), recently republished as *Les Africains et la Grande Guerre: L'appel à l'Afrique (1914–1918)* (Paris: Karthala, 2003); see also his "La génêse du recrutement de 1918 en

Afrique noire française," *Revue française d'histoire d'Outre-mer* 58, 213 (1971): 433–50; "Citoyenneté et service militaire dans les quatre communes du Sénégal au cours de la Première Guerre mondiale," in *Perspectives nouvelles sur le passé de l'Afrique noire et de Madagascar* (Paris: Publications de la Sorbonne, 1974); and "Colonisation et défense nationale: Le général Mangin et la force noire," *Guerres mondiales et conflits contempo-rains* 145 (January 1987): 27–44. And indispensible for understanding the background to the use of West Africans in the war is Charles Mangin's book *La force noire* (Paris: Hachette, 1910), as well as his articles "Troupes noires," *Revue de Paris* 16 (1 and 15 July 1909): 61–80; 383–93; "L'utilisation des troupes noires," *Bulletins et mémoires de la Société d'anthropologie de Paris* 2 (2 March 1911): 80–100; and "De l'emploi des troupes noires." *Revue anthropologique* 21 (April 1911): 9–28.

Soldiers from other regions have attracted less attention, though some important scholarship has appeared (mostly in French). On Algeria, see Gilbert Meynier, *L'Algérie révélée: La guerre de 1914–1918 et le premier quart du XXe siècle* (Geneva: Droz, 1981). On Madagascans, see Maurice Gontard, *Madagascar pendant la Première Guerre mondiale* (Tananarive: Éditions universitaires, 1969); Chantal Valensky, *Le soldat occulté: Les Mal-gaches de l'armée française, 1884–1920* (Paris: L'Harmattan, 1995); and Jacques Razafind-ranaly, *Les soldats de la grande île: D'une guerre à l'autre, 1895–1918* (Paris: L'Harmattan, 2000). Mireille Favre–Le Van Ho, "Un milieu porteur de modernisation: Travailleurs et tirailleurs vietnamiens en France pendant la Première Guerre mondiale" (doctoral the-sis, École nationale des chartes, 1986; 2 vols.); Henri Eckert, "Les militaires indochinois au service de la France (1859–1939)" (doctoral thesis, Université de Paris IV, 1998; 2 vols.); Kimloan Hill, "A Westward Journey, an Enlightened Path: Vietnamese Linh Tho, 1915–30" (Ph.D diss., University of Oregon, 2001); and Maurice Reeves and Eric Deroo, *Les Lính Tâp: Histoire des militaires indochinois au service de la France (1859–1960)* (Paris: Charles Lavauzelle, 1999) examine the experience of Indochinese soldiers. Some works do cover troops from various areas of the empire, including the eclectic collection of essays in Claude Carlier and Guy Pedroncini, eds., *Les troupes coloniales dans la Grande Guerre* (Paris: Economica, 1997); Anthony Clayton, *France, Soldiers, and Africa* (London: Brassey's Defence Publishers, 1988); and Jacques Frémeaux, *Les colonies dans la Grande Guerre: Combats et épreuves des peuples d'Outre-mer* (Paris: 14–18 Éditions, 2006).

Works that help place France's use of *troupes indigènes* during the Great War in an international and comparative perspective include Tyler Stovall, *Paris Noir: African Americans in the City of Light* (New York: Houghton Mifflin, 1996); Arthur E. Bar-beau and Florette Henri, *The Unknown Soldiers: African-American Troops in World War I* (Philadelphia: Temple University Press, 1974; rpt., New York: Da Capo Press, 1996); André Kaspi, *Le temps des Américains* (Paris: Publications de la Sorbonne, 1976); Jen-nifer Keene, *Doughboys: The Great War, and the Remaking of America* (Baltimore: Johns Hopkins University Press, 2001), and id., "French and American Racial Stereotypes Dur-ing the First World War," in William L. Chew, ed., *National Stereotypes in Perspective: Americans in France, Frenchmen in America* (Atlanta: Rodopi, 2001); Robert B. Bruce, *A Fraternity of Arms: America & France in the Great War* (Lawrence: University Press of Kansas, 2003); David Killingray, "The Idea of a British Imperial African Army," *Journal of African History* 19 (1979): 421–36; David Killingray and David Omissi, eds., *Guardians of Empire: The Armed Forces of the Colonial Powers, c. 1700–1964* (Manchester, England: Manchester University Press, 1999); Byron Farwell, *The Great War in Africa* (New York: Norton, 1986) and *The Armies of the Raj: From the Mutiny to Independence, 1858–1947* (New York: Norton, 1989); Glenford Howe, *Race, War and Nationalism: A Social History of West Indians in the First World War* (Kingston, Jamaica: Ian Randle; Oxford: James Currey, 2002); Richard Smith, *Jamaican Volunteers in the First World War: Race, Masculinity and the Development of National Consciousness* (Manchester, England: Manchester University Press, 2004).

Works that explore important aspects of the Great War in general and of France's experience in particular include Stéphane Audoin-Rouzeau and Annette Becker, *La Grande Guerre, 1914–1918* (Paris: Gallimard, 1998), and *14–18, retrouver la guerre* (Paris: Gallimard, 2000); Pierre Miquel, *Les poilus: La France sacrifiée* (Paris: Plon, 2000); Leonard V. Smith, *Between Munity and Obedience: The Case of the French Fifth Infantry Division During World War I* (Princeton, N.J.: Princeton University Press, 1994); Jean-Jacques Becker, *1914: Comment les Français sont entrés dans la guerre* (Paris: Presses de la Fondation nationale des sciences politiques, 1977), and id., *The Great War and the French People*, trans. Arnold Pomerans (Leamington Spa, England: Berg, 1985; New York: St. Martin's Press, 1986); Yves Pourcher, *Les jours de guerre: La vie des Français au jour le jour entre 1914 et 1918* (Paris: Plon, 1994); Tyler Stovall, "Colour-blind France? Colonial Workers During the First World War," *Race and Class* 35, 2 (1993): 35–55, and id., "The Color Line Behind the Lines: Racial Violence in France During the Great War," *American Historical Review* 103, 3 (June 1998): 737–69; Jean-Yves Le Naour, *Misères et tourments de la chair durant la Grande Guerre: Les mœurs sexuelles des Français, 1914–1918* (Paris: Aubier, 2002); Alistair Horne, *The Price of Glory: Verdun 1916* (New York: Penguin Books, 1962); Margaret H. Darrow, *French Women and the First World War: War Stories of the Home Front* (Oxford: Berg, 2000); Ruth Harris, "The 'Child of the Barbarian': Rape, Race, and Nationalism in France During the First World War," *Past and Present* 141 (November 1993): 170–206; Maurice Rajsfus, *La censure militaire et policière (1914–1918)* (Paris: Le Cherche Midi, 1999); Keith Nelson, "The 'Black Horror on the Rhine': Race as a Factor in Post–World War I Diplomacy," *Journal of Modern History* 42, 4 (December 1970): 606–27; Sally Marks, "Black Watch on the Rhine: A Study in Propaganda, Prejudice and Prurience," *European Studies Review* 13, 3 (1983): 297–334; Annette Becker, *War and Faith: The Religious Imagination in France, 1914–1930* (Oxford: Berg, 1998); Jean-Marie Mayeur, "La vie religieuse en France pendant la Première Guerre mondiale," in Jean Delumeau, ed., *Histoire vécu du peuple chrétien* (Paris: Privat, 1979); J. F. V. Keiger, *France and the Origins of the First World War* (New York: St. Martin's Press, 1983); Allen Douglas, *War, Memory, and the Politics of Humor: The Canard Enchaîné and World War I* (Berkeley: University of California Press, 2002); Jean-Yves le Naour, *La honte noire: L'Allemagne et les troupes coloniales françaises, 1914–1945* (Paris: Hachette, 2003); and John Horne and Alan Kramer, *German Atrocities, 1914: A History of Denial* (New Haven, Conn.: Yale University Press, 2001). Two recent general histories of the Great War place particular emphasis on the global and imperial aspects of the conflict: John H. Morrow Jr., *The Great War: An Imperial History* (New York: Routledge, 2004), and Hew Strachan, *The First World War* (New York: Viking, 2003).

On the French military, see David B. Ralston, *The Army of the Republic: The Place of the Military in the Political Evolution of France, 1871–1914* (Cambridge, Mass.: MIT Press, 1967); Douglas Porch, *The March to the Marne: The French Army, 1871–1914* (Cambridge: Cambridge University Press, 1981), id., "Bugeaud, Galliéni, Lyautey: The Development of French Colonial Warfare," 376–407, in Peter Paret, ed., *Makers of Modern Strategy from Machiavelli to the Nuclear Age* (Princeton, N.J.: Princeton University Press, 1986), and id., *The French Foreign Legion: A Complete History of the Legendary Fighting Force* (New York: Harper Collins, 1991); Jean-Charles Jauffret, *Parlement, gouvernement, commandement: L'armée de métier sous la Troisième République, 1871–1914* (Vincennes: Service historique de l'armée de terre, 1987; 2 vols.), id., "L'officier français (1871–1919)," in Claude Croubois, ed., *L'officier français des origines à nos jours* (Saint-Jean-d'Angély: Éditions Bordessoules, 1987), and "Les armes de 'la plus grande France,'" in Guy Pedroncini, ed., *Histoire militaire de la France*, vol. 3: *De 1871 à 1940* (Paris: Presses universitaires de France, 1992); John Kim Munholland, "The Emergence of the Colonial Military in France, 1880–1905" (Ph.D. diss., Princeton University, 1964); Alistair Horne, *The French Army and Politics, 1871–1970* (New York: Peter Bedrick Books, 1984); Richard D. Challener, *The French Theory of the Nation in Arms, 1866–1939* (New York: Columbia University Press, 1955); Leonard V. Smith, *Between Mutiny and Obedience: The Case of the French Fifth Infantry Division During World War I* (Princeton, N.J.: Princeton University Press, 1994); Gerd Krumeich, *Armaments and Politics in France on the Eve of the First World War: The Introduction of Three-Year Conscription*, trans. Stephen Conn (Leamington Spa, England: Berg, 1984); François Vinde, *L'affaire des fiches: Chronique d'un scandale* (Paris: Éditions universitaires, 1989); and Belkacem Recham, *Les musulmans algériens dans l'armée française (1919–1945)* (Paris: L'Harmattan, 1996). Also key to understanding the culture of the military and the officer corps under the Third Republic are two contemporary essays by Hubert Lyautey, "Du role social de l'officier," *Revue des Deux Mondes* 104 (15 March 1891): 443–59, and "Du rôle colonial de l'armée," *Revue des Deux Mondes* 157 (15 January 1900): 308–28.

For general information on the politics, culture, and society of the Third Republic, including questions of national identity, in France, see Eugen Weber, *The Nationalist Revival in France, 1905–1914* (Berkeley: University of California Press, 1968); id., *Peasants into Frenchmen: The Modernization of Rural France, 1871–1914* (Stanford, Calif.: Stanford University Press, 1976); Rogers Brubaker, *Citizenship and Nationhood in France and Germany* (Cambridge, Mass.: Harvard University Press, 1992); James R. Lehning, *To Be a Citizen: The Political Culture of the Early French Third Republic* (Ithaca, N.Y.: Cornell University Press, 2001); Edward Berenson, *The Trial of Madame Caillaux* (Berkeley: University of California Press, 1992); and Gregor Dallas, *At the Heart of a Tiger: Clemenceau and His World, 1841–1929* (New York: Carroll & Graf, 1993); On issues relating to gender, see James F. McMillan, *Housewife or Harlot: The Place of Women in French Society, 1870–1940* (New York: St. Martin's Press, 1981); Mary Louise Roberts, *Civilization Without Sexes: Reconstructing Gender in Postwar France, 1917–1927* (Chicago: University of Chicago Press, 1994); id., *Disruptive Acts: The New Woman in Fin-de-siècle France* (Chicago: University of Chicago Press, 2002); and Robert Nye, *Masculinity and Male Codes of Honor in France* (New York: Oxford University Press, 1993). On the vexed question of the declining birth rate and depopulation, see Joseph J. Spengler, *France Faces Depopulation* (1938; rpt., New York: Greenwood Press, 1968); Joshua H. Cole, *The Power of Large Numbers: Population, Politics, and Gender in Nineteenth-Century France* (Ithaca, N.Y.: Cornell University Press, 2000); Karen Offen, "Depopulation, Nationalism, and Feminism in Fin-de-Siècle France," *American Historical Review* 89, 3 (June 1984): 648–76; Richard Tomlinson, "The Disappearance of France, 1896–1940: French Politics and the Birth Rate," *Historical Journal* 28 (1985): 405–15; and John C. Hunter, "The Problem of the French Birth Rate on the Eve of World War I," *French Historical Studies* 11 (1962): 490–503. On the related question of regeneration and eugenics, see William H. Schneider, *Quality and Quantity: The Quest for Biological Regeneration in Twentieth-Century France* (Cambridge: Cambridge University Press, 1990), and "Towards the Improvement of the Human Race: The History of Eugenics in France," *Journal of Modern History* 54 (1982): 268–91.

Works that place the issue of French national identity and citizenship in a larger and longer historical perspective include David A. Bell, *The Cult of the Nation in France: Inventing Nationalism, 1680–1800* (Cambridge, Mass.: Harvard University Press, 2001); Patrick Weil, *Qu'est-ce qu'un Français? Histoire de la nationalité française depuis la Revolution* (Paris: Grasset, 2002); Tzvetan Todorov, *On Human Diversity: Nationalism, Racism, and Exoticism in French Thought* (Cambridge, Mass.: Harvard University Press, 1993); Pierre Birnbaum, *The Idea of France* (New York: Hill & Wang, 2001); James B. Collins, *From Tribes to Nation: The Making of France, 500–1799* (Toronto: Wadsworth, 2002); Renée Waldinger, Philip Dawson, and Isser Woloch, eds., *The French Revolution and the Meaning of Citizenship* (Westport, Conn.: Greenwood Press, 1993); John Torpey, *The Invention of the Passport: Surveillance, Citizenship and the State* (Cambridge: Cambridge University Press, 2000); Dale Van Kley, ed., *The French Idea of Freedom: The Old Regime and the Declaration of Rights of 1789* (Stanford, Calif.: Stanford University Press, 1994); Norman Ravitch, "Your People, My People; Your God, My God: French and American Troubles over Citizenship," *French Review* 70, 4 (March 1997): 515–27; Raoul Girardet, *Le nationalisme français: Anthologie, 1871–1914* (Paris: Seuil, 1983); Carole Reynaud Paligot, *La république raciale: Paradigme racial et idéologie républicaine (1860–1930)* (Paris: Presses universitaires de France, 2006); Dennis Ager, *Language, Community and the State* (Exeter, England: Intellect Books, 1997), and *Identity, Insecurity and Image: France and Language* (Philadelphia: Multilingual Matters, 1999); and Benedict Anderson, *Imagined Communities: Reflections on the Origin and Spread of Nationalism*, rev. ed. (New York: Verso, 1991).

The historiography of the French colonial empire is extensive and growing rapidly. Key works include Henri Brunschwig, *French Colonialism, 1871–1914: Myths and Realities,* trans. William Granville Brown (New York: Praeger, 1964), originally published as *Mythes et réalités de l'impérialisme colonial français, 1871–1914* (Paris: Armand Colin, 1960); Nicolas Bancel, Pascal Blanchard, and Françoise Vergès, *La Republique coloniale: Essai sur une utopie* (Paris: Albin Michel, 2003); Herman Lebovics, *True France: The Wars over Cultural Identity, 1900–1945* (Ithaca, N.Y.: Cornell University Press, 1992); Raoul Girardet, *L'idée coloniale en France de 1871 à 1962* (Paris: La Table Ronde, 1972); Robert Aldrich, *Greater France: A History of French Overseas Expansion* (New York: St.

Martin's Press, 1996); Jean Meyer, Jean Tarrade, Annie Rey-Goldzeigeur, and Jacques Thobie, *Histoire de la France coloniale: Des origines à 1914* (Paris: Armand Colin, 1991); Jacques Thobie, Gilbert Meynier, Catherine Coquery-Vidrovitch, and Charles-Robert Ageron, *Histoire de la France coloniale, 1914–1990* (Paris: Armand Colin, 1990); Denise Bouche, *Histoire de la colonisation française,* vol. 2: *Flux et réflux (1815–1962)* (Paris: Fayard, 1991); Christopher M. Andrew and A. S. Kanya-Forstner, *The Climax of French Imperial Expansion, 1914–1924* (Stanford, Calif.: Stanford University Press, 1981); Martin Thomas, *The French Empire Between the Wars: Imperialism, Politics and Society* (Manchester, England: Manchester University Press, 2005); Elizabeth Ezra, *The Colonial Unconscious: Race and Culture in Interwar France* (Ithaca, N.Y.: Cornell University Press, 2000); William B. Cohen, *The French Encounter with Africans: White Responses to Blacks, 1530–1880* (Bloomington: Indiana University Press, 1980); William H. Schneider, *An Empire for the Masses: The French Popular Image of Africa, 1870–1900* (Westport, Conn.: Greenwood Press, 1982); Brett A. Berliner, *Ambivalent Desire: The Exotic Black Other in Jazz-Age France* (Amherst: University of Massachusetts Press, 2002); Frederick Cooper and Ann Laura Stoler, eds., *Tensions of Empire: Colonial Cultures in a Bourgeois World* (Berkeley: University of California Press, 1997); Tony Chafer and Amanda Sackur, eds., *Promoting the Colonial Idea: Propaganda and Visions of Empire in France* (Basingstoke, England: Palgrave, 2002); Gregory Mann, *Native Sons: West African Veterans and France in the Twentieth Century* (Durham, N.C.: Duke University Press, 2006); Gregory Mann, "Locating Colonial Histories: Between France and West Africa," *American Historical Review,* 110, 2 (April 2005): 409–34; David Robinson, *Paths of Accomodation: Muslim Societies and French Colonial Authorities in Senegal and Mauritania, 1880–1920* (Athens, Ohio: Ohio University Press, 2000); J. P. Daughton, *An Empire Divided: Religion, Republicanism, and the Making of French Colonialism, 1880–1914* (New York: Oxford University Press, 2006); Gilles Manceron, *Marianne et les colonies: Une introduction à l'histoire colonial de la France* (Paris: La Découverte, 2003); Christopher Harrison, *France and Islam in West Africa, 1860–1960* (Cambridge: Cambridge University Press, 1988); Gabriel Manessy, *Le Français en Afrique noire: Mythe, stratégie, pratiques* (Paris: L'Harmattan, 1994); G. Wesley Johnson, *The Emergence of Black Politics in Senegal: The Struggle for Power in the Four Communes, 1900–1920* (Stanford, Calif.: Stanford University Press, 1971); Alice Bullard, *Exile to Paradise: Savagery and Civilization in Paris and the South Pacific, 1790–1900* (Stanford, Calif.: Stanford University Press, 2000); Philip D. Curtin, *Disease and Empire: The Health of European Troops in the Conquest of Africa* (Cambridge: Cambridge University Press, 1998); Jean de la Guérivière, *Les fous d'Afrique: Histoire d'une passion française* (Paris: Seuil, 2001); Anne Donadey, "'Y'a bon Banania': Ethics and Cultural Criticism in the Colonial Context," *French Cultural Studies* 11 (February 2000): 9–29; Stephen R. Wooten, "Colonial Administration and the Ethnography of the Family in the French Soudan," *Cahiers d'études africaines* 131, 33–3 (1993): 419–46; and John Laffey, "Racism in Tonkin Before 1914: The *Colons*' View of the Vietnamese" *French Colonial Studies* 1 (1977): 65–81.

Important works focused primarily on colonial policy include Alice Conklin, *A Mission to Civilize: The Republican Idea of Empire in France and West Africa, 1895–1930* (Stanford, Calif.: Stanford University Press, 1997); id., "Colonialism and Human Rights, a Contradiction in Terms? The Case of France and West Africa, 1895–1914," *American Historical Review* 103, 2 (April 1998): 419–42; Raymond F. Betts, *Assimilation and Association in French Colonial Theory, 1890–1914* (New York: Columbia University Press, 1961); Martin D. Lewis, "One Hundred Million Frenchmen: The Assimilationist Theory in French Colonial Policy," *Comparative Studies in Society and History* 4, 2 (1962): 129–53; Catherine Coquery-Vidrovitch, "Nationalité et citoyenneté en Afrique occidentale français: Originaires et citoyens dans le Sénégal colonial," *Journal of African History* 42, 2 (2001): 285–305; and Charles-Robert Ageron, "Clemenceau et la question coloniale," in André Wormser, ed., *Clemenceau et la justice* (Paris: Publications de la Sorbonne, 1983). Saliha Belmessous, "Assimilation and Racialism in Seventeenth- and Eighteenth-Century French Colonial Policy," *American Historical Review* 110, 2 (April 2005): 322–49, provides important background to colonial policy in the Third Republic. Albert Sarraut's *La mise en valeur des colonies françaises* (Paris: Payot, 1923) is important for his perspective on the impact of the service of *troupes indigènes* in the war on the future of the French colonies. See also id., *Grandeur et servitude coloniales* (Paris: Éditions du Sagittaire, 1931), and Clifford Rosenberg, "Albert Sarraut and Republican Racial Thought," *French Politics, Culture & Society* 20, 3 (Fall 2002): 97–114. On the place of education in the colonial project, see Denise Bouche, "L'enseignement dans les territoires français de l'Afrique occidentale de 1817 à 1920: Mission civilisatrice ou formation d'une élite?" (doctoral thesis, Université de Paris I, 1974; 2 vols.); Gail Paradise Kelly, *French Colonial Education: Essays on Vietnam and West Africa* (New York: AMS Press, 2000); and Bob H. White, "Talk About School: Education and the Colonial Project in French and British Africa (1860–1960)," *Comparative Education* 32, 1 (1996): 9–25.

Some of the most innovative studies in the field focus more specifically on gender, sexuality, and race in the colonial context. The starting point for investigations of this topic is the work of Ann Laura Stoler, especially her *Carnal Knowledge and Imperial Power: Race and the Intimate in Colonial Rule* (Berkeley: University of California Press, 2002) and *Race and the Education of Desire: Foucault's History of Sexuality and the Colonial Order of Things* (Durham, N.C.: Duke University Press, 1995). Other key works include Françoise Vergès, *Monsters and Revolutionaries: Colonial Family Romance and Métissage* (Durham, N.C.: Duke University Press, 1999); Owen White, *Children of the Empire: Miscegenation and Colonial Society in French West Africa, 1895–1960* (Oxford: Clarendon Press, 1999); Emmanuelle Saada, "Race and Sociological Reason in the Republic: Inquiries on the *Métis* in the French Empire (1908–37)," *International Sociology* 17, 3 (September 2002): 361–91; Elisa Camiscioli, "Producing Citizens, Reproducing the 'French Race': Immigration, Demography, and Pronatalism in Early Twentieth-Century France," *Gender & History* 13, 3 (November 2001): 593–621; id., "Intermarriage, Independent Nationality, and the Individual Rights of French Women: The Law of 10 August 1927," *French Politics, Culture & Society* 17, 3–4 (Summer–Fall 1999): 52–74; Elizabeth Thompson, *Colonial Citizens: Republican Rights, Paternal Privilege, and Gender in French Syria and Lebanon* (New York: Columbia University Press, 2000); Julia Clancy-Smith and Frances Gouda, eds., *Domesticating the Empire: Race, Gender, and Family Life in French and Dutch Colonialism* (Charlottesville: University Press of Virginia, 1998). On gender, sexuality, and empire in general, see Robert J. C. Young, *Colonial*

*Desire: Hybridity in Theory, Culture and Race* (New York: Routledge, 1995); Ronald Hyam, *Empire and Sexuality: The British Experience* (Manchester, England: Manchester University Press, 1990); Kenneth Ballhatchet, *Race, Sex and Class Under the Raj: Imperial Attitudes and Policies and Their Critics, 1793–1905* (London: Weidenfeld & Nicolson, 1980); Nupur Chaudhuri and Margaret Strobel, eds., *Western Women and Imperialism: Complicity and Resistance* (Bloomington: Indiana University Press, 1992); Floya Anthias and Nira Yuval-Davis, eds, *Racialized Boundaries: Race, Nation, Gender, Colour and Class and the Anti-Racist Struggle* (New York: Routledge, 1992).

On North Africa and Islam, see Patricia Lorcin, *Imperial Identities: Stereotyping, Prejudice and Race in Colonial Algeria* (London: I. B. Taurus, 1995); id., "Imperialism, Colonial Identity, and Race in Algeria, 1830–1870: The Role of the French Medical Corps," *Isis* 90, 4 (December 1999): 653–79; Jean-François Guilhaume, *Les mythes fondateurs de l'Algérie française* (Paris: L'Harmattan, 1992); William E. Watson, *Tricolor and Crescent: France and the Islamic World* (Westport, Conn.: Praeger, 2003); Ann Thomson, *Barbary and Enlightenment: European Attitudes Toward the Maghreb in the 18th Century* (Leiden: Brill, 1987); Charles-Robert Ageron, *Les Algériens musulmans et la France, 1871–1919*, 2 vols. (Paris: Presses universitaires de France, 1968); John Ruedy, *Modern Algeria: The Origins and Development of a Nation* (Bloomington: Indiana University Press, 1992); Vincent Confer, *France and Algeria: The Problem of Civil and Political Reform, 1870–1920* (Syracuse, N.Y.: Syracuse University Press, 1966); Laure Blévis, "Les avatars de la citoyenneté en Algérie coloniale ou les paradoxes d'une catégorisation," *Droit et Société* 48 (2001): 557–80; id., "La citoyenneté française au miroir ce la colonisation: Étude des demandes de naturalisation des 'sujets français' en Algérie coloniale," *Genèses* 53 (December 2003): 25–47; id., "L'usage du droit dans le rapport colonial: L'exemple de l'inscription des Algériens sur les listes électorales de métropole, 1919–1939," *Bulletin de l'Institut d'histoire du temps présent* 80 (December 2002); Jeanne Bowlan, "Polygamists Need Not Apply: Becoming a French Citizen in Colonial Algeria, 1918–1938," *Proceedings of the Western Society for French History* 24 (1997): 110–19; Augustin Bernard, *L'Afrique du nord pendant la guerre* (Paris: Presses universitaires de France, 1926); Rémy Leveau and Gilles Kepel, eds., *Les musulmans dans la société française* (Paris: Presses de la Fondation nationale des sciences politiques, 1988); Alain Boyer, *L'islam en France* (Paris: Presses universitaires de France, 1998); "France and Islam," special issue, *French Historical Studies* 30, 3 (Summer 2007); and Pascal Le Pautremat, *La politique musulmane de la France au XXe siècle: De l'Hexagone aux terres d'Islam. Espoirs, réussites, échecs* (Paris: Maisonneuve & Larose, 2003).

The legacy of French imperialism, from decolonization through current debates over immigration and citizenship, is critical for understanding French attitudes toward race and racism, both historically and today. Maxim Silverman's work is particularly important here, especially his *Deconstructing the Nation: Immigration, Racism and Citizenship in Modern France* (London: Routledge, 1992), id., *Facing Postmodernity: Contemporary French Thought on Culture and Society* (London: Routledge, 1999), and id., ed., *Race, Discourse and Power in France* (Aldershot, England: Avebury, 1991). So too is the work of Alec Hargreaves, especially *Immigration, "Race" and Ethnicity in Contemporary France* (London: Routledge, 1995); id. and Jeremy Leaman, eds., *Racism, Ethnicity and Politics in Contemporary Europe* (Aldershot, England: Edward Elgar: 1995); and id. and Mark McKinney, eds., *Post-Colonial Cultures in France* (London: Routledge, 1997). Other important works on these topics include Gérard Noiriel, *The French Melting Pot: Immigration, Citizenship, and National Identity* (Minneapolis: University of Minnesota Press, 1996); Tyler Stovall and Georges Van Den Abbeele, eds., *French Civilization and Its Discontents: Nationalism, Colonialism, Race* (Lanham, Md.: Lexington Books, 2003); Neil MacMaster, *Colonial Migrants and Racism: Algerians in France, 1900–1962* (London: Macmillan, 1997); David Beriss, *Black Skins, French Voices: Caribbean Ethnicity and Activism in Urban France* (Boulder, Colo.: Westview Press, 2004), and "Culture-as-Race or Culture-as-Culture: Caribbean Ethnicity and the Ambiguity of Cultural Identity in French Society," *French Politics, Culture & Society* 18, 3 (Fall 2000): 18–47; Paul A. Silverstein, *Algeria in France: Transpolitics, Race, and Nation* (Bloomington: Indiana University Press, 2004); Michel Wieviorka, ed., *Racisme et modernité* (Paris: La Découverte, 1993); Patrick Weil, *La France et ses étrangers: L'aventure d'une politique de l'immigration, 1938–1991* (Paris: Calmann-Lévy, 1991); id., "Lifting the Veil," *French Politics, Culture & Society* 22, 3 (Fall 2004): 142–49; Joan W. Scott, "Symptomatic Politics: The Banning of Islamic Head Scarves in French Public Schools," *French Politics, Culture & Society* 24, 4 (Winter 2005): 106–27; Tahar Ben Jelloun, *French Hospitality: Racism and North African Immigrants* (New York: Columbia University Press, 1999); Miriam Feldblum, *The Politics of Nationality Reform and Immigration in Contemporary France* (Albany: State University of New York Press, 1999); David Cesarini and Mary Fulbrook, eds., *Citizenship, Nationality and Migration in Europe* (London: Routledge, 1996); Adrian Favell, *Philosophies of Integration: Immigration and the Idea of Citizenship in France and Britain*, 2nd ed. (Basingstoke, England: Palgrave, 2001); Emmanuel Todd, *Le destin des immigrés: Assimilation et ségrégation dans les démocraties occidentales* (Paris: Seuil, 1994); id., "Le paradoxe français," *L'histoire* 193 (1995): 36–37.

Pierre-André Taguieff has published pioneering work on race and racism in France. See especially his *La force du préjugé: Essais sur le racisme et ses doubles* (Paris: La Découverte, 1988), and "Eugénisme ou décadence? L'exception française," *Ethnologie française* 24 (1994): 81–103. Other works on the history of race and racism in France include Sue Peabody and Tyler Stovall, eds., *The Color of Liberty: Histories of Race in France* (Durham, N.C.: Duke University Press, 2003); and Herrick Chapman and Laura L. Frader, eds., *Race in France: Interdisciplinary Perspectives on the Politics of Difference* (New York: Berghahn, 2004). George M. Fredrickson, *Racism: A Short History* (Princeton, N.J.: Princeton University Press, 2002); Étienne Ballibar and Immanuel Wallerstein, *Race, Nation, Class: Ambiguous Identities* (New York: Verso, 1991); and Neil MacMaster, *Racism in Europe, 1870–2000* (New York: Palgrave, 2001) are good introductions to the modern history of racism generally.